A Body of Divinity

A Body of Divinity

CONTAINED IN
SERMONS UPON THE
WESTMINSTER ASSEMBLY'S
CATECHISM BY
THOMAS WATSON

THE BANNER OF TRUTH TRUST

THE BANNER OF TRUTH TRUST
3 *Murrayfield Road, Edinburgh EH12 6EL*
P.O. Box 621, Carlisle, Pennsylvania 17013, U.S.A.

*

First published as part of A Body of Practical Divinity 1692
Reprinted 1890
First Banner of Truth Trust edition reprinted from the
1890 *edition,* 1958 (*twice*)
Reprinted 1960
Revised edition first published 1965
Reprinted 1970
Reprinted 1974
Reprinted 1978
Reprinted in limp format 1983
Reprinted 1986

ISBN 0 85151 383 2

*

Printed in Great Britain by Offset Lithography
by Billing & Sons Limited, Worcester

CONTENTS

BRIEF MEMOIR OF
THOMAS WATSON

Compiled by C. H. Spurgeon

Thomas Watson's Body of Practical Divinity is one of the most precious of the peerless works of the Puritans; and those best acquainted with it prize it most. Watson was one of the most concise, racy, illustrative, and suggestive of those eminent divines who made the Puritan age the Augustan period of evangelical literature. There is a happy union of sound doctrine, heart-searching experience and practical wisdom throughout all his works, and his Body of Divinity is, beyond all the rest, useful to the student and the minister. Although Thomas Watson issued several most valuable books, comparatively little is known of him – even the dates of his birth and death are unknown. His writings are his best memorial; perhaps he needed no other, and therefore providence forbade the superfluity. We shall not attempt to discover his pedigree, and, after the manner of antiquarians, derive his family from a certain famous Wat, whose son distinguished himself in the Crusades, or in some other insane enterprise; whether blue blood was in his veins or no is of small consequence, since we know that he was the seed-royal of the redeemed of the Lord. Some men are their own ancestors, and, for aught we know, Thomas Watson's genealogy reflected no fame upon him, but derived all its lustre from his achievements. He had the happiness to be educated at Emmanuel College, Cambridge, which in those days deserved to be called the School of Saints, the nursing mother of gigantic evangelical divines. In Kennet's 'Register and Chronicle,'* is a list of eighty-seven names of Puritan ministers, including many well-known and loved as preachers and commentators; such as Anth. Burgess, W. Jenkyn, Ralph Venning, Thomas Brooks, T. White, Samuel Slater, Thomas Watson, John Rowe, Dr. W. Bates, Stephen Charnock, Samuel Clarke, Nathaniel Vincent, Dr John Collings, William Bridge, Samuel Hildersam, Adoniram Bifield, followed by this remark, 'These are most of them mentioned in the list of sufferers for Nonconformity, and appear upon the registers to have been all of Emmanuel College, beside great numbers, no doubt of the same society, who were forward preachers up of the unhappy changes of 1641,' etc. In the margin of the book is the following observation on the foregoing: 'It may not be improper to observe how much young students, in both Universities, fell in with the prejudices of

* Vol. i. pp. 933–4.

their governors and tutors. This was the reason that this single College of Emmanuel, in Cambridge, bred more of the Puritans and Nonconformists than perhaps any seven of the other Colleges or Halls in either University." Such a fact as this should attract the prayers of all believers to our seminaries for the sons of the prophets, since upon the manner in which these institutions are conducted will depend under God the future wellbeing of our churches. The Pastors' College, for the use of whose students this work is published, earnestly petitions for a place in the intercessions of the saints.

We are not at all surprised to learn that Thomas Watson enjoyed the repute, while at Cambridge, of being a most laborious student; the great Puritanic authors must have been most industrious workers at the university, or they never would have become such pre-eminent masters in Israel. The conscientious student is the most likely man to become a successful preacher. After completing his course with honour, Watson became rector of St Stephen's, Walbrook, where in the very heart of London he executed for nearly sixteen years the office of a faithful pastor with great diligence and assiduity. Happy were the citizens who regularly attended so instructive and spiritual a ministry. The church was constantly filled, for the fame and popularity of the preacher were deservedly great. Going in and out among his flock, fired with holy zeal for their eternal welfare, his years rolled on pleasantly enough amid the growing respect of all who knew him. Calamy, in his Nonconformist Memorial, says of him:— 'He was so well known in the city for his piety and usefulness, that though he was singled out by the Friendly Debate, he yet carried a general respect from all sober persons along with him to his grave. He was a man of considerable learning, a popular, but judicious preacher (if one may judge from his writings), and eminent in the gift of prayer. Of this, the following anecdote is a sufficient proof. Once on a lecture day, before the Bartholomew Act took place, the learned Bishop Richardson came to hear him at St Stephen's, who was much pleased with his sermon, but especially with his prayer after it, so that he followed him home to give him thanks, and earnestly desired a copy of his prayer. "Alas!" (said Mr Watson) "that is what I cannot give, for I do not use to pen my prayers; it was no studied thing, but uttered, pro re nata, as God enabled me, from the abundance of my heart and affections." Upon which the good Bishop went away wondering that any man could pray in that manner extempore.'

But the hand which of old had oppressed the church was again stretched forth to vex certain of the saints. The most learned, holy, and zealous of the clergy of the Church of England found that the Act of Uniformity would not allow them to preserve a clean conscience and retain their livings, and therefore they submitted to the loss of all things for Christ's sake. Thomas Watson did not hesitate as to the course he should pursue. He was not a factious hater of royalty, a red republican, or fifth monarchy-man; in fact, he had in Cromwell's day been all too loyal to the house of Stuart; he had protested against the execution of the King, and had joined in Love's plot for the bringing in of Charles II; yet all this availed nothing, he was a Puritan, and therefore must not be tolerated by the bitter spirits then dominant in the Establishment. What seeds of discord were sown on that black Bartholomew history has not had space to record; yet the ultimate results have been fraught with results scarcely then imaginable. Comprehension might have hindered truth; the crown rights of King Jesus might have lacked advocates had monarchs and priests been more tolerant; as it was good men were forced into a truer position than they would otherwise have occupied, and the beginning of a real reformation was inaugurated. From that commencement in suffering what progress has been made! Every day the cause of the ejected gathers force and pushes on its adversary towards the brink of the precipice, adown which all establishments must fall.

With many tears and lamentations the congregation of St Stephen's saw their shepherd about to be removed from his flock, and with aching hearts they listened to his parting words. He himself speaking as one bereaved of his dearest delight, and yet suffering joyfully the loss of all things, bade them adieu, and went forth 'not knowing whither he went.'

In the collection of Farewell Sermons there are three by Mr Watson, viz.: two delivered August 17th, and the third on the Tuesday following. The first, preached in the forenoon, is on John xiii 34. 'A new commandment I give unto you, that ye love one another.' It discovers much of the spirit of the gospel, particularly in recommending love to enemies and persecutors. The second, preached in the afternoon, is on 2 Corinthians vii 1. 'Having therefore these promises, dearly beloved, let us cleanse ourselves from all filthiness of the flesh and spirit, perfecting holiness in the fear of God.' In the former part of it, he insists largely on 'the ardent affections of a right gospel minister towards his people.' This head he closes thus: 'I have now exercised my ministry among you for almost sixteen years; and I rejoice and bless God that I cannot say, the more I love you, the less I am loved: *I have received many signal demonstrations of love from you. Though other parishes have exceeded you in number of houses, yet, I think, none for strength of affection. I have with much comfort observed your reverent attention to the word preached; you rejoice in this light, not for a season, but to this day. I have observed your zeal against error in a critical time, your unity and amity. This is your honour. If there should be any interruption in my ministry among you, though I should not be permitted to preach to you again, yet I shall not cease to love you, and to pray for you. But why should there be any interruption made? Where is the crime? Some, indeed, say that we are disloyal and seditious. Beloved, what my actions and sufferings for his Majesty have been is known to not a few of you. However, we must go to heaven through good report and bad report; and it is well if we can get to glory, though we press through the pikes. I shall endeavour that I may still approve the sincerity of my love to you. I will not promise that I shall still preach among you, nor will I say that I shall not. I desire to be guided by the silver thread of God's word and providence. My heart is towards you. There is, you know, an expression in the late Act, "that we shall now shortly be as if we were naturally dead;" and if I must die, let me leave some legacy with you.' Then follow twenty admirable directions, well worthy the fervent perusal of every Christian. He closes them thus: 'I beseech you treasure them up as so many jewels in the cabinet of your breasts. Did you carry them about you, they would be an antidote to keep you from sin, and a means to preserve the zeal of piety flaming upon the altar of your hearts. I have many things yet to say to you, but I know not whether God will give another opportunity. My strength is now almost gone. I beseech you, let these things make deep impressions on all your souls. Consider what hath been said, and the Lord give you understanding in all things.'*

The last discourse, August 19th, is on Isaiah iii 10, 11. 'Say ye to the righteous, that it shall be well with him: for they shall eat the fruit of their doings. Woe unto the wicked! it shall be ill with him, for the reward of his hands shall be given him.'

After his ejectment, Watson preached occasionally whenever he could do so with safety. Fines and imprisonments were insufficient to close the mouths of the witnesses of Jesus. In barns, kitchens, outhouses, or dells and woods, the faithful few gathered to hear the message of eternal life. Those little secret assemblies were doubtless charming occasions for devout minds: the word of the Lord was precious in those days. Bread eaten in secret is proverbially sweet, and the word of God in persecution is peculiarly delightful. Little can we realise the joyful anticipation which preceded the appointed meetings, or the lingering memories which clung to them long after they were over. After the great fire in 1666, when the churches were burned, Mr Watson and several other Nonconformists fitted up large rooms for those who had an inclination to attend. Upon the Indulgence, in 1672, he licensed the great hall in Crosby House, on the east side of Bishopsgate-street, then belonging to Sir John Langham (a Nonconformist). It was a happy circumstance that the worthy baronet favoured the cause of Nonconformity, and that so noble a chamber was at his disposal. Here Watson preached for several years. Rev Stephen Charnock, B.D., became joint pastor with him at Crosby Hall in 1675, and continued so till his death in 1680. What two shepherds for the flock! Men of such most extraordinary gifts and graces were seldom if ever united in one pastorate. They both attempted a Body of Divinity, and the goodly volume on the Divine Attributes was Charnock's first stone of a colossal structure which he was not spared to complete. Our author was more modest in his attempt and the present volume shows how he succeeded.

Mr Watson at length returned to Essex, where he died suddenly, in his closet at prayer, as is supposed, about 1689 or 1690. The time either of his birth or death is nowhere mentioned.

In the life of Colonel James Gardiner, there is this remarkable account: 'In July, 1719, he had spent the evening, which was the Sabbath, in some gay company, and had an unhappy assignation with a married lady, whom he was to attend exactly at twelve. The company broke up about eleven, and he went into his chamber to kill the tedious hour. It happened that he took up a religious book, which his good mother or aunt had, without his knowledge, slipped into his portmanteau, called, "The Christian Soldier," written by Mr Watson. Guessing by the title that he should find some phrases of his own profession spiritualised in a manner which might afford him some diversion, he resolved to dip into it: while this book was in his hand, an impression was made upon his mind, which drew after it a train of the most important consequences. Suddenly he thought he saw an unusual blaze of light fall on the book while he was reading, and lifting up his eyes, he apprehended, to his extreme amazement, that there was before him, as it were suspended in the air, a visible representation of the Lord Jesus Christ upon the cross, surrounded with a glory, and was impressed as if a voice had come to him, to this effect: "O sinner, did I suffer this for thee, and are these thy returns?" He sunk down in his chair, and continued for some time insensible. He then arose in a tumult of passions, and walked to and fro in his chamber, till he was ready to drop, in unutterable astonishment and agony of heart, which continued until the October following, when his terrors were turned into un-utterable joy.'

Mr Watson published a variety of books upon practical subjects, and of a useful nature, for the titles of which, see foot-note.* But his principal work was a body of divinity, in one hundred and seventy-six sermons, upon the Assembly's Catechism, which did not appear till after his death. It was published in one volume folio, in 1692, and accompanied with a portrait of the author, by Sturt; together with a recommendatory preface by the Rev William Lorimer, and the attestation of twenty-five other ministers of principal note in that day. For many a year this volume continued to train the common people in theology, and it may still be found very commonly in the cottages of the Scottish peasantry. Rev George Rogers, Principal of the Pastors' College, has carefully superintended

---

* The following are the titles of the principal works of Thomas Watson: viz. Three treatises: 1. 'The Christian's Charter.' 2. 'The Art of Divine Contentment.' 3. 'A Discourse of Meditation,' to which is added several sermons, 1660. This volume contains, besides the three treatises, the following, viz.: 'God's Anatomy upon Man's Heart,' 'The Saint's Delight,' 'A Christian on Earth still in Heaven,' 'Christ's Loveliness,' 'The Upright Man's Character and Crown,' 'The One Thing Necessary,' 'The Holy Longing; or, the Saint's Desire to be with Christ,' 'Beatitudes; or, a Discourse upon part of Christ's Famous Sermon upon the Mount,' 1660, 'A Body of Practical Divinity,' etc., with a supplement of some sermons, 'A Divine Cordial,'' The Holy Eucharist,' 'Heaven taken by Storm,' etc., etc.

the issue of this present edition, and in a note to us he writes: 'I know of no work with so much sermon matter within the same compass. In Howe, and Charnock, and Owen, we must often read much before we are tempted to close the book and think out a whole sermon, but Watson teaches us to make short work of it. The whole may be utilised. On this account it would be, I think, of great value to all our students who have pastorates. It is for their benefit, I suppose, you wished the reprint. As several select sermons, which are usually bound up with this work, will appear with his whole works, after a time, in Nichol's series, they are not included here. This is a distinct work by itself and complete. All editions extant which we have seen, abound in errors and imperfections. These have been rectified, not entirely we fear, but in a degree as nearly approaching to accuracy as in revision of another's composition could be expected. No alteration of sentiment has been made, but every shade of the author's meaning has been scrupulously retained. The style has been modernised, so far as could be done without detracting from its own peculiar characteristics. Long sentences have been divided into two or three, where it could be done without injury to the clearness or force of the signification. Modern words have been substituted for such as had become obsolete; Latin quotations restored to their correct form, as far as their sources could be ascertained; and divisions of subjects more perspicuously arranged. The whole, in fact, has been rendered more readable, and consequently more attractive and intelligible, which in our estimation far outweighs all the supposed advantages that could arise from perpetuating the crudities and vulgarities, as they now appear to us, of former times. By popularising ancient works, their readers are multiplied and their meaning may often be more readily apprehended.'*

A PRELIMINARY DISCOURSE TO
CATECHISING

'If ye continue in the faith grounded and settled.' – Col i 23.

Intending next Lord's day to enter upon the work of catechising, it will not be amiss to give you a preliminary discourse, to show you how needful it is for Christians to be well instructed in the grounds of religion. 'If ye continue in the faith grounded and settled.'

I. *It is the duty of Christians to be settled in the doctrine of faith.*

II. *The best way for Christians to be settled is to be well grounded.*

I. *It is the duty of Christians to be settled in the doctrine of faith.* It is the apostle's prayer, 1 Pet v 10, 'The God of all grace stablish, strengthen, settle you.' That is, that they might not be meteors in the air, but fixed stars. The apostle Jude speaks of 'wandering stars' in verse 13. They are called wandering stars, because, as Aristotle says, 'They do leap up and down, and wander into several parts of the heaven; and being but dry exhalations, not made of that pure celestial matter as the fixed stars are, they often fall to the earth.' Now, such as are not settled in religion, will, at one time or other, prove wandering stars; they will lose their former steadfastness, and wander from one opinion to another. Such as are unsettled are of the tribe of Reuben, 'unstable as water,' Gen xlix 4; like a ship without ballast, overturned with every wind of doctrine. Beza writes of one Belfectius, that his religion changed as the moon. The Arians had every year a new faith. These are not pillars in the temple of God, but reeds shaken every way. The apostle calls them 'damnable heresies.' 2 Pet ii 1. A man may go to hell as well for heresy as adultery. To be unsettled in religion, argues want of judgment. If their heads were not giddy, men would not reel so fast from one opinion to another. It argues lightness. As feathers will be blown every way, so will feathery Christians. *Triticum non rapit ventus inanes palæ jactantur.* Cyprian. Therefore such are compared to children. Eph iv 14. 'That we be no more children, tossed to and fro.' Children are fickle, sometimes of one mind, sometimes of another, nothing pleases them long; so unsettled Christians are childish; the truths they embrace at one time, they reject at another; sometimes they like the Protestant religion, and soon after they have a good mind to turn Papists.

[1] It is the great end of the word preached, to bring us to a settlement in religion. Eph iv 11, 12, 14. 'And he gave some, evangelists; and some, pastors and teachers; for the edifying of the body of Christ; that we henceforth be no more children.' The word is called a hammer. Jer xxiii 29. Every blow of the hammer is to fasten the nails of the building; so the preacher's words are to fasten you the more to Christ; they weaken themselves to strengthen and settle you. This is the grand design of preaching, not only for the enlightening, but for the establishing of souls; not only to guide them in the right way, but to keep them in it. Now, if you be not settled, you do not answer God's end in giving you the ministry.

[2] To be settled in religion is both a Christian's excellence and honour. It is his excellence. When the milk is settled it turns to cream; now he will be zealous for the truth, and walk in close communion with God. And his honour. Prov xvi 31. 'The hoary head is a crown of glory, if it be found in the way of righteousness.' It is one of the best sights to see an old disciple; to see silver hairs adorned with golden virtues.

[3] Such as are not settled in the faith can never suffer for it. Sceptics in religion hardly ever prove martyrs. They that are not settled hang in suspense; when they think of the joys of heaven they will espouse the gospel, but when they think of persecution they desert it. Unsettled Christians do not consult what is best, but what is safest. 'The apostate (says Tertullian) seems to put God and Satan in balance, and having weighed both their services, prefers the devil's service, and proclaims him to be the best master: and, in this sense, may be said to put Christ to open shame.' Heb vi 6. He will never suffer for the truth, but be as a soldier that leaves his colours, and runs over to the enemy's side; he will fight on the devil's side for pay.

[4] Not to be settled in the faith is provoking to God. To espouse the truth, and then to fall away, brings an ill report upon the gospel, which will not go unpunished. Psa lxxviii 57, 59. 'They turned back, and dealt unfaithfully. When God heard this, he was wroth, and greatly abhorred Israel.' The apostate drops as a wind-fall into the devil's mouth.

[5] If ye are not settled in religion, you will never grow. We are commanded 'to grow up into the head, even Christ.' Eph iv 15. But if we are unsettled there is no growing: 'the plant which is continually removing never thrives.' He can no more grow in godliness, who is unsettled, than a bone can grow in the body that is out of joint.

[6] There is great need to be settled, because there are so many things to unsettle us. Seducers are abroad, whose work is to draw away people

[2]

from the principles of religion. I John ii 26. 'These things have I written unto you concerning them that seduce you.' Seducers are the devil's factors; they are of all others the greatest felons that would rob you of the truth. Seducers have silver tongues, that can put off bad wares; they have a sleight to deceive. Eph iv 14. The Greek word there is taken from those that can throw dice, and cast them for the best advantage. So seducers are impostors, they can throw a dice; they can so dissemble and sophisticate the truth, that they can deceive others. Seducers deceive by wisdom of words. Rom xvi 18. 'By good words and fair speeches they deceive the hearts of the simple.' They have fine elegant phrases, flattering language, whereby they work on the weaker sort. Another sleight is a pretence of extraordinary piety, that so people may admire them, and suck in their doctrine. They seem to be men of zeal and sanctity, and to be divinely inspired, and pretend to new revelations. A third cheat of seducers is, labouring to vilify and nullify sound orthodox teachers. They would eclipse those that bring the truth, like black vapours that darken the light of heaven; they would defame others, that they themselves may be more admired. Thus the false teachers cried down Paul, that they might be received Gal iv 17. The fourth cheat of seducers is, to preach the doctrine of liberty; as though men are freed from the moral law, the rule as well as the curse, and Christ has done all for them, and they need to do nothing. Thus they make the doctrine of free grace a key to open the door to all licentiousness. Another means is, to unsettle Christians by persecution. 2 Tim iii 12. The gospel is a rose that cannot be plucked without prickles. The legacy Christ has bequeathed is the Cross. While there is a devil and a wicked man in the world, never expect a charter of exemption from trouble. How many fall away in an hour of persecution! Rev xii 4. 'There appeared a great red dragon, having seven heads and ten horns; and his tail drew the third part of the stars of heaven.' The red dragon, by his power and subtilty, drew away stars, or eminent professors, that seemed to shine as stars in the firmament of the church.

To be unsettled in good is the sin of the devils. Jude 6. They are called, 'morning stars,' Job xxxviii 7, but 'falling stars;' they were holy, but mutable. As the vessel is overturned with the sail, so their sails being swelled with pride, they were overturned. 1 Tim iii 6. By unsettledness, men imitate lapsed angels. The devil was the first apostate. The sons of Sion should be like mount Sion, which cannot be removed.

II. *The second proposition is, that the way for Christians to be settled is to be well grounded.* 'If ye continue grounded and settled.' The Greek word for *grounded* is a metaphor which alludes to a building that has the foundation

[3]

well laid. So Christians should be grounded in the essential points of religion, and have their foundation well laid.

Here let me speak to two things:

[1] That we should be grounded in the knowledge of fundamentals. The apostle speaks of 'the first principles of the oracles of God.' Heb v 12. In all arts and sciences, logic, physic, mathematics, there are some *præcognita*, some rules and principles that must necessarily be known for the practice of those arts; so, in divinity, there must be the first principles laid down. The knowledge of the grounds and principles of religion is exceedingly useful.

(1.) Else we cannot serve God aright. We can never worship God acceptably, unless we worship him regularly; and how can we do that, if we are ignorant of the rules and elements of religion? We are to give God a 'reasonable service.' Rom xii 1. If we understand not the grounds of religion, how can it be a reasonable service?

(2.) Knowledge of the grounds of religion much enriches the mind. It is a lamp to our feet; it directs us in the whole course of Christianity, as the eye directs the body. Knowledge of fundamentals is the golden key that opens the chief mysteries of religion; it gives us a whole system and body of divinity, exactly drawn in all its lineaments and lively colours; it helps us to understand many of those difficult things which occur in the reading of the word; it helps to untie many Scripture knots.

(3.) It furnishes us with armour of proof; weapons to fight against the adversaries of the truth.

(4.) It is the holy seed of which grace is formed. It is *semen fidei*, the seed of faith. Psa ix 10. It is *radix amoris*, the root of love. Eph iii 17. 'Being rooted and grounded in love.' The knowledge of principles conduces to the making of a complete Christian.

[2] This grounding is the best way to being settled: 'grounded and settled.' A tree, that it may be well settled, must be well rooted; so, if you would be well settled in religion, you must be rooted in its principles. We read in Plutarch of one who set up a dead man, and he would not stand. 'Oh,' said he, 'there should be something within.' So, that we may stand in shaking times, there must be a principle of knowledge within; first grounded, and then settled. That the ship may be kept from overturning, it must have its anchor fastened. Knowledge of principles is to the soul as the anchor to the ship, that holds it steady in the midst of the rolling waves of error, or the violent winds of persecution. First grounded and then settled.

[4]

Use one: See the reason why so many people are unsettled, ready to embrace every novel opinion, and dress themselves in as many religions as fashions; it is because they are ungrounded. See how the apostle joins these two together, 'unlearned and unstable.' 2 Pet iii 16. Such as are unlearned in the main points of divinity are unstable. As the body cannot be strong that has the sinews shrunk; so neither can that Christian be strong in religion who wants the grounds of knowledge, which are the sinews to strengthen and stablish him.

Use two: See what great necessity there is of laying down the main grounds of religion in a way of catechising, that the weakest judgment may be instructed in the knowledge of the truth, and strengthened in the love of it. Catechising is the best expedient for the grounding and settling of people. I fear one reason why there has been no more good done by preaching, has been because the chief heads and articles in religion have not been explained in a catechistical way. Catechising is laying the foundation. Heb vi 1. To preach and not to catechise is to build without foundation. This way of catechising is not novel, it is apostolic. The primitive church had their forms of catechism, as those phrases imply, a 'form of sound words,' 2 Tim i 13, and 'the first principles of the oracles of God,' Heb v 12. The church had its *catechumenoi*, as Grotius and Erasmus observe. Many of the ancient fathers have written for it, as Fulgentius, Austin, Theodoret, Lactantius, and others. God has given great success to it. By thus laying down the grounds of religion catechistically, Christians have been clearly instructed and wondrously built up in the Christian faith, insomuch that Julian the apostate, seeing the great success of catechising, put down all schools and places of public literature, and instructing of youth. It is my design, therefore (with the blessing of God), to begin this work of catechising the next Sabbath day; and I intend every other Sabbath, in the afternoon, to make it my whole work to lay down the grounds and fundamentals of religion in a catechistical way. If I am hindered in this work by men, or taken away by death, I hope God will raise up some other labourer in the vineyard among you, that may perfect the work which I am now beginning.

I. Introduction

1. MAN'S CHIEF END

Q1: WHAT IS THE CHIEF END OF MAN?

A: Man's chief end is to glorify God, and to enjoy him for ever.

Here are two ends of life specified. I. *The glorifying of God*. II. *The enjoying of God*.

I. *The glorifying of God*, 1 Pet iv 11. 'That God in all things may be glorified.' The glory of God is a silver thread which must run through all our actions. 1 Cor x 31. 'Whether therefore ye eat or drink, or whatsoever ye do, do all to the glory of God.' Everything works to some end in things natural and artificial; now, man being a rational creature, must propose some end to himself, and that should be, that he may lift up God in the world. He had better lose his life than the end of his living. The great truth is asserted, that the end of every man's living should be to glorify God. Glorifying God has respect to all the persons in the Trinity; it respects God the Father who gave us life; God the Son, who lost his life for us; and God the Holy Ghost, who produces a new life in us; we must bring glory to the whole Trinity.

When we speak of God's glory, the question will be moved, *What are we to understand by God's glory?*

There is a twofold glory: [1] The glory that God has in himself, his intrinsic glory. Glory is essential to the Godhead, as light is to the sun: he is called the 'God of Glory.' Acts vii 2. Glory is the sparkling of the Deity; it is so co-natural to the Godhead, that God cannot be God without it. The creature's honour is not essential to his being. A king is a man without his regal ornaments, when his crown and royal robes are taken away; but God's glory is such an essential part of his being, that he cannot be God without it. God's very life lies in his glory. This glory can receive no addition, because it is infinite; it is that which God is most tender of, and which he will not part with. Isa xlviii 11. 'My glory I will not give to

[6]

another.' God will give temporal blessings to his children, such as wisdom, riches, honour; he will give them spiritual blessings, he will give them grace, he will give them his love, he will give them heaven; but his essential glory he will not give to another. King Pharaoh parted with a ring off his finger to Joseph, and a gold chain, but he would not part with his throne. Gen xli 40. 'Only in the throne will I be greater than thou.' So God will do much for his people; he will give them the inheritance; he will put some of Christ's glory, as mediator, upon them; but his essential glory he will not part with; 'in the throne he will be greater.' [2] The glory which is ascribed to God, or which his creatures labour to bring to him. 1 Chron xvi 29. 'Give unto the Lord the glory due unto his name.' And, 1 Cor vi 20. 'Glorify God in your body, and in your spirit.' The glory we give God is nothing else but our lifting up his name in the world, and magnifying him in the eyes of others. Phil i 20. 'Christ shall be magnified in my body.'

What is it to glorify God?

Glorifying God consists in four things: 1. Appreciation, 2. Adoration, 3. Affection, 4. Subjection. This is the yearly rent we pay to the crown of heaven.

[1] Appreciation. To glorify God is to set God highest in our thoughts, and to have a venerable esteem of him. Psa xcii 8. 'Thou, Lord, art most high for evermore.' Psa xcvii 9. 'Thou art exalted far above all gods.' There is in God all that may draw forth both wonder and delight; there is a constellation of all beauties; he is *prima causa*, the original and spring-head of being, who sheds a glory upon the creature. We glorify God, when we are God-admirers; admire his attributes, which are the glistering beams by which the divine nature shines forth; his promises which are the charter of free grace, and the spiritual cabinet where the pearl of price is hid; the noble effects of his power and wisdom in making the world, which is called 'the work of his fingers.' Psa viii 3. To glorify God is to have God-admiring thoughts; to esteem him most excellent, and search for diamonds in this rock only.

[2] Glorifying God consists in adoration, or worship. Psa xxix 2. 'Give unto the Lord the glory due unto his name; worship the Lord in the beauty of holiness.' There is a twofold worship: (1.) A civil reverence which we give to persons of honour. Gen xxiii 7. 'Abraham stood up and bowed himself to the children of Heth.' Piety is no enemy to courtesy. (2.) A divine worship which we give to God as his royal prerogative. Neh viii 6. 'They bowed their heads, and worshipped the Lord with their

faces towards the ground.' This divine worship God is very jealous of; it is the apple of his eye, the pearl of his crown; which he guards, as he did the tree of life, with cherubims and a flaming sword, that no man may come near it to violate it. Divine worship must be such as God himself has appointed, else it is offering strange fire. Lev x 1. The Lord would have Moses make the tabernacle, 'according to the pattern in the mount.' Exod xxv 40. He must not leave out anything in the pattern, nor add to it. If God was so exact and curious about the place of worship, how exact will he be about the matter of his worship! Surely here everything must be according to the pattern prescribed in his word.

[3] Affection. This is part of the glory we give to God, who counts himself glorified when he is loved. Deut vi 5. 'Thou shalt love the Lord thy God with all thy heart, and with all thy soul.' There is a twofold love: (1.) *Amor concupiscentiæ*, a love of concupiscence, which is self-love; as when we love another, because he does us a good turn. A wicked man may be said to love God, because he has given him a good harvest, or filled his cup with wine. This is rather to love God's blessing than to love God. (2.) *Amor amicitiæ*, a love of delight, as a man takes delight in a friend. This is to love God indeed; the heart is set upon God, as a man's heart is set upon his treasure. This love is exuberant, not a few drops, but a stream. It is superlative; we give God the best of our love, the cream of it. Cant viii 2. 'I would cause thee to drink of spiced wine of the juice of my pomegranate.' If the spouse had a cup more juicy and spiced, Christ must drink of it. It is intense and ardent. True saints are seraphims, burning in holy love to God. The spouse was *amore perculsa*, in fainting fits, 'sick of love.' Cant ii 5. Thus to love God is to glorify him. He who is the chief of our happiness has the chief of our affections.

[4] Subjection. This is when we dedicate ourselves to God, and stand ready dressed for his service. Thus the angels in heaven glorify him; they wait on his throne, and are ready to take a commission from him; therefore they are represented by the cherubims with wings displayed, to show how swift they are in their obedience. We glorify God when we are devoted to his service; our head studies for him, our tongue pleads for him, and our hands relieve his members. The wise men that came to Christ did not only bow the knee to him, but presented him with gold and myrrh. Matt ii 11. So we must not only bow the knee, give God worship, but bring presents of golden obedience. We glorify God when we stick at no service, when we fight under the banner of his gospel against an enemy, and say to him as David to King Saul, 'Thy servant will go and fight with this Philistine.' 1 Sam xvii 32.

[8]

A good Christian is like the sun, which not only sends forth heat, but goes its circuit round the world. Thus, he who glorifies God, has not only his affections heated with love to God, but he goes his circuit too; he moves vigorously in the sphere of obedience.

Why must we glorify God?

[1] Because he gives us our being. Psa c 3. 'It is he that made us.' We think it a great kindness in a man to spare our life, but what kindness is it in God to give us our life! We draw our breath from him; and as life, so all the comforts of life are from him. He gives us health, which is the sauce to sweeten our life; and food, which is the oil that nourishes the lamp of life. If all we receive is from his bounty, is it not reasonable we should glorify him? Should we not live to him, seeing we live by him? Rom xi 36. 'For of him, and through him, are all things.' All we have is of his fulness, all we have is through his free grace; and therefore to him should be all. It follows, therefore, 'To him be glory for ever.' God is not our benefactor only, but our founder, as rivers that come from the sea empty their silver streams into the sea again.

[2] Because God has made all things for his own glory. Prov xvi 4. 'The Lord hath made all things for himself:' that is, 'for his glory.' As a king has excise out of commodities, so God will have glory out of everything. He will have glory out of the wicked. If they will not give him glory, he will get glory upon them. Exod xiv 17. 'I will get me honour upon Pharaoh.' But especially has he made the godly for his glory; they are the lively organs of his praise. Isa xliii 21. 'This people have I formed for myself, and they shall shew forth my praise.' It is true, they cannot add to his glory, but they may exalt it; they cannot raise him in heaven, but they may raise him in the esteem of others here. God has adopted the saints into his family, and made them a royal priesthood, that they should show forth the praise of him who hath called them. 1 Pet ii 9.

[3] Because the glory of God has intrinsic value and excellence; it transcends the thoughts of men, and the tongues of angels. His glory is his treasure, all his riches lie here; as Micah said. Judges xviii 24. 'What have I more?' So, what has God more? God's glory is more worth than heaven, and more worth than the salvation of all men's souls. Better kingdoms be thrown down, better men and angels be annihilated, than God should lose one jewel of his crown, one beam of his glory.

[4] Creatures below us, and above us, bring glory to God; and do we think to sit rent free? Shall everything glorify God but man? It is a pity then that man was ever made. (1.) Creatures below us glorify God, the

inanimate creatures and the heavens glorify God. 'The heavens declare the glory of God.' Psa xix 1. The curious workmanship of heaven sets forth the glory of its Maker; the firmament is beautified and pencilled out in blue and azure colours, where the power and wisdom of God may be clearly seen. 'The heavens declare his glory:' we may see the glory of God blazing in the sun, and twinkling in the stars. Look into the air, the birds, with their chirping music, sing hymns of praise to God. Every beast in its kind glorifies God. Isa xliii 20. 'The beast of the field shall honour me.' (2.) Creatures above us glorify God: 'the angels are ministering spirits.' Heb i 14. They are still waiting on God's throne, and bring some revenues of glory into the exchequer of heaven. Surely man should be much more studious of God's glory than the angels; for God has honoured him more than the angels, in that Christ took man's nature upon him, and not the angels'. Though, in regard of creation, God made man 'a little lower than the angels,' Heb ii 7, yet in regard of redemption, God has set him higher than the angels. He has married mankind to himself; the angels are Christ's friends, not his spouse. He has covered us with the purple robe of righteousness, which is a better righteousness than the angels have. 2 Cor v 21. If then the angels bring glory to God, much more should we, being dignified with honour above angelic spirits.

[5] We must bring glory to God, because all our hopes hang upon him. Psa xxxix 7. 'My hope is in thee.' And Psa lxii 5. 'My expectation is from him;' I expect a kingdom from him. A child that is good-natured will honour his parent, by expecting all he needs from him. Psa lxxxvii 7. 'All my springs are in thee.' The silver springs of grace, and the golden springs of glory are in him.

In how many ways may we glorify God?

[1] It is glorifying God when we aim purely at his glory. It is one thing to advance God's glory, another thing to aim at it. God must be the *Terminus ad quem*, the ultimate end of all actions. Thus Christ, John viii 50, 'I seek not mine own glory, but the glory of him that sent me.' A hypocrite has a squint eye, for he looks more to his own glory than God's. Our Saviour deciphers such, and gives a caveat against them in Matthew vi 2, 'When thou givest alms, do not sound a trumpet.' A stranger would ask, 'What means the noise of this trumpet?' It was answered, 'They are going to give to the poor.' And so they did not give alms, but sell them for honour and applause, that they might have glory of men; the breath of men was the wind that blew the sails of their charity; 'verily they have their reward.' The hypocrite may make his acquittance and write, 'received in full payment.' Chrysostom calls vain-glory one of the devil's great

nets to catch men. And Cyprian says, 'Whom Satan cannot prevail against by intemperance, those he prevails against by pride and vainglory.' Oh let us take heed of self-worshipping! Aim purely at God's glory. We do this,

(1.) When we prefer God's glory above all other things; above credit, estate, relations; when the glory of God coming in competition with them, we prefer his glory before them. If relations lie in our way to heaven, we must either leap over them, or tread upon them. A child must unchild himself, and forget he is a child; he must know neither father nor mother in God's cause. Deut xxxiii 9. 'Who said unto his father and mother, I have not seen him; neither did he acknowledge his brethren.' This is to aim at God's glory.

(2.) We aim at God's glory, when we are content that God's will should take place, though it may cross ours. Lord, I am content to be a loser, if thou be a gainer; to have less health, if I have more grace, and thou more glory. Let it be food or bitter physic if thou givest it me. Lord, I desire that which may be most for thy glory. Our blessed Saviour said, 'Not as I will, but as thou wilt.' Matt xxvi 39. If God might have more glory by his sufferings, he was content to suffer. John xii 28. 'Father, glorify thy name.'

(3.) We aim at God's glory when we are content to be outshined by others in gifts and esteem, so that his glory may be increased. A man that has God in his heart, and God's glory in his eye, desires that God should be exalted; and if this be effected, let who will be the instrument, he rejoices. Phil i 15. 'Some preach Christ of envy: notwithstanding, Christ is preached, and I therein do rejoice, yea, and will rejoice'; they preached Christ of envy, they envied Paul that concourse of people, and they preached that they might outshine him in gifts, and get away some of his hearers: well, says Paul, Christ is preached, and God is like to have the glory, therefore I rejoice; let my candle go out, if the Sun of Righteousness may but shine.

[2] We glorify God by an ingenuous confession of sin. The thief on the cross had dishonoured God in his life, but at his death he brought glory to God by confession of sin. Luke xxiii 41. 'We indeed suffer justly.' He acknowledged he deserved not only crucifixion, but damnation. Josh vii 19. 'My son, give, I pray thee, glory to God, and make confession unto him.' A humble confession exalts God. How is God's free grace magnified in crowning those who deserve to be condemned! The excusing and mincing of sin casts a reproach upon God. Adam denied not that he tasted the forbidden fruit, but, instead of a full confession, he taxed God. Gen

iii 12. 'The woman whom thou gavest me, she gave me of the tree, and I did eat;' if thou hadst not given me the woman to be a tempter, I had not sinned. Confession glorifies God, because it clears him; it acknowledges that he is holy and righteous, whatever he does. Nehemiah vindicates God's righteousness; chap ix 33. 'Thou art just in all that is brought upon us.' A confession is ingenuous when it is free, not forced. Luke xv 18. 'I have sinned against heaven and before thee.' The prodigal charged himself with sin before his father charged him with it.

[3] We glorify God by believing. Rom iv 20. 'Abraham was strong in faith, giving glory to God.' Unbelief affronts God, it gives him the lie; 'he that believeth not, maketh God a liar.' 1 John v 10. But faith brings glory to God; it sets to its seal that God is true. John iii 33. He that believes flies to God's mercy and truth, as to an altar of refuge; he engarrisons himself in the promises, and trusts all he has with God. Psa xxxi 5. 'Into thy hands I commit my spirit.' This is a great way of bringing glory to God, and God honours faith, because faith honours him. It is a great honour we do to a man when we trust him with all we have, when we put our lives and estates into his hand; it is a sign we have a good opinion of him. The three children glorified God by believing. 'The God whom we serve is able to deliver us, and will deliver us.' Dan iii 17. Faith knows there are no impossibilities with God, and will trust him where it cannot trace him.

[4] We glorify God, by being tender of his glory. God's glory is dear to him as the apple of his eye. An ingenuous child weeps to see a disgrace done to his father. Psa lxix 9. 'The reproaches of them that reproached thee are fallen upon me.' When we hear God reproached, it is as if we were reproached; when God's glory suffers, it is as if we suffered. This is to be tender of God's glory.

[5] We glorify God by fruitfulness. John xv 8. 'Hereby is my Father glorified, that ye bear much fruit.' As it is dishonouring God to be barren, so fruitfulness honours him. Phil i 11. 'Filled with the fruits of righteousness, which are to the praise of his glory.' We must not be like the fig tree in the gospel, which had nothing but leaves, but like the pomecitron, that is continually either mellowing or blossoming, and is never without fruit. It is not profession, but fruit that glorifies God. God expects to have his glory from us in this way. 1 Cor ix 7. 'Who planteth a vineyard, and eateth not of the fruit of it?' Trees in the forest may be barren, but trees in the garden are fruitful. We must bring forth the fruits of love and good works. Matt v 16. 'Let your light so shine before men, that they may see your good works, and glorify your Father which is in heaven.'

[12]

Faith sanctifies our works, and works testify our faith; to be doing good to others, to be eyes to the blind, feet to the lame, much glorifies God. Thus Christ glorified his Father; 'he went about doing good.' Acts x 38. By being fruitful, we are fair in God's eyes. Jer xi 16. 'The Lord called thy name a green olive-tree, fair and of goodly fruit.' And we must bear much fruit; it is muchness of fruit that glorifies God: 'if ye bear much fruit.' The spouse's breasts are compared to clusters of grapes, to show how fertile she was. Cant vii 7. Though the lowest degree of grace may bring salvation to you, yet it will not bring much glory to God. It was not a spark of love Christ commended in Mary, but much love; 'she loved much.' Luke vii 47.

[6] We glorify God, by being contented in that state in which Providence has placed us. We give God the glory of his wisdom, when we rest satisfied with what he carves out to us. Thus Paul glorified God. The Lord cast him into as great variety of conditions as any man, 'in prisons more frequent, in deaths oft,' 2 Cor xi 23, yet he had learned to be content. Paul could sail either in a storm or a calm; he could be anything that God would have him; he could either want or abound. Phil iv 13. A good Christian argues thus: It is God that has put me in this condition; he could have raised me higher, if he pleased, but that might have been a snare to me: he has done it in wisdom and love; therefore I will sit down satisfied with my condition. Surely this glorifies God much; God counts himself much honoured by such a Christian. Here, says God, is one after mine own heart; let me do what I will with him, I hear no murmuring, he is content. This shows abundance of grace. When grace is crowning, it is not so much to be content; but when grace is conflicting with inconveniences, then to be content is a glorious thing indeed. For one to be content when he is in heaven is no wonder; but to be content under the cross is like a Christian. This man must needs bring glory to God; for he shows to all the world, that though he has little meal in his barrel, yet he has enough in God to make him content: he says, as David, Psa xvi 5, 'The Lord is the portion of mine inheritance; the lines are fallen to me in pleasant places.'

[7] We glorify God by working out our own salvation. God has twisted together his glory and our good. We glorify him by promoting our own salvation. It is a glory to God to have multitudes of converts; now, his design of free grace takes, and God has the glory of his mercy; so that, while we are endeavouring our salvation, we are honouring God. What an encouragement is this to the service of God, to think, while I am hearing and praying, I am glorifying God; while I am furthering my own

glory in heaven, I am increasing God's glory. Would it not be an encouragement to a subject, to hear his prince say to him, You will honour and please me very much, if you will go to yonder mine of gold, and dig as much gold for yourself as you can carry away? So, for God to say, Go to the ordinances, get as much grace as you can, dig out as much salvation as you can; and the more happiness you have, the more I shall count myself glorified.

[8] We glorify God by living to God. 2 Cor v 15. 'That they which live should not live to themselves, but unto him who died for them.' Rom xiv 8. 'Whether we live, we live unto the Lord.' The Mammonist lives to his money, the Epicure lives to his belly; the design of a sinner's life is to gratify lust, but we glorify God when we live to God. We live to God when we live to his service, and lay ourselves out wholly for God. The Lord has sent us into the world, as a merchant sends his factor beyond the seas to trade for him. We live to God when we trade for his interest, and propagate his gospel. God has given every man a talent; and when a man does not hide it in a napkin, but improves it for God, he lives to God. When a master in a family, by counsel and good example, labours to bring his servants to Christ; when a minister spends himself, and is spent, that he may win souls to Christ, and make the crown flourish upon Christ's head; when the magistrate does not wear the sword in vain, but labours to cut down sin, and to suppress vice; this is to live to God, and this is glorifying God. Phil i 20. 'That Christ might be magnified, whether by life or by death.' Three wishes Paul had, and they were all about Christ; that he might be found in Christ, be with Christ, and magnify Christ.

[9] We glorify God by walking cheerfully. It brings glory to God, when the world sees a Christian has that within him that can make him cheerful in the worst times; that can enable him, with the nightingale, to sing with a thorn at his breast. The people of God have ground for cheerfulness. They are justified and adopted, and this creates inward peace; it makes music within, whatever storms are without. 2 Cor i 4. 1 Thess i 6. If we consider what Christ has wrought for us by his blood, and wrought in us by his Spirit, it is a ground of great cheerfulness, and this cheerfulness glorifies God. It reflects upon a master when the servant is always drooping and sad; sure he is kept to hard commons, his master does not give him what is fitting; so, when God's people hang their heads, it looks as if they did not serve a good master, or repented of their choice, which reflects dishonour on God. As the gross sins of the wicked bring a scandal on the gospel, so do the uncheerful lives of the godly. Ps c 2. 'Serve the

Lord with gladness.' Your serving him does not glorify him, unless it be with gladness. A Christian's cheerful looks glorify God; religion does not take away our joy, but refines it; it does not break our viol, but tunes it, and makes the music sweeter.

[10] We glorify God, by standing up for his truths. Much of God's glory lies in his truth. God has intrusted us with his truth, as a master intrusts his servant with his purse to keep. We have not a richer jewel to trust God with than our souls, nor has God a richer jewel to trust us with than his truth. Truth is a beam that shines from God. Much of his glory lies in his truth. When we are advocates for truth we glorify God. Jude 3. 'That ye should contend earnestly for the truth.' The Greek word to contend signifies great contending, as one would contend for his land, and not suffer his right to be taken from him; so we should contend for the truth. Were there more of this holy contention God would have more glory. Some contend earnestly for trifles and ceremonies, but not for the truth. We should count him indiscreet that would contend more for a picture than for his inheritance; for a box of counters than for his box of title deeds.

[11] We glorify God, by praising him. Doxology, or praise, is a God-exalting work. Psa l 23. 'Whoso offereth praise glorifieth me.' The Hebrew word *Bara*, to create, and *Barak*, to praise, are little different, because the end of creation is to praise God. David was called the sweet singer of Israel, and his praising God was called glorifying God. Psa lxxxvi 12. 'I will praise thee, O Lord my God, and I will glorify thy name.' Though nothing can add to God's essential glory, yet praise exalts him in the eyes of others. When we praise God, we spread his fame and renown, we display the trophies of his excellency. In this manner the angels glorify him; they are the choristers of heaven, and do trumpet forth his praise. Praising God is one of the highest and purest acts of religion. In prayer we act like men; in praise we act like angels. Believers are called 'temples of God.' 1 Cor iii 16. When our tongues praise, then the organs in God's spiritual temple are sounding. How sad is it that God has no more glory from us in this way! Many are full of murmuring and dis-content, but seldom bring glory to God, by giving him the praise due to his name. We read of the saints having harps in their hands, the emblems of praise. Many have tears in their eyes, and complaints in their mouth, but few have harps in their hand, blessing and glorifying God. Let us honour God this way. Praise is the quit-rent we pay to God: while God renews our lease, we must renew our rent.

[12] We glorify God, by being zealous for his name. Numb xxv 11.

'Phinehas hath turned my wrath away, while he was zealous for my sake.' Zeal is a mixed affection, a compound of love and anger; it carries forth our love to God, and our anger against sin in an intense degree. Zeal is impatient of God's dishonour; a Christian fired with zeal, takes a dishonour done to God worse than an injury done to himself. Rev ii 2. 'Thou canst not bear them that are evil.' Our Saviour Christ thus glorified his Father; he, being baptized with a spirit of zeal, drove the money-changers out of the temple. John ii 14—17. 'The zeal of thine house hath eaten me up.'

[13] We glorify God, when we have an eye to God in our natural and in our civil actions. In our natural actions; in eating and drinking. 1 Cor x 31. 'Whether therefore ye eat or drink, do all to the glory of God.' A gracious person holds the golden bridle of temperance; he takes his meat as a medicine to heal the decays of nature, that he may be the fitter, by the strength he receives, for the service of God; he makes his food, not fuel for lust, but help to duty. In buying and selling, we do all to the glory of God. The wicked live upon unjust gain, by falsifying the balances, as in Hosea xii 7. 'The balances of deceit are in his hands;' and thus while men make their weights lighter, they make their sins heavier, when by exacting more than the commodity is worth, they do not for fourscore write down fifty, but for fifty four-score; when they exact double the price that a thing is worth. We buy and sell to the glory of God, when we observe that golden maxim, 'To do to others as we would have them do to us;' so that when we sell our commodities, we do not sell our consciences also. Acts xxiv 16. 'Herein do I exercise myself, to have always a conscience void of offence towards God, and towards men.' We glorify God, when we have an eye to God in all our civil and natural actions, and do nothing that may reflect any blemish on religion.

[14] We glorify God by labouring to draw others to God; by seeking to convert others, and so make them instruments of glorifying God. We should be both diamonds and loadstones; diamonds for the lustre of grace, and loadstones for attractive virtue in drawing others to Christ. Gal iv 19. 'My little children, of whom I travail,' &c. It is a great way of glorifying God, when we break open the devil's prison, and turn men from the power of Satan to God.

[15] We glorify God in a high degree when we suffer for God, and seal the gospel with our blood. John xxi 18, 19. 'When thou shalt be old, another shall gird thee, and carry thee whither thou wouldest not: this spake he, signifying by what death he should glorify God.' God's glory

[16]

shines in the ashes of his martyrs. Isa xxiv 15. 'Wherefore glorify the Lord in the fires.' Micaiah was in the prison, Isaiah was sawn asunder, Paul beheaded, Luke hanged on an olive tree; thus did they, by their death, glorify God. The sufferings of the primitive saints did honour to God, and made the gospel famous in the world. What would others say? See what a good master they serve, and how they love him, that they will venture the loss of all in his service. The glory of Christ's kingdom does not stand in worldly pomp and grandeur, as other kings'; but it is seen in the cheerful sufferings of his people. The saints of old 'loved not their lives to the death.' Rev xii 11. They embraced torments as so many crowns. God grant we may thus glorify him, if he calls us to it. Many pray, 'Let this cup pass away,' but few, 'Thy will be done.'

[16] We glorify God, when we give God the glory of all that we do. When Herod had made an oration, and the people gave a shout, saying, 'It is the voice of a God, and not of a man,' he took the glory to himself; the text says, 'Immediately the angel of the Lord smote him, because he gave not God the glory, and he was eaten of worms.' Acts xii 23. We glorify God, when we sacrifice the praise and glory of all to God. 1 Cor xv 10. 'I laboured more abundantly than they all,' a speech, one would think, savoured of pride; but the apostle pulls the crown from his own head, and sets it upon the head of free grace: 'yet not I, but the grace of God which was with me.' As Joab, when he fought against Rabbah, sent for King David, that he might carry away the crown of the victory, 2 Sam xii 28, so a Christian, when he has gotten power over any corruption or temptation, sends for Christ, that he may carry away the crown of the victory. As the silkworm, when she weaves her curious work, hides herself under the silk, and is not seen; so when we have done anything praiseworthy, we must hide ourselves under the veil of humility, and transfer the glory of all we have done to God. As Constantine used to write the name of Christ over his door, so should we write the name of Christ over our duties. Let him wear the garland of praise.

[17] We glorify God by a holy life. A bad life dishonours God. 1 Pet ii 9. 'Ye are an holy nation, that ye should shew forth the praises of him that hath called you.' Rom ii 24. 'The name of God is blasphemed among the Gentiles through you.' Epiphanius says, 'That the looseness of some Christians in his time made many of the heathens shun their company, and would not be drawn to hear their sermons.' By our exact Bible-conversation we glorify God. Though the main work of religion lies in the heart, yet our light must so shine that others may behold it. The safety of a building is the foundation, but the glory of it is in the frontis-

piece; so the beauty of faith is in the conversation. When the saints, who are called jewels, cast a sparkling lustre of holiness in the eyes of the world, then they 'walk as Christ walked.' 1 John ii 6. When they live as if they had seen the Lord with bodily eyes, and been with him upon the mount, they adorn religion, and bring revenues of glory to the crown of heaven.

Use one: This subject shows us that our chief end should not be to get great estates, not to lay up treasures upon earth; which is the degeneracy of mankind since the fall. Sometimes they never arrive at an estate, they do not get the venison they hunt for; or if they do, what have they? that which will not fill the heart any more than the mariner's breath will fill the sails of the ship. They spend their time, as Israel, in gathering straw, but remember not, that the end of living is to glorify God. Eccles v 16. 'What profit hath he that laboureth for the wind?' These things are soon gone.

Use two: It reproves such, (1.) As bring no glory to God; who do not answer the end of their creation; whose time is not time lived, but time lost; who are like the wood of the vine, Ezek xv 2; whose lives are, as St Bernard speaks 'either sinfulness or barrenness. A useless burden on the earth.' God will one day ask such a question as King Ahasuerus did, Esth vi 3. 'What honour and dignity hath been done to Mordecai?' What honour has been done to me? what revenues of glory have you brought into my exchequer? There is no one here present but God has put in some capacity of glorifying him; the health he has given you, the parts, estate, seasons of grace, all are opportunities put into your hand to glorify him; and, be assured, he will call you to account, to know what you have done with the mercies he has entrusted you with, what glory you have brought to him. The parable of the talents, where the men with the five talents and the two talents are brought to a reckoning, evidently shows that God will call you to a strict account, to know how you have traded with your talents, and what glory you have brought to him. Now, how sad will it be with them who hide their talents in a napkin, that bring God no glory at all! Matt xxv 30. 'Cast ye the unprofitable servant into outer darkness.' It is not enough for you to say, that you have not dishonoured God, you have not lived in gross sin; but what good have you done? what glory have you brought to God? It is not enough for the servant of the vineyard that he does no hurt in the vineyard, that he does not break the trees, or destroy the hedges; if he does not do service in the vineyard, he loses his pay; so, if you do not good in your place, do not glorify God, you will lose your pay, you will miss of salvation. Oh, think of this, all you that live unserviceably! Christ cursed the barren fig tree.

(2.) It reproves such as are so far from bringing glory to God, that they rob God of his glory. Mal iii 8. 'Will a man rob God? Yet ye have robbed me.' They rob God, who take the glory due to God to themselves. 1. If they have gotten an estate, they ascribe all to their own wit and industry, they set the crown upon their own head, not considering that, Deut viii 18, 'Thou shalt remember the Lord thy God, for it is he that giveth thee power to get wealth.' 2. If they do any duty of religion, they look to their own glory. Matt vi 5. 'That they may be seen of men;' that they may be set upon a theatre for others to admire and canonize them. The oil of vainglory feeds their lamp. How many by the wind of popular breath have been blown to hell! Whom the devil cannot destroy by intemperance, he does by vainglory.

(3.) It reproves those who fight against God's glory. Acts v 39. 'Lest ye be found to fight against God.' Such as oppose that whereby God's glory is promoted fight against God's glory. His glory is much promoted by the preaching of the word, which is his engine whereby he converts souls. Now, such as would hinder the preaching of the word fight against God's glory. 1 Thess ii 16. 'Forbidding us to speak to the Gentiles, that they might be saved.' Diocletian, who raised the tenth persecution against the Christians, prohibited church meetings, and would have the temples of the Christians to be razed down. Such as hinder preaching, as the Philistines that stopped the wells, stop the well of the water of life. They take away the physicians that should heal sin-sick souls. Ministers are lights, Matt v 14, and who but thieves hate the light? They directly strike at God's glory; and what an account will they have to give to God, when he shall charge the blood of men's souls upon them! Luke xi 52. 'Ye have taken away the key of knowledge; ye entered not in yourselves, and them that were entering in ye hindered.' If there be either justice in heaven, or fire in hell, they shall not go unpunished.

Use three: Exhortation. Let every one of us, in our place, make it our chief end and design to glorify God. (1.) Let me speak to magistrates. God has put much glory upon them. Psa lxxxii 6. 'I have said, Ye are Gods;' and will they not glorify him who has put so much glory upon them? (2.) Ministers should study to promote God's glory. God has entrusted them with two of the most precious things, his truth, and the souls of his people. Ministers, by virtue of their office, are to glorify God. They must glorify God, by labouring in the word and doctrine. 2 Tim iv 1. 'I charge thee before God and the Lord Jesus Christ, who shall judge the quick and the dead: preach the word, be instant in season, out of season,' etc. It was Augustine's wish, 'that Christ, at his coming, might find him either

[19]

praying or preaching.' Ministers must glorify God by their zeal and sanctity. The priests under the law, before they served at the altar, washed in the laver; so, such as serve in the Lord's house, must first be washed from gross sin in the laver of repentance. It is matter of grief and shame to think how many, who call themselves ministers, instead of bringing glory to God, dishonour him. 2 Chron xi 15. Their lives, as well as their doctrines, are heterodox; they are not free from the sins which they reprove in others. Plutarch's servant upbraided him, by saying, 'he has written a book against anger, *et ipse mihi irascitur*, yet he falls into a passion of anger with me.' So is a minister who preaches against drunkenness, yet he himself is drunk; he preaches against swearing, yet he himself swears! (3.) Masters of families must glorify God, must season their children and servants with the knowledge of the Lord; their houses should be little churches. Gen xviii 19. 'I know that Abraham will command his children, that they may keep the way of the Lord.' You that are masters have a charge of souls. For want of the bridle of family discipline youth runs wild.

It will be a great comfort in a dying hour, to think we have glorified God in our lives. It was Christ's comfort before his death: John xvii 4. 'I have glorified thee on the earth.' At the hour of death, all your earthly comforts will vanish: if you think how rich you have been, what pleasures you have had on earth; this will be so far from comforting you, that it will torment you the more. What is one the better for an estate that is spent? But to have conscience telling you, that you have glorified God on the earth, what sweet comfort and peace will this let into your soul! how will it make you long for death! The servant that has been all day working in the vineyard longs till evening comes, when he shall receive his pay. How can they who have lived, and brought no glory to God, think of dying with comfort? They cannot expect a harvest where they sowed no seed. How can they expect glory from God, who never brought any glory to him? Oh in what horror will they be at death! The worm of conscience will gnaw their souls, before the worms can gnaw their bodies.

If we glorify God, he will glorify our souls for ever. By raising God's glory, we increase our own: by glorifying God, we come at last to the blessed enjoyment of him.

II. *Man's chief end is to enjoy God for ever.* Psalm lxxiii 25. 'Whom have I in heaven but thee?' That is, What is there in heaven I desire to enjoy but thee? There is a twofold fruition or enjoying of God; the one is in this life, the other in the life to come.

[1] The enjoyment of God in this life. It is a great matter to enjoy God's ordinances, but to enjoy God's presence in the ordinances is that which a gracious heart aspires after. Psalm lxiii 2. 'To see thy glory so as I have seen thee in the sanctuary.' This sweet enjoyment of God, is, when we feel his Spirit co-operating with the ordinance, and distilling grace upon our hearts, when in the Word the Spirit quickens and raises the affections, Luke xxiv 32, 'Did not our hearts burn within us?', when the Spirit transforms the heart, leaving an impress of holiness upon it. 2 Cor iii 18. 'We are changed into the same image, from glory to glory.' When the Spirit revives the heart with comfort, it comes not only with its anointing, but with its seal; it sheds God's love abroad in the heart. Rom v 5. 'Our fellowship is with the Father, and with his Son Jesus Christ.' 1 John i 3. In the Word we hear God's voice, in the sacrament we have his kiss. The heart being warmed and inflamed in a duty is God's answering by fire. The sweet communications of God's Spirit are the first-fruits of glory. Now Christ has pulled off his veil, and showed his smiling face; now he has led a believer into the banqueting-house, and given him of the spiced wine of his love to drink; he has put in his finger at the hole of the door; he has touched the heart, and made it leap for joy. Oh how sweet is it thus to enjoy God! The godly have, in ordinances, had such divine raptures of joy, and soul transfigurations, that they have been carried above the world, and have despised all things here below.

Use one: Is the enjoyment of God in this life so sweet? How wicked are they who prefer the enjoyment of their lusts before the enjoyment of God! 2 Pet iii 3. 'The lust of the flesh, the lust of the eye, the pride of life,' is the Trinity they worship. Lust is an inordinate desire or impulse, provoking the soul to that which is evil. There is the revengeful lust, and the wanton lust. Lust, like a feverish heat, puts the soul into a flame. Aristotle calls sensual lusts brutish, because, when any lust is violent, reason or conscience cannot be heard. These lusts besot and brutalise the man. Hos iv 11. 'Whoredom and wine take away the heart;' the heart for anything that is good. How many make it their chief end, not to enjoy God, but to enjoy their lusts!; as that cardinal who said, 'Let him but keep his cardinalship of Paris, and he was content to lose his part in Paradise.' Lust first bewitches with pleasure, and then comes the fatal dart. Prov vii 23. 'Till a dart strike through his liver.' This should be as a flaming sword to stop men in the way of their carnal delights. Who for a drop of pleasure would drink a sea of wrath?

Use two: Let it be our great care to enjoy God's sweet presence in his ordinances. Enjoying spiritual communion with God is a riddle and mystery to most people. Every one that hangs about the court does not speak with the king. We may approach God in ordinances, and hang about the court of heaven, yet not enjoy communion with God. We may have the letter without the Spirit, the visible sign without the invisible grace. It is the enjoyment of God in a duty that we should chiefly look at. Psa xlii 2. 'My soul thirsteth for God, for the living God.' Alas! what are all our worldly enjoyments without the enjoyment of God! What is it to enjoy good health, a brave estate, and not to enjoy God? Job xxx 28. 'I went mourning without the sun.' So mayest thou say in the enjoyment of all creatures without God, 'I went mourning without the sun.' I have the starlight of outward enjoyments, but I want the Sun of Righteousness. 'I went mourning without the sun.' It should be our great design, not only to have the ordinances of God, but the God of the ordinances. The enjoyment of God's sweet presence here is the most contented life: he is a hive of sweetness, a magazine of riches, a fountain of delight. Psalm xxxvi 8, 9. The higher the lark flies the sweeter it sings: and the higher we fly by the wings of faith, the more we enjoy of God. How is the heart inflamed in prayer and meditation! What joy and peace is there in believing! Is it not comfortable being in heaven? He that enjoys much of God in this life carries heaven about him. Oh let this be the thing we are chiefly ambitious of, the enjoyment of God in his ordinances! The enjoyment of God's sweet presence here is an earnest of our enjoying him in heaven.

This brings us to the second thing:

[2] The enjoyment of God in the life to come. Man's chief end is to enjoy God for ever. Before the plenary fruition of God in heaven, there must be something previous and antecedent; and that is, our being in a state of grace. We must have conformity to him in grace, before we can have communion with him in glory. Grace and glory are linked and chained together. Grace precedes glory, as the morning star ushers in the sun. God will have us qualified and fitted for a state of blessedness. Drunkards and swearers are not fit to enjoy God in glory; the Lord will not lay such vipers in his bosom. Only the 'pure in heart shall see God.' We must first be, as the king's daughter, glorious within, before we are clothed with the robes of glory. As King Ahasuerus first caused the virgins to be purified and anointed, and they had their sweet odours to perfume them, and then went to stand before the king, Esth ii 12, so must we have the anointing of God, and be perfumed with the graces of the Spirit, those sweet odours, and then we shall stand before the king of heaven. Being thus divinely qualified by grace, we shall be taken up to the mount of vision, and enjoy

God for ever; and what is enjoying God for ever but to be put in a state of happiness? As the body cannot have life but by having communion with the soul, so the soul cannot have blessedness but by having immediate communion with God. God is the *summum bonum*, the chief good; therefore the enjoyment of him is the highest felicity.

He is a *universal* good; *bonum in quo omnia bona*, 'a good, in which are all goods.' The excellencies of the creature are limited. A man may have health, not beauty, learning, not parentage, riches, not wisdom; but in God are contained all excellencies. He is a good, commensurate fully to the soul; a sun, a portion, a horn of salvation; in whom dwells 'all fulness.' Col i 19. God is an *unmixed* good. There is no condition in this life but has its mixture; for every drop of honey there is a drop of gall. Solomon, who gave himself to find out the philosopher's stone, to search out for happiness here below, found nothing but vanity and vexation. Eccl i 2. God is perfect, the quintessence of good. He is sweetness in the flower. God is a *satisfying* good. The soul cries out, I have enough. Psalm xvii 15. 'I shall be satisfied with thy likeness.' Let a man who is thirsty be brought to an ocean of pure water, and he has enough. If there be enough in God to satisfy the angels, then sure there is enough to satisfy us. The soul is but finite, but God is infinite. Though God be a good that satisfies, yet he does not surfeit. Fresh joys spring continually from his face; and he is as much to be desired after millions of years by glorified souls as at the first moment. There is a fulness in God that satisfies, and yet so much sweetness, that the soul still desires. God is a *delicious* good. That which is the chief good must ravish the soul with pleasure; there must be in it rapturous delight and quintessence of joy. *In Deo quadam dulcedine delectatur anima immo rapitur* [There is a certain sweetness about God's person which delights, nay, rather, ravishes the soul]: The love of God drops such infinite suavity into the soul as is unspeakable and full of glory. If there be so much delight in God, when we see him only by faith, 1 Pet i 8, what will the joy of vision be, when we shall see him face to face! If the saints have found so much delight in God while they were suffering, oh what joy and delight will they have when they are being crowned! If flames are beds of roses, what will it be to lean on the bosom of Jesus! What a bed of roses that will be! God is a *superlative* good. He is better than anything you can put in competition with him: he is better than health, riches, honour. Other things maintain life, he gives life. Who would put anything in balance with the Deity? Who would weigh a feather against a mountain of gold? God excels all other things more infinitely than the sun the light of a taper. God is an *eternal* good. He is the Ancient of days, yet never decays, nor waxes old. Dan vii 9. The joy he gives is eternal, the crown fadeth not away. 1 Pet v 4. The glorified soul shall be ever solacing itself in God, feasting on his love, and sunning itself in the light of his countenance. We read of the river of pleasure at God's right hand; but will not this in time be dried up? No! There is a fountain at the bottom which feeds it. Psa xxxvi 9. 'With the Lord is the fountain of life.' Thus God is the chief good, and the enjoyment of God for ever is the highest felicity of which the soul is capable.

Use one: Let it be the chief end of our living to enjoy this chief good hereafter. Augustine reckons up 288 opinions among philosophers about happiness, but all were short of the mark. The highest elevation of a reasonable soul is to enjoy God for ever. It is the enjoyment of God that makes heaven. 1 Thess iv 17. 'Then shall we ever be with the Lord.' The soul trembles as the needle in the compass, and is never at rest till it comes to God. To set out this excellent state of a glorified soul's enjoyment of God: (1.) It must not be understood in a sensual manner: we must not conceive any carnal pleasures in heaven. The Turks, in their Koran, speak of a paradise of pleasure, where they have riches in abundance, and red wine served in golden chalices. The epicures of this age would like such a heaven when they die. Though the state of glory be compared to a feast, and is set out by pearls and precious stones, yet these metaphors are only helps to our faith, and to show us that there is superabundant joy and felicity in the highest heaven; but they are not carnal but spiritual delights. Our enjoyment will be in the perfection of holiness, in seeing the pure face of Christ, in feeling the love of God, in conversing with heavenly spirits; which will be proper for the soul, and infinitely exceed all carnal voluptuous delights. (2.) We shall have a lively sense of this glorious estate. A man in a lethargy, though alive, is as good as dead, because he is not sensible, nor does he take any pleasure in his life; but we shall have a quick and lively sense of the infinite pleasure which arises from the enjoyment of God: we shall know ourselves to be happy; we shall reflect with joy upon our dignity and felicity; we shall taste every crumb of that sweetness, every drop of that pleasure which flows from God. (3.) We shall be made able to bear a sight of that glory. We could not now bear that glory, it would overwhelm us, as a weak eye cannot behold the sun; but God will capacitate us for glory; our souls shall be so heavenly, and perfected with holiness, that they may be able to enjoy the blessed vision of God. Moses in a cleft of the rock saw the glory of God passing by. Exod xxxiii 22. From our blessed rock Christ, we shall behold the beatific sight of God. (4.) This enjoyment of God shall be more than a bare contemplation of him. Some of the learned move the question,

Whether the enjoyment of God shall be by way of contemplation only. That is something, but it is one half of heaven only; there shall be a loving of God, an acquiescence in him, a tasting his sweetness; not only inspection but possession. John xvii 24. 'That they may behold my glory;' there is inspection: Verse 22. 'And the glory thou hast given me, I have given them;' there is possession. 'Glory shall be revealed in us,' Rom viii 18; not only revealed to us, but in us. To behold God's glory, there is glory revealed *to* us; but, to partake of his glory, there is glory revealed *in* us. As the sponge sucks in the wine, so shall we suck in glory. (5.) There is no intermission in this state of glory. We shall not only have God's glorious presence at certain special seasons; but we shall be continually in his presence, continually under divine raptures of joy. There shall not be one minute in heaven, wherein a glorified soul may say, I do not enjoy happiness. The streams of glory are not like the water of a conduit, often stopped, so that we cannot have one drop of water; but those heavenly streams of joy are continually running. Oh how should we despise this valley of tears where we now are, for the mount of transfiguration! how should we long for the full enjoyment of God in Paradise! Had we a sight of that land of promise, we should need patience to be content to live here any longer.

Use two: Let this be a spur to duty. How diligent and zealous should we be in glorifying God, that we may come at last to enjoy him! If Tully, Demosthenes, and Plato, who had but the dim watch-light of reason to see by, fancied an elysium and happiness after this life, and took such Herculean pains to enjoy it, oh how should Christians, who have the light of Scripture to see by, bestir themselves that they may attain to the eternal fruition of God and glory! If anything can make us rise off our bed of sloth, and serve God with all our might, it should be this, the hope of our near enjoyment of God for ever. What made Paul so active in the sphere of religion? 1 Cor xv 10. 'I laboured more abundantly than they all.' His obedience did not move slow, as the sun on the dial; but swift, as light from the sun. Why was he so zealous in glorifying God, but that he might at last centre and terminate in him? 1 Thess iv 17. 'Then shall we ever be with the Lord.'

Use three: Let this comfort the godly in all the present miseries they feel. Thou complainest, Christian, thou dost not enjoy thyself, fears disquiet thee, wants perplex thee; in the day thou canst not enjoy ease, in the night thou canst not enjoy sleep; thou dost not enjoy the comforts of thy life. Let this revive thee, that shortly thou shalt enjoy God, and then shalt have more than thou canst ask or think; thou shalt have angels' joy, glory without intermission or expiration. We shall never enjoy ourselves fully till we enjoy God eternally.

2. THE SCRIPTURES

QII: WHAT RULE HATH GOD GIVEN TO DIRECT US HOW WE MAY GLORIFY AND ENJOY HIM?

A: The Word of God, which is contained in the scriptures of the Old and New Testaments, is the only rule to direct us how we may glorify and enjoy him.

2 Tim iii 16. 'All Scripture is given by inspiration of God,' &c. By Scripture is understood the sacred Book of God. It is given by divine inspiration; that is, the Scripture is not the contrivance of man's brain, but is divine in its origin. The image of Diana was had in veneration by the Ephesians, because they supposed it fell from Jupiter. Acts xix 35. The holy Scripture is to be highly reverenced and esteemed, because we are sure it came from heaven. 2 Pet i 21. The two Testaments are the two lips by which God has spoken to us.

How does it appear that the Scriptures have a Jus Divinum, *a divine authority stamped upon them?*

Because the Old and New Testament are the foundation of all religion. If their divinity cannot be proved, the foundation on which we build our faith is gone. I shall therefore endeavour to prove this great truth, that the Scriptures are the very word of God. I wonder whence the Scriptures should come, if not from God. Bad men could not be the authors of it. Would their minds be employed in inditing such holy lines? Would they declare so fiercely against sin? Good men could not be the authors of it. Could they write in such a strain? or could it stand with their grace to counterfeit God's name, and put, *Thus saith the Lord*, to a book of their own devising? Nor could any angel in heaven be the author of it, because the angels pry and search into the abyss of gospel mysteries, 1 Pet i 12, which implies their nescience of some parts of Scripture; and sure they cannot be the authors of that book which they themselves do not fully understand. Besides, what angel in heaven durst be so arrogant as to personate God and, say, 'I create,' Isa lxv 17, and, 'I the Lord have said it'? Numb xiv 35. So that it is evident, the pedigree of Scripture is sacred, and it could come from none but God himself.

Not to speak of the harmonious consent of all the parts of Scripture, there are seven cogent arguments which may evince it to be the Word of God.

[1] Its antiquity. It is of ancient standing. The grey hairs of Scripture make it venerable. No human histories extant reach further than Noah's flood: but the holy Scripture relates matters of fact that have been from the beginning of the world; it writes of things before time. That is a sure rule of Tertullian, 'That which is of the greatest antiquity, *id verum quod primum,* is to be received as most sacred and authentic.'

[2] We may know the Scripture to be the Word of God by its miraculous preservation in all ages. The holy Scriptures are the richest jewel that Christ has left us; and the church of God has so kept these public records of heaven, that they have not been lost. The Word of God has never wanted enemies to oppose, and, if possible, to extirpate it. They have given out a law concerning Scripture, as Pharaoh did the midwives, concerning the Hebrew women's children, to strangle it in the birth; but God has preserved this blessed Book inviolable to this day. The devil and his agents have been blowing at Scripture light, but could never blow it out; a clear sign that it was lighted from heaven. Nor has the church of God, in all revolutions and changes, kept the Scripture that it should not be lost only, but that it should not be depraved. The letter of Scripture has been preserved, without any corruption, in the original tongue. The Scriptures were not corrupted before Christ's time, for then Christ would not have sent the Jews to them. He said, 'Search the Scriptures.' He knew these sacred springs were not muddied with human fancies.

[3] The Scripture appears to be the Word of God, by the matter contained in it. The mystery of Scripture is so abstruse and profound that no man or angel could have known it, had it not been divinely revealed. That eternity should be born; that he who thunders in the heavens should cry in the cradle; that he who rules the stars should suck the breasts; that the Prince of Life should die; that the Lord of Glory should be put to shame; that sin should be punished to the full, yet pardoned to the full; who could ever have conceived of such a mystery, had not the Scripture revealed it to us? So, for the doctrine of the resurrection; that the same body which is crumbled into a thousand pieces, should rise *idem numero,* the same individual body, else it were a creation, not a resurrection. How could such a sacred riddle, above all human disquisition, be known, had not the Scripture made a discovery of it? As the matter of Scripture is so full of goodness, justice and sanctity, that it could be breathed from none but God; so the holiness of it shows it to be of God. Scripture is compared to silver refined seven times. Psa xii 6. The Book of God has no errata in it;

it is a beam of the Sun of Righteousness, a crystal stream flowing from the fountain of life. All laws and edicts of men have had their corruptions, but the Word of God has not the least tincture, it is of meridian splendour. Psa cxix 140. 'Thy word is very pure,' like wine that comes from the grape, which is not mixed nor adulterated. It is so pure that it purifies everything else. John xvii 17. 'Sanctify them through thy truth.' The Scripture presses holiness, so as no other book ever did: it bids us live 'soberly, righteously, and godly;' Titus ii 12; soberly, in acts of temperance; righteously, in acts of justice; godly, in acts of zeal and devotion. It commends to us, whatever is 'just, lovely, and of good report.' Phil iv 8. This sword of the Spirit cuts down vice. Eph vi 17. Out of this tower of Scripture is thrown a millstone upon the head of sin. The Scripture is the royal law which commands not only the actions, but affections; it binds the heart to good behaviour. Where is there such holiness to be found, as is digged out of this sacred mine? Who could be the author of such a book but God himself?

[4] That the Scripture is the Word of God is evident by its predictions. It prophesies of things to come, which shows the voice of God speaking in it. It was foretold by the prophet, 'A virgin shall conceive,' Isa vii 14, and, the 'Messiah shall be cut off.' Dan ix 26. The Scripture foretells things that would fall out many ages and centuries after; as how long Israel should serve in the iron furnace, and the very day of their deliverance. Exod xii 41. 'At the end of the four hundred and thirty years, even the self-same day, it came to pass that the host of the Lord went out of Egypt.' This prediction of future things, merely contingent, and not depending upon natural causes, is a clear demonstration of its divine origin.

[5] The impartiality of those men of God who wrote the Scriptures, who do not spare to set down their own failings. What man that writes a history would black his own face, by recording those things of himself that might stain his reputation? Moses records his own impatience when he struck the rock, and tells us, he could not on that account enter into the land of promise. David relates his own adultery and bloodshed, which stands as a blot in his escutcheon to succeeding ages. Peter relates his own pusillanimity in denying Christ. Jonah sets down his own passions, 'I do well to be angry to the death.' Surely had their pen not been guided by God's own hand, they would never have written that which reflects dishonour upon themselves. Men usually rather hide their blemishes than publish them to the world; but the penmen of holy Scripture eclipse their own name; they take away all glory from themselves, and give the glory to God.

[28]

[6] The mighty power and efficacy that the Word has had upon the souls and consciences of men. It has changed their hearts. Some by reading Scripture have been turned into other men; they have been made holy and gracious. By reading other books the heart may be warmed, but by reading this book it is transformed. 2 Cor iii 3. 'Ye are manifestly declared to be the epistle of Christ, written not with ink, but with the Spirit of the living God.' The Word was copied out into their hearts, and they were become Christ's epistle, so that others might read Christ in them. If you should set a seal upon marble, and it should make an impression upon the marble, and leave a print behind, there would be a strange virtue in that seal; so when the seal of the Word leaves a heavenly print of grace upon the heart, there must needs be a power going along with that Word no less than divine. It has comforted their hearts. When Christians have sat by the rivers weeping, the Word has dropped as honey, and sweetly revived them. A Christian's chief comfort is drawn out of these wells of salvation. Rom xv 4. 'That we through comfort of the Scriptures might have hope.' When a poor soul has been ready to faint, it has had nothing to comfort it but a Scripture cordial. When it has been sick, the Word has revived it. 2 Cor iv 17. 'Our light affliction, which is but for a moment, worketh for us a far more exceeding and eternal weight of glory.' When it has been deserted, the Word has dropped in the golden oil of joy. Lam iii 31. 'The Lord will not cast off for ever.' He may change his providence, not his purpose; he may have the look of an enemy, but he has the heart of a father. Thus the Word has a power in it to comfort the heart. Psa cxix 50. 'This is my comfort in mine affliction; for thy word hath quickened me.' As the spirits are conveyed through the arteries of the body, so divine comforts are conveyed through the promises of the Word. Now, the Scriptures having such an exhilarating, heart-comforting power in them, shows clearly that they are of God, and it is he that has put the milk of consolation into these breasts.

[7] The miracles by which Scripture is confirmed. Miracles were used by Moses, Elijah, and Christ, and were continued, many years after, by the apostles, to confirm the verity of the holy Scriptures. As props are set under weak vines, so these miracles were set under the weak faith of men, that if they would not believe the writings of the Word, they might believe the miracles. We read of God's dividing the waters, making a pathway in the sea for his people to go over, the iron swimming, the oil increasing by pouring out, Christ's making wine of water, his curing the blind, and raising the dead. Thus God has set a seal to the truth and divinity of the Scriptures by miracles.

The Papists cannot deny that the Scripture is divine and sacred; but they affirm quoad nos, *with respect to us, it receives its divine authority from the church; and in proof of it they bring that Scripture,* 1 Tim iii 15, *where the church is said to be the ground and pillar of truth.*

It is true, the church is the pillar of truth; but it does not therefore follow that the Scripture has its authority from the church. The king's proclamation is fixed on the pillar, the pillar holds it out, that all may read, but the proclamation does not receive its authority from the pillar, but from the king; so the church holds forth the Scriptures, but they do not receive their authority from the church, but from God. If the Word of God be divine, merely because the church holds it forth, then it will follow, that our faith is to be built upon the church, and not upon the Word, contrary to Eph ii 20. 'Built upon the foundation (that is the doctrine) of the apostles and prophets.'

Are all the books in the Bible of the same divine authority?

Those which we call canonical.

Why are the Scriptures called canonical?

Because the Word is a rule of faith, a canon to direct our lives. The Word is the judge of controversies, the rock of infallibility. That only is to be received for truth which agrees with Scripture, as the transcript with the original. All maxims in divinity are to be brought to the touchstone of Scripture, as all measures are brought to the standard.

Are the Scriptures a complete rule?

The Scripture is a full and perfect canon, containing in it all things necessary to salvation. 2 Tim iii 15. 'From a child thou hast known the holy Scriptures, which are able to make thee wise unto salvation.' It shows the *Credenda*, what we are to believe; and the *Agenda*, what we are to practise. It gives us an exact model of religion, and perfectly instructs us in the deep things of God. The Papists, therefore, make themselves guilty, who eke out Scripture with their traditions, which they consider equal to it. The Council of Trent says, that the traditions of the church of Rome are to be received *pari pietatis affectu*, with the same devotion that Scripture is to be received; so bringing themselves under the curse. Rev xxii 18. 'If any man shall add unto these things, God shall add unto him the plagues that are written in this book.'

What is the main scope and end of Scripture?

To reveal a way of salvation. It makes a clear discovery of Christ. John xx 31. 'These things are written, that ye might believe that Jesus is the Christ, and that believing ye might have life through his name.' The design of the Word is to be a test whereby our grace is to be tried; a sea-mark to show us what rocks are to be avoided. The Word is to sublimate and quicken our affections; it is to be our directory and consolatory; it is to waft us over to the land of promise.

Who should have the power of interpreting Scripture?

The Papists assert that it is in the power of the church. If you ask whom they mean by the church, they say, The Pope, who is head of it, and he is infallible; so Bellarmine. But that assertion is false, because many of the Popes have been ignorant and vicious, as Platina affirms, who writes the lives of Popes. Pope Liberius was an Arian, and Pope John XII denied the immortality of the soul; therefore Popes are not fit interpreters of Scripture; who then?

The Scripture is to be its own interpreter, or rather the Spirit speaking in it. Nothing can cut the diamond but the diamond; nothing can interpret Scripture but Scripture. The sun best discovers itself by its own beams; the Scripture interprets itself to the understanding. But the question is concerning hard places of Scripture, where the weak Christian is ready to wade beyond his depth; who shall interpret here?

The church of God has appointed some to expound and interpret Scripture; therefore he has given gifts to men. The several pastors of churches, like bright constellations, give light to dark Scriptures. Mal ii 7. 'The priest's lips should keep knowledge, and they should seek the law at his mouth.'

But this is to pin our faith upon men.

We are to receive nothing for truth but what is agreeable to the Word. As God has given to his ministers gifts for interpreting obscure places, so he has given to his people so much of the spirit of discerning, that they can tell (at least in things necessary to salvation) what is consonant to Scripture, and what is not. I Cor xii 10. 'To one is given a spirit of prophecy, to another discerning of spirits.' God has endued his people with such a measure of wisdom and discretion, that they can discern between truth and error, and judge what is sound and what is spurious. Acts xvii 11. 'The Bereans searched the Scriptures daily, whether those things were so.' They weighed the doctrine they heard, whether it was agreeable to Scripture, though Paul and Silas were their teachers. 2 Tim iii 16.

Use one: See the wonderful goodness of God, who, besides the light of nature, has committed to us the sacred Scriptures. The heathen are enveloped in ignorance. Psa cxlvii 20. 'As for his judgments they have not known them.' They have the oracles of the Sybils, but not the writings of Moses and the apostles. How many live in the region of death, where this bright star of Scripture never appeared! We have this blessed Book of God to resolve all our doubts, to point out a way of life to us. John xiv 22. 'Lord, how is it thou wilt manifest thyself unto us, and not unto the world?'

God having given us his written Word to be our directory takes away all excuses from men. No man can say, I went wrong for want of light; God has given thee his Word as a lamp to thy feet; therefore if thou goest wrong, thou dost it wilfully. No man can say, If I had known the will of God, I would have obeyed it; thou art inexcusable, O man, for God has given thee a rule to go by, he has written his law with his own finger; therefore, if thou obeyest not, thou hast no apology left. If a master leave his mind in writing with his servant, and tells him what work he will have done, and the servant neglects the work, that servant is left without excuse. John xv 22. 'Now you have no cloak for your sins.'

Use two: Is all Scripture of divine inspiration? Then it reproves, (1.) The Papists, who take away part of Scripture, and so clip the King of heaven's coin. They expunge the second commandment out of their catechisms, because it makes against images; and it is usual with them, if they meet with anything in Scripture which they dislike, either to put a false gloss upon it, or, if that will not do, to pretend it is corrupted. They are like Ananias, who kept back part of the money. Acts v 2. They keep back part of the Scripture from the people. It is a high affront to God to deface and obliterate any part of his Word, and brings us under that premunire, Rev xxii 19, 'If any man shall take away from the words of the book of this prophecy, God shall take away his part out of the book of life.' Is all Scripture of divine inspiration? (2.) It condemns the Antinomians, who lay aside the Old Testament as useless, and out of date; and call those who adhere to them Old Testament Christians. God has stamped a divine majesty upon both Testaments; and till they can show me where God has repealed the Old, it stands in force. The two Testaments are the two wells of salvation; the Antinomians would stop up one of these wells, they would dry up one of the breasts of Scripture. There is much gospel in the Old Testament. The comforts of the gospel in the New Testament have their rise from the Old. The great promise of the Messiah is in the Old Testament, 'A virgin shall conceive and bear a son.' Nay, I say more. The moral law, in some parts of it, speaks gospel – 'I am the Lord thy God;' here is the pure wine of the gospel. The saints' great charter, where God promises to 'sprinkle clean water upon them, and put his Spirit within them,' is to be found primarily in the Old Testament. Ezek xxxvi 25, 26. So that they who take away the Old Testament, as Samson pulled down the pillars, would take away the pillars of a Christian's comfort. (3.) It condemns the Enthusiasts, who, pretending to have the Spirit, lay aside the whole Bible, and say the Scripture is a dead letter, and they live above it. What impudence is this! Till we are above sin, we shall not be above Scripture. Let not men so talk of a revelation from the Spirit, but suspect it to be an imposture. The Spirit of God acts regularly, it works in and by the Word; and he that pretends to a new light, which is either above the Word, or contrary to it, abuses both himself and the Spirit: his light is borrowed from him who transforms himself into an angel of light. (4.) It condemns the slighters of Scripture; such as those who can go whole weeks and months and never read the Word. They lay it aside as rusty armour; they prefer a play or romance before Scripture. The *magnalia legis* are to them *minutula* [The weighty matters of the law are to them insignificant]. Oh how many can be looking at their faces in a glass all the morning, but their eyes begin to be sore when they look upon a Bible! Heathens die for want of Scripture, and these in contempt of it. They surely must needs go wrong who slight their guide. Such as lay the reins upon the neck of their lusts, and never use the curbing bit of Scripture to check them, are carried to hell, and never stop. (5.) It condemns the abusers of Scripture. Those who mud and poison this pure crystal fountain with their corrupt glosses, and who wrest Scripture. 2 Pet iii 16. The Greek word is, they set it upon the rack; they give wrong interpretations of it, not comparing Scripture with Scripture; as the Antinomians pervert that Scripture, Numb xxiii 21, 'He hath not beheld iniquity in Jacob;' from which they infer that God's people may take liberty in sin, because God sees no sin in them. It is true, God sees no sin in his people with an eye of revenge, but he sees it with an eye of observation. He sees not sin in them, so as to damn them; but he sees it, so as to be angry, and severely to punish them. Did not David find it so, when he cried out of his broken bones? In like manner the Arminians wrest the Scripture in John v 40, 'Ye will not come to me;' where they bring in free will. This text shows how willing God is that we should have life; and that sinners may do more than they do, they may improve the talents God has given them; but it does not prove the power of free will, for it is contrary to that Scripture, John vi 44, 'No man can come to me, except the Father which hath sent me draw him.' These, therefore, wring the text so hard, that they make the blood come out; they do not compare Scripture with Scripture. Some jest with Scripture. When they are sad, they take the Scripture as their lute or minstrel to play upon, and so drive away the sad spirit; as a drunkard I have read of, who, having drunk off his cups, called to some of his fellows, 'Give us of your oil, for our lamps are gone out.' In the fear of God, take heed of this. Eusebius tells us of one, who took a piece of Scripture to make a jest of, but was presently struck with a frenzy and ran mad. It is a saying of Luther, *Quos Deus vult perdere*, &c., 'Whom God intends to destroy, he gives them leave to play with Scripture.'

Use three: If the Scripture be of divine inspiration, then be exhorted, (1.) To study the Scripture. It is a copy of God's will. Be Scripture-men, Bible-Christians. 'I adore the fulness of Scripture,' says Tertullian. In the Book of God are scattered many truths as so many pearls. John v 39. 'Search the Scriptures.' Search as for a vein of silver. This blessed Book will fill your head with knowledge, and your heart with grace. God wrote the two tables with his own fingers; and if he took pains to write, well may we take pains to read. Apollos was mighty in the Scriptures. Acts xviii 24. The Word is our *Magna Charta* for Heaven; shall we be ignorant of our charter? Col iii 16. 'Let the word of God dwell in you richly.' The memory must be a tablebook where the Word is written. There is majesty sparkling in every line of Scripture; take but one instance, Isa lxiii 1: 'Who is this that cometh from Edom, with dyed garments from Bozrah? This that is glorious in his apparel, travelling in the greatness of his strength? I that speak in righteousness, mighty to save.' Here is a lofty, magnificent style. What angel could speak after this manner? Junius was converted by reading one verse of John; he beheld a majesty in it beyond all human rhetoric. There is a melody in Scripture. This is that blessed harp which drives away sadness of spirit. Hear the sounding of this harp a little. 1 Tim i 15. 'This is a faithful saying, and worthy of all acceptation, that Christ Jesus came into the world to save sinners;' he took not only our flesh upon him but our sins. And Matt xi 28. 'Come unto me, all ye that are heavy laden, and I will give you rest.' How sweetly does this harp of Scripture sound, what heavenly music does it make in the ears of a distressed sinner, especially when the finger of God's Spirit touches this instrument! There is divinity in Scripture. It contains the marrow and quintessence of religion. It is a rock of diamonds, a mystery of piety. The lips of Scripture have grace poured into them. The Scripture speaks of faith, self-denial, and all the graces which, as a chain of pearls, adorns a Christian. It excites to holiness; it treats of another world, it gives a prospect of eternity! Oh, then, search the Scripture! make the Word familiar to you. Had I the tongue of angels, I could not sufficiently set forth the excellency of Scripture. It is a spiritual

[34]

optic-glass, in which we behold God's glory; it is the tree of life, the oracle of wisdom, the rule of manners, the heavenly seed of which the new creature is formed. James i 18. 'The two Testaments,' says Austin, 'are the two breasts which every Christian must suck, that he may get spiritual nourishment.' The leaves of the tree of life were for healing. Rev xxii 2. So these holy leaves of Scripture are for the healing of our souls. The Scripture is profitable for all things. If we are deserted, here is spiced wine that cheers the heavy heart; if we are pursued by Satan, here is the sword of the Spirit to resist him; if we are diseased with sin's leprosy, here are the waters of the sanctuary, both to cleanse and cure. Oh, then, search the Scriptures! There is no danger in tasting this tree of knowledge. There was a penalty laid at first, that we might not taste of the tree of knowledge. Gen ii 17. 'In the day that thou eatest thereof, thou shalt surely die.' There is no danger in plucking from this tree of holy Scripture; if we do not eat of this tree of knowledge, we shall surely die. Oh, then, read the Scriptures! Time may come when the Scriptures may be kept from us.

Read the Bible with reverence. Think in every line you read that God is speaking to you. The ark wherein the law was put was overlaid with pure gold, and was carried on bars, that the Levites might not touch it. Exod xxv 14. Why was this, but to give reverence to the law? Read with seriousness. It is matter of life and death; by this Word you must be tried; conscience and Scripture are the jury God will proceed by, in judging you. Read the Word with affection. Get your hearts quickened with the Word; go to it to fetch fire. Luke xxiv 32. 'Did not our hearts burn within us?' Labour that the Word may not only be a lamp to direct, but a fire to warm. Read the Scripture, not only as a history, but as a love letter sent you from God, which may affect your hearts. Pray that the same Spirit that wrote the Word may assist you in reading it; that God's Spirit would show you the wonderful things of his law. 'Go near,' saith God to Philip, 'join thyself to this chariot.' Acts viii 29. So, when God's Spirit joins himself with the chariot of his Word, it becomes effectual.

(2.) Be exhorted to prize the written Word. Job xxiii 12. David valued the Word more than gold. What would the martyrs have given for a leaf of the Bible! The Word is the field where Christ the pearl of price is hid. In this sacred mine we dig, not for a wedge of gold, but for a weight of glory. The Scripture is a sacred collyrium, or eye-salve to illuminate us. Prov vi 23. 'The commandment is a lamp, and the law is light.' The Scripture is the chart and compass by which we sail to the new Jerusalem. It is a sovereign cordial in all distresses. What are the promises but the water of life to renew fainting spirits? Is it sin that troubles? Here is a Scripture cordial. Psa lxv 3. 'Iniquities prevail against me; as for our transgressions thou shalt purge them away;' or, as it is in the Hebrew, 'thou shalt cover them.' Do outward afflictions disquiet thee? Here is a Scripture cordial. Psa xci 15. 'I will be with him in trouble;' not only to behold, but to uphold. Thus, as in the ark manna was laid up, so promises are laid up in the ark of Scripture. The Scripture will make us wise. Wisdom is above rubies. Psa cxix 104. 'By thy precepts I get understanding.' What made Eve desire the tree of knowledge? Gen iii 6. 'It was a tree to make one wise.' The Scriptures teach a man to know himself. They discover Satan's snares and stratagems. 2 Cor ii 11. 'They make one wise to salvation.' 2 Tim iii 15. Oh, then, highly prize the Scriptures. I have read of Queen Elizabeth, that at her coronation, she received the Bible presented to her, with both her hands, and kissing it, laid it to her breast, saying, that that book had ever been her chief delight.

(3.) If the Scripture is of divine inspiration, believe it. The Romans, that they might gain credit to their laws, reported they were inspired by the gods of Rome. Oh give credence to the Word! It is breathed from God's own mouth. Hence arises the profaneness of men, that they do not believe the Scripture. Isa liii 1. 'Who hath believed our report?' Did you believe the glorious rewards the Scripture speaks of, would you not give diligence to make your election sure? Did you believe the infernal torments the Scripture speaks of, would it not put you into a cold sweat, and cause a trembling at heart for sin? But people are in part atheists, they give but little credit to the Word, therefore they are so impious, and draw such dark shadows in their lives. Learn to realize Scripture, get your hearts wrought to a firm belief of it. Some think, if God should send an angel from heaven, and declare his mind, they would believe him; or, if he should send one from the damned, and preach the torments of hell all in flames, they would believe. But, 'If they believe not Moses and the prophets, neither will they be persuaded though one arose from the dead.' Luke xvi 31. God is wise, and he thinks the fittest way to make his mind known to us is by writing; and such as shall not be convinced by the Word, shall be judged by the Word. The belief of Scripture is of high importance. It will enable us to resist temptation. 1 John ii 14. 'The Word of God abideth in you, and ye have overcome the wicked one.' It conduceth much to our sanctification; therefore sanctification of the Spirit, and belief of the truth, are put together. 2 Thess ii 13. If the Word written be not believed, it is like writing on water, which makes no impression.

(4.) Love the Word written. Psa cxix 97. 'Oh how love I thy law!'

'Lord,' said Augustine, 'let the holy Scriptures be my chaste delight.' Chrysostom compares the Scripture to a garden, every truth is a fragrant flower, which we should wear, not on our bosom, but in our heart. David counted the Word 'sweeter than honey and the honeycomb.' Psa xix 10. There is that in Scripture which may breed delight. It shows us the way to riches: Deut xxviii 5, Prov iii 10; to long life, Psa xxxiv 12; to a kingdom, Heb xii 28. Well then may we count those the sweetest hours which are spent in reading the holy Scriptures; well may we say with the prophet, Jer xv 16, 'Thy words were found, and I did eat them; and they were the joy and rejoicing of my heart.'

(5.) Conform to Scripture. Let us lead Scripture lives. Oh that the Bible might be seen printed in our lives! Do what the Word commands. Obedience is an excellent way of commenting upon the Bible. Psa lxxxvi 11. 'I will walk in thy truth.' Let the Word be the sun-dial by which you set your life. What are we the better for having the Scripture, if we do not direct all our speeches and actions according to it? What is a carpenter the better for his rule about him, if he sticks it at his back, and never makes use of it for measuring and squaring his work? So, what are we the better for the rule of the Word, if we do not make use of it, and regulate our lives by it? How many swerve and deviate from the rule! The Word teaches to be sober and temperate, but they are drunk; to be chaste and holy, but they are profane; they go quite from the rule! What a dishonour is it to religion, for men to live in contradiction to Scripture! The Word is called a 'light to our feet.' Psa cxix 105. It is not only a light to our eyes to mend our sight, but to our feet to mend our walk. Oh let us lead Bible conversations!

(6.) Contend for Scripture. Though we should not be of contentious spirits, yet we ought to contend for the Word of God. This jewel is too precious to be parted with. Prov iv 13. 'Keep her, for she is thy life.' The Scripture is beset with enemies; heretics fight against it, we must therefore 'contend for the faith once delivered to the saints.' Jude 3. The Scripture is our book of evidences for heaven; shall we part with our evidences? The saints of old were both advocates and martyrs for truth; they would hold fast Scripture, though it were with the loss of their lives.

(7.) Be thankful to God for the Scriptures. What a mercy is it that God has not only acquainted us what his will is, but that he has made it known by writing! In the old times God revealed his mind by visions, but the Word written is a surer way of knowing God's mind. 2 Pet i 18. 'This voice which came from heaven we heard, we have also a more sure word of prophecy.' The devil is God's ape, and he can transform himself into an angel of light; he can deceive with false revelations; as I have heard of one who had, as he thought, a revelation from God to sacrifice his child, as Abraham had; whereupon, following this impulse of the devil, he killed his child. Thus Satan deceives people with delusion, instead of divine revelations; therefore we are to be thankful to God for revealing his mind to us by writing. We are not left in doubtful suspense that we should not know what to believe, but we have an infallible rule to go by. The Scripture is our pole-star to direct us to heaven, it shows us every step we are to take; when we go wrong, it instructs us; when we go right, it comforts us; and it is matter of thankfulness, that the Scriptures are made intelligible, by being translated.

(8.) Adore God's distinguishing grace, if you have felt the power and authority of the Word upon your conscience; if you can say as David, Psa cxix 50, 'Thy word hath quickened me.' Christian, bless God that he has not only given thee his Word to be a rule of holiness, but his grace to be a principle of holiness. Bless God that he has not only written his Word, but sealed it upon thy heart, and made it effectual. Canst thou say it is of divine inspiration, because thou hast felt it to be of lively operation? Oh free grace! that God should send out his Word, and heal thee; that he should heal thee, and not others! That the same Scripture which to them is a dead letter, should be to thee a savour of life!

II. God and his creation

1. THE BEING OF GOD

QIII: WHAT DO THE SCRIPTURES PRINCIPALLY TEACH?

A: The Scriptures principally teach what man is to believe concerning God, and what duty God requires of man.

QIV: WHAT IS GOD?

A: God is a Spirit, infinite, eternal, and unchangeable, in his being, wisdom, power, holiness, justice, goodness, and truth.

Here is, I. *Something implied. That there is a God.* II. *Expressed. That he is a Spirit.* III. *What kind of Spirit?*

I. *Implied.* That there is a God. The question, *What is God?* takes for granted that there is a God. The belief of God's essence is the foundation of all religious worship. Heb xi 6. 'He that comes to God must believe that he is.' There must be a first cause, which gives being to all things besides. We know that there is a God.

[1] By the book of nature. The notion of a Deity is engraven on man's heart; it is demonstrable by the light of nature. I think it hard for a man to be a natural atheist; he may wish there were no God, he may dispute against a Deity, but he cannot in his judgment believe there is no God, unless by accumulated sin his conscience be seared, and he has such a lethargy upon him, that he has sinned away his very sense and reason.

[2] We know that there is a God by his works, and this is so evident a demonstration of a Godhead, that the most atheistical spirits, when they have considered these works, have been forced to acknowledge some wise and supreme maker of these things; as is reported of Galen and others. We will begin with the creation of the glorious fabric of heaven and earth. Sure there must be some architect or first cause. The world could not make itself. Who could hang the earth on nothing but the great

God? Who could provide such rich furniture for the heavens, the glorious constellations, the firmament bespangled with such glittering lights? We see God's glory blazing in the sun, twinkling in the stars. Who could give the earth its clothing, cover it with grass and corn, adorn it with flowers, enrich it with gold? God only. Job xxxviii 4. Who but God could make the sweet music in the heavens, cause the angels to join in concert, and sound forth the praises of their Maker? Job xxxviii 7. 'The morning stars sang together, and all the sons of God shouted for joy.' If a man should go into a far country, and see stately edifices there, he would never imagine that these built themselves, but that some greater power had built them. To imagine that the work of the creation was not framed by God, is as if we should conceive a curious landscape to be drawn by a pencil without the hand of an artist. Acts xvii 24. 'God that made the world, and all things therein.' To create is proper to the Deity. The wise government of all things evinces there is a God. God is the great superintendent of the world, he holds the golden reins of government in his hand, guiding all things most regularly and harmoniously to their proper end. Who that eyes Providence but must be forced to acknowledge there is a God? Providence is the queen and governess of the world; it is the hand that turns the wheel of the whole creation; it sets the sun its race, the sea its bounds. If God did not guide the world, things would run into disorder and confusion. When one looks on a clock, and sees the motion of the wheels, the striking of the hammer, the hanging of the plummets, he would say, some artificer made it; so, when we see the excellent order and harmony in the universe, the sun, that great luminary, dispensing its light and heat to the world, without which the world were but a grave or a prison; the rivers sending forth their silver streams to refresh the bodies of men, and prevent a drought; and every creature acting within its sphere, and keeping its due bounds; we must needs acknowledge there is a God, who wisely orders and governs all these things. Who could set this great army of the creatures in their several ranks and squadrons, and keep them in their constant march, but HE, whose name is THE LORD OF HOSTS? And as God does wisely dispose all things in the whole regiment of the creatures, so, by his power, he supports them. Did God suspend and withdraw his influence ever so little, the wheels of the creation would unpin, and the axletree break asunder. All motion, the philosophers say, is from something that is unmoveable. As for example, the elements are moved by the influence and motion of the heavenly bodies; the sun and moon, and these planets, are moved by the highest orb, called *Primum Mobile;* now, if one should ask, Who moves that highest orb, or is the first mover of the planets? It can be no other than God himself.

Man is a microcosm or lesser world. The excellent contexture and frame of his body is wrought curiously as with needlework. Psa cxxxix 15. 'I was curiously wrought in the lowest parts of the earth.' This body is endowed with a noble soul. Who but God could make such a union of different substances as flesh and spirit? In him we live, and move, and have our being. The quick motion of every part of the body shows there is a God. We may see something of him in the sparkling of the eye; and if the cabinet of the body be so curiously wrought, what is the jewel? The soul has a celestial brightness in it; as Damascene says, 'It is a diamond set in a ring of clay.' What noble faculties is the soul endowed with! Understanding, Will, Affections are a glass of the Trinity, as Plato speaks. The matter of the soul is spiritual, it is a divine spark lighted from heaven; and being spiritual, is immortal, as Scaliger notes; *anima non senescit;* 'the soul does not wax old,' it lives for ever. Who could create a soul ennobled with such rare angelic properties but God? We must needs say as the Psalmist, 'It is he that hath made us, and not we ourselves.' Psa c 3.

[3] We may prove a Deity by our conscience. Conscience is God's deputy or vicegerent. Conscience is a witness of a Deity. If there were no Bible to tell us there is a God, yet conscience might. Conscience, as the apostle says, 'either accuseth' or 'excuseth.' Rom ii 15. It acts in order to a higher judicatory. Natural conscience, being kept free from gross sin, excuses. When a man does virtuous actions, lives soberly and righteously, observes the golden maxim, doing to others as he would have them do to him, then conscience approves, and says, Well done. Like a bee it gives honey. Natural conscience in the wicked accuses. When men go against its light they feel the worm of conscience. *Eheu! quis intus scorpio?* [Alas! What scorpion lurks within?] Seneca. Conscience, being sinned against, spits fire in men's faces, fills them with shame and horror. When the sinner sees a handwriting on the wall of conscience, his countenance is changed. Many have hanged themselves to quiet their conscience. Tiberius the emperor, a bloody man, felt the lashes of his conscience; he was so haunted with that fury, that he told the senate, he suffered death daily. What could put a man's conscience into such an agony but the impression of a Deity, and the thoughts of coming before his tribunal? Those who are above human laws are subject to the checks of their own conscience. And it is observable, the nearer the wicked approach to death, the more they are terrified. Whence is this but from the apprehension of judgment approaching? The soul, being sensible of its immortal nature, trembles at him who never ceases to live, and therefore will never cease to punish.

[41]

[4] That there is a God, appears by the consent of nations, by the universal vote and suffrage of all men. *Nulla gens tam barbara cui non insideat hæc persuasio Deum esse.* Tully. 'No nation so barbarous,' says Tully, 'as not to believe there is a God.' Though the heathen did not worship the true God, yet they worshipped a god. They set up an altar, 'To the unknown God.' Acts xvii 23. They knew a God should be worshipped, though they knew not the God whom they ought to worship. Some worshipped Jupiter, some Neptune, some Mars. Rather than not worship something, they would worship anything.

[5] That there is a God, appears by his prediction of future things. He who can foretell things which shall surely come to pass is the true God. God foretold, that a virgin should conceive; he prefixed the time when the Messias should be cut off. Dan ix 26. He foretold the captivity of the Jews in Babylon, and who should be their deliverer. Isa xlv 1. God himself uses this argument to prove he is the true God, and that all the gods of the heathens are fictions and nullities. Isa xli 23. *Testimonium divinitatis est veritas divinationis.* Tertullian. To foretell things contingent, which depend upon no natural causes, is peculiar to Deity.

[6] That there is a God, appears by his unlimited power and sovereignty. He who can work, and none can hinder, is the true God; but God can do so. Isa xliii 13. 'I will work, and who shall let it?' Nothing can hinder action but some superior power; but there is no power above God: all power that is, is by him, therefore all power is under him; he has a 'mighty arm.' Psa lxxxix 13. He sees the designs men drive at against him, and plucks off their chariot wheels; he makes the diviners mad. Isa xliv 25. He cutteth off the spirit of princes; he bridleth the sea, gives check to the leviathan, binds the devil in chains; he acts according to his pleasure, he doth what he will. 'I will work, and who shall let it?'

[7] There are devils, therefore there is a God. Atheists cannot deny but there are devils, and then they must grant there is a God. We read of many possessed of the devil. The devils are called in Scripture 'hairy ones', because they often appeared in the form of goats or satyrs. Gerson, in his book *De probatione spirituum*, tells us how Satan on a time appeared to a holy man in a most glorious manner, professing himself to be Christ: the old man answered, 'I desire not to see my Saviour here in this desert, it shall suffice me to see him in heaven.' Now, if there be a devil, there is a God. Socrates, a heathen, when accused at his death, confessed, that, as he thought there was a *malus genius*, an evil spirit, so he thought there was a good spirit.

Use one: Seeing there is a God, it reproves such atheistical fools as deny it. Epicurus denied there was a Providence, saying that all things fell out by chance. He that says there is no God is the wickedest creature that is; he is worse than a thief, for he takes away our goods, but the atheist would take away our God from us. John xx 13. 'They have taken away my Lord.' So we may say of atheists, they would take away our God from us, in whom all our hope and comfort is laid up. Psa xiv 1. 'The fool hath said in his heart, There is no God.' He durst not speak it with his tongue, but says it in his heart: he wishes it. Sure none can be speculative atheists. 'The devils believe and tremble.' James ii 19. I have read of one Arthur, a professed atheist, who, when he came to die, cried out he was damned. Though there are few found who say, *There is no God*, yet many deny him in their practices. Tit i 16. 'In works they deny him.' Cicero said of Epicurus, *Verbis reliquit Deos resustulit* [In his words he both denies the existence of the gods, and permits them to remain]. The world is full of practical atheism; most people live as if they did not believe there was a God. Durst they lie, defraud, be unclean, if they believed there were a God who would call them to account? If an Indian who never heard of a God should come among us, and have no other means to convince him of a Deity, but the lives of men in our age, surely he would question whether there were a God; *utrum Dii sint non ausim affirmare* [I would not venture to assert that gods exist].

Use two: Seeing there is a God, he will deal righteously, and give just rewards to men. Things seem to be carried in the world very unequally; the wicked flourish. Psa lxxiii 3. They who tempt God are delivered. Mal iii 15. The ripe cluster of grapes are squeezed into their cup, and, in the meanwhile, the godly, who wept for sin, and served God, are afflicted. Psa cii 9. 'I have eaten ashes like bread, and mingled my drink with weeping.' Evil men enjoy all the good, and good men endure all the evil. But seeing there is a God, he will deal righteously with men. Gen xviii 25. 'Shall not the Judge of all the earth do right?' Offenders must come to punishment. The sinner's death-day, and dooms-day is coming. Psa xxxvii 13. 'The Lord seeth that his day is coming.' While there is a hell, the wicked shall be scourged enough; and while there is eternity, they shall lie there long enough; and God will abundantly compensate the faithful service of his people. They shall have their white robes and crowns. Psa lviii 11. 'Verily there is a reward for the righteous: verily he is a God that judgeth in the earth.' Because God is God, he will give glorious rewards to his people.

Use three: Seeing there is a God, woe to all such as have this God against them. He lives for ever to be avenged upon them. Ezek xxii 14. 'Can thine heart endure, or can thine hands be strong in the days that I shall deal with thee?' Such as pollute God's Sabbath, oppose his saints, trampling these jewels in the dust. Such as live in contradiction to God's Word engage the Infinite Majesty of heaven against them; and how dismal will their case be! Deut xxxii 41. 'If I whet my glittering sword, and mine hand take hold of judgment, I will render vengeance to mine enemies; I will make mine arrows drunk with blood,' &c. If it be so terrible to hear the lion roar, what must it be when he begins to tear his prey? Psa l 22. 'Consider this, ye that forget God, lest I tear you in pieces.' Oh that men would think of this, who go on in sin! Shall we engage the great God against us? God strikes slow but heavy. Job xl 9. 'Hast thou an arm like God?' Canst thou strike such a blow? God is the best friend, but the worst enemy. If he can look men into their grave, how far can he throw them? 'Who knows the power of his wrath?' Psa xc 11. What fools are they, who, for a drop of pleasure, drink a sea of wrath! Paracelsus speaks of a frenzy some have, which will make them die dancing; so sinners go dancing to hell.

Use four: Seeing there is a God, let us firmly believe this great article of our Creed. What religion can there be in men, if they do not believe a Deity? 'He that cometh to God must believe that he is.' To worship God, and pray to him, and not believe there is a God, is to put a high scorn and contempt upon him. Believe that God is the only true God: such a God as he has revealed himself in his Word, 'A lover of righteousness, and hater of wickedness.' Psa xlv 7. The real belief of a Deity gives life to all religious worship; the more we believe the truth and infiniteness of God, the more holy and angelic we are in our lives. Whether we are alone, or in company, God sees us; he is the heart-searcher; the belief of this would make us live always under God's eye. Psa xvi 8. 'I have set the Lord always before me.' The belief of a Deity would be a bridle to sin, and a spur to duty; it would add wings to prayer, and oil to the lamp of our devotion. The belief of a Deity would cause dependence upon God in all our straits and exigencies. Gen xvii 1. 'I am God all-sufficient;' a God that can supply all your wants, scatter all your fears, resolve all your doubts, conquer all your temptations; the arm of God's power can never be shrunk; he can create mercy for us, and therefore can help, and not be beholden to the creature. Did we believe there is a God, we should so depend on his providence as not to use any indirect means; we should not run ourselves into sin to rid ourselves out of trouble. 2 Kings i 3. 'Is it not because there is not a God in Israel, that ye go to inquire of Baal-zebub the god of Ekron?' When men run to sinful shifts, is it not because they do not believe there is a God, or that he is all-sufficient?

Use five: Seeing there is a God, let us labour to get an interest in him. Psa xlviii 14. 'This God is our God.' Since the fall we have lost likeness to God, and communion with God; let us labour to recover this lost interest, and pronounce this Shibboleth, 'My God.' Psa xliii 5. It is little comfort to know there is a God, unless he be ours. God offers himself to be our God. Jer xxxi 33. 'I will be their God.' And faith catches hold of the offer, it appropriates God, and makes all that is in him over to us to be ours; his wisdom to be ours, to teach us; his holiness ours, to sanctify us; his Spirit ours, to comfort us; his mercy ours, to save us. To be able to say, God is mine, is more than to have all mines of gold and silver.

Use six: Seeing there is a God, let us serve and worship him as God. It was an indictment brought against some in Rom i 21. 'They glorified him not as God.' Let us pray to him as to God. Pray with fervency. James v 16. 'An effectual fervent prayer availeth much.' This is both the fire and the incense; without fervency it is no prayer. Let us love him as God. Deut vi 5. 'Thou shalt love the Lord thy God with all thy heart.' To love him with all the heart, is to give him precedence in our love, to let him have the cream of our affections; to love him not only appreciatively, but intensively, as much as we can. As the sunbeams united in a burning glass burn the hotter, so all our affections should be united, that our love to God may be more ardent. Let us obey him as God. All creatures obey him, the stars fight his battles, the wind and sea obey him. Mark iv 41. Much more should man, whom God has endued with a principle of reason. He is God, and has a sovereignty over us; therefore, as we received life from him, so we must receive a law from him, and submit to his will in all things. This is to kiss him with a kiss of loyalty, and it is to glorify him as God.

II. *The thing expressed.* John iv 24. 'God is a Spirit.' God is *essentia spiritualissima*. Zanchius.

What do you mean when you say, God is a Spirit?

By a spirit I mean, God is an immaterial substance, of a pure, subtile, unmixed essence, not compounded of body and soul, without all extension of parts. The body is a dreggish thing. The more spiritual God's essence, the more noble and excellent it is. The spirits are the more refined part of the wine.

Wherein does God differ from other spirits?

[1] The angels are spirits. We must distinguish spirits. The angels are

[45]

created, God is a Spirit uncreated. The angels are finite, and capable of being annihilated; the same power which made them is able to reduce them to their first nothing; but God is an infinite Spirit. The angels are confined spirits, they cannot be *duobus locis simul*, but are confined to a place; but God is an immense Spirit, and in all places at once. The angels, though spirits, are but ministering spirits. Heb i 14. Though they are spirits, they are servants. God is a super-excellent Spirit, the Father of spirits. Heb xii 9.

[2] The soul is a spirit. Eccles xii 7. 'The spirit shall return to God that gave it.'

How does God, being a Spirit, differ from the soul?

Servetus and Osiander thought, that the soul being infused, conveyed into man the very spirit and substance of God. This is an absurd opinion, for the essence of God is incommunicable.

When it is said the soul is a spirit, it means that God has made it intelligible, and stamped upon it his likeness, not his essence.

But is it not said, that we are made partakers of the divine nature?

By divine nature there, is meant divine qualities. 2 Pet i 4. We are made partakers of the divine nature, not by identity or union with the divine essence, but by a transformation into the divine likeness. Thus you see how God differs from other spirits, angels and souls of men. He is a Spirit of transcendent excellence, the 'Father of spirits.'

Against this Vorstius and the Anthropomorphites object, that, in Scripture, a human shape and figure is given to God; he is said to have eyes and hands.

It is contrary to the nature of a spirit to have a corporeal substance. Luke xxiv 39. 'Handle me, and see me: for a spirit hath not flesh and bones, as ye see me have.' Bodily members are ascribed to God, not properly, but metaphorically, and in a borrowed sense. By the right hand of the Lord is meant his power; by the eyes of the Lord is meant his wisdom. Now that God is a Spirit, and is not capable of bodily shape or substance, is clear, for a body is visible, but God is invisible; therefore he is a Spirit. 1 Tim vi 16. 'Whom no man hath seen, nor can see;' not by an eye of sense. A body is terminated, can be but in one place at once; but God is everywhere, in all places at once; therefore he is a Spirit. Psa cxxxix 7, 8. God's centre is everywhere, and his circumference is nowhere. A body being compounded of integral parts may be dissolved; *quicquid divisibile est corruptibile:* but the Godhead is not capable of dissolution, he can have no end from whom all things have their beginning. So that it clearly appears that God is a Spirit, which adds to the perfection of his nature.

Use one: If God be a Spirit, then he is impassible; he is not capable of being hurt. Wicked men set up their banners, and bend their forces against God; they are said to fight against God. Acts v 39. But what will this fighting avail? What hurt can they do to the Deity? God is a Spirit, and therefore cannot receive any hurtful impression. Wicked men may imagine evil against the Lord. Nahum i 9. 'What do ye imagine against the Lord?' But God being a Spirit is impenetrable. The wicked may eclipse his glory, but cannot touch his essence. God can hurt his enemies, but they cannot hurt him. Julian might throw up his dagger into the air against Heaven, but could not touch the Deity. God is a Spirit, invisible. How can the wicked with all their forces hurt him, when they cannot see him? Hence all the attempts of the wicked against God are foolish, and prove abortive. Psa ii 2, 4. 'The kings of the earth set themselves against the Lord and against his anointed. He that sits in the heavens shall laugh.' He is a Spirit, he can wound them, but they cannot touch him.

Use two: If God be a Spirit, it shows the folly of the Papists, who worship him by pictures and images. As a spirit, we cannot make any image to represent him. Deut iv 12. 'The Lord spake to you out of the midst of the fire, ye heard the voice of the words, but saw no similitude.'

God being a Spirit is imperceptible, cannot be discerned; how then can there be any resemblance made of him? Isa xl 18. 'To whom then will ye liken God, or what likeness will ye compare unto him?' How can you paint the Deity? Can we make an image of that which we never saw? Ye saw no similitude. God is a Spirit. It were folly to endeavour to make a picture of the soul, because it is a spiritual thing, or to paint the angels, because they are spirits.

Are not angels in Scripture represented by the cherubim?

There is *Imago personæ et officii;* 'there is the image of the person, and the image that represents the office.' The cherubims did not represent the persons of the angels, but their office. The cherubims were made with wings, to show the swiftness of the angels in discharge of their office; and if we cannot picture the souls nor the persons of angels, because they are spirits, much less can we make an image or picture of God, who is infinite and the Father of spirits.

God is also an omnipresent Spirit; he is present in all places. Jer xxiii 24. 'Do not I fill heaven and earth? saith the Lord.' Therefore, being every-where present, it is absurd to worship him by an image. Were it not a

[47]

foolish thing to bow down to the king's picture, when the king is present? So it is to worship God's image, when God himself is present.

How then shall we conceive of God as a Spirit, if we may make no image or resemblance of him?

We must conceive of him spiritually. In his attributes; his holiness, justice, and goodness, which are the beams by which his divine nature shines forth. We must conceive of him as he is in Christ. 'Christ is the image of the invisible God.' Col i 15. Set the eyes of your faith on Christ as God-man. In Christ we see some sparklings of the divine glory; in him there is the exact resemblance of all his Father's excellencies. The wisdom, love, and holiness of God the Father, shine forth in Christ. John xiv 9. 'He that hath seen me hath seen the Father.'

Use three: If God be a Spirit, it shows us, that the more spiritual we grow, the more we grow like to God. How do earth and spirit agree? Phil iii 19. Earthly ones may give for their crest, the mole or tortoise that live in the earth. What resemblance is there between an earthly heart, and him who is a Spirit? The more spiritual any one is, the more like God.

What is it to be spiritual?

To be refined and sublimated, to have the heart still in heaven, to be thinking of God and glory, and to be carried up in a fiery chariot of love to God. Psa lxxiii 25. 'Whom have I in heaven but thee?' which Beza paraphrases thus, *Apage terra, utinam tecum in cœlo essem!* 'Begone earth! Oh that I were in heaven with thee!' A Christian, who is taken off from these earthly things, as the spirits are taken off from the lees, has a noble spiritual soul, and most resembles him who is a Spirit.

Use four: It shows that the worship which God requires of us, and is most acceptable to him, is spiritual worship. John iv 24. 'They which worship him, must worship him in spirit and in truth.' Spiritual worship is virgin worship. Though God will have the service of our bodies, our eyes and hands lifted up, to testify to others that reverence we have of his glory and majesty, yet he will have the worship of the soul chiefly. 1 Cor vi 20. 'Glorify God in your body, and in your spirit.' Spirit-worship God prizes, because it comes near to his own nature, which is a Spirit.

What is it to worship God in spirit?

(1.) To worship him without ceremonies. The ceremonies of the law, which God himself ordained, are now abrogated, and out of date. Christ the substance being come, the shadows fly away; and therefore the apostle calls the legal ceremonies carnal rites. Heb ix 10. If we may not use those Jewish ceremonies which God once appointed, then not those which he never appointed.

(2.) To worship God in spirit, is to worship him with faith in the blood of the Messiah. Heb x 19. To worship him with the utmost zeal and intenseness of soul. Acts xxvi 7. 'Our twelve tribes instantly serving God day and night,' with intenseness of spirit; not only constantly, but instantly. This is to worship God in spirit. The more spiritual any service is, the nearer it comes to God, who is a Spirit, and the more excellent it is; the spiritual part of duty is the fat of the sacrifice: it is the soul and quintessence of religion. The richest cordials are made of spirits, and the best duties are such as are of a spiritual nature. God is a Spirit, and will be worshipped in spirit; it is not pomp of worship, but purity, which God accepts. Repentance is not in the outward severities used to the body, as penance, fasting, and chastising the body, but it consists in the sacrifice of a broken heart. Thanksgiving does not stand in church-music, the melody of an organ, but rather in making melody in the heart to the Lord. Eph v 19. Prayer is not the tuning the voice into a heartless confession, or telling over a few beads, but it consists in sighs and groans. Rom viii 26. When the fire of fervency is put to the incense of prayer, than it ascends as a sweet odour. The true holy water is not that which the pope sprinkles, but is distilled from the penitent eye. Spirit-worship best pleases that God who is a Spirit. John iv 23. 'The Father seeketh such to worship him;' to show the great acceptance of such, and how God is delighted with spiritual worship. This is the savoury meat that God loves. How few mind this! They give him more dregs than spirits; they think it enough to bring their duties, but not their hearts; which makes God disclaim the very services he himself appointed. Isa i 12. Ezek xxxiii 31. Let us then give God spirit-worship, which best suits his nature. A sovereign elixir full of virtue may be given in a few drops; so a little prayer, if it be with the heart and spirit, may have much virtue and efficacy in it. The publican made but a short prayer, 'God be merciful to me a sinner,' Luke xviii 13, but it was full of life and spirit; it came from the heart, therefore it was accepted.

Use five: Let us pray to God, that as he is a Spirit, so he will give us of his Spirit. The essence of God is incommunicable; but not the motions, the presence and influences of his Spirit. When the sun shines in a room, not the body of the sun is there, but the light, heat, and influence of the sun. God has made a promise of his Spirit. Ezek xxxvi 27. 'I will put my Spirit within you.' Turn promises into prayers. 'O Lord, thou who art a

Spirit, give me of thy Spirit; I, flesh, beg thy Spirit, thy enlightening, sanctifying, quickening, Spirit.' Melanchthon prayed, 'Lord, inflame my soul with thy Holy Spirit.' How needful is his Spirit! We cannot do any duty without it, in a lively manner. When this wind blows upon our sails, we move swiftly towards heaven. Let us pray, therefore, that God would give us of the residue of his Spirit, Mal ii 15, that we may move more vigorously in the sphere of religion.

Use six: As God is a Spirit, so the rewards that he gives are spiritual. As the chief blessings he gives us in this life are spiritual blessings, Eph i 3, not gold and silver; as he gives Christ, his love; he fills us with grace; so the main rewards he gives us after this life are spiritual, 'a crown of glory that fadeth not away.' 1 Pet v 4. Earthly crowns fade, but the believer's crown being spiritual is immortal, a never-fading crown. 'It is impossible,' says Joseph Scaliger, 'for that which is spiritual to be subject to change or corruption.' This may comfort a Christian in all his labours and sufferings; he lays out himself for God, and has little or no reward here; but remember, God, who is a Spirit, will give spiritual rewards, a sight of his face in heaven, white robes, a weight of glory. Be not then weary of God's service; think of the spiritual reward, a crown of glory which fadeth not away.

III. *What kind of Spirit is God?*

He is infinite. All created beings are finite. Though infinite may be applied to all God's attributes – he is infinitely merciful, infinitely wise, infinitely holy – yet, if we take infinity it implies,

God's omnipresence. The Greek word for 'infinite' signifies 'without bounds or limits.' God is not confined to any place, he is infinite, and so is present in all places at once. His centre is everywhere, *Divina essentia nusquam inclusa aut exclusa* [In no place is God's Being either confined or excluded]. Augustine. 1 Kings viii 27. 'Behold, the heaven and heaven of heavens cannot contain thee.' The Turks build their temples open at the top, to show that God cannot be confined to them, but is in all places by his presence. God's essence is not limited either to the regions above, or to the terrestrial globe, but is everywhere. As philosophers say of the soul, it is, *Tota in tota, et tota in qualibet parte:* 'the soul is in every part of the body,' in the eye, heart, foot; so we may say of God, he is *ubique*, his essence is everywhere; his circuit is in heaven, and in earth, and sea, and he is in all places of his circuit at once. 'This is to be infinite.' God, who bounds everything else, is himself without bounds. He sets bounds to the sea; *Huc usque;* 'Hitherto shalt thou come, and no further;' he sets bounds to the angels; they, like the cherubims, move and stand at his appointment, Ezek x 16, but he is infinite, without bounds. He who can span the heavens, and weigh the earth in scales, must needs be infinite. Isa xl 22.

Vorstius maintains that God is in all places at once, but not in regard of his essence; but Virtute et potentia, *by his virtue and influence: as the body of the sun is in heaven, it only sends forth its beams and influences to the earth; or as a king, who is in all places of his kingdom authoritatively, by his power and authority, but he is personally on his throne.*

God, who is infinite, is in all places at once, not only by his influence, but by his essence; for, if his essence fills all places, then he must needs be there in person. Jer xxiii 24. 'Do not I fill heaven and earth?'

But does not God say heaven is his throne? Isa lxvi 1.

It is also said, that a humble heart is his throne. Isa lvii 15. The humble heart is his throne, in regard to his gracious presence; and heaven is his throne, in regard to his glorious presence; and yet neither of these thrones will hold him, for the heaven of heavens cannot contain him.

But if God be infinite in all places, he is in impure places, and mingles with impurity.

Though God be in all places, in the heart of a sinner by his inspection, and in hell by his justice, yet he does not mingle with the impurity, or receive the least tincture of evil. *Divina natura non est immista rebus aut sordibus inquinata* [The divine nature does not intermix with created matter, nor is contaminated by its impurities]. Augustine. No more than the sun shining on a dunghill is defiled, or its beauty spotted; or than Christ going among sinners was defiled, whose Godhead was a sufficient antidote against infection.

God must needs be infinite in all places at once, not only in regard to the simplicity and purity of his nature, but in regard to his power, which being so glorious, who can set him bounds, or prescribe him a circuit to walk in? It is as if the drop should limit the ocean, or a star set bounds to the sun.

Use one: It condemns the Papists, who would make more things infinite than the Godhead. They hold that Christ's body is in many places at once, that it is in heaven, and in the bread and wine in the sacrament. Though Christ as he is God is infinite, and in all places at once, yet as man he is not. When he was on earth, his manhood was not in heaven, though his Godhead was; and now he is in heaven, his manhood is not on earth, though his Godhead be. Heb x 5, is spoken of Christ; 'A body thou hast prepared me.' This body cannot be in all places at once; for then it is no more a body, but a spirit. Christ's body in heaven, though glorified, is not deified; it is not infinite, as it must be, if it be both in heaven, and in the bread and wine by transubstantiation.

Use two: If God be infinite, present in all places at once, then it is certain he governs all things in his own person, and needs no proxies or deputies to help him to carry on his government. He is in all places in an instant, and manages all affairs both in the earth and heaven. A king cannot be in all places of his kingdom in his own person, therefore he is fain to govern by deputies and vicegerents, and they often pervert justice; but God, being infinite, needs no deputies, he is present in all places, he sees all with his own eyes, and hears all with his own ears; he is everywhere in his own person, therefore is fit to be the judge of the world; he will do every one right.

Use three: If God be infinite by his omnipresence, then see the greatness and immenseness of the divine majesty! What a great God do we serve! 1 Chron xxix 11. 'Thine, O Lord, is the greatness, and the glory, and the majesty, and thou art exalted as head above all.' Well may the Scripture display the greatness of his glory, who is infinite in all places. He transcends our weak conceptions; how can our finite understanding comprehend him who is infinite? He is infinitely above all our praises. Neh ix 5. 'Blessed be thy glorious name, which is exalted above all blessing and praise.' Oh what a poor nothing is man, when we think of God's infiniteness! As the stars disappear at the rising of the sun, oh, how does a man shrink into nothing when infinite majesty shines forth in its glory! Isa xl 15. 'The nations are as a drop of the bucket, or the small dust of the balance!' On what a little of that drop are we! The heathens thought they had sufficiently praised Jupiter when they called him great Jupiter. Of what immense majesty is God, who fills all places at once! Psa cl 2.

Use four: If God be infinite, filling heaven and earth, see what a full portion the saints have; they have him for their portion who is infinite. His fulness is an infinite fulness; and he is infinitely sweet, as well as infinitely full. If a conduit be filled with wine, there is a sweet fulness, but still it is finite; but God is a sweet fulness, and it is infinite. He is infinitely full of beauty and of love. His riches are called unsearchable, because they are infinite. Eph iii 8. Stretch your thoughts as much as you can, there is that in God which exceeds; it is an infinite fulness. He is said to do abundantly for us, above all that we can ask. Eph iii 20. What can an ambitious spirit ask? He can ask crowns and kingdoms, millions of worlds; but God can give more than we can ask, nay, or think, because he is infinite. We can think, what if all the dust were turned to silver, if every flower were a ruby, every sand in the sea a diamond; yet God can give more than we can think, because he is infinite. Oh how rich are they who have the infinite God for their portion! Well might David say, 'The Lord is the portion of mine inheritance. The lines are fallen unto me in pleasant places, and I have a goodly heritage.' Psa xvi 5, 6. We may go with the bee from flower to flower, but we shall never have full satisfaction till we come to the infinite God. Jacob said: 'I have enough;' in the Hebrew, 'I have all,' because he had the infinite God for his portion. Gen xxxiii 11. God being an infinite fulness, there is no fear of want for any of the heirs of heaven; though there be millions of saints and angels, which have a share in God's riches, yet he has enough for them all, because he is infinite. Though a thousand men behold the sun, there is light enough for them all: put never so many buckets into the sea, there is water enough to fill them. Though an innumerable company of saints and angels are to be filled out of God's fulness, yet God, being infinite, has enough to satisfy them. God has land enough to give to all his heirs. There can be no want in that which is infinite.

Use five: If God be infinite, he fills all places, is everywhere present. This is sad to the wicked, God is their enemy, and they cannot escape him, nor flee from him, for he is everywhere present; they are never out of his eye nor out of his reach. Psa xxi 8. 'Thine hand shall find out all thine enemies.' What caves or thickets can men hide in, that God cannot find them; go where they will, he is present. Psa cxxxix 7. 'Whither shall I flee from thy presence?' If a man owes a debt to another he may make his escape, and flee into another land, where the creditor cannot find him. 'But whither shall I flee from thy presence?' God is infinite, he is in all places; so that he will find out his enemies and punish them.

But is it not said, Cain went out from the presence of the Lord? Gen iv 16.

The meaning is, he went out from the church of God, where were the visible signs of God's presence, and where God in a special manner manifested his sweet presence to his people; but Cain could not go out of God's sight; for God being infinite is everywhere present. Sinners can neither go from an accusing conscience, nor from a revenging God.

Use six: If God be everywhere present, then for a Christian to walk with God is not impossible. God is not only in heaven, but he is in earth too. Isa lxvi 1. Heaven is his throne, there he sits; the earth is his footstool, there he stands. He is everywhere present, therefore we may come to walk with

God. 'Enoch walked with God.' Gen v 22. If God was confined to heaven, a trembling soul might think, How can I converse with God, how can I walk with him who lives *in excelsis;* above the upper region? but God is not confined to heaven; he is omnipresent; he is above us, yet he is about us, he is near to us. Acts xvii 27. Though he be not far from the assembly of the saints, 'He stands in the congregation of the mighty.' Psa lxxxii 1. He is present with us, God is in every one of us; so that here on earth we may walk with God. In heaven the saints rest with him, on earth they walk with him. To walk with God is to walk by faith. We are said to draw nigh to God, Heb x 22, and to see him. Heb xi 27. 'As seeing him who is invisible:' and to have fellowship with him. 1 John i 3. 'Our fellowship is with the Father.' Thus we may take a turn with him every day by faith. It is slighting God not to walk with him. If a king be in presence, it is slighting him to neglect him, and walk with the page. There is no walk in the world so sweet as to walk with God. Psa lxxxix 15. 'They shall walk in the light of thy countenance.' Psa cxxxviii 5. 'Yea, they shall sing in the ways of the Lord.' It is like walking among beds of spices, which send forth a fragrant perfume.

Use seven: If God be infinite in his glorious essence, learn to admire where you cannot fathom. The angels wear a veil, they cover their faces, as adoring this infinite majesty. Isa vi 2. Elias wrapped himself in a mantle when God's glory passed by. Admire where you cannot fathom. Job xi 7. 'Canst thou by searching find out God?' Here we see some beams of his glory, we see him in the glass of the creation; we see him in his picture, his image shines in the saints; but who can search out all his essential glory? What angel can measure these pyramids? 'Canst thou by searching find out God?' He is infinite. We can no more search out his infinite perfections, than a man upon the top of the highest mountain can reach the firmament, or take a star in his hand. Oh, have God-admiring thoughts! Adore where you cannot fathom. There are many mysteries in nature which we cannot fathom; why the sea should be higher than the earth, yet not drown it; why the Nile should overflow in summer, when, by the course of nature, the waters are lowest; how the bones grow in the womb. Eccl xi 5. If these things pose us, how may the infinite mystery of the Deity transcend our most raised intellectuals! Ask the geometrician, if he can, with a pair of compasses, measure the breadth of the earth. So unable are we to measure the infinite perfections of God. In heaven we shall see God clearly, but not fully, for he is infinite; he will communicate himself to us, according to the bigness of our vessel, but not the immenseness of his nature. Adore then where you cannot fathom.

If God be infinite in all places, let us not limit him. Psa lxxviii 41. 'They limited the Holy One of Israel.' It is limiting God to confine him within the narrow compass of our reason. Reason thinks God must go such a way to work, or the business will never be effected. This is to limit God to our reason; whereas he is infinite, and his ways are past finding out. Rom xi 33. In the deliverance of the church, it is limiting God, either to set him a time, or prescribe him a method for deliverance. God will deliver Sion, but he will be left to his own liberty; he will not be tied to a place, to a time, or to an instrument, which were to limit him, and then he should not be infinite. God will go his own way, he will pose and nonplus reason, he will work by improbabilities, he will save in such a way as we think would destroy. Now he acts like himself, like an infinite wonder-working God.

2. THE KNOWLEDGE OF GOD

'The Lord is a God of knowledge, and by him actions are weighed.' 1 Sam ii 3. Glorious things are spoken of God; he transcends our thoughts, and the praises of angels. God's glory lies chiefly in his attributes, which are the several beams by which the divine nature shines forth. Among other of his orient excellencies, this is not the least, The Lord is a God of knowledge; or as the Hebrew word is, 'A God of knowledges.' Through the bright mirror of his own essence, he has a full idea and cognizance of all things; the world is to him a transparent body. He makes a heart-anatomy. Rev ii 23. 'I am he which searcheth the reins and the heart.' The clouds are no canopy, the night is no curtain to draw between us and his sight. Psa cxxxix 12. 'The darkness hideth not from thee.' There is not a word we whisper but God hears it. Psa cxxxix 4. 'There is not a word in my tongue, but lo, O Lord, thou knowest it altogether.' There is not the most subtle thought that comes into our mind, but God perceives it. Isa lxvi 18. 'I know their thoughts.' Thoughts speak as loud in God's ears as words do in ours. All our actions, though never so subtly contrived, and secretly conveyed, are visible to the eye of Omniscience. Isa lxvi 18. 'I know their works.' Achan hid the Babylonish garment in the earth, but God brought it to light. Josh vii 21. Minerva was drawn in such curious colours, and so lively pencilled, that which way soever one turned, Minerva's eyes were upon him; so, which way soever we turn ourselves God's eye is upon us. Job xxxvii 16. 'Dost thou know the balancing of the clouds; the wondrous works of him that is perfect in knowledge?' God knows whatever is knowable; he knows future contingencies. He foretold Israel's coming out of Babylon, and the virgin's conceiving. By this the Lord proves the truth of his Godhead against idol gods. Isa xli 23. 'Shew the things that are to come hereafter, that we may know ye are gods.' The perfection of God's knowledge is primary. He is the original, the pattern, and prototype of all knowledge; others borrow their knowledge of him; the angels light their lamps at this glorious sun. God's knowledge is pure. It is not contaminated with the object. Though God knows sin, yet it is to hate and punish it. No evil can mix or incorporate with his knowledge, any more than the sun can be defiled with the vapours which arise from the earth. God's knowledge is facile; it is without any difficulty. We study and search for knowledge. Prov ii 4. 'If thou seekest for her as for silver.' The lamp of God's knowledge is so infinitely bright, that all things are intelligible to him.

God's knowledge is infallible; there is no mistake in his knowledge. Human knowledge is subject to error. A physician may mistake the cause of a disease; but God's knowledge is unerring; he can neither deceive, nor be deceived; he cannot deceive, because he is truth, nor be deceived, because he is wisdom. God's knowledge is instantaneous. Our knowledge is successive, one thing after another. We argue from the effect to the cause. God knows things past, present, and to come, *uno intuito*, at once; they are all before him in one entire prospect.

God's knowledge is retentive; he never loses any of his knowledge; he has *reminiscentia*, as well as *intelligentia;* he remembers as well as understands. Many things elapse out of our minds, but God's knowledge is eternized. Things transacted a thousand years ago, are as fresh to him as if they were done but the last minute. Thus he is perfect in knowledge.

But is it not said, Gen xviii 21, *I will go down and see whether they have done according to the cry which is come up unto me, and I will know?*

It could not be that God was ignorant; because there is mention made of a cry; but the Lord speaks there after the manner of a judge, who will first examine the cause before he passes the sentence. When he is upon a work of justice he is not in a riot, as if he did not care where he hits; but he goes straight against offenders. 'He lays judgment to the line, and righteousness to the plummet.' Isa xxviii 17.

Hos xiii 12. *The iniquity of Ephraim is bound up, his sin is hid.*

Not that his sin is hid from God, but his sin is hid; that is, it is recorded, it is laid up against a day of reckoning. That this is the meaning, is clear by the foregoing words, his iniquity is bound up. As the clerk of the assizes binds up the indictments of malefactors in a bundle, and at the assizes brings out the indictments and reads them in court; so God binds up men's sins in a bundle, and, at the day of judgment, this bundle shall be opened, and all their sins brought to light before men and angels. God is infinite in knowledge. He cannot but be so; for he who gives being to things must needs have a clear inspection of them. Psa xciv 9. 'He that planted the ear, shall he not hear? he that formed the eye, shall he not see?' He who makes a watch or engine knows all the workmanship in it. God, that made the heart, knows all its movements. He is full of eyes, like Ezekiel's wheels, and, as Austin says, *Totus oculus,* 'All eye.' It ought to be so; for he is to be 'Judge of all the world.' Gen xviii 25. There are so many causes to be brought before him, and so many persons to be tried, that he must have a perfect knowledge, or he could not do justice. An ordinary judge cannot proceed without a jury, the jury must search the cause, and give in the verdict; but God can judge without a jury. He knows all things in and of himself, and needs no witnesses to inform him. A judge judges only matters of fact, but God judges the heart. He not only judges wicked actions, but wicked designs. He sees the treason of the heart and punishes it.

Use one: Is God infinite in knowledge? Is he light, and in him is there no darkness? Then how unlike are they to God who are darkness, and in whom is no light, who are destitute of knowledge, such as the Indians who never heard of God! And are there not many among us, who are no better than baptized heathens? who need to seek the first principles of the oracles of God. It is sad, that after the sun of the gospel has shined so long in our horizon, to this day the veil should be upon their heart. Such as are enveloped in ignorance cannot give God a reasonable service. Rom xii 1. Ignorance is the nurse of impiety. The schoolmen say, *Omne peccatum fundatur in ignorantia* [Every sin is founded upon ignorance]. Jer ix 3. 'They proceed from evil to evil, and know not me, saith the Lord.' Where ignorance reigns in the understanding, lust rages in the affections. Prov xix 2. 'That the mind be without knowledge, it is not good;' such have neither faith nor fear: no faith; for knowledge carries the torch before faith. Psa ix 10. 'They that know thy name shall put their trust in thee.' A man can no more believe without knowledge than the eye can see without light. He can have no fear of God; for how can they fear him whom they do not know? The covering of Haman's face was a sad presage of death. When people's minds are covered with ignorance, it is a covering of the face that is a fatal forerunner of destruction.

Use two: If God be a God of knowledge, then see the folly of hypocrisy. Hypocrites do not *virtutem facere*, but *fingere* [Hypocrites do not actually do good, they merely make a show of it]. Melanchthon. They carry it fair with men, but care not how bad their hearts are; they live in secret sin. Psa lxxiii 11. 'They say, How doth God know?' Psa x 11. 'God hath forgotten, he hideth his face, he will never see it.' But, Psa cxlvii 5, 'His understanding is infinite:' He has a window to look into men's breasts; he has a key for the heart; he beholds all the sinful workings of men's spirits, as in a glass-hive we can see the bees working in their combs. Matt vi 4. He sees in secret. As a merchant enters debts in his book, so God has his day-book, in which he enters every sin. Jeroboam's wife disguised herself that the prophet should not know her; but he discerned her. 1 Kings xiv 6. 'Why feignest thou thyself to be another?' The hypocrite thinks to prevaricate and juggle with God, but God will unmask him. Eccles xii 14. 'God shall bring every work into judgment, with every secret thing.' Jer xxix 23. 'They have committed villany in Israel, even I know, and am a witness, saith the Lord.' Ay, but the hypocrite hopes he shall colour over his sin, and make it look very specious. Absalom masks over his treason with the pretence of a religious vow. Judas dissembles his envy at Christ, and his covetousness, with the pretence of 'charity to the poor.' John xii 5. Jehu makes religion a stirrup to his ambitious design. 2 Kings x 16. But God sees through these fig-leaves. You may see a jade under his gilt trappings. Jer xvi 17. 'Their iniquities are not hid from mine eyes.' He that hath an eye to see will find a hand to punish.

Use three: Is God so infinite in knowledge? Then we should always feel as under his omniscient eye. *Sic vivendum est tanquam in conspectu* [Hence we ought to live as if always in full view]. Seneca. Let us set David's prospect before our eye. Psa xvi 8. 'I have set the Lord always before me.' Seneca counselled Lucilius, that whatever he was doing, he should imagine some of the Roman worthies stood before him, and then he would do nothing dishonourable. The consideration of God's omniscience would be preventive of much sin. The eye of man will restrain from sin; and will not God's eyes much more? Esther vii 8. 'Then said the king, Will he force the queen also before me?' Will we sin when our judge looks on? Would men speak so vainly, if they considered God overheard them? Latimer took heed to every word in his examination, when he heard the pen go behind the hangings: so, what care would persons have of their words, if they remembered God heard, and the pen is going on in heaven? Would men go after strange flesh if they believed God was a spectator of their wickedness, and would make them do penance in hell for it? Would they defraud in their dealings, and use false weights, if they thought God saw them, and for making their weights lighter would make their damnation heavier. Viewing ourselves as under the eye of God's omniscience, would cause reverence in the worship of God. God sees the frame and carriage of our hearts when we come before him. How would this call in our straggling thoughts? How would it animate and spirit duty? It would make us put fire to the incense. Acts xxvi 7. 'The tribes instantly served God day and night,' *omnibus viribus*, with the utmost zeal and intenseness of spirit. To think God is in this place would add wings to prayer, and oil to the flame of our devotion.

Use four: Is God's knowledge infinite? Study sincerity, be what you seem. 1 Sam xvi 7. 'The Lord looketh upon the heart.' Men judge the heart by the actions, God judges the actions by the heart; if the heart be sincere, God will see the faith and bear with the failing. Asa had his blemishes, but his heart was right with God. 2 Chron xv 17. God saw his sincerity, and pardoned his infirmity. Sincerity in a Christian is like chastity in a wife, which excuses many failings. Sincerity makes our duties acceptable, like musk among linen, that perfumes it. As Jehu said to Jehonadab, 2 Kings x 15. 'Is thy heart right with me? And he said, It is. If it be, said he, give me thy hand; and he took him up into the chariot:' so, if God sees our heart is right, that we love him, and design his glory, now, says he, give me your prayers and tears; now you shall come up with me into the chariot of glory. Sincerity makes our services to be golden, and God will not cast away the gold though it may want some weight. Is God omniscient, and his eye chiefly upon the heart? Wear the girdle of truth about you, and never leave it off.

Use five: Is God a God of infinite knowledge? Then there is comfort, (1.) To the saints in particular. (2.) To the church in general.

(1.) To saints in particular. In case of private devotion. Christian, thou settest hours apart for God, thy thoughts run upon him as thy treasure; God takes notice of every good thought. Mal iii 16. 'He had a book of remembrance written for them that thought upon his name.' Thou enterest into thy closet, and prayest to thy Father in secret; he hears every sigh and groan. Psa xxxviii 9. 'My groaning is not hid from thee.' Thou waterest the seed of thy prayer with tears, God bottles every tear. Psa lvi 8. 'Put thou my tears into thy bottle.' When the secrets of all hearts shall be opened, God will make an honourable mention of the zeal and devotion of his people, and he himself will be the herald of their praises. 1 Cor iv 5. 'Then shall every man have praise of God.'

The infiniteness of God's knowledge is a comfort, in case the saints have not a clear knowledge of themselves. They find so much corruption, that they judge they have no grace. Gen xxv 22. 'If it be so, why am I thus?' If I have grace, why is my heart in so dead and earthly a frame? Oh remember, God is of infinite knowledge, he can spy grace where thou canst not; he can see grace hid under corruption, as the stars may be hid under a cloud. God can see that holiness in thee which thou canst not discern in thyself; he can spy the flower of grace in thee, though overtopped with weeds. 1 Kings xiv 13. 'Because there is in him some good thing.' God sees some good thing in his people, when they can see no good in themselves; and though they judge themselves, he will give them an absolution.

It is comfort in respect of personal injuries. It is the saints' lot to suffer. The head being crowned with thorns, the feet must not tread upon roses. If saints find a real purgatory, it is in this life; but this is their comfort, that God sees what wrong is done to them; the apple of his eye is touched, and is he not sensible of it? Paul was scourged by cruel hands. 2 Cor xi 25. 'Thrice was I beaten with rods;' as if you should see a scullion whip the king's son. God beholds it. Exod iii 7. 'I know their sorrows.' The wicked make wounds in the backs of the saints, and then pour in vinegar; but God writes down their cruelty. Believers are a part of Christ's mystical body; and for every drop of a saint's blood spilt God puts a drop of wrath in his vial.

(2.) Comfort to the church of God in general. If God be a God of knowledge, he sees all the plots of the enemies against Zion, and can make them prove abortive. The wicked are subtile, having borrowed their skill from the old serpent; they dig deep, to hide their counsels from God, but he sees them, and can easily counterwork them. The dragon is described with seven heads in Rev xii 3, to show how he plots against the church; but God is described with seven eyes in Zech iii 9, to show that he sees all the plots and stratagems of the enemies; and when they deal proudly, he can be above them. Come, says Pharaoh, 'let us deal wisely;' Exod i 10; but he never played the fool more than when he thought to deal wisely. Exod xiv 24. 'In the morning watch the Lord looked to the host of the Egyptians by the pillar of fire, and troubled the host.' How may this, like sap in the vine, comfort the church of God in her militant state! The Lord has an eye in all the councils and combinations of the enemy; he sees them in their train, and can blow them up in their own mine.

3. THE ETERNITY OF GOD

The next attribute is, 'God is eternal.' Psa xc 2. 'From everlasting to everlasting thou art God.' The schoolmen distinguish between *aevun et aeternum*, to explain the notion of eternity. There is a threefold being.

1. Such as had a beginning; and shall have an end; as all sensitive creatures, the beasts, fowls, fishes, which at death are destroyed and return to dust; their being ends with their life. 2. Such as had a beginning, but shall have no end, as angels and the souls of men, which are eternal *a parte post;* they abide for ever. 3. Such as is without beginning, and without ending, and that is proper only to God. He is *semper existens,* from everlasting to everlasting. This is God's title, a jewel of his crown. He is called 'the King eternal.' 1 Tim i 17. Jehovah is a word that properly sets forth God's eternity; a word so dreadful, that the Jews trembled to name or read it; and used Adonai, Lord, in its place. Jehovah contains in it time past, present, and to come. Rev i 8. 'Which is, and which was, and which is to come,' interprets the word Jehovah; *(which is)* he subsists of himself, having a pure and independent being; *(which was)* God only was before time; there is no searching into the records of eternity; *(which is to come)* his kingdom has no end; his crown has no successors. Heb i 8. 'Thy throne, O God, is for ever and ever.' The doubling of the word ratifies the certainty of it, as the doubling of Pharaoh's dream. I shall prove that God only could be eternal, without beginning. Angels could not; they are but creatures, though spirits; they were made; and therefore their beginning may be known; their antiquity may be searched into. If you ask, when were they created? Some think before the world was; but not so: for what was before time was eternal. The first origin of angels reaches no higher than the beginning of the world. It is thought by the learned, that the angels were made on the day on which the heavens were made. Job xxxviii 7. 'When the morning stars sang together, and all the sons of God shouted for joy.' St Jerome, Gregory, and venerable Bede understand it, that when God laid the foundation-stone of the world, the angels being then created, sang anthems of joy and praise. It is proper to God only to be eternal, without beginning. He is Alpha and Omega, the first and the last. Rev i 8. No creature can write itself Alpha, that is only a flower of the crown of heaven. Exod iii 14. 'I am that I am,' that is, He who exists from and to eternity.

Use one: Here is thunder and lightning to the wicked. God is eternal, therefore the torments of the wicked are eternal. God lives for ever; and as long as God lives he will be punishing the damned. This should be as the handwriting upon the wall, it should 'make their joints to be loosed,' &c. Dan v 6. The sinner takes liberty to sin; he breaks God's laws, like a wild beast that breaks over the hedge, and leaps into forbidden pasture; he sins with greediness, as if he thought he could not sin fast enough. Eph iv 19. But remember, one of God's names is Eternal, and as long as

God is eternal he has time enough to reckon with all his enemies. To make sinners tremble, let them think of these three things: the torments of the damned are without intermission, without mixture, and eternal.

(1.) Without *intermission*. Their pains shall be acute and sharp, and no relaxation; the fire shall not be slackened or abated. Rev xiv 11. 'They have no rest day nor night;' like one that has his joints stretched continually on the rack, and has no ease. The wrath of God is compared to a stream of brimstone. Isa xxx 33. Why to a stream? Because a stream runs without intermission; so God's wrath runs like a stream, and pours out without intermission. In the pains of this life, there is some abatement and intermission; the fever abates; after a fit of the stone, the patient has some ease; but the pains of hell are intense and violent, *in summo gradu*. The damned soul never says, I am now more at ease.

(2.) Without *mixture*. Hell is a place of pure justice. In this life, God in anger remembers mercy, he mixes compassion with suffering. Deut xxxiii 25. Asher's shoe was of iron, but his foot was dipt in oil. Affliction is the iron shoe, but mercy is mixed with it; the foot is dipt in oil. But the torments of the damned have no mixture. Rev xiv 10. 'They shall drink of the wine of the wrath of God, which is poured out without mixture.' No mixture of mercy. How is the cup of wrath said to be full of mixture! Psa lxxv 8. 'For in the hand of the Lord there is a cup, and the wine is red; it is full of mixture: and he poureth out of the same: but the dregs thereof all the wicked of the earth shall wring them out and drink them.' Yet in the Revelation it is said to be without mixture. It is full of mixture, that is, it is full of all the ingredients that may make it bitter; the worm, the fire, the curse of God, all these are bitter ingredients. It is a cup mixed, yet it is without mixture; there shall be nothing to afford the least comfort, no mixture of mercy, and so without mixture. In the sacrifice of jealousy, Numb v 15, no oil was put to it; so, in the torments of the damned, there is no oil of mercy to abate their sufferings.

(3.) Without *cessation, eternal*. The pleasures of sin are but for a season, but the torments of the wicked are for ever. Sinners have a short feast, but a long reckoning. Origen erroneously thought, that after a thousand years the damned should be released out of their misery; but the worm, the fire, the prison, are all eternal. Rev xiv 11. 'The smoke of their torment ascendeth for ever and ever.' *Pœnæ gehennales puniunt, non finiunt* [The torments of hell keep on punishing, they never end]. Prosper. Eternity is a sea without bottom and banks. After millions of years, there is not one minute in eternity wasted; and the damned must be ever burning, but never consuming, always dying, but never dead. Rev ix 6. 'They shall seek death, but shall not find it.' The fire of hell is such, as multitudes of tears will not quench it, length of time will not finish it; the vial of God's wrath will be always dropping upon a sinner. As long as God is eternal, he lives to be avenged upon the wicked. Oh eternity! eternity! who can fathom it? Mariners have their plummets to measure the depths of the sea; but what line or plummet shall we use to fathom the depth of eternity? The breath of the Lord kindles the infernal lake, Isa xxx 33, and where shall we have engines or buckets to quench that fire? Oh eternity! If all the body of the earth and sea were turned to sand, and all the air up to the starry heaven were nothing but sand, and a little bird should come every thousand years, and fetch away in her bill but the tenth part of a grain of all that heap of sand, what numberless years would be spent before that vast heap of sand would be fetched away! Yet, if at the end of all that time, the sinner might come out of hell, there would be some hope; but that word 'Ever' breaks the heart. 'The smoke of their torment ascendeth up for ever and ever.' What a terror is this to the wicked, enough to put them into a cold sweat, to think, as long as God is eternal, he lives for ever to be avenged upon them!

Here the question may be asked, *Why should sin that is committed in a short time be punished eternally?*

We must hold with Augustine, 'that God's judgments on the wicked, *occultu esse possunt, injusta esse non possunt,* may be secret, but never unjust.' The reason why sin committed in a short time is eternally punished, is, because every sin is committed against an infinite essence, and no less than eternity of punishment can satisfy. Why is treason punished with confiscation and death, but because it is against the king's person, which is sacred; much more that offence which is against God's crown and dignity is of a heinous and infinite nature, and cannot be satisfied with less than eternal punishment.

Use two: Of comfort to the godly. God is eternal, therefore he lives for ever to reward the godly. Rom ii 7. 'To them who seek for glory and honour, eternal life'. The people of God here are in a suffering condition. Acts xx 23. 'Bonds and afflictions abide me.' The wicked are clad in purple, and fare deliciously, while the godly suffer. Goats climb upon high mountains, while Christ's sheep are in the valley of slaughter. But here is the comfort, God is eternal, and he has appointed eternal recompenses for the saints. In heaven are fresh delights, sweetness without surfeit; and that which is the crown and zenith of heaven's happiness, is, that it is 'eternal.' 1 John iii 15. Were there but the least suspicion that this glory must cease it would much eclipse, yea, embitter it; but it is eternal.

What angel can span eternity? 2 Cor iv 17. 'An eternal weight of glory.' The saints shall bathe themselves in the rivers of divine pleasure; and these rivers can never be dried up. Psa xvi 11. 'At thy right hand are pleasures for evermore.' This is the Elah, the highest strain in the apostle's rhetoric. 1 Thess iv 17. 'Ever with the Lord.' There is peace without trouble, ease without pain, glory without end, 'ever with the Lord.' Let this comfort the saints in all their troubles; their sufferings are but short, but their reward is eternal. Eternity makes heaven to be heaven; it is the diamond in the ring. Oh blessed day that shall have no night! The sunlight of glory shall rise upon the soul and never set! Oh blessed spring, that shall have no autumn, or fall of the leaf. The Roman emperors have three crowns set upon their heads, the first of iron, the second of silver, the third of gold; so the Lord sets three crowns on his children, grace, comfort, and glory; and this crown is eternal. 1 Pet v 4. 'Ye shall receive a crown of glory that fadeth not away.' The wicked have a never-dying worm, and the godly a never-fading crown. Oh how should this be a spur to virtue! How willing should we be to work for God! Though we had nothing here, God has time enough to reward his people. The crown of eternity shall be set upon their head.

Use three: Of exhortation. Study eternity. Our thoughts should chiefly run upon eternity. We all wish for the present, something that may delight the senses. If we could have lived, as Augustine says, *a cunabulis mundi*, from the infancy of the world to the world's old age, what were this? What is time, measured with eternity? As the earth is but a small point to the heaven, so time is but, nay scarce a minute to eternity! And then, what is this poor life which crumbles away so fast? Oh, think of eternity! *Annos æternos in mente habe.* Brethren, we are every day travelling to eternity; and whether we wake or sleep, we are going our journey. Some of us are upon the borders of eternity. Oh study the shortness of life and length of eternity!

More particularly think of God's eternity and the soul's eternity. Think of God's eternity. He is the Ancient of Days, who was before all time. There is a figurative description of God in Dan vii 9. 'The Ancient of Days did sit, whose garment was white as snow, and the hair of his head like the pure wool.' His white garment, wherewith he was clothed, signified his majesty; his hair, like the pure wool, his holiness; and the Ancient of Days, his eternity. The thought of God's eternity should make us have high adoring thoughts of God. We are apt to have mean, irreverent thoughts of him. Psa l 21. 'Thou thoughtest I was such an one as thyself,' weak and mortal, but if we would think of God's eternity, when all our power ceases, he is King eternal, his crown flourishes for ever, he can make us happy or miserable for ever, this would make us have adoring thoughts of God. Rev iv 10. 'The four and twenty elders fall down before him that sat upon the throne, and worship him that liveth for ever and ever; and cast their crowns before the throne.' The saints fall down, to signify by that humble posture that they are not worthy to sit in God's presence. They fall down and they worship him that liveth for ever and ever; they do as it were kiss his feet. They cast their crowns before the throne, they lay all their honour at his feet; thus they show humble adoration to the eternal essence. Study God's eternity, it will make us adore where we cannot fathom. Think of the soul's eternity. As God is eternal, so he has made us eternal. We are never-dying creatures; we are shortly entering upon an eternal state, either of happiness or misery. Have serious thoughts of this. Say, O my soul, which of these two eternities is like to be thy portion? I must shortly depart hence, and whither then shall I go, to which of these eternities, either of glory or misery? The serious meditation of the eternal state we are to pass into would work strongly with us.

(1.) Thoughts of eternal torments are a good antidote against sin. Sin tempts with its pleasure; but, when we think of eternity, it may cool the intemperate heat of lust. Shall I, for the pleasure of sin for a season, endure eternal pain? Sin, like those locusts, Rev ix 7, seems to have on its head a crown like gold, but it has in it a tail like a scorpion, verse 10, and a sting in its tail, and this sting can never be plucked out. Shall I venture eternal wrath? Is sin committed so sweet as lying in hell for ever is bitter? This thought would make us flee from sin, as Moses from the serpent.

(2.) The serious thoughts of eternal happiness would very much take us off from worldly things. What are these sublunary things to eternity! They are quickly gone, they salute us, and take their farewell. But I am to enter upon an everlasting estate; I hope to live with him who is eternal; what is the world to me? To those who stand upon the top of the Alps, the great cities of Campania are small things in their eyes; so to him who has his thoughts fixed on his eternal state after this life, all these things seem as nothing in his eye. What is the glory of this world! how poor and contemptible, compared with an eternal weight of glory!

(3.) The serious thoughts of an eternal state, either of happiness or misery, should have a powerful influence upon whatsoever we take in hand. Every work we do promotes either a blessed or cursed eternity; every good action sets us a step nearer to an eternity of happiness; every bad action sets us a step nearer to an eternity of misery. Oh what influence should the thoughts of eternity have upon our religious duties!

It should make us do them with all our might. Duty well performed lifts a Christian higher towards heaven, and sets a Christian a step nearer to a blessed eternity.

4. THE UNCHANGEABLENESS OF GOD

The next attribute is God's unchangeableness. 'I am Jehovah, I change not.' Mal iii 6. I. *God is unchangeable in his nature.* II. *In his decree.*

I. *Unchangeable in his nature.* 1. There is no eclipse of his brightness. 2. No period put to his being.

[1] No eclipse of his brightness. His essence shines with a fixed lustre. 'With whom is no variableness, neither shadow of turning.' James i 17. 'Thou art the same.' Psa cii 27. All created things are full of vicissitudes. Princes and emperors are subject to mutation. Sesostris, an Egyptian prince, having subdued divers kings in war, made them draw his chariot, like horses, as if he intended them to eat grass, as God did King Nebuchadnezzar. The crown has many successors. Kingdoms have their eclipses and convulsions. What is become of the glory of Athens? The pomp of Troy? *Jam seges est ubi Troja fuit* [Now corn grows where Troy once stood]. Though kingdoms have a head of gold, they have feet of clay. The heavens change. 'As a vesture shalt thou change them, and they shall be changed.' Psa cii 26. The heavens are the most ancient records, where God has written his glory with a sunbeam, yet these shall change. Though I do not think they shall be destroyed as to their substance, yet they shall be changed as to their qualities; they shall melt with fervent heat, and so be more refined and purified. 2 Pet iii 12. Thus the heavens shall be changed, but not he who dwells in heaven. 'With him there is no variableness, nor shadow of turning.' The best saints have their eclipses and changes. Look upon a Christian in his spiritual estate, and he is full of variation. Though the seed of grace does not die, yet its beauty and activity often wither. A Christian has his aguish fits in religion. Sometimes his faith is at a high tide, sometimes low ebb; sometimes his love flames, and at another time is like fire in the embers, and he has lost his first love. How strong was David's grace at one time! 'The God of my rock, in him will I trust.' 2 Sam xxii 3. At another time he says, 'I shall one day perish by the hand of Saul.' What Christian can say he does not find a change in his graces; that the bow of his faith never unbends, the strings of his viol never slacken? Surely we shall never meet with such Christians till we meet them in heaven. But

God is without any shadow of turning. The angels were subject to change; they were created holy, but mutable. 'The angels which kept not their first estate.' Jude 6. These morning stars of heaven were falling stars. But God's glory shines with a fixed brightness. In God there is nothing that looks like a change, for better or worse; not better, because then he were not perfect; not worse, for then he would cease to be perfect. He is immutably holy, immutably good; there is no shadow of change in him.

But when Christ, who is God, assumed the human nature, there was a change in God.

If the divine nature had been converted into the human, or the human into the divine, there had been a change, but they were not so. The human nature was distinct from the divine. Therefore there was no change. A cloud over the sun makes no change in the body of the sun; so, though the divine nature be covered with the human, it makes no change in the divine nature.

[2] There is no period put to his being. 'Who only hath immortality.' 1 Tim vi 16. The Godhead cannot die. An infinite essence cannnot be changed into finite; but God is infinite. He is eternal, *ergo*, he is not mortal. To be eternal and mortal is a contradiction.

Use one: See the excellence of the divine nature in its immutability. This is the glory of the Godhead. Mutableness denotes weakness, and is not in God, who is 'the same, yesterday, and to-day, and for ever.' Heb xiii 8. Men are fickle and mutable, like Reuben, 'unstable as water.' Gen xlix 4. They are changeable in their principles. If their faces altered as fast as their opinions, we should not know them. Changeable in their resolutions; as the wind that blows in the east, presently turns about to the west. They resolve to be virtuous, but quickly repent of their resolutions. Their minds are like a sick man's pulse, which alters every half hour. An apostle compares them to waves of the sea, and wandering stars. Jude 13. They are not pillars in God's temple, but reeds. Others are changeable in their friendship. They quickly love and quickly hate. Sometimes they will put you in their bosom, then excommunicate you out of their favour. They change as the chameleon, into several colours, but God is immutable.

Use two: See the vanity of the creature. There are changes in everything but in God. 'Men of high degree are vanity, and men of low degree are a lie.' Psa lxii 9. We look for more from the creature than God has put in it. It has two evils in it; it promises more than we find, and it fails us when we most need it. There is failure *in omni*. A man desires to have his corn ground, and the water fails; the mariner is for a voyage, and the wind does not blow, or is contrary; one depends upon another for the payment of a promise, and he fails, and is like a foot out of joint. Who would look for a fixed stability in the vain creature? It is as if one should build houses on the sand, where the sea comes in and overflows. The creature is true to nothing but deceit, and is constant only in its disappointments. It is no more wonderful to see changes fall out here below, than to see the moon dressing itself in a new shape and figure. Expect to meet with changes in everything but God.

Use three: Comfort to the godly. (1.) In case of losses. If an estate he almost boiled away to nothing, if you lose friends by death, there is a double eclipse; but the comfort is, God is unchangeable; I may lose these things, but I cannot lose my God; he never dies. When the fig-tree and olive-tree failed, God did not fail. 'I will joy in the God of my salvation.' Hab iii 18. Flowers in the garden die, but a man's portion remains; so outward things die and change, but 'thou art the strength of my heart, and my portion for ever.' Psa lxxiii 26.

(2.) In case of sadness of spirit. God seems to cast off the soul in desertion, as in Cant v 6, 'My Beloved had withdrawn himself;' yet he is unchangeable. He is immutable in his love; he may change his countenance, but not his heart. 'I have loved thee with an everlasting love.' Jer xxxi 3. Hebrew, *Olam*, a love of eternity. If once God's electing love rises upon the soul, it never sets. 'The mountains shall be removed, but my loving kindness shall not depart from thee, neither the covenant of my peace be removed.' Isa liv 10. God's love stands faster than the mountains. His love to Christ is unchangeable; and he will no more cease loving believers than he will cease loving Christ.

Use four: Of exhortation. Get an interest in the unchangeable God, then thou art as a rock in the sea, immoveable in the midst of all changes.

How shall I get a part in the unchangeable God?

By having a change wrought in thee. 'But ye are washed, but ye are sanctified.' 1 Cor vi 11. Whence we are changed, *a tenebris ad lucem* [from darkness to light], so changed, as if another soul did live in the same body. By this change we are interested in the unchangeable God.

Trust to that God only who is unchangeable. 'Cease ye from man,' Isa ii 22; leave trusting to the reed, but trust to the Rock of ages. He that is by faith engarrisoned in God, is safe in all changes; he is like a boat that is tied to an immoveable rock. He that trusts in God, trusts in that which cannot fail him; he is unchangeable. 'I will never leave thee, nor forsake thee.' Heb xiii 5. Health may leave us, riches, friends may leave us, but, says God, I will not leave thee; my power shall support thee; my Spirit shall sanctify thee; my mercy shall save thee; I will never leave thee. Oh trust in this unchangeable God! God is jealous of two things; of our love, and of our trust. He is jealous of our love, lest we love the creature more than him, therefore he makes it prove bitter; and of our trust, lest we should place more confidence in it than in him, therefore he makes it prove unfaithful. Outward comforts are given us as food by the way to refresh us, not as crutches to lean on. If we make the creature an idol, what we make our trust God will make our shame. Oh trust in the immortal God! Like Noah's dove, we have no footing for our souls, till we get into the ark of God's unchangeableness. Psa cxxv 1. 'They that trust in the Lord shall be like mount Sion, which cannot be removed.'

II. *God is unchangeable in his decree.* What he has decreed from eternity is unalterable. 'My counsel shall stand.' Isa xlvi 10. God's eternal counsel or decree is immutable. If he changed his decree, it must be from some defect of wisdom or foresight, for that is the reason why men change their purposes; they see something after, which they did not see before; but this cannot be the cause why God should alter his decree, because his knowledge is perfect, he sees all things in one entire prospect before him.

But is not God said to repent? There seems to be a change in his decree, in Jonah iii 10. '*The Lord repented of the evil that he said he would do unto them.*'

Repentance is attributed to God figuratively. Numb xxiii 19. 'He is not a man that he should repent.' There may be a change in God's work, but not in his will. He may will a change, but not change his will. 'God may change his sentence, but not his decree.' A king may cause sentence to be passed upon a malefactor whom he intends to save; so God threatened destruction to Nineveh, but the people of Nineveh repenting, God spared them. Jonah iii 10. Here God changed his sentence, but not his decree; it was what had lain in the womb of his purpose from eternity.

But if God's decree be unchangeable, and cannot be reversed, to what purpose should we use the means? Our endeavours towards salvation cannot alter his decree.

The decree of God does not affect my endeavour; for he that decreed my salvation decreed it in the use of means, and if I neglect the means I reprobate myself. No man argues thus: God has decreed how long I shall live, therefore I will not use means to preserve my life, I will not eat and drink. God has decreed the time of my life in the use of means; so God has decreed my salvation in the use of the Word and of prayer. As a man who refuses food murders himself, so he that refuses to work out his

[69]

salvation destroys himself. The vessels of mercy are said to be prepared unto glory. Rom ix 23. How are they prepared but by being sanctified? and that cannot be but in the use of means; therefore let not God's decree take thee off from holy endeavours. It is a good saying of Dr Preston, 'Hast thou a heart to pray to God? it is a sign no decree of wrath hath passed against thee.'

Use one: If God's decree be eternal and unchangeable, then God does not elect upon our faith foreseen, as the Arminians maintain. 'The children being not yet born, that the purpose of God according to election might stand, it was said, Jacob have I loved, Esau have I hated.' Rom ix 11, 13. We are not elected for holiness, but to holiness. Eph i 4. If we are not justified for our faith, much less are we elected for our faith; but we are not justified for it. We are said to be justified through faith as an instrument in Eph ii 8, but not for faith as a cause; and, if not justified for faith, then much less elected. God's decree of election is eternal and unchangeable, and therefore depends not upon faith foreseen. 'As many as were ordained to eternal life, believed.' Acts xiii 48. They were not elected because they believed, but they believed because they were elected.

Use two: If God's decree be unchangeable, it gives comfort in two cases. (1.) Concerning God's providence towards his church. We are ready to quarrel with Providence, if everything does not accord with our desire. Remember God's work goes on, and nothing falls out but what he has decreed from eternity. (2.) God has decreed troubles for the church's good. The troubles of God's church is like the angel's troubling the water, which made way for healing his people. John v 4. He has decreed troubles in the church. 'His fire is in Sion, and his furnace in Jerusalem.' Isa xxxi 9. The wheels in a watch move cross one to another, but they all carry on the motion of the watch; so the wheels of Providence often move cross to our desires, but still they carry on God's unchangeable decree. 'Many shall be made white.' Dan xii 10. God lets the waters of affliction be poured on his people to make them white. Therefore murmur not at God's dealings; his work goes on, nothing falls out but what he has wisely decreed from eternity; everything shall promote God's design, and fulfil his decree.

Use three: Comfort to the godly in regard of their salvation. 2 Tim ii 19. 'The foundation of God standeth sure, having this seal, The Lord knoweth them that are his.' God's counsel of election is unchangeable. Once elected for ever elected. 'I will not blot his name out of the book of life.' Rev iii 5. The book of God's decree has no errata in it, no blottings out. Once justified, never unjustified. 'Repentance shall be hid from mine eyes.'

[70]

Hos xiii 14. God never repents of his electing love. 'He loved them to the end.' John xiii 1. Therefore, if thou art a believer, comfort thyself with this, the immutability of God's decree.

Use four: To conclude with a word to the wicked, who march furiously against God and his people, let them know that God's decree is unchangeable. God will not alter it, nor can they break it; and while they resist God's will they fulfil it. There is a two-fold will of God, *Voluntas præcepti et decreti;* 'the will of God's precept, and of his decree.' While the wicked resist the will of God's precept, they fulfil the will of his permissive decree. Judas betrays Christ, Pilate condemns him, the soldiers crucify him; while they resist the will of God's precepts, they fulfil the will of his permissive decree. Acts iv 28. God commands one thing, they do the contrary; to keep the Sabbath, and they profane it. While they disobey his command, they fulfil his permissive decree. If a man sets up two nets, one of silk, the other of iron, the silken net may be broken, not the iron; so while men break the silken net of God's command, they are taken in the iron net of his decree; while they sit backward to God's precepts, they row forward to his decrees; his decrees to permit their sin, and to punish them for their sin permitted.

5. THE WISDOM OF GOD

The next attribute is God's wisdom, which is one of the brightest beams of the Godhead. 'He is wise in heart.' Job ix 4. The heart is the seat of wisdom. *Cor in Hebræo sumitur pro judicio.* Pineda. 'Among the Hebrews, the heart is put for wisdom.' 'Let men of understanding tell me:' Job xxxiv 34: in the Hebrew, 'Let men of heart tell me.' God is wise in heart, that is, he is most wise. God only is wise; he solely and wholly possesses all wisdom; therefore he is called, 'the only wise God.' 1 Tim i 17. All the treasures of wisdom are locked up in him, and no creature can have any wisdom but as God is pleased to give it out of his treasury. God is perfectly wise; there is no defect in his wisdom. Men may be wise in some things, but in other things may betray imprudence and weakness. But God is the exemplar and pattern of wisdom, and the pattern must be perfect. Matt v 48. God's wisdom appears in two things. I. *His infinite intelligence.* II. *His exact working.*

I. *His infinite intelligence.* He knows the most profound secrets. Dan ii 28. He knows the thoughts, which are the most intricate subtle things. Amos iv 13. 'He declareth to man what is his thought.' Let sin be contrived ever so politically, God will pull off all masks and disguises, and make a heart-anatomy. He knows all future contingencies, *et ante intuita* [and, already foreseen], all things are before him in one clear prospect.

II. *His exact curious working*. He is wise in heart; his wisdom lies in his works. These works of God are bound up in three great volumes, where we may read his wisdom.

[1] The work of creation. The creation is both a monument of God's power, and a looking-glass in which we may see his wisdom. None but a wise God could so curiously contrive the world. Behold the earth decked with variety of flowers, which are both for beauty and fragrance. Behold the heaven bespangled with lights. We may see the glorious wisdom of God blazing in the sun, twinkling in the stars. His wisdom is seen in marshalling and ordering everything in its proper place and sphere. If the sun had been set lower, it would have burnt us; if higher, it would not have warmed us with its beams. God's wisdom is seen in appointing the seasons of the year. 'Thou hast made summer and winter.' Psa lxxiv 17. If it had been all summer, the heat would have scorched us; if all winter, the cold would have killed us. The wisdom of God is seen in chequering the dark and the light. If it had been all night, there had been no labour; if all day, there had been no rest. Wisdom is seen in mixing the elements, as the earth with the sea. If it had been all sea, we had wanted bread; if it had been all earth, we had wanted water. The wisdom of God is seen in preparing and ripening the fruits of the earth, in the wind and frost that prepare the fruits, and in the sun and rain that ripen the fruits. God's wisdom is seen in setting bounds to the sea, and so wisely contriving it, that though the sea be higher than many parts of the earth, yet it should not overflow the earth; so that we may cry out with the Psalmist, 'O Lord, how manifold are thy works! in wisdom hast thou made them all.' Psa civ 24. There is nothing to be seen but miracles of wisdom. God's wisdom is seen in ordering things in the body politic, that one shall have need of another. The poor need the rich man's money, and the rich need the poor man's labour. God makes one trade depend upon another, that one may be helpful to another, and that mutual love may be preserved.

[2] The second work wherein God's wisdom shines forth is the work of redemption. (1.) Here was the masterpiece of divine wisdom, to contrive a way to happiness between the sin of man and the justice of God. We may cry out with the apostle, 'O the depth of the riches both of the wisdom and knowledge of God.' Rom xi 33. This astonished men and angels. If God had put us to find out a way of salvation when we were lost, we could neither have had a head to devise, nor a heart to desire,

what God's infinite wisdom had found out for us. Mercy had a mind to save sinners, and was loath that the justice of God should be wronged. It is a pity, says Mercy, that such a noble creature as man should be made to be undone; and yet God's justice must not be a loser. What way then shall be found out? Angels cannot satisfy for the wrong done to God's justice, nor is it fit that one nature should sin, and another nature suffer. What then? Shall man be for ever lost? Now, while Mercy was thus debating with itself, what to do for the recovery of fallen man, the Wisdom of God stepped in; and thus the oracle spake:—Let God become man; let the Second Person in the Trinity be incarnate, and suffer; and so for fitness he shall be man, and for ability he shall be God; thus justice may be satisfied, and man saved. O the depth of the riches of the wisdom of God, thus to make justice and mercy to kiss each other! Great is this mystery, 'God manifest in the flesh.' 1 Tim iii 16. What wisdom was this, that Christ should be made sin, yet know no sin; that God should condemn the sin, yet save the sinner! Here was wisdom, to find out the way of salvation. (2.) The means by which salvation is applied sets forth God's wisdom; that salvation should be by faith, not by works. Faith is a humble grace, it gives all to Christ; it is an adorer of free grace; and free grace being advanced here, God has his glory; and it is his highest wisdom to exalt his own glory. (3.) The way of working faith declares God's wisdom. It is wrought by the word preached. 'Faith comes by hearing.' Rom x 17. What is the weak breath of a man to convert a soul? It is like whispering in the ears of a dead man. This is foolishness in the eye of the world; but the Lord loves to show his wisdom by that which seems folly. 'He hath chosen the foolish things of the world to confound the wise.' 1 Cor i 27. Why so? verse 29. 'That no flesh should glory in his presence.' Should God convert by the ministry of angels, then we should be ready to glory in angels, and give that honour to them which is due to God; but when God works by weak tools, makes use of men who are of like passions with ourselves, and by them converts, then the power is plainly seen to be of God. 'We have this treasure in earthen vessels, that the excellency of the power may be of God and not of us.' 2 Cor iv 7. Herein is God's wisdom seen, that no flesh may glory in his Presence.

[3] The wisdom of God wonderfully appears in the works of his providence. Every providence has a mercy or a wonder wrapt up in it. The wisdom of God, in his works of providence, appears. (1.) By effecting great things by small contemptible means. He cured the stung Israelites by a brazen serpent. If some sovereign antidote had been used, if the balm of Gilead had been brought, there had been some likelihood of a cure;

but what was there in a brazen serpent? It was a mere image, and not applied to him that was wounded, he was to look upon it only; yet this wrought a cure. The less probability in the instrument, the more is God's wisdom seen. (2.) The wisdom of God is seen in doing his work by that which to the eye of flesh seems quite contrary. God intended to advance Joseph, and to make all his brethrens' sheaves bow to his sheaf. Now, what way does he take? First Joseph is thrown into the pit; then sold into Egypt; then after that put in prison. Gen xxxix 20. By his imprisonment God made way for his advancement. For God to save in an ordinary way would not so much display his wisdom. But when he goes strangely to work, and saves in that very way in which we think he will destroy, his wisdom shines forth in a most conspicuous manner. God would make Israel victorious, and what way does he take? He lessens Gideon's army. 'The people that are with thee are too many.' Judg vii 2. He reduces the army of two and thirty thousand to three hundred; and by taking away the means of victory makes Israel victorious. God had a design to bring his people out of Egypt, and a strange course he takes to effect it. He stirred up the hearts of the Egyptians to hate them. 'He turned their heart to hate his people.' Psa cv 25. The more they hated and oppressed Israel, the more God plagued the Egyptians, and the more glad they were to let Israel go. Exod xii 33. The Egyptians were urgent upon Israel, that they might send them out of the land in haste. God had a mind to save Jonah when he was cast into the sea, and he let the fish swallow him up, and so brought him to the shore. God would save Paul, and all that were in the ship with him, but the ship must break, and they all came safe to land upon the broken pieces of the ship. Acts xxvii 44. In reference to the church, God often goes by contrary means, and makes the enemy do his work. He can make a straight stroke with a crooked stick. He has often made his church grow and flourish by persecution. 'The showers of blood have made her more fruitful,' says Julian. Exod i 10. 'Come, let us deal wisely with them, lest they multiply;' and the way they took to suppress them, made them multiply. Verse 12. 'The more they afflicted them, the more they multiplied;' like ground, the more it is harrowed, the better crop it bears. The apostles were scattered by reason of persecution, and their scattering was like the scattering of seed; they went up and down, and preached the gospel, and brought daily converts. Paul was put in prison, and his bonds were the means of spreading the gospel. Phil i 12.

(3.) The wisdom of God is seen in making the most desperate evils turn to the good of his children. As several poisonable ingredients, wisely tempered by the skill of the artist, make a sovereign medicine, so God makes the most deadly afflictions co-operate for the good of his children. He purifies them, and prepares them for heaven. 2 Cor iv 17. These hard frosts hasten the spring flowers of glory. The wise God, by a divine chemistry, turns afflictions into cordials. He makes his people gainers by losses, and turns their crosses into blessings.

(4.) The wisdom of God is seen in this, that the sins of men shall carry on God's work; yet he should have no hand in their sin. The Lord permits sin, but does not approve it. He has a hand in the action in which sin is, but not in the sin of the action. As in the crucifying of Christ, so far as it was a natural action, God concurred; if he had not given the Jews life and breath, they could not have done it; but as it was a sinful action, so God abhorred it. A musician plays upon a viol out of tune; the musician is the cause of the sound, but the jarring and discord is from the viol itself; so men's natural motion is from God, but their sinful motion is from themselves. When a man rides on a lame horse, his riding is the cause why the horse goes, but the lameness is from the horse itself. Herein is God's wisdom, that the sins of men carry on his work, yet he has no hand in them.

(5.) The wisdom of God is seen in helping in desperate cases. God loves to show his wisdom when human help and wisdom fail. Exquisite lawyers love to wrestle with niceties and difficulties in the law, to show their skill the more. God's wisdom is never at a loss; but when providences are darkest, then the morning star of deliverance appears. 'Who remembered us in our low estate.' Psa cxxxvi 23. Sometimes God melts away the spirits of his enemies. Josh ii 24. Sometimes he finds them other work to do, and sounds a retreat to them, as he did to Saul when he was pursuing David. 'The Philistines are in the land.' 'In the mount will God be seen.' When the church seems to be upon the altar, her peace and liberty ready to be sacrificed, then the angel comes.

(6.) God's wisdom is seen in befooling wise men, and in making their wisdom the means of their overthrow. Ahithophel had deep policy. 2 Sam xvi 23. 'The counsel of Ahithophel, which he counselled, was as if a man had enquired at the oracle of God;' but he consulted his own shame. 'The Lord turned his counsel into foolishness.' 2 Sam xv 31. 'God taketh the wise in their own craftiness;' Job v 13; that is, when they think to deal wisely, he not only disappoints them, but ensnares them. The snares they lay for others catch themselves. 'In the net which they hid is their own foot taken.' Psa ix 15. God loves to counterplot politicians; he makes use of their own wit to undo them, and hangs Haman upon his own gallows.

Use one: Adore the wisdom of God. It is an infinite deep; the angels cannot search into it. 'His ways are past finding out.' Rom xi 33. As we should adore, so we should rest in the wisdom of God. God sees what condition is best for us. Did we believe the wisdom of God, it would keep us from murmuring. Rest in God's wisdom. (1.) In want of spiritual comfort. God is wise; he sees it good sometimes that we should be without comfort. Perhaps we should be lifted up with spiritual enlargements, as Paul, with his revelations. 2 Cor xii 7. It is hard to have the heart low when comfort is high. God sees humility to be better for us than joy. It is better to want comfort, and be humble, than to have it, and be proud. (2.) In want of bodily strength, rest in God's wisdom. He sees what is best. Perhaps the less health the more grace; weaker in body, the stronger in faith. 'Though our outward man perish, yet the inward man is renewed day by day.' 2 Cor iv 16. At Rome there were two laurel trees; when the one withered, the other flourished. The inward man is renewed. When God shakes the tree of the body, he is gathering the fruits of righteousness. Heb xii 11. Sickness is God's lance, to let out the imposthume of sin. Isa xxvii 9. (3.) In case of God's providences to his church. When we wonder what God is doing with us, and are ready to kill ourselves with care; let us rest in God's wisdom. He knows best what he has to do. 'His footsteps are not known.' Psa lxxvii 19. Trust him where you cannot trace him. God is most in his way, when we think he is most out of the way. When we think God's church is, as it were, in the grave, and there is a tombstone laid upon her, his wisdom can roll away the stone from the sepulchre. 'Christ cometh leaping over mountains.' Cant ii 8. Either his power can remove the mountain, or his wisdom knows how to leap over it. (4.) In case we are low in the world, or have but little oil in our cruse, let us rest in God's wisdom. He sees it best; it is to cure pride and wantonness. God knew if thy estate had not been lost, thy soul had been lost. God saw riches would be a snare unto thee. 1 Tim vi 9. Art thou troubled that God has prevented a snare? God will make thee rich in faith. What thou lackest in temporals shall be made up in spirituals. God will give thee more of his love. Thou art weak in estate, but God will make thee strong in assurance. Oh rest in God's wisdom! he will carve the best piece for thee. (5.) In case of the loss of dear friends, a wife, or child, or husband, let us rest satisfied in God's wisdom. God takes away these, because he would have more of our love; he breaks these crutches, that we may live more upon him by faith. God would have us learn to go without crutches.

Use two: If God be infinitely wise, let us go to him for wisdom, as Solomon did. 'Give thy servant an understanding heart; and the speech pleased the Lord.' 1 Kings iii 9. Here is encouragement for us; 'If any one lack wisdom, let him ask of God, who giveth liberally, and upbraideth not.' James i 5. Wisdom is in God, *tanquam in fonte*, 'as in the fountain'; his wisdom is imparted, not impaired; his stock is not spent by giving. Go then to God. Lord, do thou light my lamp; in thy light shall I see light; give me wisdom, to know the fallacy of my heart, the subtleties of the old serpent; to walk jealously towards myself, religiously towards thee, prudently towards others; guide me by thy counsel, and afterwards receive me to glory.

6. THE POWER OF GOD

The next attribute is God's power. Job ix 19. 'If I speak of strength, lo, he is strong.' In this chapter is a magnificent description of God's power. 'Lo, he is strong.' The Hebrew word for strong signifies a conquering, prevailing strength. 'He is strong.' The superlative degree is intended here; viz., He is most strong. He is called *El-shaddai*, God almighty. Gen xvii 1. His almightiness lies in this, that he can do whatever is feasible. Divines distinguish between authority and power. God has both.

I. *He has a sovereign right and authority over man.* He can do with his creatures as he pleases. Who shall dispute with God? who shall ask him a reason of his doings? Dan iv 35. 'He doeth according to his will in the army of heaven, and among the inhabitants of the earth; and none can stay his hand, or say unto him, What doest thou?' God sits judge in the highest court; he calls the monarchs of the earth to the bar, and is not bound to give a reason of his proceedings. Psa lxxv 7. 'He putteth down one, and raiseth up another.' He has salvation and damnation in his power. He has the key of justice in his hand, to lock up whom he will in the fiery prison of hell; and he has the key of mercy in his hand, to open heaven's gate to whom he pleases. The name engraven upon his vesture is, 'King of kings, and Lord of lords.' Rev xix 16. He sits Lord paramount, and who can call him to account? Isa xlvi 10. 'I will do all my pleasure.' The world is God's diocese, and shall not he do what he will in his own diocese? He it was that turned King Nebuchadnezzar to eat grass, and threw the angels to hell when they sinned; that broke the head of the Babylonish empire. 'How art thou fallen from heaven, O Lucifer! Thy pomp is brought down to the grave.' Isa xiv 12. 'Who sets bounds to the sea, and bridles the proud waves.' Job xxxviii 11. God is the supreme monarch, all power is seated originally in him. 'The powers that be are ordained of God.' Rom xiii 1. Kings hold their crowns of him. 'By me kings reign.' Prov viii 15.

II. *As God has authority, so he has infinite power.* What is authority without power? 'He is mighty in strength.' Job ix 4. This power of God is seen.

[1] In the creation. To create requires infinite power. All the world cannot make a fly. God's power in creating is evident; because he needs no instruments to work with; he can work without tools; because he needs no matter to work upon; he creates matter, and then works upon it; and because he works without labour; 'He spake, and it was done.' Psa xxxiii 9.

[2] The power of God is seen in the conversion of souls. The same power draws a sinner to God that drew Christ out of the grave to heaven. Eph i 19. Greater power is put forth in conversion than in creation. When God made the world, he met with no opposition; as he had nothing to help him, so he had nothing to hinder him; but when he converts a sinner, he meets with opposition. Satan opposes him, and the heart opposes him; a sinner is angry with converting grace. The world was the 'work of God's fingers.' Psa viii 3. Conversion is the 'work of God's arm.' Luke i 51. In the creation, God wrought but one miracle, he spake the word; but, in conversion, he works many miracles; the blind is made to see, the dead is raised, the deaf hears the voice of the Son of God. Oh the infinite power of Jehovah! Before his sceptre, angels veil and prostrate themselves, and kings cast their crowns at his feet. 'He toucheth the land, and it shall melt.' Amos ix 5. 'He removeth the earth out of her place.' Job ix 6. An earthquake makes the earth tremble upon her pillars, but God shakes it out of its place; he can remove the earth from its centre. He can do what he will; his power is as large as his will. Were men's power as large as their will, what work would they make in the world! God's power is of equal extent with his will. He with a word can unpin the wheels, and break the axletree of the creation. He can do 'more than we can think.' Eph iii 20. He can suspend natural agents. He sealed up the lions' mouths; he made the fire not to burn; he made the waters to stand up on a heap; he caused the sun to go ten degrees backward in the dial of Ahaz. Isa xxxviii 8. What can pose Omnipotence? 'The Lord cuts off the spirit of princes.' Psa lxxvi 12. He counterworks his enemies; he pulls down their flags and banners of pride, infatuates their counsels, breaks their forces; and he does it with ease, with the turning of his hand; 'with his breath,' Psa xxxiii 6, Isa xl 24; a look, a glance of his eye is all it needs cost God to destroy his enemies, 'the Lord looked into the host of the Egyptians through the pillar of fire, and troubled their host.' Exod xiv 24.

Who shall stop him in his march? God commands, and all creatures in heaven and earth obey him. Xerxes, the Persian monarch, threw fetters into the sea, when its waves swelled, as if he would have chained the waters; but when God speaks, the wind and sea obey him. If he say but the word, the stars fight in their courses against Sisera; if he stamp with his foot, an army of angels shall presently be in battalia. What cannot omnipotent power do? 'The Lord is a man of war.' Exod xv 3. 'He hath a mighty arm.' Psa lxxxix 13. 'God's power is a glorious power.' Col i 11. It is an irresistible power. Rom ix 19. 'Who hath resisted his will?' To contest with him, is as if the thorns should set themselves in battle array against the fire; or, as if an infirm child should fight with an archangel. If the sinner be once taken in God's iron net, there is no escape. 'There is none that can deliver out of my hand.' Isa xliii 13. God's power is inexhaustible; it is never spent or wasted. Men, while they exercise their strength, weaken it; but God has an everlasting spring of strength in himself. Isa xxvi 4. Though he spends his arrows upon his enemies, yet he does not spend his strength. Deut xxxii 23. 'He fainteth not, neither is weary.' Isa xl 28.

God cannot do all things, because he cannot deny himself.

Though God can do all things, he cannot do that which stains the glory of his Godhead. He cannot sin; he cannot do that which implies a contradiction. To be a God of truth, and yet deny himself, is a contradiction.

Use one: If God be infinite in power, let us fear him. We fear such as are in power. 'Fear ye not me? saith the Lord: will ye not tremble at my presence?' Jer v 22. He has power to cast our souls and bodies into hell. 'Who knows the power of his wrath?' Psa xc 11. The same breath that made us can dissolve us. 'His fury is poured out like fire; the rocks are thrown down by him.' Nahum i 6. Solomon says, 'Where the word of a king is, there is power, much more where the word of a God is. Eccles viii 4. Oh let us fear this mighty God! The fear of God will drive out all other base fear.

Use two: See the deplorable condition of wicked men. (1.) This power of God is not for them: (2.) It is against them.

(1.) This power of God is not for them. They have no union with God, therefore they have no warrant to lay claim to his power. His power is no relief to them. He has power to forgive sins, but he will not put forth his power towards an impenitent sinner. God's power is an eagle's wing, to carry the saints to heaven; but what privilege is that to the wicked? Though a man will carry his child in his arms over a dangerous stream, yet he will not carry an enemy. God's power is not engaged to help those that fight against him. Let miseries come upon the wicked, they have none to help them; they are like a ship in a storm without a pilot, and driven upon the rocks.

(2.) This power of God is against the wicked. God's power will not be the sinner's shield to defend him, but a sword to wound him. God's power will bind the sinner in chains. His power serves to revenge the wrong done to his mercy. He will be Almighty to damn the sinner. Now, in what condition is every unbeliever? God's power is engaged against him, and 'it is a fearful thing to fall into the hands of the living God.' Heb x 31.

Use three: It reproves such as do not believe the power of God. We say we do not doubt of God's power, but his will. But indeed it is his power that we question. 'Is anything too hard for God?' Jer xxxii 27. We stagger through unbelief, as if the arm of God's power were shrunk, and he could not help in desperate cases. Take away a king's power, and we unking him; take away the Lord's power, and we ungod him. Yet how guilty of this are we! Did not Israel question God's power? 'Can he prepare a table in the wilderness?' Psa lxxviii 19. They thought the wilderness was a fitter place for making graves than spreading a table. Did not Martha doubt Christ's power? 'He hath been dead four days.' John xi 39. If Christ had been there while Lazarus was sick, or when he had been newly dead, Martha did not question but he could have raised him; but he had lain in the grave four days, and now she seemed to question his power. Christ had as much ado to raise her faith as to raise her dead brother. Moses, though a holy man, limited God's power through unbelief. 'The people among whom I am, are six hundred thousand footmen; and thou hast said, I will give them flesh for a whole month: shall the flocks and the herds be slain for them to suffice them? or shall all the fish of the sea be gathered for them to suffice? And the Lord said unto Moses, Is the Lord's hand waxed short?' Numb xi 21. This is a great affront to God, to deny his power. That men doubt of God's power appears by their taking indirect courses; for they would not defraud in their dealings, and use false weights, if they believed the power of God could provide for them; and by depending more upon second causes than upon God. 'In his disease, he sought not to the Lord, but to the physicians.' 2 Chron xvi 12.

Use four: If God be infinite in power, let us take heed of hardening our hearts against him. 'Who hath hardened himself against him and prospered?' Job ix 4. Job sends a challenge to all creatures in heaven and earth. Who ever took up the buckler against God, and came off conqueror? For a person to go on daringly in any sin is to harden his heart against God, and to raise a war against heaven. Let him remember God is *El-Shaddai*, almighty; he will be too hard for them that oppose him. 'Hast thou an arm like God?' Job xl 9. Such as will not bow to his golden sceptre shall be broken with his iron rod. Julian hardened his heart against God, he opposed him to his face; but what got he at last? Did he prosper? Being wounded in battle, he threw up his blood into the air, and said to Christ, *Vicisti Galilæe*, 'O Galilean, thou hast overcome!' I acknowledge thy power, whose name and truth I have opposed. Will folly contend with wisdom; weakness with power; finite with infinite? Oh take heed of hardening your heart against God! He can send legions of angels to avenge his quarrel. It is better to meet God with tears in your eyes than weapons in your hand. You may overcome him sooner by repentance than by resistance.

Use five: Get an interest in God, and then this glorious power is engaged for you. He gives it under his hand, that he will put forth the whole power of his Godhead for the good of his people. 'The Lord of hosts is the God of Israel, even a God to Israel.' 1 Chron xvii 24. This almightiness of God's power is a wonderful support and comfort to the believer. It was Samson's riddle. 'Out of the strong came forth sweetness;' Judges xiv 14; so out of the attribute of God's power, out of this strong comes forth sweetness. It is comfort in several cases.

(1.) In case of strong corruption. My sins, says a child of God, are potent. I have no power against this army that comes against me; I pray, and humble my soul by fasting; but my sins return upon me. Ay, but dost thou believe the power of God? The strong God can conquer thy strong corruption; though sin be too hard for thee, yet not for him; he can soften hard hearts and quicken the dead. 'Is any thing too hard for the Lord?' Gen xviii 14. Set his power to work, by faith and prayer. Say, Lord! it is not for thy honour that the devil should have so strong a party within me; oh, break the head of this leviathan! Abba, Father, all things are possible to thee.

(2.) In case of strong temptation. Satan is called the strong man; but remember the power of God. Christ is called, 'The Lion of the tribe of Judah,' he has broken the serpent's head upon the cross. Satan is a chained enemy, and a conquered enemy. Michael is stronger than the dragon.

(3.) Comfort in case of weakness of grace, and fear of falling away. I pray, but I cannot send out strong cries. I believe, but the hand of my faith shakes and trembles. Cannot God strengthen weak grace? 'My strength is made perfect in weakness: most gladly therefore will I rather glory in my infirmities, that the power of Christ may rest upon me.'

2 Cor xii 9. I fear I shall not hold out. Christian, dost thou believe the power of God? Has not God preserved thy grace thus far? Mayest thou not set up thy Ebenezer? God has kept thy grace hitherto as a spark in the main ocean; and is not he able still to keep it? 'We are kept by the power of God,' &c. 1 Pet i 5. God's mercy pardons us, but his power preserves us. He who by his power keeps the stars that they do not fall from their orbs, keeps our grace that it does not fail or annihilate.

(4.) Comfort in case of deficiency in thy estate. God can multiply the oil in the cruse; miraculously he can raise up supplies. Cannot he who provides for the birds of the air provide for his children? Cannot he that clothes the lilies clothe his lambs?

(5.) Comfort in regard of the resurrection. It seems difficult to believe, that the bodies of men, when eaten up by worms, devoured by beasts and fishes, or consumed to ashes, should be raised the same numerical bodies; but if we believe the power of God, it is no great wonder. Which is harder, to create, or raise the dead? He that can make a body of nothing, can restore it to its parts when mingled and confounded with other substances. 'With God all things are possible.' Matt xix 26. If we believe the first article of the creed, That God is almighty, we may quickly believe the other article, the resurrection of the body. God can raise the dead because of his power, and he cannot but raise them because of his truth.

(6.) It is comfort in reference to the church of God. He can save and deliver it when it is brought low. The enemies have power in their hand, but the remainder of wrath God will restrain. Psa lxxvi 10. He can either confine the enemy's power or confound it. 'If God be for us, who can be against us?' God can create Jerusalem a rejoicing. Isa lxv 18. The church in Ezekiel is compared to dry bones, but God made breath to enter into them, and they lived. Ezek xxxvii 10. The ship of the church may be tossed, because sin is in it, but it shall not be overwhelmed, because Christ is in it. Psa xlvi 5. *Deus in medio.* All the church's pangs shall help forward her deliverance.

7. THE HOLINESS OF GOD

The next attribute is God's holiness. Exod xv 11. 'Glorious in holiness.' Holiness is the most sparkling jewel of his crown; it is the name by which God is known. Psa cxi 9. 'Holy and reverend is his name.' He is 'the holy One.' Job vi 10. Seraphims cry, 'Holy, holy, holy, is the Lord of hosts, the whole earth is full of his glory.' Isa vi 3. His power makes him mighty, his holiness makes him glorious. God's holiness consists in his perfect love of righteousness, and abhorrence of evil. 'Of purer eyes than to behold evil, and cannot look on iniquity.' Hab i 13.

I. *God is holy intrinsically.* He is holy in his nature; his very being is made up of holiness, as light is of the essence of the sun. He is holy in his Word. The Word bears a stamp of his holiness upon it, as the wax bears an impression of the seal. 'Thy Word is very pure.' Psa cxix 140. It is compared to silver refined seven times. Psa xii 6. Every line in the Word breathes sanctity, it encourages nothing but holiness. God is holy in his operations. All he does is holy; he cannot act but like himself; he can no more do an unrighteous action than the sun can darken. 'The Lord is holy in all his works.' Psa cxlv 17.

II. *God is holy primarily.* He is the original and pattern of holiness. Holiness began with him who is the Ancient of Days.

III. *God is holy efficiently.* He is the cause of all that is holiness in others. 'Every good and perfect gift comes from above.' James i 17. He made the angels holy. He infused all holiness into Christ's human nature. All the holiness we have is but a crystal stream from this fountain. We borrow all our holiness from God. As the lights of the sanctuary were lighted from the middle lamp, so all the holiness of others is a lamp lighted from heaven. 'I am the Lord which sanctify you.' Lev xx 8. God is not only a pattern of holiness, but he is a principle of holiness: his spring feeds all our cisterns, he drops his holy oil of grace upon us.

IV. *God is holy transcendently.* 'There is none holy as the Lord.' 1 Sam ii 2. No angel in heaven can take the just dimensions of God's holiness. The highest seraphim is too low of stature to measure these pyramids; holiness in God is far above holiness in saints or angels.

[1] It is above holiness in saints. It is a pure holiness. The saints' holiness is like gold in the ore, imperfect; their humility is stained with pride; he that has most faith needs pray, 'Lord, help my unbelief:' but the holiness of God is pure, like wine from the grape; it has not the least dash or tincture of impurity mixed with it. It is a more unchangeable holiness. Though the saints cannot lose the habit of holiness (for the seed of God remains), yet they may lose some degrees of their holiness. 'Thou hast left thy first love.' Rev ii 4. Grace cannot die, yet the flame of it may go out. Holiness in the saints is subject to ebbing, but holiness in God is unchangeable; he never lost a drop of his holiness; as he cannot have more holiness, because he is perfectly holy; so he cannot have less holiness, because he is unchangeably holy.

[2] The holiness of God is above the holiness of angels. Holiness in the angels is only a quality, which may be lost, as we see in the fallen angels; but holiness in God is his essence, he is all over holy, and he can as well lose his Godhead as his holiness.

But is he not privy to all the sins of men? How can he behold their impurities, and not be defiled?

God sees all the sins of men, but is no more defiled with them than the sun is defiled with the vapours that rise from the earth. God sees sin, not as a patron to approve it, but as a judge to punish it.

Use one: Is God so infinitely holy? Then see how unlike to God sin is. Sin is an unclean thing, it is hyperbolically evil. Rom i 23. It is called an abomination. Deut vii 25. God has no mixture of evil in him; sin has no mixture of good, it is the spirit and quintessence of evil; it turns good into evil; it has deflowered the virgin soul, made it red with guilt, and black with filth; it is called the accursed thing. Josh vii 11. No wonder, therefore, that God hates sin, being so unlike to him, nay, so contrary to him: it strikes at his holiness; it does all it can to spite God; if sin could help it, God should be God no longer.

Use two: Is God the Holy One, and is holiness his glory? How impious are they that are haters of holiness! As the vulture hates perfumes, so they hate the sweet perfume of holiness in the saints; their hearts rise against holiness; as a man's stomach at a dish he has an antipathy against. There is not a greater sign of a person devoted to hell, than to hate one for the thing wherein he is most like God. Others are despisers of holiness. They despise the glory of the Godhead. 'Glorious in holiness.' The despising holiness is seen in deriding it; and is it not sad that men should deride that which should save them? Sure that patient will die who derides the physic. Deriding the grace of the Spirit comes near to despiting the Spirit of grace. Scoffing Ishmael was cast out of Abraham's house. Gen xxi 9. Such as scoff at holiness shall be cast out of heaven.

Use three: Is God so infinitely holy? Then let us endeavour to imitate God in holiness. 'Be ye holy, for I am holy.' 1 Pet i 16. There is a twofold holiness; a holiness of equality, and a holiness of similitude. A holiness of equality no man or angel can reach to. Who can be equally holy with God? Who can parallel him in sanctity? But there is a holiness of similitude, and that we must aspire after, to have some analogy and resemblance of God's holiness in us, to be as like him in holiness as we can. Though a taper does not give so much light as the sun, yet it resembles it. We must imitate God in holiness.

If we must be like God in holiness, wherein does our holiness consist?

In two things. In our suitableness to God's nature, and in our subjection to his will.

Our holiness consists in our suitableness to the nature of God. Hence the saints are said to partake of the divine nature, which is not partaking of his essence, but his image. 2 Pet i 4. Herein is the saints' holiness, when they are the lively pictures of God. They bear the image of God's meekness, mercifulness, heavenliness; they are of the same judgment with God, of the same disposition; they love what he loves, and hate what he hates.

Our holiness consists also in our subjection to the will of God. As God's nature is the pattern of holiness, so his will is the rule of holiness. It is our holiness when we do his will, Acts xiii 22; when we bear his will, Micah vii 9; when what he inflicts wisely we suffer willingly. Our great care should be, to be like God in holiness. Our holiness should be qualified as God's; as his is a real holiness, ours should be. 'Righteousness and true holiness.' Eph iv 24. It should not be the paint of holiness, but the life; it should not be like the Egyptian temples, beautified without merely, but like Solomon's temple, gold within, Psa xlv 13. 'The king's daughter is all glorious within.' That I may press you to resemble God in holiness consider,

(1.) How illustrious every holy person is. He is a fair glass in which some of the beams of God's holiness shine forth. We read that Aaron put on his garments for glory and beauty. Exod xxviii 2. When we wear the embroidered garment of holiness, it is for glory and beauty. A good Christian is ruddy, being sprinkled with Christ's blood; and white, being adorned with holiness. As the diamond to a ring, so is holiness to the soul; that, as Chrysostom says, they that oppose it cannot but admire it.

(2.) It is the great design God carries on in the world, to make a people like himself in holiness. What are all the showers of ordinances for, but to rain down righteousness upon us, and make us holy? What are the promises for, but to encourage holiness? What is the sending of the Spirit into the world for, but to anoint us with the holy unction? 1 John ii 20. What are all afflictions for, but to make us partakers of God's holiness? Heb xii 10. What are mercies for, but loadstones to draw us to holiness? What is the end of Christ's dying, but that his blood might wash away our unholiness? 'Who gave himself for us, to purify unto himself a peculiar people.' Titus ii 14. So that if we are not holy, we cross God's great design in the world.

(3.) Our holiness draws God's heart to us. Holiness is God's image; and God cannot choose but love his image where he sees it. A king loves to see his effigies upon a piece of coin. 'Thou lovest righteousness.' Psa xlv 7. And where does righteousness grow, but in a holy heart? Isa lxii 4. 'Thou shalt be called *Hephzibah*, for the Lord delighteth in thee.' It was her holiness that drew God's love to her. 'They shall call them the holy people.' Verse 12. God values not any by their high birth, but their holiness.

(4.) Holiness is the only thing that distinguishes us from the reprobate part of the world. God's people have his seal upon them. 'The foundation of God standeth sure, having this seal, the Lord knoweth them that are his. And let all that name the name of Christ depart from iniquity.' 2 Tim ii 19. The people of God are sealed with a double seal. Election, 'The Lord knows who are his:' and Sanctification, 'Let every one depart from iniquity.' As a nobleman is distinguished from another by his silver star; as a virtuous woman is distinguished from a harlot by her chastity; so holiness distinguishes between the two seeds. All that are of God have Christ for their captain, and holiness is the white colour they wear. Heb ii 10.

(5.) Holiness is our honour. Holiness and honour are put together. 1 Thess iv 4. Dignity goes along with sanctification. 'He hath washed us from our sins in his blood, and hath made us kings unto God.' Rev i 5. When we are washed and made holy, then we are kings and priests to God. The saints are called vessels of honour; they are called jewels, for the sparkling of their holiness, because filled with wine of the Spirit. This makes them earthly angels.

(6.) Holiness gives us boldness with God. 'Thou shalt put away iniquity far from thy tabernacles, and shalt lift up thy face unto God.' Job xxii 23, 26. Lifting up the face is an emblem of boldness. Nothing can make us so ashamed to go to God as sin. A wicked man in prayer may lift up his hands, but he cannot lift up his face. When Adam had lost his holiness, he lost his confidence; he hid himself. But the holy person goes to God as a child to its father; his conscience does not upbraid him with allowing any sin, therefore he can go boldly to the throne of grace, and have mercy to help in time of need. Heb iv 16.

(7.) Holiness gives peace. Sin raises a storm in the conscience; *ubi peccatum ibi procella* [where there is sin, there is tumult]. 'There is no peace to the wicked.' Isa lvii 21. Righteousness and peace are put together. Holiness is the root which bears this sweet fruit of peace; righteousness and peace kiss each other.

(8.) Holiness leads to heaven. It is the King of heaven's highway. 'An highway shall be there, and it shall be called the way of holiness.' Isa xxxv 8. At Rome there were temples of virtue and honour, and all were to go through the temple of virtue to the temple of honour; so we must go through the temple of holiness to the temple of heaven. Glory begins in virtue. 'Who hath called us to glory and virtue.' 2 Pet i 3. Happiness is nothing else but the quintessence of holiness; holiness is glory militant, and happiness holiness triumphant.

What shall we do to resemble God in holiness?

(1.) Have recourse to Christ's blood by faith. This is *lavacrum animæ* [the washing of the soul]. Legal purifications were types and emblems of it. 1 John i 7. The Word is a glass to show us our spots, and Christ's blood is a fountain to wash them away.

(2.) Pray for a holy heart. 'Create in me a clean heart, O God.' Psa li 10. Lay thy heart before the Lord, and say, Lord, my heart is full of leprosy; it defiles all it touches; Lord, I am not fit to live with such a heart, for I cannot honour thee; nor die with such a heart, for I cannot see thee. Oh create in me a clean heart; send thy Spirit into me, to refine and purify me, that I may be a temple fit for thee the holy God to inhabit.

(3.) Walk with them that are holy. 'He that walketh with the wise shall be wise.' Prov xiii 20. Be among the spices and you will smell of them. Association begets assimilation. Nothing has a greater power and energy to effect holiness than the communion of saints.

8. THE JUSTICE OF GOD

The next attribute is God's justice. All God's attributes are identical, and are the same with his essence. Though he has several attributes whereby he is made known to us, yet he has but one essence. A cedar tree may have several branches, yet it is but one cedar. So there are several attributes of God whereby we conceive of him, but only one entire essence. Well, then, concerning God's justice. Deut xxxii 4. 'Just and right is he.' Job xxxvii 23. 'Touching the Almighty, we cannot find him out: he is excellent in plenty of justice.' God is said to dwell in justice. Psa lxxxix 14. 'Justice and judgment are the habitation of thy throne.' In God, power and justice meet. Power holds the sceptre, and justice holds the balance.

I. *What is God's justice?*

'Justice is to give every one his due.' God's justice is the rectitude of his nature, whereby he is carried to the doing of that which is righteous

[87]

and equal. Prov xxiv 12. 'Shall not he render to every man according to his works?' God is an impartial judge. He judgeth the cause. Men often judge the person, but not the cause; which is not justice, but malice. Gen xviii 21. 'I will go down and see whether they have done according to the cry which is come up unto me.' When the Lord is upon a punitive act, he weighs things in the balance, he does not punish rashly; he does not go in the way of a riot, but a circuit, against offenders. Concerning God's justice, I shall lay down these six positions:—

[1] God cannot but be just. His holiness is the cause of his justice. Holiness will not suffer him to do anything but what is righteous. He can no more be unjust than he can be unholy.

[2] God's will is the supreme rule of justice; it is the standard of equity. His will is wise and good. God wills nothing but what is just; and therefore it is just because he wills it.

[3] God does justice voluntarily. Justice flows from his nature. Men may act unjustly, because they are bribed or forced: God will not be bribed, because of his justice; he cannot be forced, because of his power. He does justice out of love to justice. Psa xlv 7. 'Thou lovest righteousness.'

[4] Justice is the perfection of the divine nature. Aristotle says, 'Justice comprehends in it all virtues.' To say God is just, is to say, he is all that is excellent: perfections meet in him, as lines in a centre. He is not only just, but justice itself.

[5] God never did nor can do the least wrong to his creatures. God's justice has been wronged, but never did any wrong. God does not go according to the *summum jus*, or rigour of the law; he abates something of his severity. He might inflict heavier penalties than he does. 'Thou hast punished us less than our iniquities deserve.' Ezra ix 13. Our mercies are more than we deserve, and our punishments less.

[6] God's justice is such that it is not fit for any man or angel to expostulate with him, or demand a reason of his actions. God has not only authority on his side, but equity. 'He lays judgment to the line, and righteousness to the plummet.' Isa xxviii 17. It is below him to give an account to us of his proceedings. Which of these two is more fit to take place, God's justice or man's reason? Rom ix 20. 'Who art thou, O man, that repliest against God?' The plumb line of our reason is too short to fathom the depth of God's justice. Rom xi 33. 'How unsearchable are his judgments!' We are to adore God's justice, where we cannot see a reason of it.

II. *God's justice runs in two channels.* It is seen in two things, the distribution of rewards and punishments.

[1] In rewarding the virtuous. Psa lviii 11. 'Verily there is a reward for the righteous.' The saints shall not serve him for nought, he will reward *præces et lachrymas;* though they may be losers for him, they shall not be losers by him. 'God is not unrighteous to forget your work and labour of love, which ye have shewed to his name.' Heb vi 10. He gives a reward, not because we have deserved it, but because he has promised it.

[2] He is just in punishing offenders. He is just. (1.) Because he punishes sinners by a law. 'Where there is no law, there is no transgression.' Rom iv 15. But God has given men a law, and they break it, therefore he punishes them justly. (2.) God is just in punishing the wicked, because he never punished them but upon full proof and evidence. What greater evidence than for a man's own conscience to be witness against him! There is nothing God charges upon a sinner but conscience sets its seal to the truth of it.

Use one: See here another flower of God's crown, he is just and righteous. He is the exemplar and pattern of justice.

But how does it seem to stand with God's justice, that the wicked should prosper in the world? 'Wherefore doth the way of the wicked prosper?' Jer xii 1. This has been a great stumbling, and has led many to question God's justice. Such as are highest in sin are highest in power. Diogenes seeing Harpalus a thief go on prosperously, said, 'Sure God hath cast off the government of the world, and mindeth not how things go on here below.'

(1.) The wicked may be sometimes instruments to do God's work. Though they do not design his glory, yet they may promote it. Cyrus (Ezra i 7) was instrumental in the building of God's temple in Jerusalem. There is some kind of justice, that they should have a temporal reward. God lets those prosper under whose wing his people are sheltered. God will not be in any man's debt. 'Who hath kindled a fire on my altar for nought?' Mal i 10.

(2.) God lets men go on in sin, and prosper, that he may leave them more inexcusable. 'I gave her space to repent of her fornication.' Rev ii 21. God adjourns the sessions, spins out his mercies towards sinners; and if they repent not, his patience will be a witness against them, and his justice will be more cleared in their condemnation. 'That thou mightest be justified when thou speakest, and be clear when thou judgest.' Psa li 4.

(3.) God does not always let the wicked prosper in their sin. Some he punishes openly, that his justice may be taken notice of. 'The Lord is known by the judgment which he executeth:' Psa ix 16: that is, his justice is seen by striking men dead in the very act of sin. Thus he struck Zimri and Cozbi in the act of uncleanness.

(4.) If God lets men prosper a while in their sin, his vial of wrath is all this while filling; his sword is all this time whetting: and though God may forbear men a while, yet long forbearance is no forgiveness. The longer God is in taking his blow, the heavier it will be at last. As long as there is eternity, God has time enough to reckon with his enemies.

Justice may be as a lion asleep, but at last the lion will awake, and roar upon the sinner. Do not Nero, and Julian, and Cain, now meet with God's justice?

But God's own people suffer great afflictions; they are injured and persecuted. 'All the day long have I been plagued, and chastened every morning.' Psa lxxiii 14. *How does this stand with God's justice?*

(1.) That is a true rule of Austin, *Judicia Dei possunt esse occulta, non injusta;* 'God's ways of judgment are sometimes secret, but never unjust.' The Lord never afflicts his people without a cause; so that he cannot be unjust. There is some good in the godly, therefore the wicked afflict them; there is some evil in them, therefore God afflicts them. God's own children have their blemishes. 'Are there not with you, even with you, sins against the Lord?' 2 Chron xxviii 10. These spiritual diamonds, have they no flaws? Do we not read of the spots of God's children? Deut xxxii 5. Are not they guilty of much pride, censoriousness, passion, worldliness? Though, by their profession, they seem to resemble the birds of paradise, to fly above, and feed upon the dew of heaven; yet, as the serpent, they lick the dust. And these sins of God's people do more provoke God than others. 'Because of the provoking of his sons and daughters.' Deut xxxii 19. The sins of others pierce Christ's side, these wound his heart. Therefore is not God just in all the evils that befall them? 'You only have I known of all the families of the earth, therefore I will punish you for your iniquities.' Amos iii 2. I will punish you sooner, surer, sorer, than others.

(2.) The trials and sufferings of the godly are to refine and purify them. God's furnace is in Sion. Isa xxxi 9. Is it any injustice in God to put his gold into the furnace to purify it? Is it any injustice in God, by afflicting his people, to make them partakers of his holiness? Heb xii 10. What more proclaims God's faithfulness, than to take such a course with them as may make them better? 'In faithfulness thou hast afflicted me.' Psa cxix 75.

(3.) What injustice is it in God to inflict a less punishment, and prevent a greater? The best of God's children have that in them which is meritorious of hell. Does God do them any wrong, if he uses only the rod, where they have deserved the scorpion? Is the father unjust, if he only corrects his child, who has deserved to be disinherited? If God deals so favourably with his children, he only puts wormwood in their cup, whereas he might put fire and brimstone. They should rather admire his mercy than complain of his injustice.

How can it stand with God's justice, that all men being equally guilty by nature, he should pass by one and save another? Why does he not deal with all alike?

'Is there unrighteousness with God? God forbid.' Rom ix 14. 'Doth the Almighty pervert justice?' Job viii 3.

(1.) God is not bound to give an account of his actions to his creatures. If none may say to a king, 'What doest thou?' Eccles viii 4, much less to God. It is sufficient, God is Lord paramount; he has a sovereign power over his creatures, therefore can do no injustice. 'Hath not the potter power over the clay, of the same lump to make one vessel to honour, and another to dishonour?' Rom ix 21. God has liberty in his own breast, to save one, and not another; and his justice is not at all impeached or blemished. If two men owe you money, you may, without any injustice, remit the debt to one, and exact it of the other. If two malefactors be condemned to die, the king may pardon the one and not the other: he is not unjust if he lets one suffer, because he offended the law; nor if he save the other, because he will make use of his prerogative as he is king.

(2.) Though some are saved and others perish, yet there is no unrighteousness in God; because, whoever perishes, his destruction is of himself. 'O Israel, thou hast destroyed thyself.' Hos xiii 9. God offers grace, and the sinner refuses it. Is God bound to give grace? If a surgeon comes to heal a man's wound, and he will not be healed, is the surgeon bound to heal him? 'I have called, and ye refused.' Prov i 24. 'Israel would none of me.' Psa lxxxi 11. God is not bound to force his mercies upon men. If they wilfully oppose the offer of grace, their sin is to be regarded as the cause of their perishing, and not God's justice.

Use two: See the difference between God and a great part of the world. They are unjust. (1.) In their courts of judicature they pervert justice. 'They decree unrighteous decrees.' Isa x 1. The Hebrew word for a judge's robe signifies prevarication, deceit, or injustice, which is more often true of the judge than of the robe. What is a good law without a good judge? Injustice lies in two things, either not to punish where there is a fault, or, to punish where there is no fault. Again (2.) Men are unjust in their dealings. This is, [1] In using false weights. 'The balances of deceit are in his hand.' Hos xii 7. It is sad to have the Bible in one hand, and

[91]

false weights in the other. Or, [2] In adulterating commodities. 'Thy wine is mixed with water,' Isa i 22: when bad grain is mixed with good, and sold for pure grain. I can never believe he is good in the first table who is not good in the second. He cannot be godly who is not just. Though God does not bid you be as omnipotent as he is, yet he bids you be as just.

Use three: Imitate God in justice. Let Christ's golden maxim be observed, 'What you would have men to do to you, do ye even so to them.' Matt vii 12. You would not have them wrong you, neither do you them; rather suffer wrong than do wrong. 'Why do ye not rather take wrong?' 1 Cor vi 7. Oh be exemplary for justice! Let justice be your ornament. 'I put on righteousness (viz. justice) as a robe and a diadem.' Job xxix 14. A robe for its graceful beauty; and I put it on, *et induebam justitiam* [and I was clothed in righteousness]. A judge puts on his robe, and puts it off again at night; but Job did so put on justice, as he did not put it off till death; *semper vestitus* [forever clothed]. We must not lay off this robe of justice till we lay down our tabernacle. If you have anything of God in you, you will be like him. By every unjust action you deny yourselves to be Christians, you stain the glory of your profession. Heathens will rise up in judgment against you. The sun might sooner alter his course than God could be turned from doing justice.

Use four: If God be just, there will be a day of judgment. Now things are out of course; sin is rampant, saints are wronged, they are often cast in a righteous cause, they can meet with no justice here, justice is turned into wormwood; but there is a day coming, when God will set things right; he will do every man justice; he will crown the righteous and condemn the wicked. 'He hath appointed a day,' &c. Acts xvii 31. If God be a just God, he will take vengeance. God has given men a law to live by, and they break it. There must be a day for the execution of offenders. A law not executed is but like a wooden dagger, for a show. At the last day, God's sword shall be drawn out against offenders; then his justice shall be revealed before all the world. 'God will judge in righteousness.' Acts xvii 31. 'Shall not the Judge of all the earth do right?' Gen xviii 25. The wicked shall drink a sea of wrath, but not sip one drop of injustice. At that day shall all mouths be stopped, and God's justice shall be fully vindicated from all the cavils and clamours of unjust men.

Use five: Comfort to the true penitent. As God is a just God, he will pardon him. *Homo agnoscit, Deus ignoscit* [Man acknowledges his sin, God spares him]. 'If we confess our sins (i.e. *confess and forsake*), he is just to forgive us our sins.' 1 John i 9. Not only merciful but just. Why just?

Because he has promised to forgive such. Prov xxviii 13. If thy heart has been broken for and from sin, thou mayest not only plead God's mercy, but his justice for the pardoning of thy sin. Show him his hand and seal, and he cannot deny himself.

9. THE MERCY OF GOD

The next attribute is God's goodness or mercy. Mercy is the result and effect of God's goodness. Psa xxxiii 5. So then this is the next attribute, God's goodness or mercy. The most learned of the heathens thought they gave their god Jupiter two golden characters when they styled him *good* and *great*. Both these meet in God, *goodness and greatness*, majesty and mercy. God is essentially good in himself and relatively good to us. They are both put together in Psa cxix 68. 'Thou art good, and doest good.' This relative goodness is nothing else but his mercy, which is an innate propenseness in God to pity and succour such as are in misery.

I. *Concerning God's mercy I shall lay down these twelve positions.*

[1] It is the great design of the Scripture to represent God as merciful. This is a loadstone to draw sinners to him. 'The Lord, merciful, gracious, long-suffering, abundant in goodness,' &c. Exod xxxiv 6. Here are six expressions to set forth God's mercy, and but one to set forth his justice: 'who will by no means clear the guilty.' Psa lvii 10. 'God's mercy is far above the heavens.' Psa cviii 4. God is represented as a king, with a rainbow about his throne. Rev iv 3. The rainbow was an emblem of mercy. The Scripture represents God in white robes of mercy more often than with garments rolled in blood; with his golden sceptre more often than his iron rod.

[2] God is more inclinable to mercy than wrath. Mercy is his darling attribute, which he most delights in. Mic vii 18. Mercy pleases him. It is delightful to the mother, says Chrysostom, to have her breasts drawn; so it is to God to have the breasts of his mercy drawn. 'Fury is not in me,' Isa xxvii 4; that is, I do not delight in it. Acts of severity are rather forced from God; he does not afflict willingly. Lam iii 33. The bee naturally gives honey, it stings only when it is provoked; so God does not punish till he can bear no longer. 'So that the Lord could bear no longer, because of the evil of your doings.' Jer xliv 22. Mercy is God's right hand that he is most used to; inflicting punishment is called his strange work. Isa xxviii 21. He is not used to it. When the Lord would shave off the pride of a

nation, he is said to hire a razor, as if he had none of his own. 'He shall shave with a razor that is hired.' Isa vii 20. 'He is slow to anger,' Psa ciii 8, but 'ready to forgive.' Psa lxxxvi 5.

[3] There is no condition, but we may spy mercy in it. When the church was in captivity, she cried out, 'It is of the Lord's mercies that we are not consumed.' Lam iii 22. Geographers write of Syracuse in Sicily, that it is so situated that the sun is never out of sight. In all afflictions we may see some sunshine of mercy. That outward and inward troubles do not come together is mercy.

[4] Mercy sweetens all God's other attributes. God's holiness without mercy, and his justice without mercy were terrible. When the water was bitter, and Israel could not drink, Moses cast a tree into the waters, and then they were made sweet. How bitter and dreadful were the other attributes of God, did not mercy sweeten them! Mercy sets God's power on work to help us; it makes his justice become our friend; it shall avenge our quarrels.

[5] God's mercy is one of the most orient pearls of his crown; it makes his Godhead appear amiable and lovely. When Moses said to God, 'I beseech thee shew me thy glory;' the Lord answered him, 'I will make all my goodness pass before thee, and I will shew thee mercy.' Exod xxxiii 19. God's mercy is his glory. His holiness makes him illustrious; his mercy makes him propitious.

[6] Even the wo forst taste God's mercy; such as fight against God's mercy, taste of it; the wicked have some crumbs from mercy's table. 'The Lord is good to all.' Psa cxlv 9. Sweet dewdrops are on the thistle, as well as on the rose. The diocese where mercy visits is very large. Pharaoh's head was crowned though his heart was hardened.

[7] Mercy coming to us in a covenant is sweetest. It was mercy that God would give Israel rain, and bread to the full, and peace, and victory over their enemies, Lev xxvi 4—6, but it was a greater mercy that God would be their God, verse 12. To have health is a mercy, but to have Christ and salvation is a greater mercy; it is like the diamond in the ring, which casts a more sparkling lustre.

[8] One act of mercy engages God to another. Men argue thus, I have shown you kindness already, therefore trouble me no more; but, because God has shown mercy, he is more ready still to show mercy; his mercy in election makes him justify, adopt, glorify; one act of mercy engages God to more. A parent's love to his child makes him always giving.

[9] All the mercy in the creature is derived from God, and is but a drop of this ocean. The mercy and pity a mother has to her child is from God; he that puts the milk in her breast puts the compassion in her heart. God is called, 'The Father of mercies,' because he begets all the mercies in the world. 2 Cor i 3. If God has put any kindness into the creature, how much kindness is in him who is the Father of mercy!

[10] As God's mercy makes the saints happy, so it should make them humble. Mercy is not the fruit of our goodness, but the fruit of God's goodness. Mercy is an alms that God bestows. They have no cause to be proud that live upon the alms of God's mercy. 'If I be righteous, yet will I not lift up my head,' Job x 15: all my righteousness is the effect of God's mercy, therefore I will be humble and will not lift up my head.

[11] Mercy stays the speedy execution of God's justice. Sinners continually provoke God, and make 'the fury come up in his face.' Ezek xxxviii 18. Whence is it God does not presently arrest and condemn them? It is not that God cannot do it, for he is armed with omnipotence, but it is from his mercy. Mercy gets a reprieve for the sinner, and stops the speedy process of justice. God would, by his goodness, lead sinners to repentance.

[12] It is dreadful to have mercy as a witness against any one. It was sad with Haman when the queen herself accused him. Esth vii 6. So will it be when this queen of mercy shall stand up against a person and accuse him. It is only mercy that saves a sinner; how sad then to have mercy become an enemy! If mercy be an accuser, who shall be our advocate? The sinner never escapes hell when mercy draws up the indictment.

I might show you several species or kinds of mercy; as preventing mercy, sparing mercy, supplying mercy, guiding mercy, accepting mercy, healing mercy, quickening mercy, supporting mercy, forgiving mercy, correcting mercy, comforting mercy, delivering mercy, crowning mercy; but I shall speak of,

II. *The qualifications or properties of God's mercy.*

[1] God's mercy is free. To set up merit is to destroy mercy. Nothing can deserve mercy, because we are polluted in our blood; nor force it. We may force God to punish us, but not to love us. 'I will love them freely.' Hos xiv 4. Every link in the chain of salvation is wrought and interwoven with free grace. Election is free. 'He hath chosen us in him, according to the good pleasure of his will.' Eph i 4. Justification is free. 'Being justified freely by his grace.' Rom iii 24. Salvation is free. 'According to his mercy he saved us.' Titus iii 5. Say not then, I am unworthy; for mercy is free.

If God should show mercy to such only as are worthy, he would show none at all.

[2] God's mercy is an overflowing mercy; it is infinite. 'Plenteous in mercy.' Psa lxxxvi 5. 'Rich in mercy.' Eph ii 4. 'Multitude of mercies.' Psa li 1. The vial of wrath drops, but the fountain of mercy runs. The sun is not so full of light as God is of mercy. God has morning mercies. 'His mercies are new every morning.' Lam iii 23. He has night mercies. 'In the night his song shall be with me.' Psa xlii 8. God has mercies under heaven, which we taste; and in heaven, which we hope for.

[3] God's mercy is eternal. 'The mercy of the Lord is from everlasting to everlasting.' Psa ciii 17. 'His mercy endureth for ever,' is repeated twenty-six times in one psalm. Psa cxxxvi. The souls of the blessed shall be ever bathing themselves in this sweet and pleasant ocean of God's mercy. God's anger to his children lasts but a while, 'but his mercy lasts for ever.' Psa ciii 9. As long as he is God he will be showing mercy. As his mercy is overflowing, so it is everflowing.

Use one: We are to look upon God in prayer, not in his judgment robes, but clothed with a rainbow full of mercy and clemency. Add wings to prayer. When Jesus Christ ascended up to heaven, that which made him go up thither with joy was, 'I go to my Father;' so that which should make our hearts ascend with joy in prayer, is, 'We are going to the Father of mercy, who sits upon the throne of grace.' Go with confidence in this mercy; as when one goes to a fire, not doubtingly, saying, perhaps it will warm me, perhaps not.

Use two: Believe in his mercy. 'I will trust in the mercy of God for ever.' Psa lii 8. God's mercy is a fountain opened. Let down the bucket of faith and you may drink of this fountain of salvation. What greater encouragement to believe than God's mercy? God counts it his glory to be scattering pardons; he is desirous that sinners should touch the golden sceptre of his mercy and live. This willingness to show mercy appears two ways:—

(1.) By entreating sinners to come and lay hold on his mercy. 'Whosoever will, let him come, and take the water of life freely.' Rev xxii 17. Mercy woos sinners, it even kneels down to them. It were strange for a prince to entreat a condemned man to accept of pardon. God says, Poor sinner, suffer me to love thee, be willing to let me save thee.

(2.) By his joyfulness when sinners lay hold on his mercy. What is God the better whether we receive his mercy or not? What is the fountain profited that others drink of it? Yet such is God's goodness, that he rejoices at the salvation of sinners, and is glad when his mercy is accepted.

[96]

When the prodigal son came home the father was glad, and made a feast to express his joy; so, God rejoices when a poor sinner comes in, and lays hold of his mercy. What an encouragement is here to believe in God! He is a God of pardons. Neh ix 17. Mercy pleases him. Mic vii 18. Nothing prejudices us but unbelief. Unbelief stops the current of God's mercy from running. It shuts up God's bowels, closes the orifice of Christ's wounds, so that no healing virtue will come out. 'He did not many mighty works there, because of their unbelief.' Matt xiii 58. Why dost thou not believe in God's mercy? Do thy sins discourage thee? God's mercy can pardon great sins, nay, because they are great. Psa xxv 11. The sea covers the rocks as well as the sands. Some that had a hand in crucifying Christ found mercy. As far as the heavens are above the earth, so far is God's mercy above our sins. Isa lv 9. What will tempt us to believe, if not the mercy of God?

Use three: Take heed of abusing the mercy of God. Suck not poison out of the sweet flower of God's mercy. Think not that because God is merciful, you may go on in sin; this is to make mercy your enemy. None might touch the ark but the priests, who by their office were more holy; so none may touch the ark of God's mercy but such as are resolved to be holy. To sin because mercy abounds is the devil's logic. He that sins because of mercy, is like one that wounds his head because he has a plaster. He that sins because of God's mercy, shall have judgment without mercy. Mercy abused turns to fury. 'If he bless himself, saying, I shall have peace though I walk after the imaginations of my heart, to add drunkenness to thirst, the Lord will not spare him, but the anger of the Lord, and his jealousy, shall smoke against that man.' Deut xxix 19, 20. Nothing is sweeter than mercy, when it is improved; nothing fiercer, when it is abused; as nothing is colder than lead when taken out of the mine, and nothing more scalding when it is heated. Nothing is blunter than iron, yet nothing is sharper when it is whetted. 'The mercy of the Lord is upon them that fear him.' Psa ciii 17. Mercy is not for them that sin and fear not, but for them that fear and sin not. God's mercy is a holy mercy; where it pardons it heals.

What shall we do to be interested in God's mercy?

(1.) Be sensible of your wants. See how much you stand in need of pardoning, saving mercy. See yourselves orphans. 'In thee the fatherless find mercy.' Hos xiv 3. God bestows the alms of mercy only on such as are indigent. Be emptied of all opinion of self-worthiness. God pours the golden oil of mercy into empty vessels.

(2.) Go to God for mercy. 'Have mercy upon me, O God!' Psa li 1. Put me not off with common mercy that reprobates may have; give me not only acorns but pearls; give me not only mercy to feed and clothe me, but mercy to save me; give me the cream of thy mercies; Lord! let me have mercy and lovingkindness. 'Who crowneth thee with lovingkindness and tender mercies.' Psa ciii 4. Give me such mercy as speaks thy electing love to my soul. Oh pray for mercy! God has treasures of mercy; prayer is the key that opens these treasures; and in prayer, be sure to carry Christ in your arms, for all the mercy comes through Christ. 'Samuel took a sucking lamb'; 1 Sam vii 9; carry the lamb Christ in your arms, go in his name, present his merits; say, Lord! here is Christ's blood, which is the price of my pardon; Lord! show me mercy, because Christ has purchased it. Though God may refuse us when we come for mercy in our own name, yet he will not when we come in Christ's name. Plead Christ's satisfaction, and this is an argument that God cannot deny.

Use four: Such as have found mercy are exhorted to three things. (1.) To be upon *Gerizim,* the mount of blessing and praising. They have not only heard the King of heaven is merciful, but they have found it so; the honeycomb of God's mercy has dropped upon them; when in wants, mercy supplied them; when they were nigh unto death, mercy raised them from the sick-bed; when covered with guilt, mercy pardoned them. 'Bless the Lord, O my soul, and all that is within me, bless his holy name.' Psa ciii 1. Oh how should the vessels of mercy run over with praise! 'Who was before a persecutor, and injurious; but I obtained mercy.' 1 Tim i 13. I was bemiracled with mercy; as the sea overflows and breaks down the banks, so the mercy of God broke down the banks of my sin, and mercy sweetly flowed into my soul. You that have been monuments of God's mercy, should be trumpets of praise; you that have tasted the Lord is gracious, tell others what experiences you have had of God's mercy, that you may encourage them to seek to him for mercy. 'I will tell you what God hath done for my soul;' Psa lxvi 16; that when I found my heart dead, God's Spirit came upon me mightily, and the blowing of that wind made the withering flowers of my grace revive. Oh tell others of God's goodness, that you may set others blessing him, and that you may make God's praises live when you are dead.

(2.) To love God. Mercy should be the attraction of love. 'I will love thee, O Lord, my strength.' Psa xviii 1. The Hebrew word for love signifies love out of the inward bowels. God's justice may make us fear him, his mercy makes us love him. If mercy will not produce love, what will? We are to love God for giving us our food, much more for giving us grace; for sparing mercy, much more for saving mercy. Sure that heart is made of marble, which the mercy of God will not dissolve in love. 'I would hate my own soul,' says Augustine, 'if I did not find it loving God.'

(3.) To imitate God in showing mercy. As God is the Father of mercy, show yourselves to be his children, by being like him. Ambrose says, 'The sum and definition of religion is, Be rich in works of mercy, be helpful to the bodies and souls of others. Scatter your golden seeds; let the lamp of your profession be filled with the oil of charity. Be merciful in giving and forgiving. "Be ye merciful, as your heavenly Father is merciful."'

10. THE TRUTH OF GOD

The next attribute is God's truth. 'A God of truth and without iniquity; just and right is he.' Deut xxxii 4. 'For thy mercy is great unto the heavens, and thy truth unto the clouds.' Psa lvii 10. 'Plenteous in truth.' Psa lxxxvi 15.

I. *God is the truth.* He is true in a physical sense; true in his being: he has a real subsistence, and gives a being to others. He is true in a moral sense; he is true *sine errore*, without errors; *et sine fallacia*, without deceit. God is *prima veritas*, the pattern and prototype of truth. There is nothing true but what is in God or comes from God.

II. *God's truth, as it is taken from his veracity in making good his promises.* 'There hath not failed one word of all his good promise.' 1 Kings viii 56. The promise is God's bond; God's truth is the seal set to his bond.

There are two things to be observed in the promises of God to comfort us. [1] The power of God, whereby he is able to fulfil the promise. God has promised to subdue our corruption. 'He will subdue our iniquities.' Micah vii 19. Oh, says a believer, my corruption is so strong, that I am sure I shall never get the mastery of it. Abraham looked at God's power. 'Being fully persuaded that what God had promised he was able to perform.' Rom iv 21. He believed that God, who could make a world, could make dry breasts give suck. It is faith's support that there is nothing too hard for God. He that could bring water out of a rock is able to bring to pass his promises.

[2] The truth of God in the promises. God's truth is the seal set to the promise. 'In hope of eternal life, which God that cannot lie hath promised.' Tit i 2. *Eternal life*, there is the sweetness of the promise: *God which*

[99]

cannot lie, there is the certainty of it. *Mercy* makes the promise, *truth* fulfils it. God's providences are uncertain, but his promises are the 'sure mercies of David.' Acts xiii 34. 'God is not a man that he should repent.' I Sam xv 29. The word of a prince cannot always be taken, but God's promise is inviolable. God's truth is one of the richest jewels of his crown, and he has pawned it in a promise. 'Although my house be not so with God, yet he hath made with me an everlasting covenant, ordered in all things and sure.' 2 Sam xxiii 5. Although my *house be not so*, that is, though I fail much of that exact purity the Lord requires, yet he has made with me an everlasting *covenant*, that he will pardon, adopt, and glorify me; and this covenant is ordered in all things and *sure*. 'The elements shall melt with fervent heat;' but this covenant abides firm and inviolable, being sealed with the truth of God. Nay, God has added to his word his oath, wherein he pawns his being, life, and righteousness to make good the promise. Heb vi 17. If as often as we break our vows with God, he should break promise with us, it would be very sad; but his truth is engaged in his promise, therefore it is like the law of the Medes and Persians, which cannot be altered. 'We are not,' says Chrysostom, 'to believe our senses so much as we are to believe the promises.' Our senses may fail us, but the promise cannot, being built upon the truth of God. God will not deceive the faith of his people, nay, he cannot. 'God, who cannot lie, hath promised;' he can as well part with his Deity as his verity. God is said to be abundant in truth. Exod xxxiv 6. What is that? If God has made a promise of mercy to his people, he will be so far from coming short of his word that he will be better than his word. He often does more than he has said, never less. He is abundant in truth.

(1.) The Lord may sometimes delay a promise, but he will not deny. He may delay a promise. God's promise may lie a good while as seed under ground, but at last it will spring up into a crop. He promised to deliver Israel from the iron furnace, but this promise was above four hundred years in travail before it brought forth. Simeon had a promise that he should not depart hence, 'till he had seen the Lord's Christ,' Luke ii 26, but it was a long time first, but a little before his death, that he did see Christ. But though God delay the promise, he will not deny. Having given his bond, in due time the money will be paid.

(2.) God may change his promise, but he will not break it. Sometimes God changes a temporal promise into a spiritual. 'The Lord shall give that which is good,' Psa lxxxv 12; which may not be fulfilled in a temporal sense, but a spiritual. God may let a Christian be cut short in temporals, but he makes it up in spirituals. If he does not increase the basket and the store, he gives increase of faith, and inward peace. Here he changes his promise, but he does not break it, he gives that which is better. If a man promises to pay me in farthings, and he pays me in a better coin, as in gold, he does not break his promise. 'I will not suffer my faithfulness to fail.' Psa lxxxix 33. In the Hebrew it is, to lie.

How does it consist with the truth of God, that he will have all *to be* saved, *and yet some perish?* 1 Tim ii 4.

Augustine understands it, not of every individual person, but some of all sorts shall be saved. As in the ark, God saved all the living creatures; not every bird or fish was saved, for many perished in the flood; but all, that is, some of every kind were saved; so he will have all to be saved, that is, some of all nations.

It is said, Christ died for all. 'He is the Lamb of God that takes away the sins of the world.' John i 29. *How does this consist with God's truth, when some are* vessels of wrath? Rom ix 22.

(1.) We must qualify the term *world*. The world is taken either in a limited sense, for the world of the elect; or in a larger sense, for both elect and reprobates. 'Christ takes away the sins of the world,' that is, the world of the elect.

(2.) We must qualify also Christ's dying for the world. Christ died sufficiently for all, not effectually. There is the value of Christ's blood, and the virtue. Christ's blood has value enough to redeem the whole world, but the virtue of it is applied only to such as believe. Christ's blood is meritorious for all, not efficacious. All are not saved, because some put away salvation from them, as in Acts xiii 46, and vilify Christ's blood, counting it an unholy thing. Heb x 29.

Use one: The truth of God is a great pillar for our faith. Were not he a God of truth, how could we believe in him? Our faith were fancy; but he is truth itself, and not a word which he has spoken shall fall to the ground. 'Truth is the object of trust.' The truth of God is an immovable rock, on which we may venture our salvation. Isa lix 15. 'Truth faileth:' truth on earth does, but not truth in heaven. God can as well cease to be God, as cease to be true. Has God said, he 'will do good to the soul that seeks him,' Lam iii 25, and he will 'give rest to the weary?' Matt xi 28. Here is a safe anchor-hold, he will not alter the thing which is gone out of his lips. The public faith of heaven is engaged for believers. Can we have better security? The whole earth hangs upon the word of God's power, and shall not our faith hang upon the word of God's truth? Where can we rest our faith but upon God's faithfulness? There is nothing else we can believe in but the truth of God. To trust in ourselves is to build upon quicksands; but the truth of God is a golden pillar for faith to stay upon. God cannot deny himself. 'If we believe not, yet he abideth faithful: he cannot deny himself.' 2 Tim ii 13. Not to believe God's veracity, is to affront God. 'He that believeth not, hath made God a liar.' 1 John v 10. A person of honour cannot be more affronted or provoked, than when he is not believed. He that denies God's truth makes the promise no better than a forged deed; and can there be a greater affront offered to God?

Use two: If God is a God of truth, he is true to his threatenings. The threatenings are a flying roll against sinners. God has threatened to 'wound the hairy scalp of every one that goes on still in his trespasses.' Psa lxviii 21. He has threatened to judge adulterers. Heb xiii 4. To be avenged upon the malicious. Psa x 14. 'Thou beholdest mischief and spite, to requite it with thine own hand;' and to 'rain fire and brimstone upon the sinner.' Psa xi 6. God is as true to his threatenings as to his promises. To show his truth he has executed his threatenings, and let his thunderbolts of judgment fall upon sinners in this life. He struck Herod in the act of his pride. He has punished blasphemers. Olympius, an Arian bishop, reproached and blasphemed the blessed Trinity, and immediately lightning fell down from the heaven upon him and consumed him. Let us fear the threatening that we may not feel it.

Use three: Is God a God of truth? Let us be like God in truth. (1.) We must be true in our words. Pythagoras being asked what made men like God, answered, 'When they speak truth.' It is the note of a man that shall go to heaven. 'He speaketh the truth in his heart.' Psa xv 2. Truth in words is opposed (i) To lying. 'Putting away lying, speak every one truth to his neighbour.' Eph iv 25. Lying is when one speaks that for truth which he knows to be false. A liar is most opposite to the God of truth. There are, as Augustine says, two sorts of lies. *An officious lie,* when a man tells a lie for his profit; as, when a tradesman says his commodity cost him so much, when perhaps it did not cost him half so much. He that will lie in his trade shall lie in hell. *A jesting lie,* when a man tells a lie in sport, to make others merry, and goes laughing to hell. He who tells a lie makes himself like the devil. 'The devil is a liar, and the father of it.' John viii 44. He deceived our first parents by a lie. Some are so wicked, that they will not only speak an untruth, but will swear to it; nay, they will wish a curse upon themselves, if that untruth be not true. I have read of a woman, one Anne Avarie, who in 1575, being in a shop, wished that she might sink if she had not paid for the wares she took, and fell down speechless immediately and died. A liar is not fit to live in a commonwealth. Lying takes away all society and converse with men. How can you converse with a man when you cannot believe what he says? Lying shuts men out of heaven. 'Without are dogs, and whosoever loveth and maketh a lie.' Rev xxii 15. As it is a great sin to tell a lie, so it is a worse sin to teach a lie. 'The prophet that teacheth lies.' Isa ix 15. He who broacheth error teacheth lies; he spreads the plague; he not only damns himself, but helps to damn others. (ii) Truth in words is opposed to dissembling. The heart and tongue should go together, as the dial goes exactly with the sun. To speak fair to one's face, and not to mean what one speaks, is no better than a lie. 'His words were smoother than oil, but war was in his heart.' Psa lv 21. Some have an art to flatter and hate. Jerome, speaking of the Arians, says, 'they pretended friendship, they kissed my hands, but plotted mischief against me.' 'A man that flattereth his neighbour, spreadeth a net for his feet.' Prov xxix 5. *Impia sub dulci melle venena latent* [Cruel poison can be hidden under sweet honey]. Falsehood in friendship is a lie. Counterfeiting friendship is worse than counterfeiting money.

(2.) We must be true in our profession of religion. Let practice go along with profession. 'Righteousness and true holiness.' Eph iv 24. Hypocrisy in religion is a lie. The hypocrite is like a face in a glass, which is the show of a face, but no true face. He makes show of holiness, but has no truth in it. Ephraim pretended to be that which he was not; and what says God of him? 'Ephraim compasseth me about with lies.' Hos xi 12. By a lie in our words we deny the truth; by a lie in our profession we disgrace it. Not to be to God what we profess is telling a lie; and the Scripture makes it little better than blasphemy. 'I know the blasphemy of them that say they are Jews, and are not.' Rev ii 9. Oh! I beseech you, labour to be like God. He is a God of truth. He can as well part with his Deity as his verity. Be like God, be true in your words, be true in your profession. God's children are children that will not lie. Isa lxiii 8. When God sees 'truth in the inward parts,' and 'lips in which is no guile,' he sees his own image, which draws his heart towards us. Likeness produces love.

11. THE UNITY OF GOD

QV: ARE THERE MORE GODS THAN ONE?

A: There is but one only, the living and true God.

That there is a God has been proved; and those that will not believe the verity of his essence, shall feel the severity of his wrath. 'Hear, O Israel, the Lord our God is one Lord.' Deut vi 4. He is 'the only God.' Deut iv 39.

'Know therefore this day, and consider it in thy heart, that the Lord he is God in heaven above, and upon the earth beneath, there is none else.' 'A just God and a Saviour; there is none beside me.' Isa xlv 21. There are many titular gods. Kings represent God; their regal sceptre is an emblem of his power and authority. Judges are called gods. 'I have said, Ye are gods,' Psa lxxxii 6, viz., set in God's place to do justice; but dying gods. 'Ye shall die like men.' Verse 7. 'There be that are called gods, but to us there is but one God.' 1 Cor viii 5, 6.

I. *There is but one First Cause that has its Being of itself, and on which all other beings depend.* As in the heavens, the *primum mobile* moves all the other orbs, so God gives life and motion to everything that exists. There can be but one God, because there is but one First Cause.

II. *There is but one infinite Being, therefore there is but one God.* There cannot be two infinites. 'Do not I fill heaven and earth, saith the Lord?' Jer xxiii 24. If there be one infinite, filling all places at once, how can there be any room for another infinite to subsist?

III. *There is but one Omnipotent Power.* If there be two Omnipotents, then we must always suppose a contest between these two: that which one would do, the other power, being equal, would oppose, and so all things would be brought into confusion. If a ship should have two pilots of equal power, one would be ever crossing the other; when one would sail, the other would cast anchor; there would be confusion, and the ship must perish. The order and harmony in the world, or the constant and uniform government of all things, is a clear argument that there is but one Omnipotent, one God that rules all. 'I am the first, and I am the last, and beside me there is no God.' Isa xliv 6.

Use one: Of information, (1.) If there be but one God, then it excludes all other gods. Some have feigned that there were two gods; as the Valentinians: others, that there were many gods; as the Polytheists. The Persians worshipped the sun; the Egyptians the lion and elephant; the Grecians worshipped Jupiter. These 'err, not knowing the Scriptures.' Matt xxii 29. Their faith is a fable. 'God hath given them up to strong delusions, to believe a lie, that they may be damned.' 2 Thess ii 11.

(2.) If there be but one God, then there can be but one true religion in the world. 'One Lord, one faith.' Eph iv 5. If there were many gods, then there might be many religions, every God would be worshipped in his way; but if there be but one God, there is but one religion; one Lord, one faith. Some say, we may be saved in any religion; but it is absurd to imagine that God who is *One in essence,* should appoint several religions in which he will be worshipped. It is as dangerous to set up a false religion, as to set up a false god. There are many ways to hell; men may go thither which way their fancy leads them; but there is only one direct road to heaven, viz., faith and holiness. There is no way to be saved but this. As there is but one God, so there is but one true religion.

(3.) If there be but one God, then there is but One whom you need chiefly to study to please, and that is God. If there were divers gods, we should be hard put to it to please them all. One would command one thing, another the contrary; and to please two contrary masters is impossible: but there is only one God. Therefore you have but One to please. As in a kingdom there is but one king, therefore every one seeks to ingratiate himself into his favour, Prov xix 6, so there is but one true God; therefore our main work is to please him. Be sure to please God, whoever else you displease. This was Enoch's wisdom. He had this testimony before he died, that 'he pleased God.' Heb xi 5.

What doth this pleasing God imply?

(1.) We please God when we comply with his will. It was Christ's meat and drink to do his Father's will, John iv 34, and so he pleased him, Matt iii 17. A voice came from heaven, saying, 'This is my beloved Son, in whom I am well pleased.' It is the will of God that we should be holy. 1 Thess iv 3. Now, when we are bespangled with holiness, our lives are walking Bibles. This is according to God's will, and it pleases him.

(2.) We please God when we do the work that he sets us about. 'I have finished the work which thou gavest me to do,' viz., my mediatory work. John xvii 4. Many finish their lives, but do not finish their work. The work God has cut out for us is, to observe the first and second tables. In the first is set down our duty towards God; in the second our duty towards man. Such as make morality the chief and sole part of religion, set the second table above the first; nay, they take away the first table; for, if prudence, justice, temperance, be enough to save, then what needs the first table? Thus our worship towards God will be quite left out; but those two tables which God has joined together, let no man put asunder.

(3.) We please God when we dedicate our hearts to give him the best of everything. Abel gave God the fat of the offering. Gen iv 4. Domitian would not have his image carved in wood, or iron, but in gold. We please God when we serve him with love, fervency, and alacrity. These are golden services. There is but one God, therefore there is but One whom we have chiefly to please, namely, God.

[105]

(4.) If there be but one God, then we must pray to none but God. The Papists pray to saints and angels. (i) To saints. A Popish writer says, 'when we pray to the saints departed, they being touched with compassion, say the like to God for us as the disciples did to Christ for the Canaanitish woman. "Send her away, for she crieth after us."' Matt xv 23. The saints above know not our wants; if they did, we have no warrant to pray to them. 'Abraham is ignorant of us.' Isa lxiii 16. Prayer is a part of divine worship, which must be given to God only. (ii) They pray to angels. Angel-worship is forbidden. Col ii 18, 19. That we may not pray to angels is clear from Rom x 14. 'How shall they call on him in whom they have not believed?' We may not pray to any but whom we may believe in; but we may not believe in any angel, therefore we may not pray to him. There is but one God, and it is a sin to invoke any but God.

(5.) If there be but one God, who is 'above all,' Eph iv 6, then he must be loved above all. We must love him with a love of *appreciation;* set the highest estimate on him, who is the only fountain of being and bliss. We must love him with a love of *complacency. Amor est complacentia amantis amato* [The lover's effort to please the beloved, this is love]. Aquinas. Our love to other things must be more indifferent. Some drops of love may run beside to the creature, but the full stream must run towards God. The creature may have the milk of our love, but we must keep the cream for God. He who is above all, must be loved above all. 'There is none on earth whom I desire in comparison of thee.' Psa lxxiii 25.

Use two: Of caution. If there be but one God, then let us take heed of setting up more gods than one. 'Their sorrows shall be multiplied, that hasten after another god; their drink-offerings of blood will I not offer, nor take up their names into my lips.' Psa xvi 4. God is a jealous God, and he will not endure that we should have other gods. It is easy to commit idolatry with the creature. (1.) Some make a god of pleasure. 'Lovers of pleasures more than lovers of God.' 2 Tim iii 4. Whatever we love more than God we make a god. (2.) Others make money their god. The covetous man worships the image of gold, therefore he is called an idolater. Eph v 5. That which a man trusts to he makes his god; but he makes the wedge of gold his hope; he makes money his creator, redeemer, and comforter. It is his creator; if he has money, he thinks he is made: it is his redeemer; if he be in danger, he trusts in his money to redeem him: it is his comforter; if at any time he be sad, the golden harp drives away the evil spirit: so that money is his god. God made man of the dust of the earth, and man makes a god of the dust of the earth. (3.) Another makes a god of his child, sets his child in God's room, and so provokes God to take it away. If you lean too hard upon glass it will break, so many break their children by leaning too hard upon them. (4.) Others make a god of their belly. 'Whose god is their belly.' Phil iii 19. Clement of Alexandria writes of a fish that has its heart in its belly; an emblem of epicures, their heart is in their belly, they mind nothing but indulging the sensual appetite; *sacrificant lari* [They worship home comforts]; their belly is their god, and to this they pour drink-offerings. Thus men make many gods. The apostle names the wicked man's trinity, 'The lust of the flesh, the lust of the eye, and the pride of life,' 1 John ii 16: the lust of the flesh is pleasure; the lust of the eye, money; the pride of life, honour. Oh take heed of this! Whatever you deify beside God will prove a bramble, and fire will come out of it and devour you. Judg ix 15.

Use three: Of reproof. If the Lord Jehovah be the only true God, it re-proves those who renounce the true God, I mean such as seek to familiar spirits, which is too much practised among them that call themselves Christians. It is a sin condemned by the law of God. 'There shall not be found among you any one that consults with familiar spirits.' Deut xviii 11. How common is this! If people have lost any of their goods, they send to wizards to know how they may obtain them again. What is this but consulting with the devil! and so renouncing God and their baptism. What! because you have lost your goods, will you lose your souls too? 'Thus saith the Lord, Is it not because there is not a God in Israel, that thou sendest to enquire of Beelzebub?' 2 Kings i 6. So, is it not because you think there is not a God in heaven that you ask counsel of the devil? If any here be guilty, be deeply humbled, ye have renounced the true God. Better be without the goods ye have lost than have the devil help you to them again.

Use four: Of exhortation. (1.) If there be but one God, as God is one, so let them that serve him be one. This is what Christ prayed so heartily for. 'That they all may be one.' John xvii 21. Christians should be one, (i) In judgment. The apostle exhorts to be all of one mind. 1 Cor i 10. How sad is it to see religion wearing a coat of divers colours; to see Christians of so many opinions, and going so many different ways! It is Satan that has sown these tares of division. Matt xiii 39. He first divided men from God, and then one man from another. (ii) One in affection. They should have one heart. 'The multitude of them that believed were of one heart, and of one soul.' Acts iv 32. As in music, though there be several strings of a viol, yet all make one sweet harmony; so, though there are several Christians, yet there should be one sweet harmony of affection among them. There is but one God, and they that serve him should be one. There is nothing that would render the true religion more lovely, or make more proselytes to it, than to see the professors of it tied together with the heart-strings of love. 'Behold how good and how pleasant a thing it is, to see brethren live together in unity!' Psa cxxxiii 1. It is as the sweet dew on Hermon, and the fragrant ointment poured on Aaron's head. If God be one, let all that profess him be of one mind, and one heart, and thus fulfil Christ's prayer, 'that they all may be one.'

(2.) If there be but one God, let us labour to make clear the title that this God is ours. 'This God is our God.' Psa xlviii 14. What comfort can it be to hear that there is a God, and that he is the only God, unless he be our God? What is Deity without property in him? Oh let us labour to make clear the title! Beg the Holy Spirit. The Spirit works by faith. By faith we are one with Christ, and through Christ we come to have God for our God, and thus all his glorious fulness is made over to us by a deed of gift.

Use five: Of gratitude. What cause have we to be thankful, that we have the knowledge of the only true God! How many are brought up in blindness! Some worship Mahomet. Many of the Indians worship the devil; they light a candle to him, that he may not hurt them. Such as know not the true God must needs stumble into hell in the dark. Oh let us be thankful that we are born in such a land, where the light of the gospel hath shone. To have the knowledge of the true God is more than if we had mines of gold, rocks of diamonds, islands of spices; especially if God has savingly revealed himself to us; if he has given us eyes to see the light; if we so know God as to be known of him, to love him, and believe in him. Matt xi 25. We can never be thankful enough to God, that he has hid the knowledge of himself from the wise and prudent of the world, and has revealed it unto us.

12. THE TRINITY

Qvi: HOW MANY PERSONS ARE THERE IN THE GODHEAD?

A: Three persons, yet but one God.

'There are three that bear record in heaven, the Father, the Word, and the Holy Ghost, and these three are one.' 1 John v 7.

God is but one, yet are there three distinct persons subsisting in one Godhead. This is a sacred mystery, which the light within man could never have discovered. As the two natures in Christ, yet but one person, is a wonder; so three persons, yet but one Godhead. Here is a great deep, the Father God, the Son God, the Holy Ghost God; yet not three Gods, but one God. The three persons in the blessed Trinity are distinguished, but not divided; three substances, but one essence. This is a divine riddle, where one makes three, and three make one. Our narrow thoughts can no more comprehend the Trinity in Unity, than a nut-shell will hold all the water in the sea. Let me shadow it out by a similitude. In the body of the sun, there are the substance of the sun, the beams, and the heat; the beams are begotten of the sun, the heat proceeds both from the sun and the beams; but these three, though different, are not divided; they all three make but one sun: so in the blessed Trinity, the Son is begotten of the Father, the Holy Ghost proceeds from both; yet though they are three distinct persons, they are but one God. First, let me speak of the Unity in Trinity; then of the Trinity in Unity.

I. *Of the Unity in Trinity.* The Unity of the persons in the Godhead consists of two things.

[1] The identity of essence. In the Trinity there is a oneness in essence. The three persons are of the same divine nature and substance; so that *in Deo nonest magis et minus*, 'there are no degrees in the Godhead'; one person is not God more than another.

[2] The Unity of the persons in the Godhead consists in the mutual in-being of them, or their being in one together. The three persons are so united that one person is in another, and with another. 'Thou, Father, art in me, and I in thee.' John xvii 21.

II. *Let me speak of the Trinity in Unity.*

[1] The first person in the Trinity is God the Father. He is called the first person, in respect of *order*, not *dignity:* for God the Father has no essential perfection which the other persons have not; he is not more wise, more holy, more powerful than the other persons are. There is a priority, not a superiority.

[2] The second person in the Trinity is Jesus Christ, who is begotten of the Father before all time. 'I was set up from everlasting, from the beginning, or ever the earth was. When there were no depths I was brought forth; when there were no fountains abounding with water. Before the mountains were settled, before the hills, was I brought forth.' Prov viii 23—25. This Scripture declares the eternal generation of the Son of God. This second person in the Trinity, who is Jehovah, is become our Jesus. The Scripture calls him the branch of David, Jer xxiii 5, and I may call him the flower of our nature. 'By him all that believe are justified.' Acts xiii 39.

[3] The third person in the Trinity is the Holy Ghost, who proceeds from the Father and the Son, whose work is to illuminate the mind, and enkindle sacred motions. The essence of the Spirit is in heaven, and everywhere; but the influence of it is in the hearts of believers. This is that blessed Spirit who gives us the holy unction. 1 John ii 20. Though Christ merits grace for us, it is the Holy Ghost that works it in us. Though Christ makes the purchase, it is the Holy Ghost that makes the assurance, and seals us to the day of redemption. Thus I have spoken of all the three persons. The Trinity of persons may be proved out of Matt iii 16. 'Jesus, when he was baptized, went up straightway out of the water, and he saw the Spirit of God descending like a dove, and lighting upon him; and lo, a voice from heaven, saying, This is my beloved Son.' Here are three names given to the three persons. He who spake with a voice from heaven was God the Father; he who was baptized in Jordan was God the Son; he who descended in the likeness of a dove was God the Holy Ghost. Thus I have shown you the Unity of essence, and the Trinity of persons.

Use one: For confutation. (1.) This confutes the Jews and Turks, who believe only the first person in the Godhead. Take away the distinction of the persons in the Trinity, and you overthrow man's redemption; for God the Father being offended with man for sin, how shall he be pacified without a mediator? This mediator is Christ, who makes our peace. Christ having died, and shed his blood, how shall this blood be applied but by the Holy Ghost? Therefore, if there be not three persons in the Godhead, man's salvation cannot be wrought out; if there be no second person in the Trinity, there is no redeemer; if no third person, there is no comforter. Thus the plank is taken away by which we get to heaven.

(2.) It confutes the execrable opinion of the Socinians, who deny the Divinity of the Lord Jesus, and make him to be a creature only, but of a higher rank. As the Papists blot out the second commandment, so the Socinians do the second person in the Trinity. If to oppose Christ's members be a sin, what is it to oppose Christ himself? Jesus Christ is co-equal with God the Father. He thought it no robbery to be equal with God. Phil ii 6. He is co-eternal with God the Father: 'I was from the beginning,' Prov viii 23: if not, there was a time when God was without a Son, and so he would be no Father; nay, there was a time when God was without his glory, for Christ is 'the brightness of his Father's glory.' Heb i 3. He is co-essential with God the Father. The Godhead subsists in Christ. 'In whom dwells all the fulness of the Godhead bodily.' Col ii 9. It is said, not only that Christ was with God before the beginning, but that he was God. John i 1, and 1 Tim iii 16. 'God manifest in the flesh.'

The title of Lord, so often given to Christ, in the New Testament, answers to the title of Jehovah in the Old. Deut vi 5; Matt xxii 37. Christ has a co-eternity, and co-substantiality with his Father. 'I and my Father are one.' John x 30. It were blasphemy for an angel to speak thus. Yet further to prove Christ's Godhead, consider (i) The glorious incommunicable attributes belonging to God the Father are ascribed to Christ. Is God the Father omnipotent? So is Jesus Christ. He is the almighty, Rev i 8, and he creates, Col i 16. Is God the Father infinitely immense, filling all places? Jer xxiii 24. So is Jesus Christ. While Christ was on the earth by his bodily presence, he was at the same time in the bosom of the Father by his divine presence. John iii 13. (ii) The same *jura regalia*, or prerogatives royal, which belong to God the Father, belong also to Christ. Does God the Father seal pardons? This is a flower of Christ's crown. 'Thy sins be forgiven thee.' Matt ix 2. Nor does Christ remit sin *organice* only, as ministers do, by virtue of a power delegated to them from God; but he does it by his own power and authority. Is God the Father the adequate object of faith? Is he to be believed in? So is his Son. John xiv 1. Does adoration belong to God the Father? So it does to the Son. 'Let all the angels of God worship him.' Heb i 6. How sacrilegious therefore is the Socinian, who would rob Christ of his Godhead, the best flower of his crown. They that deny Christ to be God, must greatly wrest, or else deny the Scripture to be the Word of God.

(3.) It confutes the Arians, who deny the Holy Ghost to be God. The eternal Godhead subsists in the Holy Ghost. 'He shall guide you into all truth.' John xvi 13. Christ speaks not there of an attribute, but of a person. That the Godhead subsists in the person of the Holy Ghost appears in this; that the Spirit, who gives diversity of gifts, is said to be the same Lord, and the same God. 1 Cor xii 5, 6. The black and unpardonable sin is said, in a special manner, to be committed against the Godhead subsisting in the Holy Ghost. Matt xii 32. The mighty power of God is made manifest by the Holy Ghost; for he changes the hearts of men. The devil would have Christ prove himself to be God, by turning stones into bread; but the Holy Ghost shows his Godhead by turning stones into flesh. 'I will take away the stony heart; and give you a heart of flesh.' Ezek xxxvi 26. Yet further, the power and Godhead of the Holy Ghost appeared in effecting the glorious conception of our Lord Jesus Christ. The very shadow of the Holy Ghost made a virgin conceive. Luke i 35. The Holy Ghost works miracles, which transcend the sphere of nature; as raising the dead. Rom viii 11. To him belongs divine worship; our souls and bodies are the temples of the Holy Ghost, 1 Cor vi 19, in which temples he is to be worshipped, verse 20. We are baptized in the name of the Holy

Ghost; therefore we must believe his Godhead, or renounce our baptism in his name. Methinks it were better for such men not to have so much as heard whether there be any Holy Ghost, Acts xix 2, than to deny his Deity. They who would wittingly and willingly blot out the third person, shall have their names blotted out of the book of life.

Use two: For exhortation. (1.) Believe this doctrine of the Trinity of persons in the unity of essence. The Trinity is purely an object of faith; the plumbline of reason is too short to fathom this mystery; but where reason cannot wade, there faith may swim. There are some truths in religion that may be demonstrated by reason; as that there is a God: but the Trinity of persons in the Unity of essence is wholly supernatural, and must be believed by faith. This sacred doctrine is not against reason, but above it. Those illuminated philosophers, that could find out the causes of things, and discourse of the magnitude and influence of the stars, the nature of minerals, could never, by their deepest search, find out the mystery of the Trinity. This is of divine revelation, and must be adored with humble believing. We can be no good Christians, without the firm belief of the Trinity. How can we pray to God the Father but in the name of Christ, and through the help of the Spirit? How believe the glorious Trinity? How are the Quakers to be abhorred, who go under the name of Christians, and yet undervalue and renounce Jesus Christ! I have read of some Quakers who speak thus: 'We deny the person of him whom you call Christ, and affirm, That they who expect to be saved by that Christ without works, will be damned in that faith!' Could the devil himself speak worse blasphemy? They would pull up all religion by the roots, and take away that corner stone, on which the hope of our salvation is built.

(2.) If there be one God subsisting in three persons, then let us give equal reverence to all the persons in the Trinity. There is not more or less in the Trinity; the Father is not more God than the Son and Holy Ghost. There is an order in the Godhead, but no degrees; one person has not a majority or supereminence above another, therefore we must give equal worship to all the persons. 'That all men should honour the Son even as they honour the Father.' John v 23. Adore Unity in Trinity.

(3.) Obey all the persons in the blessed Trinity; for all of them are God. Obey God the Father. Christ himself, as man, obeyed God the Father, John iv 34, much more must we. Deut xxvii 10.

Obey God the Son. 'Kiss the Son, lest he be angry.' Psa ii 12. Kiss him with a kiss of obedience. Christ's commands are not grievous. 1 John v 3. Whatever he commands is for our interest and benefit. Oh then kiss the Son! Why do the elders throw down their crowns at the feet of Christ, and fall down before the Lamb? Rev iv 10, 11. To testify their subjection, and to profess their readiness to serve and obey him.

Obey God the Holy Ghost. Our souls are breathed into us by the glorious Spirit. 'The Spirit of God hath made me.' Job xxxiii 4. Our souls are adorned by the blessed Spirit. Every grace is a divine spark lighted in the soul by the Holy Ghost. Nay, more, the Spirit of God sanctified Christ's human nature; he united it with the divine, and fitted the man Christ to be our Meditator. Well then does this third person in the Trinity, the Holy Ghost, deserve to be obeyed; for he is God, and this tribute of homage and obedience is due to him from us.

13. THE CREATION

QVII: WHAT ARE THE DECREES OF GOD?

A: The decrees of God are his eternal purpose, according to the counsel of his will, whereby, for his own glory, he has foreordained whatsoever shall come to pass.

I have already spoken something concerning the decrees of God under the attribute of his immutability. God is unchangeable in his essence, and he is unchangeable in his decrees; his counsel shall stand. He decrees the issue of all things, and carries them on to their accomplishment by his providence; I shall proceed therefore to the execution of his decrees.

QIX: The next question is, WHAT IS THE WORK OF CREATION?

A: It is God's making all things from nothing by the word of his power. Gen i 1. 'In the beginning God created the heaven and the earth.'

The creation is glorious to behold, and it is a pleasant and profitable study. Some think that when Isaac went abroad into the fields to meditate, it was in the book of the creatures. The creation is the heathen man's Bible, the ploughman's primer, and the traveller's perspective glass, through which he receives a representation of the infinite excellencies which are in God. The creation is a large volume, in which God's works are bound up; and this volume has three great leaves in it, heaven, earth, and sea.

The author of the creation is God, as it is in the text, 'God created.' The world was created in time, and could not be from eternity, as Aristotle thought. The world must have a maker, and could not make itself. If one should go into a far country, and see stately edifices, he would never imagine that they could build themselves, but that there had been some artificer to raise such goodly structures; so this great fabric of the world could not create itself, it must have some builder or maker, and that is God. 'In the beginning God created.' To imagine that the work of the creation was not framed by the Lord Jehovah, is as if we should conceive a curious landscape to be drawn without the hand of an artist. 'God that made the world and all things therein.' Acts xvii 24.

In the work of creation there are two things to be considered: I. *The making.* II. *The adorning.*

I. *The making of the world.* Here consider, [1] God made the world without any pre-existent matter. This is the difference between generation and creation. In generation there is *materia habilis et disposita* [suitable material at hand], some matter to work upon; but in creation there is no pre-existent matter. God brought all this glorious fabric of the world out of the womb of nothing. Our beginning was of nothing. Some brag of their birth and ancestry; but how little cause have they to boast who came from nothing.

[2] God made the world with a word. When Solomon had to build a temple he needed many workmen, and they all had tools to work with, but God wrought without tools. 'By the word of the Lord were the heavens made.' Psa xxxiii 6. The disciples wondered that Christ could with a word calm the sea; but it was more with a word to make the sea.

[3] God made all things at first very good, Gen i 31, without any defect or deformity. The creation came out of God's hands a curious piece; it was a fair copy, without any blot, written with God's own fingers. Psa viii 3. His work was perfect.

II. *The adorning of the world.* God made this great lump and mass, *Rudis indigestaque moles* [with neither shape nor order], and then beautified it. He divided the sea and the earth, he decked the earth with flowers, the trees with fruit; but what is beauty when it is masked over? Therefore, that we might behold this glory, God made the light. The heavens were bespangled with the sun, moon, and stars, that so the world's beauty might be beheld and admired. God, in the creation, began with things less noble and excellent, rocks and vegetables; and then the rational creatures, angels and men. Man is the most exquisite piece in the creation. He is a microcosm, or little world. Man was made with deliberation and counsel. 'Let us make man.' Gen i 26. It is the manner of artificers to be more than ordinarily accurate when they are about their masterpieces.

Man was to be the masterpiece of this visible world, therefore God consulted about making so rare a piece. A solemn council of the sacred persons in the Trinity was called. 'Let us make man, and let us make him in our own image.' On the king's coin his own image or effigy is stamped; so God stamped his image on man, and made him partaker of many divine qualities.

I shall speak, [1] Of the parts of man's body. (1.) The head, the most excellent architectural part, is the fountain of spirits, and the seat of reason. In nature the head is the best piece, but in grace the heart excels. (2.) The eye is the beauty of the face; it shines and sparkles like a lesser sun in the body. The eye occasions much sin, and therefore may well have tears in it. (3.) The ear is the conduit-pipe through which knowledge is conveyed. Better lose our seeing than our hearing, for 'faith cometh by hearing.' Rom x 17. To have an ear open to God is the best jewel on the ear. (4.) The tongue. David calls the tongue his glory, Psa xvi 9, because it is an instrument to set forth the glory of God. The soul at first was a viol in tune to praise God, and the tongue made the music. God has given us two ears, but one tongue, to show that we should be swift to hear, but slow to speak. God has set a double fence before the tongue, the teeth, and the lips, to teach us to be wary that we offend not with our tongue. (5.) The heart is a noble part, and the seat of life.

[2] The soul of man. This is the man of the man. Man, in regard of his soul, partakes with the angels; nay, as Plato says, the understanding, will, and conscience, are a glass that resemble the Trinity. The soul is the diamond in the ring, it is a vessel of honour; God himself is served in this vessel. It is a spark of celestial brightness, says Damascene. David admired the rare contexture and workmanship of his body. 'I am wonderfully made, I was curiously wrought in the lowest parts of the earth.' Psa cxxxix 14, 15. If the cabinet be so curiously wrought, what is the jewel? How richly is the soul embroidered! Thus you see how glorious a work the creation is, and man especially, who is the epitome of the world.

But why did God make the world?

(1.) *Negatively.* Not for himself; for he did not need it, being infinite. He was happy in reflecting upon his own sublime excellencies and perfections before the world was. God did not make the world to be a mansion for us, since we are not to abide here for ever. Heaven is the mansion house. John xiv 2. The world is only a passage-room to eternity; the world is to us as the wilderness was to Israel, not to rest in, but to travel through to the glorious Canaan. The world is a dressing-room to dress our souls in, not a place where we are to stay for ever. The apostle tells us of the world's funeral. 'The elements shall melt with fervent heat, the earth also and the works that are therein shall be burnt up.' 2 Pet iii 10.

(2.) *Positively.* God made the world to demonstrate his own glory. The world is a looking glass, in which we may see the power and goodness of God shine forth. 'The heavens declare the glory of God.' Psa xix 1. The world is like a curious piece of tapestry, in which we may see the skill and wisdom of him that made it.

Use one: Did God create this world? (1.) This convinces us of the truth of his Godhead. To create is proper to a Deity. Acts xvii 24. Plato was convinced of a Deity when he saw that all the world could not make a fly. Thus God proves himself to be the true God, and distinguishes himself from idols. Jer x 11. It is written in Chaldee, 'Thus shall ye say to them, The gods that have not made the heavens and the earth, even they shall perish.' Who but God can create? The creation is enough to convince the heathen that there is a God. There are two books out of which God will judge and condemn the heathen, viz., the book of Conscience, 'Which shew the work of the law written in their hearts,' Rom ii 15, and the book of the Creation, 'The invisible things of him are clearly seen by the things that are made, even his eternal power and Godhead.' Rom i 20. The world is full of emblems and hieroglyphics. Every star in the sky, every bird that flies in the air, is a witness against the heathen. A creature could not make itself.

(2.) It is a mighty support of faith that God creates. He that made all things with a word, what cannot he do? He can create strength in weakness; he can create a supply of our wants. What a foolish question was that, 'Can he prepare a table in the wilderness?' Psa lxxviii 19. Cannot he that made the world do much more? 'Our help is in the name of the Lord, who made heaven and earth.' Psa cxxiv 8. Rest on this God for help, who made heaven and earth. As the work of creation is a monument of God's power, so it is a stay to faith. Is thy heart hard? He can with a word create softness. Is it unclean? He can create purity. 'Create in me a clean heart, O God.' Psa li 10. Is the church of God low? He can create Jerusalem a praise. Isa lxv 18. There is no such golden pillar for faith to stay upon as a creating power.

(3.) Did God make this world full of beauty and glory, everything very good? Then, what an evil thing is sin, that has put out of frame the whole creation! Sin has much eclipsed the beauty, soured the sweetness, and marred the harmony of the world. How bitter is that gall, a drop whereof can embitter a whole sea! Sin has brought vanity and vexation into the world, yea, a curse. God cursed the ground for man's sake. Gen iii. There were several fruits of the curse.

'In sorrow shalt thou eat of it.' Verse 17. By sorrow is to be understood all the troubles and cares of this life. 'In the sweat of thy face shalt thou eat bread.' Verse 19. In innocence Adam tilled the ground, for he must not live idly; but it was rather a delight than a labour. That tilling was without toiling. The eating in sorrow, and the sweat of the brow, came in after sin. 'Thorns and thistles shall the ground bring forth.' Verse 18. Did the earth in innocence bear thorns, though they were afterwards threatened as a punishment? It is likely it did bear thorns; for, when God had done creating, he made no new species or kinds of things; but the meaning is, Now, after sin, the earth should bring forth more plentifully of thorns, and now those thorns should be hurtful, and choke the corn, which hurtful quality was not in them before. Ever since the fall, all the comforts of this life have a thorn and a thistle in them! The fourth fruit of the curse was the driving of man out of paradise. 'So he drove out the man.' Verse 24. God at first brought Adam into paradise as into a house ready furnished, or as a king into his palace. 'Have dominion over every living thing that moveth.' Gen i 28. God's driving Adam out of paradise signified his dethroning and banishing him, that he might look after a heavenly and a better paradise. A fifth fruit of the curse was death. 'To dust thou shalt return.' Verse 19. Death was not natural to Adam, but came in after sin. Josephus is of opinion that man would have died, though he would have had a longer term of years added to his life; but, out of question, death grew out of the root of sin, as the apostle says. 'By sin came death.' Rom v 12. See then how cursed a thing sin is, that has brought so many curses upon the creation. If we will not hate sin for its deformity, let us hate it for the curse it brings.

(4.) Did God make this glorious world? Did he make everything good? Was there in the creature so much beauty and sweetness? Oh! then what sweetness is there in God? *Quicquid efficit tale, illud est magis tale;* 'the cause is always more noble than the effect.' Think with yourselves, is there so much excellence in house and lands? Then how much more is there in God, that made them! Is there beauty in a rose? What beauty then is there in Christ, the Rose of Sharon! Does oil make the face shine? Psa civ 15. How will the light of God's countenance make it shine! Does wine cheer the heart? Oh! what virtue is there in the true vine! How does the blood of this grape cheer the heart! Is the fruit of the garden sweet? How delicious are the fruits of the Spirit! Is a gold mine so precious? How precious is he who founded this mine! What is Christ, in whom are hid all treasures? Col ii 3. We should ascend from the creature to the

Creator. If there be any comfort below, how much more is there in God, who made all these things! How unreasonable is it that we should delight in the world, and not much more in him that made it! How should our hearts be set on God, and how should we long to be with God, who has infinitely more sweetness in him than any creature!

Use two: Of exhortation. (1.) Did God create the world? Let us wisely observe the works of creation. God has given us not only the book of the Scriptures to read in, but the book of the creation. Look up to the heavens, for they show much of God's glory. The sun gilds the world with its bright beams. Behold the stars, their regular motion in their orbs, their magnitude, their light and their influence. We may see God's glory blazing in the sun and twinkling in the stars. Look into the sea, and see the wonders of God in the deep. Psa cvii 24. Look into the air, there the birds make melody, and sing forth the praises of their Creator. Look into the earth, there we may wonder at the nature of minerals, the power of the loadstone, the virtue of herbs. See the earth decked as a bride with flowers. All these are the glorious effects of God's power. God has wrought the creation as with curious needlework, that we may observe his wisdom and goodness, and give him the praise due to him. 'O Lord, how manifold are thy works! in wisdom hast thou made them all.' Psa civ 24.

(2.) Did God create all things? Let us obey our Maker. We are his *jure creationis* [By right of creation], we owe ourselves to him. If another gives us our maintenance we think ourselves bound to serve him; much more should we serve and obey God who gives us our life. 'In him we live and move.' Acts xvii 28. God has made everything for man's service; the corn for nourishment, the beasts for usefulness, the birds for music, that man should be for God's service. The rivers come from the sea, and they run into the sea again. All we have is from God. Let us honour our Creator, and live to him that made us.

(3.) Did God make our bodies out of the dust, and that dust out of nothing? Let this keep down pride. When God would humble Adam he uses this expression, 'Out of the dust wast thou taken.' Gen iii 19. Why art thou proud, O dust and ashes? Thou art made but of coarse metal. *Cum sis humillimus, cur non humillimus?* [Since you are humble, why do you not walk humbly?] Bernard. David says, 'I was curiously wrought.' Psa cxxxix 15. Thy being curiously wrought, may make thee thankful; but being made of the dust, may keep thee humble. If thou hast beauty, it is but well-coloured earth. Thy body is but air and dust mingled together, and this dust will drop into the dust. When the Lord had said of the judges, they were gods, Psa lxxxii 6, lest they should grow proud he told them they were dying gods. 'Ye shall die like men.' Verse 7.

(4.) Did God create our souls after his image, but we lost it? Let us never rest till we are restored to God's image again. We have now got the devil's image in pride, malice, and envy. Let us get God's image restored, which consists in knowledge and righteousness. Col. iii 10. Eph iv 24. Grace is our best beauty, it makes us like God and angels. As the sun is to the world, so is holiness to the soul. Let us go to God to repair his image in us. Lord! thou hast once made me, make me anew; sin has defaced thy image in me, oh draw it again by the pencil of the Holy Ghost.

14. THE PROVIDENCE OF GOD

QXI: WHAT ARE GOD'S WORKS OF PROVIDENCE?

A: God's works of providence are the acts of his most holy, wise, and powerful government of his creatures, and of their actions.

Of the work of God's providence Christ says, 'My Father worketh hitherto and I work.' John v 17. God has rested from the works of creation, he does not create any new species of things. 'He rested from all his works;' Gen ii 2; and therefore it must needs be meant of his works of providence: 'My Father worketh and I work.' 'His kingdom ruleth over all;' Psa ciii 19; *i.e.*, his providential kingdom. Now, for the clearing of this point, I shall—

I. *Show you that there is a providence.* II. *What that providence is; and* III. *Lay down some maxims or propositions concerning the providence of God.*

I. *That there is a providence.* There is no such thing as blind fate, but there is a providence that guides and governs the world. 'The lot is cast into the lap, but the whole disposing thereof is of the Lord.' Prov xvi 33.

II. *What this providence is.* I answer, Providence is God's ordering all issues and events of things, after the counsel of his will, to his own glory.

[1] I call providence God's ordering things, to distinguish it from his decrees. God's decree ordains things that shall fall out, God's providence orders them.

[2] I call providence the ordering of things after the counsel of God's will.

[3] God orders all events of things, after the counsel of his will, to his own glory, his glory being the ultimate end of all his actings, and the centre

where all the lines of providence meet. The providence of God is *Regina mundi*, 'the queen and governess of the world': it is the eye that sees, and the hand that turns all the wheels in the universe. God is not like an artificer that builds a house, and then leaves it, but like a pilot he steers the ship of the whole creation.

III. *Propositions about God's providence.*

[1] God's providence reaches to all places, persons, and occurrences. (1.) To all places. 'Am I a God at hand, and not a God afar off?' Jer xxiii 23. The diocese where Providence visits is very large; it reaches to heaven, earth, and sea. 'They that go down to the sea, see the wonders of God in the deep.' Psa cvii 23, 24. Now, that the sea, which is higher than the earth, should not drown the earth, is a wonder of Providence. The prophet Jonah saw the wonders of God in the deep, when the very fish which devoured him and swallowed him brought him safe to shore. (2.) God's providence reaches to all persons, especially the persons of the godly, who in a special manner are taken notice of. God takes care of every saint in particular, as if he had none else to care for. 'He careth for you,' 1 Pet v 7, *i.e.*, the elect in a special manner. 'The eye of the Lord is upon them that fear him; to preserve them from death, and to keep them alive in famine.' Psa xxxiii 18, 19. God by his providential care shields off dangers from his people, and sets a life-guard of angels about them. Psa xxxiv 7. God's providence keeps the very bones of the saints. Psa xxxiv 20. It bottles their tears. Psa lvi 8. It strengthens the saints in their weakness. Heb xi 34. It supplies all their wants out of its alms basket. Psa xxiii 5. Thus Providence wonderfully supplies the wants of the elect. When the Protestants in Rochelle were besieged by the French king, God by his providence sent a great number of small fishes to feed them, such as were never seen before in that haven. So the raven, that unnatural creature (that will hardly feed its own young), providentially brought sustenance to the prophet Elijah. 1 Kings xvii 6. The Virgin Mary, through bearing and bringing forth the Messiah, helped to make the world rich, yet she herself was very poor; and now, being warned of the angel to go into Egypt, Matt ii 13, she had scarce enough to bear her charges thither; but see how God provides for her beforehand. By his providence he sends wise men from the east, who bring costly gifts, gold, myrrh, and frankincense, and present them to Christ; and now she has enough to defray her charges into Egypt. God's children sometimes scarce know how they are fed, except that providence feeds them. 'Verily thou shalt be fed.' Psa xxxvii 3. If God will give his people a kingdom when they die, he will not deny them daily bread while they live. (3.) God's providence reaches

to all affairs and occurrences in the world. There is nothing that stirs in the world but God has, by his providence, the over-ruling of it. Is it the raising of a man to honour? Psa lxxv 7. He puts down one, and raises up another. Success and victory in battle is the result of providence. Saul had the victory, but God wrought the salvation. 1 Sam xi 13. That among all virgins brought before the king, Esther should find favour in the eyes of the king, was not without God's special providence; for, by this means, the Lord saved the Jews alive that were destined to destruction. Providence reaches to the least of things, to birds and ants. Providence feeds the young raven, when the dam forsakes it, and will give it no food. Psa cxlvii 9. Providence reaches to the very hairs of our head. 'The hairs of your head are all numbered.' Matt x 30. Surely if providence reaches to our hairs, much more to our souls. Thus you have seen that God's providence reaches to all places, to all persons, to all occurrences and affairs. Now there are two objections against this doctrine.

Some say, There are many things done in the world which are very disorderly and irregular; and surely God's providence is not in these things.

Yes, the things that seem to us irregular, God makes use of to his own glory. Suppose you were in a smith's shop, and should see there several sorts of tools, some crooked, some bowed, others hooked, would you condemn all these things, because they do not look handsome? The smith makes use of them all for doing his work. Thus it is with the providences of God; they seem to us to be very crooked and strange, yet they all carry on God's work. I shall make this clear to you in two particular cases.

God's people are sometimes low. It seems to be out of order that they who are best should be in the lowest condition; but there is much wisdom in this providence, as appears thus: 1. Perhaps the hearts of the godly were lifted up with riches, or with success; now God comes with a humbling providence to afflict them and fleece them. Better is the loss that makes them humble than the success that makes them proud. Again. 2. If the godly were not sometimes afflicted, and suffered an eclipse in their outward comforts, how could their graces be seen, especially their faith and patience? If it were always sunshine we should see no stars; so if we should have always prosperity, it would be hard to see the acting of men's faith. Thus you see God's providences are wise and regular, though to us they seem very strange and crooked.

Here is another case. The wicked flourish. This seems to be very much out of order; but God, in his providence, sees good sometimes that the worst of men should be exalted; that they may do some work for God, though it be against their will. Isa x 7. God will be in no man's debt.

He makes use of the wicked sometimes to protect and shield his church; and sometimes to refine and purify it. 'Thou hast ordained them for correction.' Hab i 12. As if the prophet had said, Thou hast ordained the wicked to correct thy children. Indeed, as Augustine says well, 'We are beholden to wicked men, who against their wills do us good,' As the corn is beholden to the flail to thresh off its husks, or as the iron is beholden to the file to brighten it, so the godly are beholden to the wicked, though it be against their will, to brighten and refine their graces. Now, then, if the wicked do God's own work, though against their will, he will not let them be losers by it; he will raise them in the world, and give them a full cup of earthly comforts. Thus you see those providences are wise and regular, which to us seem strange and crooked.

But, some may say, if God has a hand in ordering all things that fall out, he has a hand in the sins of men.

I answer, No, by no means, he has no hand in any man's sin. God cannot go contrary to his own nature, he cannot do any unholy action, any more than the sun can be said to be darkened. Here you must take heed of two things; as you must take heed of making God ignorant of men's sins, so you must take heed of making God to have a hand in men's sins. Is it likely that God is the author of sin, and the avenger of it? Is it a likely thing that God should make a law against sin, and then have a hand in breaking his own law? God in his providence permits men's sins. 'He suffered all nations to walk in their own ways.' Acts xiv 16. God permitted their sin, which he never would, if he could not bring good out of it. Had not sin been permitted, God's justice in punishing sin, and his mercy in pardoning sin, had not been so well known. The Lord is pleased to permit it, but he has no hand in sin.

But is it not said that God hardened Pharaoh's heart? Here is more than barely permitting sin.

God does not infuse evil into men, he withdraws the influence of his graces, and then the heart hardens of itself; even as the light being withdrawn, darkness presently follows in the air; but it were absurd to say, that therefore the light darkens the air; and therefore you will observe, that Pharaoh is said to harden his own heart. Exod viii 15. God is the cause of no man's sin. It is true God has a hand in the action where sin is, but no hand in the sin of the action. A man may play upon a jarring instrument, but the jarring is from itself; so here, the actions of men, so far as they are natural, are from God; but so far as they are sinful, they are from men themselves, and God has no hand at all in them. So much for the first position, that God's providence reaches to all places, to all persons, and to all occurrences.

[2] A second proposition is, that providences, which are casual and accidental to us, are pre-determined by the Lord. The falling of a tile upon one's head, the breaking out of a fire, is casual to us, but it is ordered by a providence of God. You have a clear instance of this in 1 Kings xxii 34. 'A certain man drew a bow at a venture, and smote the king of Israel between the joints of the harness.' This accident was casual as to the man that drew the bow; but it was divinely ordered by the providence of God. God's providence directed the arrow to hit the mark. Things that seem to fall out casual, and by chance, are the issues of God's decrees, and the interpretation of his will.

[3] God's providence is greatly to be observed, but we are not to make it the rule of our actions. 'Whoso is wise will observe these things.' Psa cvii 43. It is good to observe providence, but we must not make it our rule to walk by. Providence is a Christian's diary, but not his Bible. Sometimes a bad cause prevails and gets ground; but it is not to be liked because it prevails. We must not think the better of what is sinful, because it is successful. This is no rule for our actions to be directed by.

[4] Divine providence is irresistible. There is no standing in the way of God's providence to hinder it. When God's time was come for Joseph's release, the prison could hold him no longer. 'The king sent and loosed him.' Psa cv 20. When God would indulge the Jews with liberty in their religion, Cyrus, by a providence, puts forth a proclamation to encourage the Jews to go and build their temple at Jerusalem, and worship God. Ezra i 2, 3. If God will shield and protect Jeremiah's person in captivity, the very king of Babylon shall nurse up the prophet, and give charge concerning him that he wants nothing. Jer xxxix 11, 12.

[5] God is to be trusted when his providences seem to run contrary to his promises. God promised to give David the crown, to make him king; but providence ran contrary to his promise. David was pursued by Saul, and was in danger of his life, but all this while it was David's duty to trust God. Pray observe, that the Lord by cross providences often brings to pass his promise. God promised Paul the lives of all that were with him in the ship; but the providence of God seemed to run quite contrary to his promise, for the winds blew, the ship split and broke in pieces. Thus God fulfilled his promise; upon the broken pieces of the ship they all came safe to shore. Trust God when providences seem to run quite contrary to promises.

[6] The providences of God are chequer-work, they are intermingled. In the life to come there shall be no more mixture; in hell there will be nothing but bitter; in heaven nothing but sweet; but in this life the providences of God are mixed, there is something of the sweet in them, and something of the bitter. Providences are just like Israel's pillar of cloud, that conducted them in their march, which was dark on one side and light on the other. In the ark were laid up the rod and manna, so are God's providences to his children; there is something of the rod and something of the manna; so that we may say with David, 'I will sing of mercy and judgment.' When Joseph was in prison there was the dark side of the cloud; but God was with Joseph, there was the light side of the cloud. Asher's shoes were of brass, but his feet were dipped in oil. Deut xxxiii 24. So affliction is the shoe of brass that pinches; but there is mercy mingled with the affliction, for there is the foot dipped in oil.

[7] The same action, as it comes from God's providence, may be good, and as it comes from men may be evil. For instance, Joseph being sold into Egypt by his brethren was evil, very wicked, for it was the fruit of their envy; but as it was an act of God's providence it was good; for by this means Jacob and all his family were preserved alive in Egypt. Another instance is in Shimei's cursing David. Shimei cursed David, it was wicked and sinful, for it was the fruit of his malice; but as his cursing was ordered by God's providence, it was an act of God's justice to punish David, and to humble him for his adultery and murder. As the crucifying of Christ came from the Jews, it was an act of hatred and malice to Christ; and Judas's betraying him was an act of covetousness; but as each was an act of God's providence, so there was good in it; for it was an act of God's love in giving Christ to die for the world. Thus I have made clear to you the doctrine of God's providence in these several positions. Let me now speak something by way of application.

Use one: By way of exhortation in these particulars. (1.) Admire God's providence. The providence of God keeps the whole creation upon the wheels, or else it would soon be dissolved, and the very axletree would break in pieces. If God's providence should be withdrawn but for a while, creatures would be dissolved, and run into their first nothing. Without this wise providence of God there would be anxiety and confusion in the whole world, just like an army when it is routed and scattered. The providence of God infuses comfort and virtue into everything we enjoy. Our clothes would not warm us, our food would not nourish us, without the special providence of God. And does not all this deserve your admiration of providence?

(2.) Learn quietly to submit to divine providence. Do not murmur at things that are ordered by divine wisdom. We may no more find fault with the works of providence than we may with the works of creation. It is a sin as much to quarrel with God's providence as to deny his providence. If men do not act as we would have them, they shall act as God would have them. His providence is his master-wheel that turns these lesser wheels, and God will bring his glory out of all at last. 'I was dumb and opened not my mouth, because thou didst it.' Psa xxxix 9. It may be, we think sometimes we could order things better if we had the government of the world in our hands; but alas! should we be left to our own choice we should choose those things that are hurtful for us. David earnestly desired the life of his child, which was the fruit of his sin, but had the child lived it would have been a perpetual monument of his shame. Let us be content that God should rule the world; learn to acquiesce in his will, and submit to his providence. Does any affliction befall you? Remember God sees it is that which is fit for you, or it would not come. Your clothes cannot be so fit for you as your crosses. God's providence may sometimes be secret, but it is always wise; and though we may not be silent under God's dishonour, yet we should learn to be silent under his displeasure.

(3.) You that are Christians, believe that all God's providence shall conspire for your good at last. The providences of God are sometimes dark, and our eyes dim, and we can hardly tell what to make of them; but when we cannot unriddle providence, let us believe that it will work together for the good of the elect. Rom viii 28. The wheels in a clock seem to move contrary one to the other, but they help forward the motion of the clock, and make the larum strike: so the providences of God seem to be cross wheels; but for all that, they shall carry on the good of the elect. The pricking of a vein is in itself evil and hurtful; but as it prevents a fever, and tends to the health of the patient, it is good; so affliction in itself is not joyous, but grievous; but the Lord turns it to the good of his saints. Poverty shall starve their sins, and afflictions shall prepare them for a kingdom. Therefore, Christians, believe that God loves you, and that he will make the most cross providences to promote his glory and your good.

(4.) Let it be an antidote against immoderate fear, that nothing comes to pass but what is ordained by God's decree, and ordered by his providence. We sometimes fear what the issue of things will be, when men grow high in their actings; but let us not make things worse by our fear. Men are limited in their power, and cannot go one hair's breadth further than God's providence permits. He might let Sennacherib's army march towards Jerusalem, but he shall not shoot one arrow against it. 'Then the angel of the Lord went forth and smote in the camp of the Assyrians an hundred and fourscore and five thousand.' Isa xxxvii 36. When Israel was encompassed between Pharaoh and the Red Sea, no question, some of their hearts began to tremble, and they looked upon themselves as dead men; but Providence so ordered it, that the sea was a safe passage to Israel, and a sepulchre to Pharaoh and all his host.

(5.) Let the merciful providence of God cause thankfulness. We are kept alive by a wonderful-working Providence. Providence makes our clothes to warm us, and our meat to nourish us. We are fed every day out of the alms-basket of God's providence. That we are in health, that we have an estate, is not our diligence, but God's providence. 'Thou shalt remember the Lord thy God, for he it is that gives thee power to get wealth.' Deut viii 18. Especially if we go a step higher, we may see cause for thankfulness, that we were born and bred in a gospel land, and that we live in such a place where the Sun of Righteousness shines, which is a signal providence. Why might we not have been born in such places where Paganism prevails? That Christ should make himself known to us, and touch our hearts with his Spirit, when he passes by others; whence is this but from the miraculous providence of God, which is the effect of his free grace?

Use two: Comfort in respect of the church of God. God's providence reaches in a more special manner to his church. 'Sing ye unto her, A vineyard of red wine.' Isa xxvii 2. God waters this vineyard with his blessings, and watches over it by his providence. 'I the Lord keep it night and day.' Such as think totally to ruin the church, must do it in a time when it is neither day nor night, for the Lord keeps it by his providence night and day. What a miraculous conduct of Providence had Israel! God led them by a pillar of fire, gave them manna from heaven, and water from the rock. God by his providence preserves his church in the midst of enemies; a spark kept alive in the ocean, or a flock of sheep among wolves. God saves his church strangely. (1.) By giving unexpected mercies to his church, when she looked for nothing but ruin. 'When the Lord turned the captivity of Zion, we were like them that dream.' Psa cxxvi 1. How strangely did God raise up Queen Esther to preserve alive the Jews, when Haman had got a bloody warrant signed for their execution! (2.) Strangely, by saving in that very way in which we think he will destroy. God works sometimes by contraries. He raises his church by bringing it low. The blood of the martyrs has watered the church, and made it more fruitful. Exod i 12. 'The more they afflicted them the more they multiplied.' The church is like that plant which Gregory Nazianzen speaks of, it lives by dying, and grows by cutting. (3.) Strangely, in that he makes the enemy to do his work. When the people of Ammon and Moab and Mount Seir came against Judah, God set the enemy one against another. 'The children of Ammon and Moab stood up against them of Mount Seir to slay them; and when they had made an end of the inhabitants of Seir, every one helped to destroy another.' 2 Chron xx 23. In the powder treason he made the traitors to be their own betrayers. God can do his work by the enemy's hand. God made the Egyptians send away the people of Israel laden with jewels. Exod xii 36. The church is the apple of God's eye, and the eyelid of his providence daily covers and defends it.

Use three: See here, that which may make us long for the time when the great mystery of God's providence shall be fully unfolded to us. Now we scarce know what to make of God's providence, and are ready to censure what we do not understand; but in heaven we shall see how all his providences (sickness, losses, sufferings) contributed to our salvation. Here we see but some dark pieces of God's providence, and it is impossible to judge of his works by pieces; but when we come to heaven, and see the full body and portrait of his providence drawn out into its lively colours, it will be glorious to behold. Then we shall see how all God's providences helped to fulfil his promises. There is no providence but we shall see a wonder or a mercy in it.

III. The fall

1. THE COVENANT OF WORKS

Qxii: I proceed to the next question, WHAT SPECIAL ACT OF PROVIDENCE DID GOD EXERCISE TOWARDS MAN IN THE ESTATE WHEREIN HE WAS CREATED?

A: When God had created man, he entered into a covenant of life with him upon condition of perfect obedience, forbidding him to eat of the tree of knowledge upon pain of death.

For this, consult with Gen ii 16, 17: 'And the Lord commanded the man, saying, Of every tree of the garden thou mayest freely eat; but of the tree of the knowledge of good and evil, thou shalt not eat; for in the day thou eatest of it, thou shalt surely die.' The subject of our next discourse is this *covenant of works*.

I. *This covenant was made with Adam and all mankind;* for Adam was a public person, and the representative of the world.

For what reason did God make a covenant with Adam and his posterity in innocence?

(1.) To show his sovereignty over us. We were his creatures, and as he was the great Monarch of heaven and earth, he might impose upon us terms of a covenant. (2.) God made a covenant with Adam to bind him fast to him: as God bound himself to Adam, so Adam was bound to him by the covenant.

What was the covenant?

God commanded Adam not to eat of the tree of knowledge; but gave him leave to eat of all the other trees of the garden. God did not envy him any happiness; but said, 'Meddle not with this tree of knowledge,' because he would try Adam's obedience. As King Pharaoh made Joseph chief ruler of his kingdom, and gave him a ring off his finger, and a chain of gold, but said he must not 'touch his throne.' Gen xli 40. In like manner

God dealt with Adam. He gave him a sparkling jewel, knowledge; and put upon him the garment of original righteousness; only, said he, touch not the tree of knowledge, for that is aspiring after omniscience. Adam had power to keep this law: he had the copy of God's law written in his heart. This covenant of works had a promise annexed to it, and a threatening. 1. The promise was, 'Do this and live.' In case man had stood, it is probable he would not have died, but would have been translated to a better paradise. 2. The threatening, 'Thou shalt die the death;' Heb. 'In dying thou shalt die;' that is, thou shalt die both a natural death and an eternal, unless some expedient be found out for thy restoration.

Why did God give Adam this law, seeing he foresaw that Adam would transgress it?

(1.) It was Adam's fault that he did not keep the law. God gave him a stock of grace to trade with, but by his own neglect he failed. (2.) Though God foresaw Adam would transgress, yet that was not a sufficient reason that no law should be given him; for, by the same reason, God should not have given his written Word to men, to be a rule of faith and manners, because he foresaw that some would not believe, and others would be profane. Shall laws not be made in the land, because some will break them? (3.) Though God foresaw Adam would break the law, he knew how to turn it to greater good in sending Christ. The first covenant being broken, he knew how to establish a second, and a better.

II. *Concerning the first covenant, consider these four things:—*

[1] The form of the first covenant in innocence was working; 'Do this and live.' Working was the ground and condition of man's justification. Gal iii 12. Not but that working is required in the covenant of grace, for we are bid to work out our salvation, and be rich in good works. But works in the covenant of grace are not required under the same notion as in the first covenant with Adam. Works are not required for the justification of our persons, but as an attestation of our love to God; not as the cause of our salvation, but as an evidence of our adoption. Works are required in the covenant of grace, not so much in our own strength as in the strength of another. 'It is God which worketh in you.' Phil ii 13. As the teacher guides the child's hand, and helps him to form his letters, so that it is not so much the child's writing as the master's, so our obedience is not so much our working as the Spirit's co-working.

[2] The covenant of works was very strict. God required of Adam and all mankind, (1.) Perfect obedience. Adam must do all things written in the 'book of the law,' and not fail, either in the matter or manner. Gal iii 10.

Adam was to live up to the whole breadth of the moral law, and go exactly according to it, as a well-made dial goes with the sun. One sinful thought would have forfeited the covenant. (2.) Personal obedience. Adam must not do his work by a proxy, or have any surety bound for him; but it must be done in his own person. (3.) Perpetual obedience. He must continue in all things written in 'the book of the law.' Gal iii 10. Thus it was very strict. There was no mercy in case of failure.

[3] The covenant of works was not built upon a very firm basis; and therefore must needs leave men full of fears and doubts. The covenant of works rested upon the strength of man's inherent righteousness; which though in innocence was perfect, yet was subject to change. Adam was created holy, but mutable; having a power to stand and a power to fall. He had a stock of original righteousness to begin the world with, but he was not sure he would not break. He was his own pilot, and could steer right in the time of innocence; but he was not so secured but that he might dash against the rock of temptation, and he and his posterity be shipwrecked; so that the covenant of works must needs leave jealousies and doubtings in Adam's heart, as he had no security given him that he should not fall from that glorious state.

[4] The covenant of works being broken by sin, man's condition was very deplorable and desperate. He was left in himself helpless; there was no place for repentance; the justice of God being offended set all the other attributes against him. When Adam lost his righteousness, he lost his anchor of hope and his crown; there was no way for relief, unless God would find out such a way as neither man nor angel could devise.

Use one: See (1.) The condescension of God, who was pleased to stoop so low as to make a covenant with us. For the God of glory to make a covenant with dust and ashes; for God to bind himself to us, to give us life in case of obedience; for him to enter into covenant with us was a sign of friendship, and a royal act of favour.

(2.) See what a glorious condition man was in, when God entered into covenant with him. He was placed in the garden of God, which for the pleasure of it was called paradise. Gen ii 8. He had his choice of all the trees, one only excepted; he had all kinds of precious stones, pure metals, rich cedars; he was a king upon the throne, and all the creation did obeisance to him, as in Joseph's dream all his brethren's sheaves bowed to his sheaf. Man, in innocence, had all kinds of pleasure that might ravish his senses with delight, and be as baits to allure him to serve and worship his Maker. He was full of holiness. Paradise was not more adorned with fruit than Adam's soul was with grace. He was the coin on which God had stamped his lively image. Light sparkled in his understanding, so that he was like an earthly angel; and his will and affections were full of order, tuning harmoniously to the will of God. Adam was a perfect pattern of sanctity. Adam had intimacy of communion with God and conversed with him, as a favourite with his prince. He knew God's mind, and had his heart. He not only enjoyed the light of the sun in paradise, but the light of God's countenance. This was Adam's condition when God entered into a covenant with him; but this did not long continue; for 'man being in honour abideth not,' lodged not for a night. Psa xlix 12. His teeth watered at the apple, and ever since it has made our eyes water.

(3.) Learn from Adam's fall, how unable we are to stand in our own strength. If Adam, in the state of integrity, did not stand, how unable are we now, when the lock of our original righteousness is cut. If purified nature did not stand, how then shall corrupt nature? We need more strength to uphold us than our own.

(4.) See in what a sad condition all unbelievers and impenitent persons are. As long as they continue in their sins they continue under the curse, under the first covenant. Faith entitles us to the mercy of the second covenant; but while men are under the power of their sins they are under the curse of the first covenant; and if they die in that condition, they are damned to eternity.

(5.) See the wonderful goodness of God, who was pleased when man had forfeited the first covenant, to enter into a new covenant with him. Well may it be called *fœdus gratiæ*, a covenant of grace; for it is bespangled with promises as the heaven with stars. When the angels, those glorious spirits, fell, God did not enter into a new covenant with them to be their God, but he let those golden vessels lie broken; yet has he entered into a second covenant with us, better than the first. Heb viii 6. It is better, because it is surer; it is made in Christ, and cannot be reversed. Christ has engaged his strength to keep every believer. In the first covenant we had a *posse stare*, a power of standing; in the second we had a *non posse cadere*, an impossibility of falling finally. 1 Pet i 5.

(6.) Whosoever they are that look for righteousness and salvation by the power of their freewill, or the inherent goodness of their nature, or by virtue of their merit, as the Socinians and Papists, they are all under the covenant of works. They do not submit to the righteousness of faith, therefore they are bound to keep the whole law, and in case of failure they are condemned. The covenant of grace is like a court of Chancery, to relieve the sinner, and help him who is cast by the first covenant. It says, 'Believe in the Lord Jesus, and be saved'; but such as will stand upon their own inherent righteousness, free-will and merit, fall under the first covenant of works, and are in a perishing estate.

Use two: Let us labour by faith to get into the second covenant of grace, and then the curse of the first covenant will be taken away by Christ. If we once get to be heirs of the covenant of grace, we are in a better state than before. Adam stood on his own legs, and therefore he fell; we stand in the strength of Christ. Under the first covenant, the justice of God, as an avenger of blood, pursues us; but if we get into the second covenant we are in the city of refuge, we are safe, and the justice of God is pacified towards us.

2. SIN

QXIV: WHAT IS SIN?

A: Sin is any want of conformity to the law of God, or transgression of it. 'Sin is the transgression of the law.' 1 John iii 4. Of sin in general:

[1] Sin is a violation or transgression. The Latin word, *transgredior*, to transgress, signifies to go beyond one's bounds. The moral law is to keep us within the bounds of duty. Sin is going beyond our bounds.

[2] The law of God is not the law of an inferior prince, but of Jehovah, who gives laws as well to angels as men; it is a law that is just, and holy, and good. Rom vii 12. It is just, there is nothing in it unequal; holy, nothing in it impure; good, nothing in it prejudicial. So that there is no reason to break this law, no more than for a beast, that is in a fat pasture, to break over the hedge, or to leap into a barren heath or quagmire.

I shall show what a heinous and execrable thing sin is. It is *malorum colluvies*, the complication of all evil; it is the spirits of mischief distilled. The Scripture calls it the "accursed thing.' Josh vii 13. It is compared to the venom of serpents, and the stench of sepulchres. The apostle uses this expression of sin, 'Out of measure sinful,' Rom vii 13, or, as it is in the Greek, 'Hyperbolically sinful.' The devil would paint sin with the vermilion colour of pleasure and profit, that he may make it look fair; but I shall pull off the paint that you may see its ugly face. We are apt to have slight thoughts of sin, and say to it, as Lot of Zoar, 'Is it not a little one?' Gen xix 20. But that you may see how great an evil sin is, consider these four things:

I. *The origin of sin, from whence it comes.* It fetches its pedigree from hell; sin is of the devil. 'He that committeth sin is of the devil.' 1 John iii 8.

Satan was the first actor of sin, and the first tempter to sin. Sin is the devil's first-born.

II. *Sin is evil in the nature of it.*

[1] It is a defiling thing. Sin is not only a defection, but a pollution. It is to the soul as rust is to gold, as a stain to beauty. It makes the soul red with guilt, and black with filth. Sin in Scripture is compared to a 'menstruous cloth,' Isa xxx 22, and to a 'plague-sore.' 1 Kings viii 38. Joshua's filthy garments, in which he stood before the angel, were nothing but a type and hieroglyphic of sin. Zech iii 3. Sin has blotted God's image, and stained the orient brightness of the soul. It makes God loathe a sinner, Zech xi 8; and when a sinner sees his sin, he loathes himself. Ezek xx 43. Sin drops poison on our holy things, it infects our prayers. The high priest was to make atonement for sin on the altar, to typify that our holiest services need Christ to make an atonement for them. Exod xxix 36. Duties of religion in themselves are good, but sin corrupts them, as the purest water is polluted by running through muddy ground. If the leper, under the law, had touched the altar, the altar would not have cleansed him, but he would have defiled the altar. The apostle calls sin, 'Filthiness of flesh and spirit.' 2 Cor vii 1. Sin stamps the devil's image on a man. Malice is the devil's eye, hypocrisy his cloven foot. It turns a man into a devil. 'Have not I chosen you twelve, and one of you is a devil?' John vi 70.

[2] Sin is grieving God's Spirit. 'Grieve not the Holy Spirit of God.' Eph iv 30. To grieve is more than to anger.

How can the Spirit be said to be grieved? For, seeing he is God, he cannot be subject to any passion.

This is spoken metaphorically. Sin is said to grieve the Spirit, because it is an injury offered to the Spirit, and he takes it unkindly, and, as it were, lays it to heart. And is it not much thus to grieve the Spirit? The Holy Ghost descended in the likeness of a dove; and sin makes this blessed dove mourn. Were it only an angel, we should not grieve him, much less the Spirit of God. Is it not sad to grieve our Comforter?

[3] Sin is an act of contumacy against God; a walking antipodes to heaven. 'If ye will walk contrary to me.' Lev xxvi 27. A sinner tramples upon God's law, crosses his will, does all he can to affront, yea, to spite God. The Hebrew word for sin, *Pasha*, signifies rebellion; there is the heart of a rebel in every sin. 'We will do whatsoever proceedeth out of our own mouth, to burn incense to the queen of heaven.' Jer xliv 17. Sin strikes at the very Deity; *Peccatum est Deicidium.* [Sin is God's would-be murderer].

[133]

Sin would not only unthrone God, but un-God him. If the sinner could help it, God would no longer be God.

[4] Sin is an act of disingenuity and unkindness. God feeds the sinner, keeps off evils from him, bemiracles him with mercy; but the sinner not only forgets God's mercies, but abuses them. He is the worse for mercy; like Absalom, who, as soon as David had kissed him, and taken him into favour, plotted treason against him. 2 Sam xv 10. Like the mule, who kicks the dam after she has given it milk. 'Is this thy kindness to thy friend?' 2 Sam xvi 17. God may upbraid the sinner. 'I have given thee,' he may say, 'thy health, strength, and estate; but thou requitest me evil for good, thou woundest me with my own mercies; is this thy kindness to thy friend? Did I give thee life to sin? Did I give thee wages to serve the devil?'

[5] Sin is a disease. 'The whole head is sick;' Isa i 5. Some are sick of pride, others of lust, others of envy. Sin has distempered the intellectual part, it is a leprosy in the head, it has poisoned the vitals. 'Their conscience is defiled.' Tit i 15. It is with a sinner as with a sick patient, his palate is distempered, the sweetest things taste bitter to him. The word which is 'sweeter than the honey-comb,' Psa xix 10, tastes bitter to him, he puts 'sweet for bitter.' Isa v 20. This is a disease, and nothing can cure this disease but the blood of the Physician.

[6] Sin is an irrational thing. It makes a man act not only wickedly, but foolishly. It is absurd and irrational to prefer the less before the greater; the pleasures of life, before the rivers of pleasures at God's right-hand for evermore. Is it not irrational to lose heaven for the satisfying or indulging of lust? As Lysimachus, who, for a draught of water, lost a kingdom. Is it not irrational to gratify an enemy? In sin we do so. When lust or rash anger burns in the soul, Satan warms himself at this fire. Men's sins feast the devil.

[7] Sin is a painful thing. It costs men much labour to pursue their sins. How do they tire themselves in doing the devil's drudgery! 'They weary themselves to commit iniquity.' Jer ix 5. What pains did Judas take to bring about his treason! He goes to the high priest, and then after to the band of soldiers, and then back again to the garden. Chrysostom says, 'Virtue is easier than vice.' It is more pains to some to follow their sins, than to others to worship their God. While the sinner travails with his sin, in sorrow he brings forth; which is called 'serving divers lusts.' Tit iii 3. Not enjoy, but serve. Why so? Because not only of the slavery in sin, but the hard labour; it is 'serving divers lusts.' Many a man goes to hell in the sweat of his brow.

[8] Sin is the only thing God has an antipathy against. God does not hate a man because he is poor, or despised in the world; as you do not hate your friend because he is sick; but that which draws forth the keenness of God's hatred, is sin. 'Oh, do not this abominable thing that I hate.' Jer xliv 4. And sure, if the sinner dies under God's hatred, he cannot be admitted into the celestial mansions. Will God let the man live with him whom he hates? God will never lay a viper in his bosom. The feathers of the eagle will not mix with the feathers of other fowls; so God will not mix and incorporate with a sinner. Till sin be removed, there is no coming where God is.

III. *See the evil of sin, in the price paid for it.* It cost the blood of God to expiate it. 'O man,' says Augustine, 'consider the greatness of thy sin, by the greatness of the price paid for sin.' All the princes on earth, or angels in heaven, could not satisfy for sin; only Christ. Nay, Christ's active obedience was not enough to make atonement for sin, but he must suffer upon the cross; for, without blood is no remission. Heb ix 22. Oh what an accursed thing is sin, that Christ should die for it! The evil of sin is not so much seen in that one thousand are damned for it, as that Christ died for it.

IV. *Sin is evil in its effects.*

[1] Sin has degraded us of our honour. Reuben by incest lost his dignity; and though he was the first-born, he could not excel. Gen xlix 4. God made us in his own image, a little lower than the angels; but sin has debased us. Before Adam sinned, he was like a herald that has his coat of arms upon him: all reverence him, because he carries the king's coat of arms; but let this coat be pulled off, and he is despised, no man regards him. Sin has done this, it has plucked off our coat of innocence, and now it has debased us, and turned our glory into shame. 'And there shall stand up a vile person.' Dan xi 21. This was spoken of Antiochus Epiphanes, who was a king, and his name signifies illustrious; yet sin degraded him, he was a vile person.

[2] Sin disquiets the peace of the soul. Whatever defiles, disturbs. As poison tortures the bowels, corrupts the blood, so sin does the soul. Isa lvii 21. Sin breeds a trembling at the heart; it creates fears, and there is 'torment in fear.' 1 John iv 18. Sin makes sad convulsions in the conscience. Judas was so terrified with guilt and horror, that he hanged himself to quiet his conscience. And is not he like to be ill cured, that throws himself into hell for ease?

[3] Sin produces all temporal evil. 'Jerusalem has grievously sinned, therefore she is removed.' Lam i 8. It is the Trojan horse, that has sword and famine, and pestilence, in its belly. Sin is a coal, that not only blacks, but burns. Sin creates all our troubles; it puts gravel into our bread, wormwood in our cup. Sin rots the name, consumes the estate, buries relations. Sin shoots the flying roll of God's curses into a family and kingdom. Zech v 4. It is reported of Phocas, that having built a wall of mighty strength about his city, there was a voice heard, 'Sin is within the city, and that will throw down the wall.'

[4] Sin unrepented of brings final damnation. The canker that breeds in the rose is the cause of its perishing; and corruptions that breed in men's souls are the cause of their damning. Sin, without repentance, brings the 'second death,' that is *mors sine morte,* Bernard 'a death always dying,' Rev xx 14. Sin's pleasure will turn to sorrow at last; like the book the prophet did eat, sweet in the mouth, but bitter in the belly. Ezek iii 3. Rev x 9. Sin brings the wrath of God, and what bucket or engines can quench that fire? 'Where the worm never dies, and the fire is not quenched.' Mark ix 44.

Use one: See how deadly an evil sin is, and how strange is it that any one should love it! 'How long will ye love vanity?' Psa iv 2. 'Who look to other gods, and love flagons of wine.' Hos iii 1. Sin is a dish men cannot forbear, though it makes them sick. Who would pour rose-water into a kennel? What pity is it so sweet an affection as love should be poured upon so filthy a thing as sin! Sin brings a sting in the conscience, a curse in the estate; yet men love it. A sinner is the greatest self-denier; for his sin he will deny himself a part in heaven.

Use two: Do anything rather than sin. Oh, hate sin! There is more evil in the least sin than in the greatest bodily evils that can befall us. The ermine rather chooses to die than defile her beautiful skin. There is more evil in a drop of sin than in a sea of affliction. Affliction is but like a rent in a coat, sin a prick at the heart. In affliction there is *aliquid mellis,* some good: in this lion there is some honey to be found. 'It is good for me that I was afflicted.' Psa cxix 71. *Utile est animâ si in hâc area mundi flagellis trituretur corpus.* Augustine. 'Affliction is God's flail to thresh off our husks; not to consume, but to refine.' There is no good in sin; it is the spirit and quintessence of evil. Sin is worse than hell; for the pains of hell are a burden to the creature only; but sin is a burden to God. 'I am pressed under your iniquities, as a cart is pressed under the sheaves.' Amos ii 13.

Use three: Is sin so great an evil? Then how thankful should you be to God, if he has taken away your sin! 'I have caused thy iniquity to pass from thee.' Zech iii 4. If you had a disease on your body, plague or dropsy, how thankful would you be to have it taken away! Much more to have sin taken away. God takes away the guilt of sin by pardoning grace, and the power of sin by mortifying grace. Oh be thankful that this sickness is 'not unto death;' that God has changed your nature, and, by grafting you into Christ, made you partake of the sweetness of that olive; that sin, though it live, does not reign, but the elder serves the younger; sin the elder serves grace the younger.

3. ADAM'S SIN

Qxv: WHAT WAS THE SIN WHEREBY OUR FIRST PARENTS FELL FROM THE ESTATE WHEREIN THEY WERE CREATED?

A: That sin was eating the forbidden fruit.

'She took of the fruit thereof, and did eat, and gave also to her husband.' Gen iii 6.

Here is implied, I. *That our first parents fell from their estate of innocence.* II. *The sin by which they fell, was eating the forbidden fruit.*

I. *Our first parents fell from their glorious state of innocence.* 'God made man upright, but they have sought out many inventions.' Eccl vii 29. Adam was perfectly holy, he had rectitude of mind, and liberty of will to good; but his head ached till he had invented his own and our death; he sought out many inventions. 1. His fall was voluntary. He had a *posse non peccare*, a power not to fall. Free-will was a sufficient shield to repel temptation. The devil could not have forced him unless he had given his consent. Satan was only a suitor to woo, not a king to compel; but Adam gave away his own power, and suffered himself to be decoyed into sin; like a young gallant, who at one throw loses a fair lordship. Adam had a fair lordship, he was lord of the world. 'Have dominion over the fish of the sea, and over the fowl of the air, and over every living thing that moveth.' Gen i 28. But he lost all at one throw. Soon as he sinned, he forfeited paradise. 2. Adam's fall was sudden; he did not long continue in his royal majesty.

How long did Adam continue in paradise before he fell?

Tostatus says, he fell the next day. Pererius says, he fell the eighth day after his creation. The most probable and received opinion is, that he fell the very same day in which he was created. So Irenæus, Cyril, Epiphanius, and many others. The reasons which incline me to believe so are,

(1.) It is said, Satan was a murderer, 'from the beginning.' John viii 44. Now, whom did he murder? Not the blessed angels, he could not reach them; nor the cursed angels, for they had before destroyed themselves. How then was Satan a murderer from the beginning? As soon as Satan fell, he began to tempt mankind to sin; this was a murdering temptation. By which it appears Adam did not stay long in Paradise; soon after his creation the devil set upon him, and murdered him by his temptation.

(2.) Adam had not yet eaten of the tree of life. 'And now, lest he put forth his hand, and take also of the tree of life, and eat; the Lord sent him forth of the garden.' Gen iii 22, 23. This tree of life, being one of the choicest fruits in the garden, and being placed in the midst of Paradise, it is very likely Adam would have eaten of this tree of life one of the first, had not the serpent beguiled him with the tree of knowledge. So that I conclude, Adam fell the very day of his creation, because he had not tasted the tree of life, that tree that was most in his eye, and had such delicious fruit growing upon it.

(3.) 'Man being in honour, abideth not.' Psalm xlix 12. The Rabbins read it thus, 'Adam being in honour, lodged not one night.' The Hebrew word for *abide*, signifies, 'To stay or lodge all night.' Adam then, it seems, did not take up one night's lodging in Paradise.

Use one: From Adam's sudden fall learn the weakness of human nature. Adam, in a state of integrity, quickly made a defection from God, he soon lost the robe of innocence and the glory of Paradise. If our nature was thus weak when it was at the best, what is it now when it is at the worst? If Adam did not stand when he was perfectly righteous, how unable are we to stand when sin has cut the lock of our original righteousness! If purified nature did not stand, how shall corrupt nature? If Adam, in a few hours, sinned himself out of Paradise, how quickly would we sin ourselves into hell, if we were not kept by a greater power than our own! But God puts underneath his everlasting arms. Deut xxxiii 27.

Use two: From Adam's sudden fall, learn how sad it is for a man to be left to himself. Adam being left to himself, fell. Oh then, what will become of us, how soon fall, if God should leave us to ourselves! A man without God's grace, left to himself, is like a ship in a storm, without pilot or anchor, and is ready to dash upon every rock. Make this prayer to God, 'Lord, do not leave me to myself. If Adam fell so soon who had strength, how soon shall I fall who have no strength!' Oh! urge God with his hand and seal. 'My strength shall be made perfect in weakness.' 2 Cor xii 9.

II. *The sin by which our first parents fell was eating the forbidden fruit;* where, consider two things:

[1] The occasion of it was the serpent's temptation. The devil crept into the serpent, and spake in the serpent, as the angel in Balaam's ass; where, consider,

(1.) The subtlety of Satan's temptation. His wiles are worse than his darts. Satan's subtlety in tempting; (i) He dealt all along as an impostor, he ushered in his temptation by lies. 1st Lie. 'Ye shall not surely die.' Gen iii 4. 2nd Lie. That God did envy our first parents their happiness. 'God knows, that in the day ye eat, your eyes shall be opened;' verse 5 *q. d.* It is God's envying your felicity, that he forbids you this tree. 3rd Lie. That they should be thereby made like unto God. 'Ye shall be as gods.' Verse 5. Here was his subtlety in tempting. The devil was first a liar, then a murderer.

(ii) In that he set upon our first parents so quickly, before they were confirmed in their obedience. The angels in heaven are fully confirmed in holiness; they are called stars of the morning, Job xxxviii 7, and they are fixed stars; but our first parents were not confirmed in their obedience, they were not fixed in their orb of holiness. Though they had a possibility of standing, they had not an impossibility of falling; they were holy, but mutable. There was Satan's subtlety, in tempting our first parents before they were confirmed in their obedience.

(iii) His subtlety in tempting was, That he set upon Eve first because he thought she was less able to resist. Satan broke over the hedge where it was weakest; he knew he could more easily insinuate and wind himself into her by a temptation. An expert soldier, when about to storm or enter a castle, observes warily where there is a breach, or how he may enter with more facility; so did Satan the weaker vessel. He tempted Eve first, because he knew, if once he could prevail with her, she would easily draw her husband. Thus the devil handed over a temptation to Job by his wife. 'Curse God and die.' Job ii 9. Agrippina poisoned the Emperor Commodus, with wine in a perfumed cup; the cup being perfumed and given him by his wife it was the less suspected. Satan knew a temptation coming to Adam from his wife would be more prevailing, and would be less suspected. Oh bitter! sometimes relations prove temptations. A wife may be a snare, when she dissuades her husband from doing his duty, or entices him to evil. 'Ahab sold himself to work wickedness, whom his wife Jezebel stirred up.' 1 Kings xxi 25. She blew the coals, and made his sin flame out the more. Satan's subtlety was in tempting Adam by his wife; he thought she would draw him to sin.

(iv) Satan's subtlety in tempting was in assaulting Eve's faith. He would persuade her that God had not spoken truth: 'Ye shall not surely die.' Gen iii 4. This was Satan's masterpiece, to weaken her faith. When he had shaken that, and had brought her once to distrust; then 'she yielded,' she presently put forth her hand to evil.

(2.) Satan's cruelty in tempting. Soon as Adam was invested in all his glory, the devil cruelly, as it were on the day of Adam's coronation, would dethrone him, and bring him and all his posterity under a curse. See how little love Satan has to mankind; he has an implacable antipathy against us, and antipathies can never be reconciled. So much for the occasion of Adam's sin, or his being tempted by the serpent.

[2] The sin itself, 'Eating the forbidden fruit.' This was very heinous, and that appears three ways. (1.) In respect of the person that committed it. (2.) The aggravation of the sin. (3.) The dreadfulness of the effect.

(1.) It was very heinous in respect of the person that committed it. Adam had excellent and noble endowments; he was illumined with knowledge, embellished with holiness; he knew his duty, and it was as easy to him to obey God's command as to know it; he might have chosen whether he would sin or no; yet he wilfully did eat of the forbidden tree.

(2.) The aggravation of Adam's sin.

Wherein did it appear to be so great? It was but raptus pomi [*the seizing of an apple*]. *Was it such a great matter to pluck an apple?*

It was against an infinite God. It was *malum complexum*, a voluminous sin, there were many twisted together in it; as Cicero says of parricide, 'He who is guilty of it, *Plurima committit peccata in uno*, he commits many sins in one;' so there were many sins in this one sin of Adam. It was a big-bellied sin, a chain with many links. Ten sins were in it.

(i) Incredulity. Our first parents did not believe what God had spoken was truth. God said, They shall die the death in the day they eat of that tree. They believed not that they should die; they could not be persuaded that such fair fruit had death at the door. Thus, by unbelief they made God a liar; nay, which was worse, they believed the devil rather than God.

(ii) Unthankfulness, which is the epitome of all sin. Adam's sin was committed in the midst of Paradise. God had enriched him with variety of mercies; he had stamped his own image upon him; he had made him lord of the world; gave him of all the trees of the garden to eat (one only excepted), and now to take of that tree! This was high ingratitude; it was like the dye to the wool, which makes it crimson. When Adam's eyes were opened, and he saw what he had done, well might he be ashamed, and hide himself. How could he who sinned in the midst of Paradise, look God in the face without blushing!

(iii) In Adam's sin was discontent. Had he not been discontented, he would never have sought to have altered his condition. Adam, one would think, had enough, he differed but little from the angels, he had the robe of innocence to clothe him, and the glory of Paradise to crown him; yet he was not content, he would have more; he would be above the ordinary rank of creatures. How wide was Adam's heart, that a whole world could not fill it!

(iv) Pride, in that he would be like God. This worm, that was but newly crept out of the dust, now aspired after Deity. 'Ye shall be as gods,' said Satan, and Adam hoped to have been so indeed; he supposed the tree of knowledge would have anointed his eyes, and made him omniscient. But, by climbing too high, he got a fall.

(v) Disobedience. God said, 'Thou shalt not eat of the tree;' but he would eat of it, though it cost him his life. Disobedience is a sin against equity. It is right we should serve him from whom we have our subsistence. God gave Adam his allowance, therefore it was but right he should give God his allegiance. How could God endure to see his laws trampled on before his face? This made him place a flaming sword at the end of the garden.

(vi) Curiosity. He meddled with that which was out of his sphere, and did not belong to him. God smote the men of Bethshemesh for looking into the ark. 1 Sam vi 19. Adam would be prying into God's secrets, and tasting what was forbidden.

(vii) Wantonness. Though Adam had a choice of all the other trees, yet his palate grew wanton, and he must have this tree. Like Israel, God sent them manna, angels' food, ay, but they had a hankering after quails. It was not enough that God supplied their wants, unless he should satisfy their lusts. Adam had not only for necessity, but for delight; yet his wanton palate lusted after forbidden fruit.

(viii) Sacrilege. The tree of knowledge was none of Adam's, yet he took of it, and did sacrilegiously rob God of his due. It was counted a great crime in Harpalus to rob the temple, and steal the silver vessels; so it was in Adam to steal fruit from that tree which God had peculiarly enclosed for himself. Sacrilege is double theft.

(ix) Murder. Adam was a public person, and all his posterity were involved and wrapped up in him; and he, by sinning, at once destroyed all his posterity, if free grace did not interpose. If Abel's blood cried so loud in God's ears, 'The voice of thy brother's blood crieth unto me from the ground,' Gen iv 10; how loud did the blood of all Adam's posterity cry against him for vengeance!

(x) Presumption. Adam presumed of God's mercy; he blessed himself, saying he should have peace; he thought, though he did transgress, he should not die; that God would sooner reverse his decree than punish him. This was great presumption. What a heinous sin was Adam's breach of covenant!

One sin may have many sins in it. We are apt to have slight thoughts of sin, and say it is but a little one. How many sins were in Adam's sin! Oh take heed of any sin! As in one volume there may be many works bound up, so there may be many sins in one sin.

[3] The dreadfulness of the effect. It has corrupted man's nature. How rank is that poison a drop whereof could poison a whole sea! And how deadly is that sin of Adam, that could poison all mankind, and bring a curse upon them, till it be taken away by him who was made a curse for us.

4. ORIGINAL SIN

Qxvi: did all mankind fall in adam's first transgression?

A: The covenant being made with Adam, not only for himself, but for his posterity, all mankind descending from him, by ordinary generation, sinned in him, and fell with him in his first transgression.

'By one man sin entered into the world, and death by sin,' &c. Rom v 12.

Adam being a representative person, while he stood, we stood; when he fell, we fell, We sinned in Adam; so it is in the text, 'In whom all have sinned.'

Adam was the head of mankind, and being guilty, we are guilty, as the children of a traitor have their blood stained. *Omnes unus ille Adam fuerunt.* 'All of us,' says Augustine, 'sinned in Adam, because we were part of Adam.'

If when Adam fell, all mankind fell with him; why, when one angel fell, did not all fall?

The case is not the same. The angels had no relation to one another. They are called morning-stars; the stars have no dependence one upon another; but it was otherwise with us, we were in Adam's loins; as a child is a branch of the parent, we were part of Adam; therefore when he sinned, we sinned.

How is Adam's sin made ours?

(1.) By imputation. The Pelagians of old held, that Adam's transgression is hurtful to posterity by imitation only, not by imputation. But the text, 'In whom all have sinned,' confutes that.

(2.) Adam's sin is ours by propagation. Not only is the guilt of Adam's sin imputed to us, but the depravity and corruption of his nature is transmitted to us, as poison is carried from the fountain to the cistern. This is that which we call original sin. 'In sin did my mother conceive me.' Psa li 5. Adam's leprosy cleaves to us, as Naaman's leprosy did to Gehazi. 2 Kings v 27. This original concupiscence is called,

(1.) The 'old man.' Eph iv 22. It is said to be the old man, not that it is weak, as old men are, but for its long standing, and for its deformity. In old age the fair blossoms of beauty fall; so original sin is the old man, because it has withered our beauty, and made us deformed in God's eye.

(2.) Original concupiscence is called the law of sin. Rom vii 25. Original sin has *vim coactivam*, the power of a law which binds the subject to allegiance. Men must needs do what sin will have them, when they have both the love of sin to draw them, and the law of sin to force them.

I. *In original sin there is something privative, and something positive.*

[1] Something privative. *Carentia Justitiæ debitæ* [The lack of that righteousness which should be ours]. We have lost that excellent quintessential frame of soul which once we had. Sin has cut the lock of original purity, where our strength lay.

[2] Something positive. Original sin has contaminated and defiled our virgin nature. It was death among the Romans to poison the springs. Original sin has poisoned the spring of our nature, it has turned beauty into leprosy; it has turned the azure brightness of our souls into midnight darkness.

Original sin has become co-natural to us. A man by nature cannot but sin; though there were no devil to tempt, no bad examples to imitate, yet there is such an innate principle in him that he cannot forbear sinning. 2 Pet ii 14. *A peccato cessare nesciunt*, who cannot cease to sin, as a horse that is lame cannot go without halting. In original sin there is,

(1.) An aversion from good. Man has a desire to be happy, yet opposes that which should promote his happiness. He has a disgust of holiness, he hates to be reformed. Since we fell from God, we have no mind to return to him.

(2.) A prospensity to evil. If, as the Pelagians say, there is so much goodness in us since the fall, why is there not as much natural proneness to good as there is to evil? Our experience tells us, that the natural bias of the soul is to that which is bad. The very heathens by the light of nature saw this. Hierocles the philosopher said, 'it is grafted in us by nature to sin.' Men roll sin as honey under their tongue. 'They drink iniquity as water,' Job xv 16. Like a hydropsical person, that thirsts for drink, and is not satisfied; they have a kind of drought on them, they thirst for sin. Though they are tired out in committing sin, yet they sin. Eph iv 19. 'They weary themselves to commit iniquity'; as a man that follows his game while he is weary, yet delights in it, and cannot leave it off. Jer ix 5. Though God has set so many flaming swords in the way to stop men in their sin, yet they go on in it; which all shows what a strong appetite they have to the forbidden fruit.

II. *That we may further see the nature of original sin, consider,*

[1] The universality of it. It has, as poison, diffused itself into all the parts and powers of the soul. 'The whole head is sick, and the whole heart is faint.' Isa i 5. Like a sick patient, that has no part sound, his liver is swelled, his feet are gangrened, his lungs are perished; such infected, gangrened souls have we, till Christ, who has made a medicine of his blood, cures us.

(1.) Original sin has depraved the intellectual part. As in the creation 'darkness was upon the face of the deep,' Gen i 2, so it is with the understanding; darkness is upon the face of this deep. As there is salt in every drop of the sea, bitterness in every branch of wormwood, so there is sin in every faculty. The mind is darkened, we know little of God. Ever since Adam did eat of the tree of knowledge, and his eyes were opened, we lost our eye-sight. Besides ignorance in the mind, there is error and mistake; we do not judge rightly of things, we put bitter for sweet, and sweet for bitter. Isa v 20. Besides this, there is much pride, superciliousness and prejudice, and many fleshly reasonings. 'How long shall thy vain thoughts lodge within thee?' Jer iv 14.

(2.) Original sin has defiled the heart. The heart is deadly wicked. Jer xvii 9. It is a lesser hell. In the heart are legions of lusts, obdurateness, infidelity, hypocrisy, sinful estuations; it boils as the sea with passion and revenge. 'Madness is in their heart while they live.' Eccl ix 3. The heart is, *Officina diaboli,* 'the devil's shop or workhouse,' where all mischief is framed.

(3.) The will. Contumacy is the seat of rebellion. The sinner crosses God's will, to fulfil his own. 'We will burn incense to the queen of heaven.' Jer xliv 17. There is a rooted enmity in the will against holiness;

it is like an iron sinew, it refuses to bend to God. Where is then the freedom of the will, when it is so full not only of indisposition, but opposition to what is spiritual?

(4.) The affections. These, as the strings of a viol, are out of tune. They are the lesser wheels, which are strongly carried by the will, the master-wheel. Our affections are set on wrong objects. Our love is set on sin, our joy on the creature. Our affections are naturally as a sick man's appetite, who desires things which are noxious and hurtful to him; he calls for wine in a fever. So we have impure lustings instead of holy longings.

[2] The adhesion of original sin. It cleaves to us, as blackness to the skin of the Ethiopian, so that we cannot get rid of it. Paul shook off the viper on his hand, but we cannot shake off this inbred corruption. It may be compared to a wild fig-tree growing on a wall, the roots of which are pulled up, and yet there are some fibres of it in the joints of the stonework, which will not be eradicated, but will sprout forth till the wall be pulled in pieces. Original concupiscence comes not, as a lodger, for a night, but as an indweller. 'Sin which dwelleth in me.' Rom vii 17.

It is a *malus genius*, 'an evil spirit' that haunts us wheresoever we go. 'The Canaanite would dwell in that land.' Josh xvii 12.

[3] Original sin retards and hinders us in the exercise of God's worship. Whence is 'all that dulness and deadness in religion? It is the fruit of original sin. This it is that rocks us asleep in duty. 'The good that I would, I do not.' Rom vii 19. Sin is compared to a weight. Heb xii 1. A man that has weights tied to his legs cannot run fast. It is like that fish Pliny speaks of, a sea lamprey, that cleaves to the keel of the ship, and hinders its progress when it is under sail.

[4] Original sin, though latent in the soul, and as a spring which runs under ground, often breaks forth unexpectedly. Christian, thou canst not believe that evil which is in thy heart, and which will break forth suddenly, if God should leave thee. 'Is thy servant a dog that he should do this great thing?' 2 Kings viii 13. Hazael could not believe he had such a root of bitterness in his heart, that he should rip up the women with child. Is thy servant a dog? Yes, and worse than a dog, when that original corruption within is stirred up. If one had come to Peter and said, Peter, within a few hours thou wilt deny Christ, he would have said, 'Is thy servant a dog?' But alas! Peter did not know his own heart, nor how far that corruption within would prevail upon him. The sea may be calm, and look clear; but when the wind blows how it rages and foams! so though now thy heart seems good, yet, when temptation blows, how

may original sin discover itself, making thee foam with lust and passion. Who would have thought to have found adultery in David, and drunkenness in Noah, and cursing in Job? If God leave a man to himself, how suddenly and scandalously may original sin break forth in the holiest men on the earth!

[5] Original sin mixes and incorporates itself with our duties and graces.

(1.) With our duties. As the hand which is paralytic or palsied cannot move without shaking, as wanting some inward strength; so we cannot do any holy action without sinning, as wanting a principle of original righteousness. As whatever the leper touched became unclean; such a leprosy is original sin; it defiles our prayers and tears. We cannot write without blotting. Though I do not say that the holy duties and good works of the regenerate are sins, for that were to reproach the Spirit of Christ, by which they are wrought; yet this I say, that the best works of the godly have sin cleaving to them. Christ's blood alone makes atonement for our holy things.

(2.) With our graces. There is some unbelief mixed with faith, lukewarmness with zeal, pride with humility. As bad lungs cause an asthma or shortness of breath, so original corruption has infected our hearts, so that our graces breathe very faintly.

[6] Original sin is a vigorous active principle within us. It does not lie still, but is ever exciting and stirring us up to evil; it is an inmate very unquiet. 'What I hate, that do I.' Rom vii 15. How came Paul to do so? Original sin irritated and stirred him up to it. Original sin is like quicksilver, always in motion. When we are asleep, sin is awake in the fancy. Original sin sets the head plotting evil, and the hands working it. It has in it *principium motûs*, not *quietis* [a principle of restlessness, not of tranquillity]; it is like the pulse, ever beating.

[7] Original sin is the cause of all actual sin. It is *fomes peccati* [the kindling-wood of sin], it is the womb in which all actual sins are conceived. Hence come murders, adulteries, rapines. Though actual sins may be more scandalous, yet original sin is more heinous; the cause is more than the effect.

[8] It is not perfectly cured in this life. Though grace does subdue sin, yet it does not wholly remove it. Though we are like Christ, having the first fruits of the Spirit, yet we are unlike him, having the remainders of the flesh. There are two nations in the womb. Original sin is like that tree, in Dan iv 23, though the branches of it were hewn down, and the main body of it, yet the stumps and root of the tree were left. Though the

Spirit be still weakening and hewing down sin in the godly, yet the stump of original sin is left. It is a sea that will not, in this life, be dried up.

But why does God leave original corruption in us after regeneration? He could free us from it if he pleased.

(1.) He does it to show the power of his grace in the weakest believer. Grace shall prevail against a torrent of corruption. Whence is this? The corruption is ours, but the grace is God's.

(2.) God leaves original corruption to make us long after heaven, where there shall be no sin to defile, no devil to tempt. When Elias was taken up to heaven his mantle dropped off; so, when the angels shall carry us up to heaven, this mantle of sin shall drop off. We shall never more complain of an aching head, or an unbelieving heart.

Use one: If original sin be propagated to us, and will be inherent in us while we live here, it confutes the Libertines and Quakers, who say thay are without sin. They hold perfection; they show much pride and ignorance; but we see the seeds of original sin remain in the best. 'There is not a just man lives and sins not.' Eccl vii 20. And Paul complained of a 'body of death.' Rom vii 24. Though grace purifies nature, it does not perfect it.

But does not the apostle say of believers, that their 'old man is crucified;' Rom vi 6, and they are 'dead to sin?' Rom vi 11.

They are dead. (1.) Spiritually. They are dead as to the *reatus*, the guilt of it; and as to the *regnum*, the power of it; the love of sin is crucified.

(2.) They are dead to sin legally. As a man that is sentenced to death is dead in law, so they are legally dead to sin. There is a sentence of death gone out against sin. It shall die, and drop into the grave; but at the present, sin has its life lengthened out. Nothing but the death of the body can quite free us from the body of this death.

Use two: Let us lay to heart original sin, and be deeply humbled for it. It cleaves to us as a disease, it is an active principle in us, stirring us up to evil. Original sin is worse than all actual sin; the fountain is more than the stream. Some think, as long as they are civil, they are well enough; ay, but the nature is poisoned. A river may have fair streams, but vermin at the bottom. Thou carriest a hell about thee, thou canst do nothing but thou defilest it; thy heart, like muddy ground, defiles the purest water that runs through it. Nay, though thou art regenerate, there is much of the old man in the new man. Oh how should original sin humble us!

This is one reason God has left original sin in us, because he would have it as a thorn in our side to humble us. As the bishop of Alexandria, after the people had embraced Christianity, destroyed all their idols but one, that the sight of that idol might make them loathe themselves for their former idolatry; so God leaves original sin to pull down the plumes of pride. Under our silver wings of grace are black feet.

Use three: Let the sense of this make us daily look up to heaven for help. Beg Christ's blood to wash away the guilt of sin, and his Spirit to mortify the power of it; beg further degrees of grace; *gratiam Christi eo obnoxiam ambiamus.* Though grace cannot make sin not to be, yet it makes it not to reign; though grace cannot expel sin, it can repel it. And for our comfort, where grace makes a combat with sin, death shall make a conquest.

Use four: Let original sin make us walk with continual jealousy and watchfulness over our hearts. The sin of our nature is like a sleeping lion, the least thing that awakens it makes it rage. Though the sin of our nature seems quiet, and lies as fire hid under the embers, yet if it be a little stirred and blown up by a temptation, how quickly may it flame forth into scandalous evils! therefore we need always to walk watchfully. 'I say to you all, Watch.' Mark xiii 37. A wandering heart needs a watchful eye.

5. MAN'S MISERY BY THE FALL

QXIX: WHAT IS THE MISERY OF THAT ESTATE WHEREINTO MAN FELL?

A: All mankind by their fall lost communion with God, are under his wrath and curse, and so made liable to all the miseries in this life, to death itself, and to the pains of hell for ever.

'And were by nature children of wrath.' Eph ii 3. Adam left an unhappy portion to his posterity, *Sin and Misery.* Having considered the first of these, original sin, we shall now advert to the misery of that state. In the first, we have seen mankind offending; in the second, we shall see him suffering. The misery ensuing from original sin is two-fold.

I. *Privative.* By this first hereditary sin we have lost communion with God. Adam was God's familiar, his favourite; but sin has put us all out of favour. When we lost God's image, we lost his acquaintance. God's banishing Adam out of paradise hieroglyphically showed how sin has banished us out of God's love and favour.

II. *Positive*. In four things. 1. Under the power of Satan. 2. Heirs of God's wrath. 3. Subject to all the miseries of this life. 4. Exposed to hell and damnation.

[1] The first misery is, that by nature we are 'under the power of Satan,' who is called 'The prince of the power of the air.' Eph ii 2. Before the fall man was a free denizen, now a slave; before, a king on the throne, now in fetters. And whom is man enslaved to? To one that is a hater of him. This was an aggravation of Israel's servitude. 'They that hated them ruled over them.' Psa cvi 41. By sin we are enslaved to Satan, who is a hater of mankind, and writes all his laws in blood. Sinners before conversion are under Satan's command; as the ass at the command of the driver, so he does all the devil's drudgery. No sooner Satan tempts but he obeys. As the ship is at the command of the pilot, who steers it which way he will, so is the sinner at the command of Satan; and he ever steers the ship into hell's mouth. The devil rules all the powers and faculties of a sinner.

(1.) He rules the understanding. He blinds men with ignorance, and then rules them; as the Philistines first put out Samson's eyes, and then bound him. Satan can do what he will with an ignorant man; because he does not see the error of his way, the devil can lead him into any sin. You may lead a blind man any whither. *Omne peccatum fundatur in ignorantia* [Every sin is founded upon ignorance].

(2.) Satan rules the will. Though he cannot force the will, yet he can, by temptation, draw it. 'The lusts of your father ye will do.' John viii 44. He hath got your hearts, and him ye will obey. 'We will burn incense to the queen of heaven.' Jer xliv 17. When the devil spurs a sinner by a temptation, he will over hedge and ditch break all God's laws, that he may obey Satan. Where then is free will, when Satan has such power over the will? 'His lusts ye will do.' There's not any member of the body but is at the devil's service: the head to plot sin, the hands to work it, the feet to run the devil's errand. *Grave jugum servitutis*. Cicero. 'Slavery is hateful to a noble spirit.' Satan is the worst tyrant; the cruelty of a cannibal, or Nero, is nothing to his. Other tyrants do but rule over the bodies, he over the conscience. Other tyrants have some pity on their slaves; though they work in the galley, they give them meat, let them have hours for rest; but Satan is a merciless tyrant, he lets them have no rest. What pains did Judas take! The devil would let him have no rest till he had betrayed Christ, and afterwards imbrued his hands in his own blood.

Use one: See here our misery by original sin; enslaved to Satan. Eph ii 2. Satan is said to work effectually in the children of disobedience. What a sad plague is it for a sinner to be at the will of the devil! Just like a slave, if the Turks bid him dig in the mines, hew in the quarries, tug at the oar, the slave must do it, he dares not refuse. If the devil bids a man lie or steal, he does not refuse; and, what is worse, he willingly obeys this tyrant. Other slaves are forced against their will: 'Israel sighed by reason of their bondage,' Exod ii 23; but sinners are willing to be slaves, they will not take their freedom; they kiss their fetters.

Use two: Let us labour to get out of this deplorable condition into which sin has plunged us, and get from under the power of Satan. If any of your children were slaves, you would give great sums of money to purchase their freedom; and when your souls are enslaved, will ye not labour for their freedom? Improve the gospel. The gospel proclaims a jubilee to captives. Sin binds men, but the gospel looses them. Paul's preaching was 'to turn men from the power of Satan to God.' Acts xxvi 18. The gospel star leads you to Christ; and if you get Christ, then you are made free, though not from the being of sin, yet from Satan's tyranny. 'If the Son make you free, ye shall be free indeed.' John viii 36. You hope to be kings to reign in heaven, and will you let Satan reign in you now? Never think to be kings when you die, and slaves while you live. The crown of glory is for conquerors, not for captives. Oh get out of Satan's jurisdiction; get your fetters of sin filed off by repentance.

[2] 'And were by nature the children of wrath.' Tertullian's exposition here is wrong, who by *children of wrath*, understands subjectively, that is, subject to wrath and passion; offending often in the irascible faculty of a wrathful spirit. By *children of wrath*, the apostle passively means *heirs of wrath*, exposed to God's displeasure. God was once a friend, but sin broke the knot of friendship; now God's smile is turned into a frown; we are now bound over to the sessions, and become children of wrath. 'And who knows the power of God's wrath?' Psa xc 11. 'The wrath of a king is as the roaring of a lion.' Prov xix 12. How did Haman's heart tremble, when the king rose up from the banquet in wrath! Esth vii 7. But God's wrath is infinite, all other is but as a spark to a flame: wrath in God is not a passion, as in us; but it is an act of God's holy will, whereby he abhors sin, and decrees to punish it. This wrath is very dismal; it is this wrath of God that embitters afflictions in this life, for when sickness comes attended with God's wrath, it puts conscience into an agony. The mingling of the fire with the hail made it most terrible. Exod ix 24. So mingling God's wrath with affliction, makes it torturing; it is the nail in the yoke. God's wrath, when but in a threatening (as a shower hanging in the cloud), made Eli's ears to tingle; what is it then, when this wrath

is executed? It is terrible when the king rates and chides a traitor; but it is more dreadful when he causes him to be set upon the rack, or to be broke upon the wheel. 'Who knows the power of God's wrath?' While we are children of wrath we have nothing to do with any of the promises; they are as the tree of life, bearing several sorts of fruit, but we have no right to pluck one leaf. 'Children of wrath.' Eph ii 3. 'Strangers to the covenants of promise,' verse 12. The promises are as a fountain sealed. While we are in the state of nature, we see nothing but the flaming sword; and, as the apostle says, 'There remains nothing but a fearful looking for of fiery indignation.' Heb x 27. While children of wrath we are 'heirs to all God's curses.' Gal iii 10. How can the sinner eat and drink in that condition? Like Damocles' banquet, who while he sat at meat with a sword hanging over his head by a small thread could have little stomach to eat; so the sword of God's wrath and curse hangs every moment over a sinner's head. We read of a flying roll, written with curses. Zech v 3. A roll written with curses goes out against every person that lives and dies in sin. God's curse blasts wherever it comes. There is a curse on the sinner's name, a curse on his soul, a curse on his estate and posterity, a curse on the ordinances. Sad, if all a man eats should turn to poison; yet the sinner eats and drinks his own damnation at God's table. Thus it is before conversion. As the love of God makes every bitter thing sweet, so the curse of God makes every sweet thing bitter.

Use one: See our misery by the fall. *Heirs of wrath.* And is this estate to be rested in? If a man be fallen under the king's displeasure, will he not labour to re-ingratiate himself into his favour? Oh let us flee from the wrath of God! And whither should we fly, but to Jesus Christ? There is none else to shield off the wrath of God from us. 'Jesus hath delivered us from the wrath to come.' I Thess i 10.

[3] Subject to all outward miseries. All the troubles incident to man's life are the bitter fruits of original sin. The sin of Adam has 'subjected the creature to vanity.' Rom viii 20. Is it not a part of the creature's vanity, that all the comforts below will not fill the heart, any more than the mariner's breath can fill the sails of a ship? 'In the midst of his sufficiency he shall be in straits.' Job xx 22. There is still something wanting, and a man would have more; the heart is always hydropsical; it thirsts, and is not satisfied. Solomon put all the creatures into a crucible; and when he came to extract the spirit and quintessence, there was nothing but froth, 'all was vanity.' Eccl i 2. Nay, it is vexing vanity; not only emptiness, but bitterness, our life is labour and sorrow: we come into the world with a

cry, and go out with a groan. Psa xc 10. Some have said, that they would not live the life they have lived over again, because their life has had more water in it than wine; more water of tears, than wine of joy. *Quia est diu vivere nisi diu torqueri* [Long life is merely long torment]. Augustine. 'Man is born to trouble.' Job v 7. Every one is not born heir to land, but he is born heir to trouble. As well separate weight from lead as trouble from man. We do not finish our troubles in this life, but change them. Trouble is the vermin bred out of the putrid matter of sin. Whence all our fears but from sin? 'There is torment in fear.' 1 John iv 18. Fear is the ague of the soul, sets it shaking; some fear want, others alarms, others fear loss of relations; if we rejoice, it is with trembling. Whence all our disappointments of hopes but from sin? Where we look for comfort, there is a cross; where we expect honey, there we taste wormwood. Whence is it that the earth is filled with violence, that the wicked oppresses the man who is more righteous than he? Hab i 13. Whence so much fraudulence in dealing, so much falseness in friendship, such crosses in relations? Whence is it children prove undutiful, and they that should be as the staff of the parents' age are a sword to pierce their hearts? Whence is it that servants are unfaithful to their masters? The apostle speaks of some who have entertained angels in their houses; Heb xiii 2; but how oft, instead of entertaining angels in their houses, do some entertain devils! Whence all the mutinies and divisions in a kingdom? 'In those days there was no peace to them that went out, nor to him that came in.' 2 Chron xv 5. All this is but the sour core in the apple which our first parents ate, the fruit of original sin. Besides, all the deformities and diseases of the body, fevers, convulsions, catarrhs are from sin, *Macies et nova febrium terris incubuit cohors* [Famine and a new crop of fevers oppressed the lands]. There had never been a stone in the kidneys, if there had not been first a stone in the heart. Yea, the death of the body is the fruit and result of original sin. 'Sin entered into the world, and death by sin.' Rom v 12. Adam was made immortal, conditionally, if he had not sinned. Sin dug Adam's grave. Death is terrible to nature. Louis, king of France, forbade all that came into his court to mention the name of death in his ears. The Socinians say, that death comes only from the infirmities of the constitution. But the apostle says, Sin ushered in death into the world: by sin came death. Certainly, had not Adam ate of the tree of knowledge he had not died. 'In the day thou eatest, thou shalt surely die,' Gen ii 17: implying, if Adam had not eaten, he should not have died. Oh then see the misery ensuing upon original sin! Sin dissolves the harmony and good temperature of the body, and pulls its frame in pieces.

[4] Original sin without repentance exposes to hell and damnation. This is the second death. Rev xx 14. Two things are in it:

(1.) *Pœna damni*, Punishment of loss. The soul is banished from the beatific presence of God, in whose presence is fulness of joy.

(2.) *Pœna sensus*, Punishment of sense. The sinner feels scalding vials of God's wrath. It is penetrating, abiding, John iii 36, and reserved, 2 Pet ii 17. If when God's anger be kindled but a little, and a spark or two of it flies into a man's conscience in this life, it be so terrible, what will it be when God stirs up all his anger? In hell there is the worm and the fire. Mark ix 44. Hell is the very accent and emphasis of misery; there is judgment without mercy. Oh what flames of wrath, what seas of vengeance, what rivers of brimstone, are poured out there upon the damned! Bellarmine is of opinion, That one glimpse of hell-fire were enough to make the most flagitious sinner to turn Christian; nay, live like a hermit, a most strict mortified life. What is all other fire to this but painted fire? *Ejus adesse intolerabile, ejus abesse impossibile;* 'to bear it will be intolerable, to avoid it will be impossible.' And these hell torments are for ever, they have no period put to them. 'They shall seek death, and shall not find it.' Rev ix 6. Origen fancied a fiery stream in which the souls of sinful men were to be purged after this life, and then to pass into heaven; but it is for ever. The breath of the Lord kindles that fire; and where shall we find engines or buckets to quench it? 'And the smoke of their torment ascendeth up for ever and ever, and they have no rest day nor night.' Rev xiv 11. Thank original sin for all.

Use one: What sad thoughts should we have of this primitive original sin, that hath created so many miseries! What honey can be got out of this lion? What grapes can we gather off this thorn? It sets heaven and earth against us. While we choose this bramble to rule, fire comes out of the bramble to devour us.

Use two: How are all believers bound to Jesus Christ, who has freed them from that misery to which sin has exposed them! 'In whom we have redemption through his blood.' Eph i 7. Sin has brought trouble and a curse into the world: Christ has sanctified the trouble, and removed the curse. Nay, he has not only freed believers from misery, but purchased for them a crown of glory and immortality. 'When the chief Shepherd shall appear, ye shall receive a crown of glory that fadeth not away.' 1 Pet v 4.

IV. The covenant of grace and its mediator

1. THE COVENANT OF GRACE

QXX: DID GOD LEAVE ALL MANKIND TO PERISH IN THE ESTATE OF SIN AND MISERY?

A: No! He entered into a covenant of grace to deliver the elect out of that state, and to bring them into a state of grace by a Redeemer.

'I will make an everlasting covenant with you.' Isa lv 3. Man being by his fall plunged into a labyrinth of misery, and having no way left to recover himself, God was pleased to enter into a new covenant with him, and to restore him to life by a Redeemer.

The great proposition I shall go upon is, *that there is a new covenant ratified between God and the elect.*

What is the new covenant?

It is a solemn compact and agreement made between God and fallen man, wherein the Lord undertakes to be our God, and to make us his people.

What names are given to the covenant?

(1.) It is called the covenant of peace in Ezek xxxvii 26, because it seals up reconciliation between God and humble sinners. Before this covenant there was nothing but enmity. God did not love us, for a creature that offends cannot be loved by a holy God; and we did not love him, since a God that condemns cannot be loved by a guilty creature; so that there was war on both sides. But God has found out a way in the new covenant to reconcile differing parties, so that it is fitly called the covenant of peace.

(2.) It is called a covenant of grace, and well it may; for, (i) It was of grace, that, when we had forfeited the first covenant, God should enter into a new one, after we had cast away ourselves. The covenant of grace is *tabula post naufragium*, 'as a plank after shipwreck.' Oh the free grace of God, that he should parley with sinners, and set his wisdom and mercy to work to bring rebels into the bond of the covenant!

[154]

(ii) It is a covenant of grace, because it is a royal charter, all made up of terms of grace; that 'God will cast our sins behind his back;' that 'he will love us freely;' Hos xiv 4; that he will give us a will to accept of the mercy of the covenant, and strength to perform the conditions of the covenant. Ezek xxxvi 27. All this is pure grace.

Why should God make a covenant with us?

It is out of indulgence, favour, and regard to us. A tyrant will not enter into a covenant with slaves, he will not show them such respect. God's entering into a covenant with us, to be our God, is a dignity he puts upon us. A covenant is *insigne honoris*, a note of distinction between God's people and heathens. 'I will establish my covenant with thee.' Ezek xvi 60. When the Lord told Abraham that he would enter into a covenant with him, Abraham fell upon his face, as being amazed that the God of glory should bestow such a favour upon him. Gen xvii 2.

God makes a covenant with us, to tie us fast to him; as it is called in Ezekiel, the 'bond of the covenant.' God knows we have slippery hearts, therefore he will have a covenant to bind·us. It is horrid impiety to go away from God after covenant. If one of the vestal nuns, who had vowed herself to religion, was deflowered, the Romans caused her to be burnt alive. It is perjury to depart from God after solemn covenant.

How does the covenant of grace differ from the first covenant made with Adam?

(1.) The terms of the first covenant were more strict and severe. For, (i) The least failing would have made the covenant with Adam null and void, but many failings do not annul the covenant of grace. I grant, the least sin is a trespass upon the covenant, but it does not make it null and void. There may be many failings in the conjugal relation, but every failing does not break the marriage bond. It would be sad, if, as oft as we break covenant with God he should break covenant with us; but God will not take advantage of every failing, but in 'anger remember mercy.'

(ii) The first covenant being broken, allowed the sinner no remedy, all doors of hope were shut; but the new covenant allows the sinner a remedy: it leaves room for repentance, and provides a mediator. 'Jesus the mediator of the new covenant.' Heb xii 24.

(2.) The first covenant ran all upon 'working,' the second is upon 'believing.' Rom iv 5.

But are not works required in the covenant of grace?

Yes. 'This is a faithful saying, that they which believe in God, be careful to maintain good works.' Tit iii 8. But the covenant of grace does not require works in the same manner as the covenant of works did. In the first covenant, works were required as the condition of life; in the second, they are required only as the signs of life. In the first covenant, works were required as grounds of salvation; in the new covenant, they are required as evidences of our love to God. In the first, they were required to the justification of our persons; in the new, to the manifestation of our grace.

What is the condition of the covenant of grace?

The main condition is faith.

Why is faith more the condition of the new covenant than any other grace?

To exclude all glorying in the creature. Faith is a humble grace. If repentance or works were the condition of the covenant, a man would say, It is my righteousness that has saved me; but if it be of faith, where is boasting? Faith fetches all from Christ, and gives all the glory to Christ; it is a most humble grace. Hence it is that God has singled out this grace to be the condition of the covenant.

If faith be the condition of the covenant of grace, it excludes desperate presumptuous sinners from the covenant. They say there is a covenant of grace, and they shall be saved: but did you ever know a bond without a condition? The condition of the covenant is faith, and if thou hast no faith, thou hast no more to do with the covenant, than a foreigner or a country farmer with the city charter.

Use one: Of information. See the amazing goodness of God, to enter into covenant with us. He never entered into covenant with angels when they fell. It was much condescension in God to enter into covenant with us in a state of innocence, but more so when we were in a state of enmity. In this covenant of grace, we may see the cream of God's love, and the working of his bowels to sinners. This is a marriage covenant. "I am married to you, saith the Lord." Jer iii 14. In the new covenant, God makes himself over to us, and what can he give more? He makes over his promises to us, and what better bonds can we have?

Use two: Of trial. Whether we are in covenant with God. There are three characters.

(1.) God's covenant-people are a humble people. "Be ye clothed with humility." 1 Pet v 5. God's people esteem others better than themselves; they shrink into nothing in their own thoughts. Phil ii 3. David cries out, "I am a worm, and no man:" though a saint, though a king, yet a worm. Ps. xxii 6. When Moses' face shined, he covered it with a veil. When

God's people shine most in grace, they are covered with the veil of humility. Pride excludes from the covenant, for "God resisteth the proud," 1 Pet v 5, and sure such are not in covenant with God whom he resists.

(2.) A people in covenant with God are a willing people; though they cannot serve God perfectly, they serve him willingly. They do not grudge God a little time spent in his worship; they do not hesitate or murmur at sufferings; they will go through a sea and a wilderness, if God call. "Thy people shall be a willing people:' Ps cx 3: 'a people of willingness.' Heb. This spontaneity and willingness is from the attractive power of God's Spirit: the Spirit does not *impellere*, force, but *trahere*, sweetly draws the will; and this willingness in religion makes all our services accepted. God does sometimes accept of willingness without the work, but never the work without willingness.

(3.) God's covenant people are a consecrated people, they have holiness to the Lord written upon them. 'Thou art a holy people to the Lord thy God.' Deut vii 6. God's covenant people are separated from the world, and sanctified by the Spirit. The priests under the law were not only to wash in the great laver, but were arrayed with glorious apparel. Exod xxviii 2. This was typical, to show God's people are not only washed from gross sins, but adorned with holiness of heart: they bear not only God's name, but image. Tamerlane refused a pot of gold, when he saw it had not his father's stamp upon it, but the Roman stamp. Holiness is God's stamp; if he does not see this stamp upon us, he will not own us for his covenant people.

Use three: Of exhortation. To such as are out of covenant, labour to get into covenant, and have God for your God. How glad would the old world have been of an ark! How industrious should we be to get within the ark of the covenant! Consider, (1.) The misery of such as live and die out of covenant with God. Such have none to go to in an hour of distress. When conscience accuses, when sickness approaches (which is but a harbinger to bespeak a lodging for death), then what will you do? Whither will you flee? Will you look to Christ for help? He is a mediator only for such as are in covenant. Oh, how will you be filled with horror and despair! and be as Saul, when he said, 'The Philistines make war against me, and the Lord is departed.' 1 Sam xxviii 15. Till you are in covenant with God, there is no mercy. The mercy-seat was placed upon the ark, and the mercy-seat was no larger than the ark; to show, that the mercy of God reaches no further than the covenant.

(2.) The excellency of the covenant of grace. It is a better covenant than the covenant made with Adam, first because it is more friendly and propitious. Those services which would have been rejected in the first covenant are accepted in the second. Here God accepts of the will for the deed, 2 Cor viii 12; here sincerity is crowned in the covenant of grace; wherein we are weak, God will give strength; and wherein we come short, God will accept of a surety. Secondly it is a better covenant, because it is surer. 'Thou hast made with me an everlasting covenant, ordered in all things, and sure.' 2 Sam xxiii 5. The first covenant was not sure, it stood upon a tottering foundation of works. Adam had no sooner a stock of righteousness to trade with, but he broke; but the covenant of grace is sure; it is confirmed with God's decree, and it rests upon two mighty pillars, the oath of God, and the blood of God. Thirdly it has better privileges. The covenant of grace brings preferment. Our nature now is more ennobled, we are raised to higher glory than in innocence, we are advanced to sit upon Christ's throne. Rev iii 21. We are, by virtue of the covenant of grace, nearer to Christ than the angels: they are his friends, we his spouse. God is willing to be in covenant with you. Why does God woo and beseech you by his ambassadors to be reconciled, if he were not willing to be in covenant?

I would fain be in covenant with God, but I have been a great sinner, and I fear God will not admit me into covenant.

If thou seest thy sins, and loathest thyself for them, God will take thee into covenant. 'Thou hast wearied me with thy iniquities; I, even I, am he that blotteth out thy transgressions.' Isa xliii 24, 25. As the sea covers great rocks, so God's covenant mercy covers great sins. Some of the Jews that crucified Christ had their sins washed away in his blood.

But I am not worthy that God should admit me into covenant.

It never came into God's thoughts to make a new covenant upon terms of worthiness. If God should show mercy to none but such as are worthy, then must he show mercy to none. But it is God's design in the new covenant to advance the riches of grace, to love us freely; and when we have no worthiness of our own, to accept us through Christ's worthiness. Therefore let not unworthiness discourage you; it is not unworthiness that excludes any from the covenant, but unwillingness.

What shall we do that we may be in covenant with God?

(1.) Seek to God by prayer. *Exige a Domino misericordiam* [Demand compassion from the Lord]. Augustine. 'Lord, be my God in covenant.' The Lord has made an express promise, that, upon our prayer to him, the covenant should be ratified, he will be our God, and we shall be his people. 'They shall call upon my name, and I will hear them: I will say,

It is my people: and they shall say, The Lord is my God.' Zech xiii 9. Only it must be an importunate prayer; come as earnest suitors, resolve to take no denial.

(2.) If you would be in covenant with God, break off the covenant with sin. Before the marriage-covenant there must be a divorce. 'If ye return to the Lord with all your hearts, put away the strange gods; and they put away Ashtaroth,' 1 Sam vii 3, viz. their female gods. Will any king enter into covenant with that man who is in league with his enemies?

(3.) If you would enter into the bond of the covenant, get faith in the blood of the covenant. Christ's blood is the blood of atonement; believe in this blood, and you are safely arked in God's mercy. 'Ye are made nigh by the blood of Christ.' Eph ii 13.

Use four: Of comfort to such as can make out their covenant interest in God. (1.) You that are in covenant with God, all your sins are pardoned. Pardon is the crowning mercy. 'Who forgiveth thy iniquity, who crown-eth thee,' &c. Psa ciii 3. This is a branch of the covenant. 'I will be their God, and I will forgive their iniquity,' Jer xxxi 33, 34. Sin being pardoned, all wrath ceases. How terrible is it when but a spark of God's wrath flies into a man's conscience! But sin being forgiven, there is no more wrath. God does not appear now in the fire or earthquake, but covered with a rainbow full of mercy.

(2.) All your temporal mercies are fruits of the covenant. Wicked men have mercies by Providence, not by virtue of a covenant; with God's leave, not with his love. But such as are in covenant have their mercies sweetened with God's love, and they swim to them in the blood of Christ. As Naaman said to Gehazi, 'Take two talents,' 2 Kings v 23, so says God to such as are in covenant, take two talents, take health, and take Christ with it; take riches, and take my love with them; take the venison, and take the blessing with it: take two talents.

(3.) You may upon all occasions plead the covenant. If you are haunted with temptations, plead the covenant. Lord, thou hast promised to bruise Satan under my feet shortly; wilt thou suffer thy child to be thus worried? Take off the roaring lion. If in want, plead the covenant: Lord, thou hast said, 'I shall want no good thing;' wilt thou save me from hell, and not from want? wilt thou give me a kingdom, and deny me daily bread?

(4.) If in covenant with God all things shall co-operate for your good. *Etiam mala cidunt in bonum.* Psa xxv 10. Not only golden paths, but his bloody paths are for good. Every wind of Providence shall blow them nearer heaven. Affliction shall humble and purify. Heb xii 10. Out of the bitterest drug God distils your salvation. Afflictions add to the saints' glory. The more the diamond is cut, the more it sparkles; the heavier the saints' cross is, the heavier shall be their crown.

(5.) If thou art in covenant once, then for ever in covenant. The text calls it an 'everlasting covenant.' Such as are in covenant are elected; and God's electing love is unchangeable. 'I will make an everlasting covenant with them, that I will not turn away from them; but I will put my fear in their heart, that they shall not depart from me.' Jer xxxii 40. God will so love the saints that he will not forsake them; and the saints shall so fear God that they shall not forsake him. It is a covenant of eternity. It must be so; for whom is this covenant made with? Is it not with believers? and have not they coalition and union with Christ? Christ is the head, they are the body. Eph i 22, 23. This is a near union, much like that union between God the Father and Christ. 'As thou, Father, art in me, and I in thee, that they also may be one in us.' John xvii 21. Now, the union between Christ and the saints being so inseparable, it can never be dissolved, or the covenant made void; so that you may die with comfort.

(6.) Thou art in covenant with God, and thou art going to thy God. Behold a death-bed cordial; death breaks the union between the body and the soul, but perfects the union between Christ and the soul. This has made the saints desire death as the bride the wedding-day. Phil i 23. *Cupio dissolvi,* 'Lead me, Lord, to that glory,' said one, 'a glimpse whereof I have seen, as in a glass darkly.'

Use five: Of direction. To show you how you should walk who have tasted of covenant-mercy, live as a people in covenant with God. As you differ from others in respect of dignity, so you must in point of carriage.

(1.) You must love this God. God's love to you calls for love. It is *Amor gratiatus,* a free love. Why should God pass by others, and take you into a league of friendship with himself? In the law, God passed by the lion and eagle, and chose the dove; so he passes by the noble and mighty. It is *Amor plenus,* a full love. When God takes you into covenant, you are his *Hephzibah;* Isa lxii 4; his delight is in you; he gives you the key of all his treasure, he heaps pearls upon you, he settles heaven and earth upon you; he gives you a bunch of grapes by the way, and says, 'Son, all I have is thine.' And does not all this call for love? Who can tread upon these hot coals, and his heart not burn in love to God?

(2.) Walk holily. The covenant has made you a royal nation, therefore be a holy people. Shine as lights in the world; live as earthly angels. God has taken you into covenant, that you and he may have communion together; and what is it that keeps up your communion with God but holiness?

[160]

(3.) Walk thankfully. Psa ciii 1. God is your God in covenant; he has done more for you than if he had made you ride upon the high places of the earth, and given you crowns and sceptres. Oh take the cup of salvation, and bless the Lord! Eternity will be little enough to praise him. Musicians love to play on their music where there is the loudest sound; and God loves to bestow his mercies where he may have the loudest praises. You that have angels' reward, do angels' work. Begin that work of praise here, which you hope to be always doing in heaven.

2. CHRIST THE MEDIATOR OF THE COVENANT

'Jesus the Mediator of the New Covenant,' &c. Heb xii 24.

Jesus Christ is the sum and quintessence of the gospel; the wonder of angels; the joy and triumph of saints. The name of Christ is sweet, it is as music in the ear, honey in the mouth, and a cordial at the heart.

I shall waive the context, and only speak of that which concerns our present purpose. Having discoursed of the covenant of grace, I shall speak now of the Mediator of the covenant, and the restorer of lapsed sinners, 'Jesus the Mediator of the new covenant.'

There are several names and titles in Scripture given to Christ, as the great restorer of mankind: [1] Sometimes he is called a Saviour. 'His name shall be called Jesus.' Matt i 21. The Hebrew word for JESUS signifies a Saviour, and whom he saves from hell he saves from sin; where Christ is a Saviour he is a sanctifier. 'He shall save his people from their sins.' Matt i 21. There is no other saviour. 'Neither is there salvation in any other.' Acts iv 12. As there was but one ark to save the world from drowning, so there is but one Jesus to save sinners from damning. As Naomi said to her daughters-in-law, 'Are there yet any more sons in my womb?' Ruth i 11, so has God any other sons in the womb of his eternal decree, to be saviours to us, besides Christ? Where shall wisdom be found? The depth saith, It is not in me: and the sea saith, It is not with me.' Job xxviii 12, 14. Where shall salvation be found? The angel says, It is not in me; mortality says, It is not in me; the ordinance says, It is not in me. Christ alone is the well-spring of life; the ordinance is the conduit-pipe that conveys salvation, but Christ is the spring that feeds it. 'Neither is there salvation in any other.'

[2] Sometimes Christ is called a Redeemer. 'The Redeemer shall come to Sion.' Isa lix 20. Some understand it of Cyrus, others of an angel; but the most ancient Jewish doctors understood it of Christ, the Redeemer of

the elect. 'My Redeemer liveth.' Job xix 25. The Hebrew word for Redeemer signifies such a one as is near akin, and has right to redeem a mortgage; so Christ is near of kin to us, being our elder brother, therefore has the best right to redeem us.

[3] Christ is called a Mediator in the text. 'Jesus the Mediator of the new covenant.' The Greek word for Mediator signifies a middle person, one that makes up the breach between two disagreeing parties. God and we were at variance by sin, now Christ mediates and becomes umpire between us; he reconciles us to God through his blood, therefore he is called the Mediator of the new covenant. There is no way of communion and intercourse between God and man but in and through a Mediator. Christ takes away the enmity in us, and the wrath of God, and so makes peace. Nor is Christ a Mediator of reconciliation only, but intercession. 'Christ is entered, not into the holy place made with hands, but into heaven itself, now to appear in the presence of God for us.' Heb ix 24. When the priest had slain the sacrifice he was to go with the blood before the altar and mercy-seat, and show it to the Lord. Now, in Christ, our blessed Mediator, consider two things. I. *His person.* II. *His graces.*

I. *His person.* His person is amiable; he is made up of all love and beauty. He is the effigy of his Father. 'The express image of his person.' Heb i 3. Consider,

[1] Christ's person in two natures. (1.) Look upon his human nature as incarnate. The Valentinians deny his human nature; but John i 14 says, 'The Word was made flesh.' It is spoken of Christ the promised Messiah. Christ took our flesh, that the same nature which sinned might suffer; and 'The Word was made flesh,' that through the glass of his human nature we might look upon God.

Why is Christ called the Word?

Because, as a word is the interpreter of the mind, and reveals what is in a man's breast; so Jesus Christ reveals his Father's mind to us concerning the great matters of our salvation. John i 18. Were it not for Christ's manhood, the sight of the Godhead would be formidable to us; but through Christ's flesh we may look upon God without terror. And Christ took our flesh, that he might know how to pity us; he knows what it is to be faint, sorrowful, tempted. 'He knows our frame.' Psa ciii 14. And he took our flesh, that he might (as Augustine says) ennoble our human nature with honour. Christ having married our flesh has exalted it above the angelic nature.

[162]

(2.) Look upon Christ's divine nature. Christ may be fitly compared to Jacob's ladder, which reacheth from earth to heaven. Gen xxviii 12. Christ's human nature was the foot of the ladder, which stood upon earth; his divine nature the top of the ladder, which reaches to heaven. This being a grand article of our faith I shall amplify it. I know the Arians, Socinians, and Ebionites would rob Christ of the best jewel of his crown, his Godhead; but the Apostolical, Nicene, Athanasian creeds, affirm Christ's Deity; and to this the churches of Helvetia, Bohemia, Wittenberg, Transylvania, &c., give their full consent. The Scripture is clear for it. He is called 'the mighty God.' Isa ix 6. 'And in him dwells the fulness of the Godhead.' Col ii 9. He is of the same nature and essence with the Father. So Athanasius, Basil, Chrysostom. Is God the Father called Almighty? So is Christ. 'The Almighty.' Rev i 8. Is God the Father the heart-searcher? So is Christ. 'He knew their thoughts.' John ii 25. Is God the Father omnipresent? So is Christ. 'The Son of Man which is in heaven.' John iii 13. Christ as God was then in heaven, when as man he was upon the earth.

Is Christ eternal?

Christ is the everlasting Father, Isa ix 6, may be urged against the Cerinthian heretics, who denied the pre-existence of Christ's Godhead, and held that Christ had no being till he derived it from the Virgin Mary.

Does divine worship belong to the first person in the Trinity? So it does to Christ. John v 23. 'Let all the angels of God worship him.' Heb i 6. Is creation proper to the Deity? this is a flower of Christ's crown. 'By him were all things created.' Col i 16. Is invocation proper to the Deity? this is given to Christ. 'Lord Jesus, receive my spirit.' Acts vii 59. Is recumbency and trust peculiar to God the Father? this is given to Christ. 'Ye believe in God, believe also in me.' John xiv 1. Christ must needs be God, not only that the divine nature might support the human from sinking under God's wrath, but also to give value and weight to his sufferings.

Christ being God, his death and passion are meritorious. Christ's blood is called *sanguis Dei*, the blood of God, in Acts xx 28, because the person who was offered in sacrifice was God as well as man. This is an invincible support to believers; it was God who was offended, and it was God who satisfied. Thus Christ's person is in two natures.

[2] Consider Christ's two natures in one person, God-man. 'God manifest in the flesh.' 1 Tim iii 16. Christ had a twofold substance, divine and human, yet not a twofold subsistence; both natures make but one Christ.

A scion may be grafted into another tree – a pear-tree into an apple; which, though it bear different fruits, is but one tree; so Christ's manhood is united to the Godhead in an ineffable manner; yet though there are two natures, yet but one person. This union of the two natures in Christ was not by transmutation, the divine nature changed into the human, or the human into the divine; nor by mixture, the two natures mingled together, as wine and water are mixed; but both the natures of Christ remain distinct, and yet make not two distinct persons, but one person; the human nature not God, yet one with God.

II. *Consider Christ, our Mediator, in his graces.* These are the sweet savour of his ointments, that make the virgins love him. Christ, our blessed Mediator, is said to be 'full of grace and truth.' John i 14. He had the anointing of the Spirit without measure. John iii 34. Grace in Christ is after a more eminent and glorious manner than it is in any of the saints.

[1] Jesus Christ, our Mediator, has perfection in every grace. Col i 19. He is a panoply, magazine and storehouse of all heavenly treasure, all fulness. This no saint on earth has; he may excel in one grace, but not in all; as Abraham was eminent for faith, Moses for meekness; but Christ excels in every grace.

[2] There is a never-failing fulness of grace in Christ. Grace in the saints is ebbing and flowing, it is not always in the same degree and proportion; at one time David's faith was strong, at another time so faint and weak, that you could hardly feel any pulse. 'I said, I am cut off from before thine eyes.' Psalm xxxi 22. But grace in Christ is a never-failing fulness, it never abated in the least degree, he never lost a drop of his holiness. What was said of Joseph in Gen xlix 23, may more truly be applied to Christ. 'The archers shot at him, but his bow abode in strength.' Men and devils shot at him, but his grace remained in its full vigour and strength; 'his bow abode in strength.'

[3] Grace in Christ is communicative. His grace is for us; the holy oil of the Spirit was poured on the head of this blessed Aaron, that it might run down upon us. The saints have not grace to bestow on others. When the foolish virgins would have bought oil of their neighbour virgins, saying, 'Give us of your oil, for our lamps are gone out,' Matt xxv 8, the wise virgins answered, 'Not so, lest there be not enough for us and you.' The saints have no grace to spare for others; but Christ diffuses his grace to others. Grace in the saints is as water in the vessel, grace in Christ is as water in the spring. 'Of his fulness have all we received and grace for grace.' John i 16. Set a glass under a still and it receives water from it,

[164]

drop by drop; so the saints have the drops and influences of Christ's grace distilling upon them. What a rich consolation is this to those who either have no grace, or their stock is low! They may go to Christ, the Mediator, as a treasury of grace: Lord, I am indigent; but whither shall I carry my empty vessel, but to a full fountain? 'All my springs are in thee.' Psa lxxxvii 7. I am guilty, thou hast blood to pardon me; I am polluted, thou hast grace to cleanse me; I am sick unto death, thou hast the balm of Gilead to heal me. Joseph opened all the storehouses of corn: Christ is our Joseph, that opens all the treasuries and storehouses of grace, and communicates to us. He is not only sweet as the honey-comb, but drops as the honey-comb. In Christ our Mediator there is a cornucopia, and fulness of all grace; and Christ is desirous that we should come to him for grace, like the full breast that aches till it be drawn.

Use one: Admire the glory of this Mediator; he is God-man, he is co-essentially glorious with the Father. All the Jews that saw Christ in the flesh, did not see his Godhead; all that saw the man did not see the Messiah. The temple of Solomon within was embellished with gold; travellers, as they passed along, might see the outside of the temple, but only the priests saw the glory which sparkled within the temple; so believers only, who are made priests unto God, see Christ's glorious inside, the Godhead shining through the manhood. Rev i 16.

Use two: If Christ be God-man in one person, then look unto Jesus Christ alone for salvation. There must be something of the Godhead to fasten our hope upon; in Christ there is Godhead and manhood hypostatically united. If we could weep rivers of tears, out-fast Moses on the mount, if we were exact moralists, touching the law blameless, if we could arrive at the highest degree of sanctification in this life, all this would not save us, without looking to the merits of him who is God. Our perfect holiness in heaven is not the cause of our salvation, but the righteousness of Jesus Christ. To this therefore did Paul flee, as to the horns of the altar. 'That I may be found in him, not having my own righteousness.' Phil iii 9. It is true, we may look to our graces as evidences of salvation, but to Christ's blood only as the cause. In time of Noah's flood, all that trusted to the high hills and trees, and not to the ark, were drowned. 'Looking unto Jesus;' and so look unto him, as to believe in him, that so Christ may not only be united to our nature, but to our persons. Heb xii 2. 'That believing, you may have life through his name.' John xx 31.

Use three: Is Jesus Christ God and man in one person? This, as it shows the dignity of believers, that they are nearly related to one of the greatest persons that is, 'In him dwells the fulness of the Godhead bodily,' so it is

[165]

of unspeakable comfort. Col ii 9. Christ's two natures being married together, the divine and human, all that Christ in either of his natures can do for believers, he will do. In his human nature he prays for them, in his divine nature he merits for them.

Use four: Admire the love of Christ our Mediator; that he should humble himself, and take our flesh, that he might redeem us. Believers should put Christ in their bosom, as the spouse did. 'Lie betwixt my breasts.' Cant i 13. What was said of Ignatius, that the name of Jesus was found written in his heart, should be verified of every saint; he should have Jesus Christ written in his heart.

3. CHRIST'S PROPHETIC OFFICE

'*The Lord thy God will raise up unto thee a Prophet,*' &c. Deut xviii 15.

Having spoken of the person of Christ, we are next to speak of the offices of Christ. These are Prophetic, Priestly, and Regal.

'The Lord thy God will raise up unto thee a Prophet.' *Enunciatur hic locus de Christo.* 'It is spoken of Christ.' There are several names given to Christ as a Prophet. He is called 'the Counsellor' in Isa ix 6. *In uno Christo Angelus fœderis completur* [The Messenger of the Covenant appears in Christ alone]. Fagius. 'The Angel of the covenant.' Mal iii 1. 'A Lamp.' 2 Sam xxii 19. 'The Morning Star.' Rev xxii 16. Jesus Christ is the great Prophet of his church. The woman of Samaria gave a shrewd guess. John iv 19. He is the best teacher; he makes all other teaching effectual. 'Then opened he their understanding.' Luke xxiv 45. He not only opened the Scriptures, but opened their understanding. He teaches to profit. 'I am the Lord thy God, who teacheth thee to profit.' Isa xlviii 17.

How does Christ teach?

(1.) Externally, by his Word. 'Thy word is a lamp to my feet.' Psa cxix 105. Such as pretend to have a light or revelation above the Word, or contrary to it, never had their teaching from Christ. Isa viii 20.

(2.) Christ teaches these sacred mysteries, inwardly, by the Spirit. John xvi 13. The world knows not what it is. 'The natural man receives not the things of God, neither can he know them.' 1 Cor ii 14. He knows not what it is to be transformed by the renewing of the mind, Rom xii 2, or what the inward workings of the Spirit mean; these are riddles and paradoxes to him. He may have more insight into the things of the world than a believer, but he does not see the deep things of God. A swine may see an acorn under a tree, but he cannot see a star. He who is taught of Christ sees the *arcana imperii* [state secrets], the secrets of the kingdom of heaven.

What are the lessons which Christ teaches?

He teaches us to see into our own hearts. Take the most mercurial wits, the greatest politicians, that understand the mysteries of state, they know not the mysteries of their own hearts, they cannot believe the evil that is in them. 'Is thy servant a dog?' 2 Kings viii 13. *Grande profundum est homo.* Augustine. The heart is a great deep, which is not easily fathomed. But when Christ teaches he removes the veil of ignorance, and lights a man into his own heart; and now that he sees swarms of vain thoughts, he blushes to see how sin mingles with his duties, his stars are mixed with clouds; he prays, as Augustine, that God would deliver him from himself.

The second lesson Christ teaches is the vanity of the creature. A natural man sets up his happiness here, and worships the golden image; but he that Christ has anointed with his eye-salve has a spirit of discerning; he looks upon the creature in its night-dress, sees it to be empty and unsatisfying, and not commensurate to a heaven-born soul. Solomon had put all the creatures into a still, and when he came to extract the spirit and quintessence, all was vanity. Eccles ii 11. The apostle calls it a show or apparition, having no intrinsic goodness. 1 Cor vii 31.

The third lesson is the excellency of things unseen. Christ gives the soul a sight of glory, a prospect of eternity. 'We look not at things which are seen, but at things which are not seen.' 2 Cor iv 18. Moses saw him who is 'invisible.' Heb xi 27. And the patriarchs saw a better country, viz. an heavenly, where are delights of angels, rivers of pleasure, the flower of joy, fully ripe and blown. Heb xi 16.

How does Christ's teaching differ from other teaching?

Several ways.

(1.) Christ teaches the heart. Others may teach the ear, Christ the heart. 'Whose heart the Lord opened.' Acts xvi 14. All that the dispensers of the word can do is but to work knowledge, Christ works grace: they can but give the light of the truth; Christ gives the love of the truth; they can only teach what to believe, Christ teaches how to believe.

(2.) Christ gives us a taste of the word. Ministers may set the food of the word before you, and carve it out to you; but it is only Christ can cause you to taste it. 'If so be ye have tasted that the Lord is gracious.' 1 Pet ii 3. 'Taste and see that the Lord is good.' Psa xxxiv 8. It is one thing to hear a truth preached, another thing to taste it; one thing to read a promise, another thing to taste it. David had got a taste of the word. 'Thou hast taught me: How sweet are thy words unto my taste! yea, sweeter than honey to my mouth.' Psalm cxix 102, 103. The apostle calls it the savour of knowledge. 2 Cor ii 14. The light of knowledge is one thing, the savour another. Christ makes us taste a savouriness in the word.

(3.) When Christ teaches, he makes us obey. Others may instruct, but cannot command obedience: they teach to be humble, but men remain proud. The prophet had been denouncing judgments against the people of Judah, but they would not hear. 'We will do whatsoever goeth out of our own mouth, to burn incense unto the queen of heaven.' Jer xliv 17. Men come as it were, armed in a coat of mail that the sword of the word will not enter; but when Christ comes to teach, he removes this obstinacy; he not only informs the judgment, but inclines the will. He does not only come with the light of his word, but the rod of his strength, and makes the stubborn sinner yield to him. His grace is irresistible.

(4.) Christ teaches easily. Others teach with difficulty. They have difficulty in finding out a truth, and in inculcating it. 'Precept *must be* upon precept, and line upon line.' Isa xxviii 10. Some may teach all their lives, and the word take no impression. They complain, 'I have spent my labour in vain;' Isa xlix 4, plowed on rocks; but Christ the great Prophet teaches with ease. He can with the least touch of his Spirit convert: he can say, 'Let there be light;' with a word he can convey grace.

(5.) When Christ teaches he makes men willing to learn. Men may teach others, but they have no mind to learn. 'Fools despise instruction.' Prov i 7. They rage at the word, as if a patient should rage at the physician when he brings him a cordial; thus backward are men to their own salvation. But Christ makes his people a 'willing people.' Psa cx 3. They prize knowledge, and hang it as a jewel upon their ear. Those that Christ teaches say, as Isa ii 3, 'Come let us go up to the mountains of the Lord, and he will teach us of his ways, and we will walk in them;' and as Acts x 33; 'We are all here present before God, to hear all things commanded.'

(6.) When Christ teaches, he not only illuminates but animates. He so teaches, that he quickens. 'I am the light of the world: he that follows me shall have *lumen vitæ*, the light of life.' John viii 12. By nature we are dead, therefore unfit for teaching. Who will make an oration to the dead? But Christ teaches them that are dead! he gives the light of life. As when Lazarus was dead, Christ said, 'Come forth,' and he made the dead to hear, for Lazarus came forth: so when he says to the dead soul, Come forth of the grave of unbelief, he hears Christ's voice, and comes forth, it is the light of life. The philosophers say, *calor et lux concrescunt*, 'heat and light increase together.' Where Christ comes with his light, there is the heat of spiritual life going along with it.

Use one: Of information. (1.) See here an argument of Christ's Divinity. Had he not been God, he could never have known the mind of God, or revealed to us those *arcana cæli* [the secrets of Heaven], those deep mysteries, which no man or angel could find out. Who but God can anoint the eyes of the blind, and give not only light, but sight? Who but he, who has the key of David, can open the heart? Who but God can bow the iron sinew of the will? He only who is God can enlighten the conscience, and make the stony heart bleed.

(2.) See what a *cornucopia*, or plenty of wisdom is in Christ, who is the great doctor of his church, and gives saving knowledge to all the elect. The body of the sun must needs be full of clearness and brightness, which enlightens the whole world. Christ is the great luminary; in him are hid all treasures of knowledge. Col ii 3. The middle lamp of the sanctuary gave light to all the other lamps; so Christ diffuses his glorious light to others. We are apt to admire the learning of Aristotle and Plato; alas! what is this poor spark of light to that which is in Christ, from whose infinite wisdom both men and angels light their lamps.

(3.) See the misery of man in the state of nature. Before Christ becomes their prophet they are enveloped in ignorance and darkness. Men know nothing in a sanctified manner, they know nothing as they ought to know. 1 Cor viii 2. This is sad. Men in the dark cannot discern colours; so in the state of nature they cannot discern between morality and grace; they take one for the other, *pro dea nubem* [They mistake the cloud for the goddess herself]. In the dark the greatest beauty is hid. Let there be rare flowers in the garden, and pictures in the room, in the dark their beauty is veiled over; so, though there be such transcendent beauty in Christ as amazes the angels, man in the state of nature sees none of this beauty. What is Christ to him? or heaven to him? The veil is upon his heart. A man in the dark is in danger every step he takes; so man in the state of nature is in danger, at every step, of falling into hell. Thus it is before Christ teaches us; nay, the darkness in which a sinner is, while in an unregenerate state, is worse than natural darkness; for natural darkness affrights. 'An horror of great darkness fell upon Abraham.' Gen xv 12. But the spiritual darkness is not accompanied with horror, men tremble not at their condition; nay, they like their condition well enough. 'Men loved darkness.' John iii 19. This is their sad condition, till Jesus Christ comes as a prophet to teach them, and to turn them from darkness to light, and from the power of Satan to God.

[169]

(4.) See the happy condition of the children of God. They have Christ to be their prophet. 'All thy children shall be taught of the Lord.' Isa liv 13. 'He is made to us wisdom.' 1 Cor i 30. One man cannot see by another's eyes; but believers see with Christ's eyes. 'In his light they see light.' Christ gives them the light of grace and the light of glory.

Use two: Labour to have Christ for your prophet. He teaches savingly: he is an interpreter of a thousand, he can untie those knots which puzzle angels. Till Christ teach, we never learn any lesson; till Christ is made to us wisdom, we shall never be wise to salvation.

What shall we do to have Christ for our teacher?

(1.) See your need of Christ's teaching. You cannot see your way without this morning star. Some speak much of the light of reason improved: alas! the plumb-line of reason is too short to fathom the deep things of God; the light of reason will no more help a man to believe, than the light of a candle will help him to understand. A man can no more by the power of nature reach Christ, than an infant can reach the top of the pyramids, or the ostrich fly up to the stars. See your need of Christ's anointing and teaching in Rev iii 18.

(2.) Go to Christ to teach you. 'Lead me in thy truth, and teach me.' Psa xxv 5. As one of the disciples said, 'Lord, teach us to pray,' Luke xi 1, so say, Lord, teach me to profit. Do thou light my lamp, O thou great prophet of thy church! Give me a spirit of wisdom and revelation, that I may see things in another manner than I ever saw them before; teach me in the word to hear thy voice, and in the sacrament to discern thy body. 'Lighten mine eyes,' &c. Psa xiii 3. *Cathedram habet in cœlo qui corda docet in terra.* Augustine. 'He has his pulpit in heaven who converts souls.' That we may be encouraged to go to our great Prophet:

(i) Jesus Christ is very willing to teach us. Why else did he enter into the calling of the ministry, but to teach the mysteries of heaven? 'Jesus went about teaching and preaching the gospel of the kingdom, and healing all manner of sickness and all manner of disease among the people.' Matt iv 23. Why did he take the prophetic office upon him? Why was Christ so angry with them that kept away the key of knowledge? Luke xi 52. Why was Christ anointed with the Spirit without measure, but that he might anoint us with knowledge? Knowledge is in Christ for us as milk in the breast for the child. Oh then go to Christ for teaching. None in the gospel came to Christ for sight, but he restored their eyesight; and sure Christ is more willing to work a cure upon a blind soul than ever he was to do so upon a blind body.

(ii) There are none so dull and ignorant but Christ can teach them,

Every one is not fit to make a scholar of; *ex omni ligno non fit Mercurius;* but there is none so dull but Christ can make him a good scholar. Even such as are ignorant, and of low parts, Christ teaches in such a manner that they know more than the great sages and wise men of the world. Hence that saying of Augustine, *surgunt indocti, et rapiunt cœlum;* the un-learned men rise up, and take heaven; they know the truths of Christ more savingly than the great admired Rabbis. The duller the scholar the more is his skill seen that teaches. Hence it is, that Christ delights in teaching the ignorant, to get himself more glory. 'The eyes of the blind shall be opened, and the ears of the deaf shall be unstopped.' Isa xxxv 5. Who would go to teach a blind or a deaf man? Yet such dull scholars Christ teaches. Such as are blinded with ignorance shall see the mysteries of the gospel, and the deaf ears shall be unstopped.

(3.) Wait upon the means of grace which Christ has appointed. Though Christ teaches by his Spirit, yet he teaches in the use of ordinances. Wait at the gates of wisdom's door. Ministers are teachers under Christ. 'Pastors and teachers.' Eph iv 11. We read of pitchers, and lamps within the pitchers. Judges vii 16. Ministers are earthen vessels, but these pitchers have lamps within them to light souls to heaven. Christ is said to speak to us from heaven now, by his ministers, as the king speaks by his am-bassador. Heb xii 25. Such as wean themselves from the breast of ordin-ances seldom thrive; either they grow light in their head, or lame in their feet. The word preached is Christ's voice in the mouth of the minister; and those that refuse to hear Christ speaking in the ministry, Christ will refuse to hear speaking on their death-bed.

(4.) If you would have the teachings of Christ, walk according to the knowledge which you have already. Use your little knowledge well, and Christ will teach you more. 'If any man will do his will, he shall know of the doctrine, whether it be of God, or whether I speak of myself.' John vii 17. A master seeing his servant improve a little stock well gives him more to trade with.

Use three: If you have been taught by Christ savingly, be thankful. It is your honour to have God for your teacher, and that he should teach you, and not others, is a matter of admiration and congratulation. Oh how many knowing men are ignorant! They are not taught of God; they have Christ's Word to enlighten them, but not his Spirit to sanctify them. But that you should have the inward as well as the outward teaching, that Christ should anoint you with the heavenly unction of his Spirit, that you can say, as he in John ix 25, 'One thing I know, that whereas I was blind, now I see.' Oh, how thankful should you be to Christ, who has revealed his Father's bosom secrets unto you! 'No man hath seen God at any time; the only begotten Son, which is in the bosom of the Father, he hath declared him.' John i 18. If Alexander thought himself so much obliged to Aristotle for the philosophic instruction he received from him, oh, how are we obliged to Jesus Christ, this great Prophet, for opening to us the eternal purposes of his love, and revealing to us the mysteries of the kingdom of heaven!

4. CHRIST'S PRIESTLY OFFICE

Qxxv: HOW DOES CHRIST EXECUTE THE OFFICE OF A PRIEST?

A: In his once offering up of himself a sacrifice to satisfy divine justice, and reconcile us to God, and in making continual intercession for us.

'Now once in the end of the world hath he appeared to put away sin by the sacrifice of himself.' Heb ix 26.

What are the parts of Christ's priestly office?

Christ's priestly office has two parts—his satisfaction and intercession.

I. *His Satisfaction;* and this consists of two branches. [1] His active obedience. 'He fulfilled all righteousness.' Matt iii 15. Christ did everything which the law required; his holy life was a perfect commentary upon the law of God; and he obeyed the law for us.

[2] His passive obedience. Our guilt being transferred and imputed to him, he suffered the penalty which was due to us; he appeared to put away sin by the sacrifice of himself. The paschal lamb slain was a type of Christ who was offered up in sacrifice for us. Sin could not be done away without blood. 'Without blood is no remission.' Heb ix 22. Christ was not only a lamb without spot, but a lamb slain.

Why was it requisite there should be a priest?

There needed a priest to be an umpire, to mediate between a guilty creature and a holy God.

How could Christ suffer, being God?

Christ suffered only in the human nature.

But if only Christ's humanity suffered, how could this suffering satisfy for sin?

The human nature being united to the divine, the human nature suffered, the divine satisfied. Christ's Godhead supported the human nature that it did not faint, and gave virtue to his sufferings. The altar sanctifies the thing offered on it. Matt xxiii 19. The altar of Christ's divine nature sanctified the sacrifice of his death, and made it of infinite value.

Wherein does the greatness of Christ's sufferings appear?

(1.) In the sufferings of his body. He suffered truly, not in appearance only. The apostle calls it *mors crucis*, the death of the cross. Phil ii 8. Cicero, when speaking of this kind of death, says, *quid dicam in crucem tollere?* [How can I describe being raised up on a cross?] Though he was a great orator he wanted words to express it. The thoughts of this made Christ sweat great drops of blood in the garden. Luke xxii 44. It was an ignominious, painful, cursed death. Christ suffered in all his senses. His eyes beheld two sad objects, his enemies insulting, and his mother weeping. His ears were filled with the revilings of the people. 'He saved others, himself he cannot save.' Matt xxvii 42. His smell was offended when their spittle fell upon his face. His taste; when they gave him gall and vinegar to drink. His feeling; when his head suffered with thorns, his hands and feet with the nails. *Totum pro vulnere corpus* [His whole body one great wound]; now was this white lily dyed with purple colour.

(2.) In the sufferings of his soul. He was pressed in the wine-press of his Father's wrath. This caused that vociferation and outcry on the cross, 'My God, my God,' *cur deseruisti?* Christ suffered a double eclipse upon the cross, an eclipse of the sun, and an eclipse of the light of God's countenance. How bitter was this agony! The evangelists use three words to express it. 'He began to be amazed.' 'He began to be faint.' 'To be exceeding sorrowful' Mark xiv 33; Matt xxvi 38. Christ felt the pains of hell in his soul, though not locally, yet equivalently.

Why did Christ suffer?

Surely not for any desert of his own. 'The Messiah shall be cut off, but not for himself,' it was for us. Dan ix 26; Isa liii 6. *Unus peccat, alius plectitur* [One man sins, another takes the punishment]; he suffered, that he might satisfy God's justice for us. We, by our sins, had infinitely wronged God; and, could we have shed rivers of tears, offered up millions of holocausts and burnt-offerings, we could never have pacified an angry Deity; therefore Christ must die, that God's justice may be satisfied.

It is hotly debated among divines, whether God could have forgiven sin freely without a sacrifice. Not to dispute what God could have done,

[173]

when he was resolved to have the law satisfied, and to have man saved in a way of justice as well as mercy; it was necessary that Christ should lay down his life as a sacrifice.

(1.) To fulfil the predictions of Scripture. 'Thus it behoved Christ to suffer.' Luke xxiv 46.

(2.) To bring us into favour with God. It is one thing for a traitor to be pardoned, and another thing to be made a favourite. Christ's blood is not only called a sacrifice, whereby God is appeased, but a propitiation, whereby God becomes gracious and friendly to us. Christ is our mercy-seat, from which God gives answers of peace to us.

(3.) Christ died, that he might make good his last will and testament with his blood. There were many legacies which Christ bequeathed to believers, which had been all null and void had he not died, and by his death confirmed the will. Heb ix 16. A testament is in force after men are dead; the mission of the Spirit, the promises, those legacies, were not in force till Christ's death; but Christ by his blood has sealed them, and believers may lay claim to them.

(4.) He died that he might purchase for us glorious mansions; therefore heaven is called not only a promised, but a 'purchased possession.' Eph i 14. Christ died for our preferment; he suffered that we might reign; he hung upon the cross that we might sit upon the throne. Heaven was shut, &c. *crux Christi, clavis Paradisi:* the cross of Christ is the ladder by which we ascend to heaven. His crucifixion is our coronation.

Use one: In the bloody sacrifice of Christ, see the horrid nature of sin. Sin, it is true, is odious as it banished Adam out of paradise, and threw the angels into hell; but that which most of all makes it appear horrid is this, that it made Christ veil his glory, and lose his blood. We should look upon sin with indignation, and pursue it with a holy malice, and shed the blood of those sins which shed Christ's blood. The sight of Cæsar's bloody robe incensed the Romans against them that slew him. The sight of Christ's bleeding body should incense us against sin. Let us not parley with it; let not that be our joy, which made Christ a man of sorrow.

Use two: Is Christ our priest sacrificed? See God's mercy and justice displayed. I may say as the apostle, 'Behold the goodness and severity of God.' Rom xi 22.

(1.) The goodness of God in providing a sacrifice. Had not Christ suffered upon the cross, we must have lain in hell for ever, satisfying God's justice.

(2.) The severity of God. Though it were his own Son, the Son of his love, and our sins were but imputed to him, yet God did not spare him, but his wrath did flame against him. Rom viii 32. If God was thus severe to his own Son, how dreadful will he be one day to his enemies! Such as die in wilful impenitence, must feel the same wrath as Christ did; and because they cannot bear it at once, therefore they must endure it for ever.

Use three: Is Christ our priest, who was sacrificed for us? Then see the endeared affection of Christ to us sinners. 'The cross,' says Augustine, 'was a pulpit, in which Christ preached his love to the world.' That Christ should die, was more than if all the angels had been turned to dust; and especially that Christ should die as a malefactor, having the weight of all men's sins laid upon him, and that he should die for his enemies. Rom v 10. The balm-tree weeps out its precious balm, to heal those that cut and mangle it; so Christ shed his blood, to heal those that crucified him. He died freely. It is called the offering of the body of Jesus. Heb x 10. Though his sufferings were so great, that they made him sigh, and weep, and bleed; yet they could not make him repent. 'He shall see of the travail of his soul, and be satisfied.' Isa liii 11. Christ had hard travail upon the cross, yet he does not repent of it, but thinks his sweat and blood well bestowed, because he sees redemption brought forth to the world. Oh infinite, amazing love of Christ! a love that passeth knowledge! that neither man nor angel can parallel. Eph iii 19. How should we be affected with this love! If Saul was so affected with David's kindness in sparing his life, how should we be affected with Christ's kindness in parting with his life for us! At Christ's death and passion, the very stones cleave asunder, 'The rocks rent.' Matt xxvii 51. Not to be affected with Christ's love in dying, is to have hearts harder than rocks.

Use four: Is Christ our sacrifice? Then see the excellence of his sacrifice.

(1.) It is perfect. 'By one offering, he hath perfected them that are sanctified.' Heb x 14. Therefore, how impious are the Papists, in joining their merits and the prayers of saints with Christ's sacrifice! They offer him up daily in the mass, as if Christ's sacrifice on the cross were imperfect. This is a blasphemy against Christ's priestly office.

(2.) Christ's sacrifice is meritorious. He not only died for our example, but to merit salvation. The person who suffered being God as well as man, put virtue into his sufferings; and our sins were expiated, and God appeased. No sooner did the messengers say, 'Uriah is dead,' but David's anger was pacified. 2 Sam xi 21. No sooner did Christ die, but God's anger was pacified.

(3.) This sacrifice is beneficial. Out of the dead lion Samson had honey. It procures justification of our persons, acceptance of our service, access to God with boldness, and entrance into the holy place of heaven. Heb x 19. *Per latus Christi patescit nobis in cælum* [Through the side of Christ a way to Heaven lies open to us]. Israel passed through the Red sea to Canaan; so through the red sea of Christ's blood, we enter into the heavenly Canaan.

Use five: (1.) Let us apply this blood of Christ. All the virtue of a medicine is in the application; though the medicine be made of the blood of God, it will not heal, unless applied by faith. As fire is to the chemist, so is faith to the Christian; the chemist can do nothing without fire, so there is nothing done without faith. Faith makes Christ's sacrifice ours. 'Christ Jesus my Lord.' Phil iii 8. It is not gold in the mine that enriches, but gold in the hand. Faith is the hand that receives Christ's golden merits. It is not a cordial in the glass that refreshes the spirit, but a cordial drunk down. *Per fidem Christi sanguinem sugimus* [By faith we drink the blood of Christ], Cyprian. Faith opens the orifice of Christ's wounds, and drinks the precious cordial of his blood. Without faith Christ himself will not avail us.

(2.) Let us love a bleeding Saviour, and let us show our love to Christ, by being ready to suffer for him. Many rejoice at Christ's suffering for them, but dream not of their suffering for him. Joseph dreamed of his preferment, but not of his imprisonment. Was Christ a sacrifice? Did he bear God's wrath for us? We should bear man's wrath for him. Christ's death was voluntary. 'Lo, I come to do thy will, O God.' Heb x 7. 'I have a baptism to be baptized with, and how am I straitened till it be accomplished!' Luke xii 50. Christ calls his sufferings a baptism; he was to be (as it were) baptized in his own blood; and how did he thirst for that time! 'How am I straitened!' Oh then, let us be willing to suffer for Christ! Christ has taken away the venom and sting of the saints' sufferings: there is no wrath in their cup. Our sufferings Christ can make sweet. As there was oil mixed in the peace-offering, so God can mix the oil of gladness with our sufferings. 'The ringing of my chain is sweet music in my ears.' *Landgrave of Hesse.* Life must be parted with shortly; what is it to part with it a little sooner, as a sacrifice to Christ, as a seal of sincerity, and a pledge of thankfulness!

Use six: This sacrifice of Christ's blood may infinitely comfort us. This is the blood of atonement. Christ's cross is *cardo salutis* [the hinge of our deliverance], Calvin; the hinge and fountain of our comfort. (1.) This blood comforts in case of guilt! Oh, says the soul, my sins trouble me, but Christ's blood was shed for the remission of sin. Matt xxvi 28. Let us see our sins laid on Christ, and then they are no more ours but his. (2.) In case of pollution. Christ's blood is a healing and cleansing blood. It is healing. 'With his stripes we are healed.' Isa liii 5. It is the best weapon-salve, it heals at a distance. Though Christ be in heaven, we may feel the virtue of his blood healing our bloody issue. And it is cleansing. It is therefore compared to fountain-water. Zech xiii 1. The word is a glass to show us our spots, and Christ's blood is a fountain to wash them away; it turns leprosy into purity. 'The blood of Jesus cleanseth us from all our sin.' 1 John i 7. There is indeed one spot so black, that Christ's blood does not wash away, viz. the sin against the Holy Ghost. Not but that there is virtue enough in Christ's blood to wash it away; but he who has sinned that sin will not be washed; he contemns Christ's blood, and tramples it under foot. Heb x 29. Thus we see what a strong cordial Christ's blood is; it is the anchor-hold of our faith, the spring of our joy, the crown of our desires, and the only support both in life and death. In all our fears, let us comfort ourselves with the propitiatory sacrifice of Christ's blood. Christ died both as a purchaser and as a conqueror: as a purchaser in regard of God, having by his blood obtained our salvation, and as a conqueror in regard of Satan, the cross being his triumphant chariot, wherein he has led hell and death captive.

Use seven: Bless God for this precious sacrifice of Christ's death. 'Bless the Lord, O my soul.' Psa ciii 1. And for what does David bless him? 'Who redeemeth thy life from destruction!' Christ gave himself a sin-offering for us; let us give ourselves a thank-offering to him. If a man redeem another out of debt, will he not be grateful? How deeply do we stand obliged to Christ, who has redeemed us from hell and damnation! 'And they sung a new song, saying Thou art worthy to take the book, and open the seals; for thou wast slain, and hast redeemed us to God by thy blood.' Rev v 9. Let our hearts and tongues join in concert to bless God, and let us show thankfulness to Christ by fruitfulness; let us bring forth (as spice trees) the fruits of humility, zeal, and good works. This is to live unto him who died for us. 2 Cor v 15. The wise men not only worshipped Christ, but presented him with gifts; gold, and frankincense, and myrrh. Matt ii 11. Let us present Christ with the fruits of righteousness, which are unto the glory and praise of God.

II. *His Intercession.* 'Who also maketh intercession for us.' Rom viii 34.

When Aaron entered into the holy place, his bells gave a sound; so Christ having entered into heaven, his intercession makes a melodious sound in the ears of God. Though Christ be exalted to glory, he has not laid aside his bowels of compassion, but is still mindful of his mystic body, as Joseph was mindful of his father and brethren, when he was exalted to the court. 'Who also maketh intercession for us.' To intercede is to make request in behalf of another. Christ is the great Master of requests in heaven. *Christus est catholicus Patris Sacerdos* [Christ is the universal Priest of the Father]. Tertullian.

What are the qualifications of our intercessor?

(1.) He is holy. 'For such an high priest became us, who is holy, undefiled, separated from sinners.' Heb vii 26. 'Christ knew no sin.' 2 Cor v 21. He knew sin in its weight, not in the act. It was requisite, that he, who was to do away the sins of others, should himself be without sin. Holiness is one of the precious stones which shine on the breast-plate of our high priest.

(2.) He is faithful. 'It behoved him to be like unto his brethren, that he might be a faithful high priest.' Heb ii 17. Moses was faithful as a servant, Christ as a Son. Heb iii 5. He does not forget any cause he has to plead, nor does he use any deceit in pleading. An ordinary attorney may leave out some word which might make for the client, or put in a word against him, having received a fee on both sides; but Christ is true to the cause he pleads. We may leave our matters with him, we may trust our lives and souls in his hand.

(3.) He never dies. While the office of the priests under the law lived, they themselves died. 'They were not suffered to continue, by reason of death.' Heb vii 23. But 'Christ ever lives to make intercession.' Heb vii 25. He has no succession in his priesthood.

Whom does Christ intercede for?

Not for all promiscuously, but for the elect. John xvii 9. The efficacy of Christ's prayer reaches no further than the efficacy of his blood; but his blood was shed only for the elect, therefore his prayers reach them only. The high priest went into the sanctuary with the names of the twelve tribes only upon his breast: so Christ goes into heaven with the names of the elect only upon his breast. Christ intercedes for the weakest believers, and for all the sins of believers. John xvii 20. In the law there were some sins for which the high priest was neither to offer sacrifice, nor prayer. 'The soul that doeth ought presumptuously shall be cut off.' Numb xv 30. The priest might offer up prayers for sins of ignorance, but not of presumption; but Christ's intercession extends to all the sins of the elect. Of what a bloody colour was David's sin; yet it did not exclude him from Christ's intercession.

What does Christ in the work of intercession?

Three things.

(1.) He presents the merit of his blood to his Father, and, in the virtue of that price paid, pleads for mercy. The high priest was herein a lively type of Christ. Aaron was to do four things. Kill the beasts. Enter with the blood into the holy of holies. Sprinkle the mercy-seat with the blood. Kindle the incense, and with the smoke of it cause a cloud to arise over the mercy-seat; and thus atonement was made. Lev xvi 11-16. Christ our high priest exactly answered to this type. He was offered up in sacrifice, which answers to the priest's killing the bullock; and he is gone up into heaven, which answers to the priest's going into the holy of holies; and he spreads his blood before his Father which answers to the priest's sprinkling the blood upon the mercy-seat; and he prays to his Father, that for his blood's sake, he would be propitious to sinners, which answers to the cloud of incense going up; and through his intercessions God is pacified, which answers to the priest's making atonement.

(2.) Christ by his intercession answers all bills of indictment brought in against the elect. Do what they can, sin, and then Satan, accuses believers to God, and conscience accuses them to themselves; but Christ, by his intercession, answers all these accusations. 'Who shall lay anything to the charge of God's elect? it is Christ that maketh intercession for us.' Rom viii 33, 34. When Esculus was accused for some impiety, his brother stood up for him, and showed the magistrates how he had lost his hand in the service of the state, and so obtained his pardon: thus, when Satan accuses the saints, or when the justice of God lays anything to their charge, Christ shows his own wounds, and by virtue of his bloody sufferings answers all the demands and challenges of the law, and counterworks Satan's accusations.

(3.) Christ, by his intercession, calls for acquittance. Lord, he says, let the sinner be absolved from guilt; and in this sense he is called an advocate. 1 John ii 1. He requires that the sinner be set free in the court. An advocate differs much from an orator; an orator uses rhetoric to persuade and entreat the judge to show mercy to another; but an advocate tells the judge what is law. Thus Christ appears in heaven as an advocate, he represents what is law. When God's justice opens the debt-book, Christ opens the law-book. Lord, says he, thou art a just God, and wilt not be pacified without blood; lo, here the blood is shed, therefore in justice give me a discharge for these distressed creatures. The law being satisfied, the

[179]

sinner should be acquitted. Upon Christ's plea, God sets his hand to the sinner's pardon.

In what manner does Christ intercede?

(1.) Freely. He pleads our cause in heaven, and takes no fee. An ordinary lawyer will have his fee, and sometimes a bribe too; but Christ is not mercenary. How many causes does he plead every day in heaven, and will take nothing! As Christ laid down his life freely, so he intercedes freely. John x 15, 18.

(2.) Feelingly. He is as sensible of our condition as his own. 'We have not an high priest which cannot be touched with the feeling of our infirmity.' Heb iv 15. As a tender-hearted mother would plead with a judge for a child ready to be condemned. Oh, how would her bowels work! how would her tears trickle down! what weeping rhetoric would she use to the judge for mercy! So the Lord Jesus is full of sympathy and tenderness, that he might be a merciful high priest. Heb ii 17. Though he has left his passion, yet not his compassion. An ordinary lawyer is not affected with the cause he pleads, nor does he care which way it goes; it is profit that makes him plead, not affection; but Christ intercedes feelingly; and that which makes him intercede with affection is, it is his own cause which he pleads. He has shed his blood to purchase life and salvation for the elect; and if they should not be saved, he would lose his purchase.

(3.) Efficaciously. It is a prevailing intercession. Christ never lost any cause he pleaded, he was never non-suited. Christ's intercession must needs be effectual, if we consider,

(i) The excellency of his person. If the prayer of a saint be so prevalent with God, as Moses' prayer bound God's hand, 'Let me alone,' Exod xxxii 10; and Jacob, as a prince, prevailed with God, Gen xxxii 28; and Elijah by prayer opened and shut heaven, James v 17; then what is Christ's prayer! He is the Son of God, the Son in whom he is well pleased. Matt iii 17. What will not a father grant a son! "I know that thou hearest me always.' John xi 42. If God could forget that Christ were a Priest, he could not forget that he is a Son.

(ii) Christ prays for nothing but what his Father has a mind to grant. There is but one will between Christ and his Father. Christ prays, 'Sanctify them through thy truth;' and 'This is the will of God, even your sanctification.' 1 Thess iv 3. So then, if Christ prays for nothing but what God the Father has a mind to grant, then he is like to succeed.

(iii) Christ prays for nothing but what he has power to give. What he prays for as he is man, that he has power to give as he is God. 'Father,

I will.' John xvii 24. *Father, there he prays as a man; I will, there he gives as God.* It is a great comfort to a believer, when his prayer is weak, and he can hardly pray for himself, that Christ's prayer in heaven is mighty and powerful. Though God may refuse prayer as it comes from us, yet he will not as it comes from Christ.

(iv) Christ's intercession is always ready at hand. The people of God have sins of daily occurrence; and, besides these, they sometimes lapse into great sins, and God is provoked, and his justice is ready to break forth upon them: but Christ's intercession is ready at hand, he daily makes up the breaches between God and them; he presents the merits of his blood to his Father, to pacify him. When the wrath of God began to break out upon Israel, Aaron presently stepped in with his censer, and offered incense, and so the plague was stayed. Numb xvi 47. So, no sooner does a child of God offend, and God begin to be angry, but immediately Christ steps in and intercedes. Father, he says, it is my child that has offended; though he has forgotten his duty, thou hast not lost thy bowels. Oh, pity him, and let thy anger be turned away from him. Christ's intercession is ready at hand, and, upon the least failings of the godly, he stands up and makes request for them in heaven.

What are the fruits of Christ's intercession?

(1.) Justification. In justification there are two things. Guilt is remitted and righteousness is imputed. 'The Lord our righteousness.' Jer xxxiii 16. We are reputed not only righteous, as the angels, but as Christ, having his robes put upon us. 2 Cor v 21. But whence is it that we are justified? It is from Christ's intercession. Rom viii 33, 34. Lord, says Christ, these are the persons I have died for; look upon them as if they had not sinned, and repute them righteous.

(2.) The unction of the Spirit. 'Ye have an unction from the Holy One.' 1 John ii 20. This unction or anointing is nothing else but the work of sanctification in the heart, whereby the Spirit makes us partakers of the divine nature. 2 Pet i 4. Such as speak of the philosopher's stone suppose it to have such a property, that when it touches the metal it turns it into gold. Such a property has the Spirit of God upon the soul; when it touches the soul, it puts into it a divine nature; it makes it to be holy and to resemble God. The sanctifying work of the Spirit is the fruit of Christ's intercession. 'The Holy Ghost was not yet given, because Jesus was not yet glorified.' John vii 39. Christ being glorified, and in heaven, he prays the Father, and the Father sends the Spirit, who pours out the holy anointing upon the elect.

(3.) The purification of our holy things. It is Christ's work in heaven, not only to present his own prayers to his Father, but he prays our prayers over again. 'Another angel came, having a golden censer, and there was given to him much incense, that he should offer it with the prayers of all saints upon the golden altar.' Rev viii 3. This angel was Christ; he takes the golden censer of his merits, and puts our prayers into this censer, and with the incense of his intercession makes our prayers go up as a sweet perfume in heaven. It is observable in Lev xvi 16. 'Aaron shall make atonement for the holy place.' This was typical, to show that our holy duties need to have atonement made for them. Our best services, as they come from us, are mixed with corruption, as wine that tastes of the cask. 'They are filthy rags.' Isa lxiv 6. But Christ purifies and sweetens these services, mixing the sweet odours of his intercession with them; and then God accepts and crowns them. What would become of our duties without a high priest? Christ's intercession is to our prayers, as the fan to the chaff. It winnows it from the corn; so Christ winnows out the chaff which intermixes with our prayers.

(4.) Access with boldness unto the throne of grace. Heb iv 16. We have a great high priest that is passed into the heavens, let us come boldly to the throne of grace. We have a friend at court that speaks a good word for us, and is following our cause in heaven; let this animate and encourage us in prayer. Do we think it too much boldness for such sinners as we to come for pardon, and that we shall be denied? Surely this is a sinful modesty. Did we indeed come in our own name in prayer it were presumption, but Christ intercedes for us in the force and efficacy of his blood. To be afraid to come to God in prayer is a dishonour to Christ's intercession.

(5.) Sending the Comforter. 'I will pray the Father, and he shall give you another Comforter.' John xiv 16. The comfort of the Spirit is distinct from the anointing. Here is sweet comfort, sweeter than the honey-drops from the comb; it is the manna in the golden pot, it is *vinum in pectore;* a drop of this heavenly comfort is enough to sweeten a sea of wordly sorrow. It is called the 'earnest of the Spirit.' An earnest assures us of the whole sum. 2 Cor i 22. The Spirit gives us an earnest of heaven in our hand. Whence is this comforting work of the Spirit? Thank Christ's intercession for it. 'I will pray the Father, and he shall give the Comforter.'

(6.) Perseverance in grace. 'Keep through thine own name those whom thou hast given me.' John xvii 11. It is not our prayer, or watchfulness, or grace that keeps us, but it is God's care and maintenance; he holds us, that we do not fall away. Whence is it that God preserves us? It is from Christ's intercession. 'Father, keep them.' The prayer of Christ for Peter,

'I have prayed for thee, that thy faith fail not,' Luke xxii 32, is the copy of his prayer now in heaven. Peter's faith did fail in some degree, when he denied Christ; but Christ prayed that it might not totally fail. The saints persevere in believing, because Christ perseveres in praying.

(7.) Absolution at the day of judgment. Christ shall judge the world. 'God has committed all judgment to the Son.' John v 22. Those for whom Christ has so prayed he will absolve when he sits upon the bench of judicature. Will Christ condemn those for whom he prays? Believers are his spouse, and will he condemn his own spouse?

Use one: Of instruction. (1.) See here the constancy of Christ's love to the elect. He not only died for them, but intercedes for them in heaven. When Christ has done dying, he has not done loving. He is now at work in heaven for the saints, he carries their names on his breast, and will never leave praying till that prayer be granted. 'Father, I will that those whom thou hast given me, be with me where I am.' John xvii 24.

(2.) See whence it is that the prayers of the saints are so powerful with God. Jacob, as an angel, prevailed with God. Moses' prayer tied God's hands. *Precibus suis tanquam inquam vinculis ligatum tenuit Deum* [By his prayers, I say, he held God bound as if by chains]; 'Let me alone.' Exod xxxii 10. Whence is this? It is Christ's prayer in heaven that makes the saints' prayers so available. Christ's divine nature is the altar on which he offers up our prayers, and so they prevail. Prayer, as it comes from the saints is but weak and languid; but when the arrow of a saint's prayer is put into the bow of Christ's intercession it pierces the throne of grace.

(3.) It shows that a Christian when he prays must chiefly fix his eye on Christ's intercession. We are to look up to the mercy-seat, but to hope for mercy through Christ's intercession. We read in Lev xvi that Aaron made atonement by the incense as well as by the blood. So we must look to the cloud of incense, viz., the intercession of Christ. Christian, look up to thy Advocate, one to whom God can deny nothing. A word from Christ's mouth is more than if all the angels in heaven were pleading for thee. If a man had a suit depending in the Court of Chancery, and had a skilful lawyer to plead, it would much encourage him. Christ is at the court appearing for us, Heb ix 24, and he has great power in heaven, which should much encourage us to look up to him, and hope for audience in prayer. We might indeed be afraid to offer our petitions, if we had not Christ to present them.

(4.) The sad condition of an unbeliever. He has none in heaven to speak a word for him. 'I pray not for the world.' John xvii 9. As good be shut out of heaven as shut out of Christ's prayer. Christ pleads for the saints, as Queen Esther did for the Jews, when they would have been destroyed. 'Let my people be given at my request.' Esth vii 3. When the devil shows the blackness of their sins, Christ shows the redness of his wounds. How sad is the condition of that man for whom Christ will not pray, nay, against whom he will pray! Then Queen Esther petitioned against Haman, and then his face was covered, and he was led away to execution. Esth vii 8. It is sad when the law shall be against the sinner, and conscience, and judge, and no friend to speak a word for him; there is no way, then, but for the jailor to take the prisoner.

(5.) If Christ makes intercession, then we have nothing to do with other intercessors. The Church of Rome distinguishes between mediators of redemption and intercession, and says, the angels do not redeem us, but intercede for us, and then pray to them; 'but Christ only can intercede for us *ex officio*. God has consecrated him as high priest. 'Thou art a priest for ever.' Heb v 6. Christ intercedes *vi pretii* [by virtue of his merit], in the virtue of his blood; he pleads his merits to his Father; but the angels have no merits to bring to God, and therefore cannot be intercessors for us. Whoever is our advocate must be our propitiation to pacify God. 'We have an advocate with the Father.' 1 John ii 1. 'And he is our propitiation.' Verse 2. The angels cannot be our propitiation, and not therefore our advocates.

Use two: Of trial. How shall we know that Christ intercedes for us? They have little ground to think Christ prays for them who never pray for themselves. Well, but how shall we know?

(1.) If Christ be praying for us, his Spirit is praying in us. 'He hath sent forth his Spirit into your hearts, crying, Abba, Father. Gal. iv 6. The Spirit helps us with sighs and groans; not only with gifts but groans. Rom viii 26. We need not climb up the firmament, to see if the sun be there, we may see the beauty of it upon the earth: so we need not go up into heaven to see if Christ be there interceding for us; but let us look into our hearts, if they are quickened and inflamed in prayer, and we can cry, Abba, Father. By this interceding of the Spirit within us we may know Christ is interceding above for us.

(2.) If we are given to Christ, then he intercedes for us. 'I pray for them whom thou hast given me.' John xvii 9. It is one thing for Christ to be given to us, another thing for us to be given to Christ.

How know you that?

If thou art a believer, then thou art one given to Christ, and he prays for thee. Faith is an act of recumbency. We rest on Christ as the stones in the building rest upon the corner-stone. Faith throws itself into

Christ's arms; it says, Christ is my priest, his blood is my sacrifice, his divine nature is my altar, and here I rest. This faith is seen by its effects; it is a refining work and a resigning work. It purifies the heart, there is the refining work; it makes a deed of gift to Christ, it gives up its use, its love to him, there is the resigning work of faith. They who believe are given to Christ, and have a part in his prayer. 'Neither pray I for these alone, but for them also which shall believe on me through their word.' John xvii 20.

Use three: Of exhortation. It stirs us up to several duties. (1.) If Christ appears for us in heaven, then we must appear for him upon earth. Christ is not ashamed to carry our names on his breast, and shall we be ashamed of his truth? Does he plead our cause, and shall we not stand up in his cause? What a mighty argument is this to stand up for the honour of Christ in times of apostasy! Christ is interceding for us. Does he present our names in heaven, and shall not we profess his name on earth?

(2.) If Christ lays out all his interest for us at the throne of grace, we must lay out all our interest for him. 'That Christ may be magnified.' Phil i 20. Trade your talents for Christ's glory; there is no man but has some talent to trade, one learning, another estate. Oh, trade for Christ's glory: spend and be spent for him. Let your heart study for Christ, your hands work for him, your tongue speak for him. If Christ be an advocate for us in heaven, we must be agents for him on earth, every one in his sphere must act vigorously for him.

(3.) Believe in this glorious intercession of Christ; that he now intercedes for us, and that for his sake God will accept us, as in the text, 'Who maketh intercession for us.' If we believe not we dishonour Christ's intercession. If a poor sinner may not go to Christ as his high priest, believing in his intercession, then are we Christians in a worse condition under the gospel than the Jews were under the law? When they had sinned they had their high priest to make atonement; and shall not we have our High Priest? Is not Christ our Aaron, who presents his blood and incense before the mercy seat? Oh look up by faith to Christ's intercession! Christ did not only pray for his disciples and apostles, but for the weakest believer.

(4.) Love your Intercessor. 'If any man love not the Lord Jesus Christ, let him be anathema.' 1 Cor xvi 22. Kindness invites love. Had you a friend at court, who, when you were questioned for delinquency or debt, should plead with the judge for you, and bring you off your troubles, would you not love that friend? How often does Satan put in his bills against us in the court! Now Christ is at the judge's hand; he sits at his Father's right hand, ever to plead for us, and to make our peace with God. Oh, how should our hearts be fired with love to Christ! Love him with a sincere and superlative love, above estate and relations. Bernard. *Plusquam tua, tuos* [more than your possessions, and your family]. Our fire of love should be as fire on the altar, never to go out. Lev vi 13.

Use four: Of comfort to believers. Christ is at work for you in heaven; he makes intercession for you.

Oh! but I am afraid Christ does not intercede for me. I am a sinner; and for whom does Christ intercede?

'He made intercession for the transgressors.' Isa liii 12. Did Christ open his sides for thee, and will he not open his mouth to plead for thee?

But I have offended my High Priest, by distrusting his blood, abusing his love, grieving his Spirit; and will he ever pray for me?

Which of us may not say so? But, Christian, dost thou mourn for unbelief? Be not discouraged, thou mayest have a part in Christ's prayer. 'The congregation murmured against Aaron;' but though they had sinned against their high priest, Aaron ran in with his censer, and 'stood between the dead and the living.' Numb xvi 41, 48. If so much bowels in Aaron, who was but a type of Christ, how much more bowels are in Christ, who will pray for them who have sinned against their High Priest! Did he not pray for them that crucified him, 'Father, forgive them'?

But I am unworthy; what am I, that Christ should intercede for me?

The work of Christ's intercession is a work of free grace. Christ's praying for us is from his pitying us. He looks not at our worthiness, but our wants.

But I am followed with sad temptations.

But though Satan tempts, Christ prays, and Satan shall be vanquished. Thou mayest lose a single battle, but not the victory. Christ prays that thy faith fail not; therefore, Christian, say, 'Why art thou cast down, O my soul?' Christ intercedes. It is man that sins, it is God that prays. The Greek word for advocate signifies comforter. It is a sovereign comfort that Christ makes intercession.

5. CHRIST'S KINGLY OFFICE

Qxxvi: HOW DOES CHRIST EXECUTE THE OFFICE OF A KING?

A: In subduing us to himself, in ruling and defending us, and in restraining and conquering all his and our enemies.

Let us consider now Christ's regal office. 'And he hath on his vesture, and on his thigh, a name written, "King of kings, and Lord of lords".' Rev xix 16.

Jesus Christ is of mighty renown, he is a king; (1.) he has a kingly title. 'High and Lofty.' Isa lvii 15. (2.) He has his *insignia regalia*, his ensigns of royalty; *corona est insigne regæ potestatis* [a crown is the symbol of royal power]. He has his crown; Rev vi 2; his sword, 'Gird thy sword upon thy thigh;' Psa xlv 3; his sceptre, 'A sceptre of righteousness is the sceptre of thy kingdom.' Heb i 8. (3.) He has his *escutcheon*, or coat of armour; he inserts the lion in his coat of arms. 'The lion of the tribe of Judah.' Rev v 5. The text says 'he is King of kings.' He has a pre-eminence of all other kings, and is called, 'The Prince of the kings of the earth.' Rev i 5. He must needs be so, for 'by him kings reign.' Prov viii 15. They hold their crowns by immediate tenure from this great King. Christ infinitely outvies all other princes; he has the highest throne, the largest dominions, and the longest possession. 'Thy throne, O God, is for ever and ever.' Heb i 8. He has many heirs, but no successors. Well may he be called 'King of kings,' for he has an unlimited power. The power of other kings is limited, but Christ's power is unlimited. 'Whatsoever he pleased, that did he, in heaven and earth, and in the seas.' Psa cxxxv 6. Christ's power is as large as his will. The angels take the oath of allegiance to him. 'Let all the angels of God worship him.' Heb i 6.

How came Christ to be king?

Not by usurpation, but legally. He holds his crown by immediate tenure from heaven. God the Father has decreed him to be king. 'I have set my king upon my holy hill: I will declare the decree.' Psa ii 6, 7. God has anointed and sealed him to his regal office. 'Him hath God the Father sealed.' John vi 27. God has set the crown upon his head.

In what sense is Christ king?

Two ways. I. *In reference to his people.* And, II. *In reference to his enemies.*

I. *In reference to his people.*

[1.] To govern them. It was prophesied of Christ before he was born, 'And thou, Bethlehem, art not the least among the princes of Judah; for out of thee shall come a governor that shall rule my people Israel.' Matt ii 6. It is a vain thing for a king to have a crown on his head, unless he have a sceptre in his hand to rule.

Where does Christ rule as king?

His kingdom is spiritual. He rules in the hearts of men. He sets up his throne where no other king does; he rules the will and affections, his power binds the conscience; he subdues men's lusts. 'He will subdue our iniquities.' Mic vii 19.

What does Christ rule by?

By *law*, and by *love*. (1.) He rules by law. It is one of the *jura regalia*, the flowers of the crown to enact laws. Christ as a king makes laws, and by his laws he rules; as the law of faith; 'believe in the Lord Jesus:' and the law of sanctity; 'Be ye holy in all manner of conversation;' 1 Pet i 15. Many would admit Christ to be their advocate to plead for them, but not their king to rule over them.

(2.) He rules by love. He is a king full of mercy and clemency; as he has a sceptre in his hand, so an olive branch of peace in his mouth. Though he be the Lion of the tribe of Judah for majesty, yet he is the Lamb of God for meekness. His regal rod has honey at the end of it. He sheds abroad his love into the hearts of his subjects; he rules them with promises as well as precepts. This makes all his subjects become volunteers; they are willing to pay their allegiance to him. 'Thy people shall be a willing people.' Psa cx 3.

[2.] Christ is a king to defend his people. As Christ has a sceptre to rule them, so he has a shield to defend them. 'Thou, O Lord, art a shield for me.' Psa iii 3. When Antiochus raged furiously against the Jews, took away the vessels of the Lord's house, and set up an idol in the temple, this great king, called Michael, stood up for them to defend them. Dan xii 1. Christ preserves his church as a spark in the ocean, as a flock of sheep among wolves. That the sea should be higher than the earth, and yet not drown it, is a wonder; so, that the wicked should be so much higher than the church in power, and not devour it, is, because Christ has this inscription on his vesture and his thigh, KING OF KINGS. 'If it had not been the Lord, who was on our side, they had swallowed us up.' Psa cxxiv 2, 3. They say, lions are *insomnes*, they have little or no sleep; it is true of the Lion of the tribe of Judah, he never slumbers or sleeps, but watches over his church to defend it. 'Sing ye unto her, A vineyard of red wine. I the Lord do keep it: lest any hurt it, I will keep it night and day.' Isa xxvii 2, 3. If the enemies destroy the church, it must be at a time when it is neither night nor day, for Christ keeps it day and night. Christ is said to carry his church, as the eagle her young ones upon her wings. Exod xix 4. The arrow must first hit the eagle before it can hurt the young ones, and shoot through her wings: the enemies must first strike through Christ, before they can destroy his church. Let the wind and storms be up, and the church almost covered with waves, yet Christ is in the ship of the church, and there is no danger of shipwreck. Nor will Christ defend his church only, as he is king, but deliver it. 'He delivered me out of the mouth of the lion,' viz. Nero. 2 Tim iv 17. 'The Lord saved them by a great deliverance.' 1 Chron xi 14. Sometimes Christ is said to command deliverance. Psa xliv 4. Sometimes to create deliverance. Isa xlv 8. Christ as a king commands deliverance, and as a God creates it. And deliverance shall come in his time. 'I the Lord will hasten it in his time.' Isa lx 22.

When is the time that this king will deliver his people?

When the hearts of his people are most humble, when their prayers are most fervent, when their faith is strongest, when their forces are weakest, when their enemies are highest; then is the usual time that Christ puts forth his kingly power for their deliverance. Isa xxxiii 2, 8, 9.

[3.] Christ is a king to reward his people. There is nothing lost by serving this king. He rewards his subjects in this life. He gives them inward peace and joy; a bunch of grapes by the way; and oft-times riches and honour. 'Godliness hath the promise of this life.' 1 Tim iv 8. These are, as it were, the saints' veils. But the great reward is to come. 'An eternal weight of glory.' 2 Cor iv 17. Christ makes all his subjects kings. 'I will give thee a crown of life.' Rev ii 10. This crown will be full of jewels, and it will 'never fade.' 1 Pet v 4.

II. *Christ is a king in reference to his enemies, in subduing and conquering them.* He pulls down their pride, befools their policy, restrains their malice. That stone cut out of the mountain without hands, which smote the image, was an emblem, says Augustine, of Christ's monarchical power, conquering and triumphing over his enemies. Dan ii 34. Christ will make his enemies his footstool. Psa cx 1. He can destroy them with ease. 'It is nothing for thee, Lord, to help.' 2 Chron xiv 11. He can do it with weak means, and without means. He can make the enemies destroy themselves. He set the Persians against the Grecians; and the children of Ammon helped to destroy one another. 2 Chron xx 23. Thus Christ is king in vanquishing the enemies of his church.

It is a great ground of comfort to the church of God in the midst of all the combinations of the enemy, that 'Christ is king;' and he can not only bound the enemies' power, but break it. The church has more with her than against her; she has Emmanuel on her side, even that great KING to whom all knees must bend.

Christ is called 'a man of war.' Exod xv 3. He understands all the policy of chivalry; he is described with seven eyes and seven horns.

Rev v 6. The seven eyes are to discern the conspiracies of his enemies, and the seven horns are to push and vex his enemies.

Christ is described with a crown and a bow. 'He that sat upon the white horse had a bow, and a crown was given unto him, and he went forth conquering and to conquer.' Rev vi 2. The crown is an ensign of his kingly office, and the bow is to shoot his enemies to death.

Christ is described with a vesture dipped in blood. Rev xix 13. He has a golden sceptre to rule his people, but an iron rod to break his enemies. 'The ten horns thou sawest are ten kings; these shall make war with the Lamb, but the Lamb shall overcome them; for he is the King of kings.' Rev xvii 12, 14. The enemies may set up their standard, but Christ will set up his trophies at last. 'And the angel gathered the vine of the earth, and cast it into the great wine-press of the wrath of God, and the wine-press was trodden, and blood came out of the wine-press.' Rev xiv 19, 20. The enemies of Christ shall be but as so many clusters of ripe grapes, to be cast into the great wine-press of the wrath of God, and to be trodden by Christ till their blood come out. Christ will at last come off victor, and all his enemies shall be put under his feet. *Gaudeo quod Christus Dominus est, alioque desperassem;* 'I am glad Christ reigns, else I should have despaired,' said Myconius in an epistle to Calvin.

Use one: (1.) It is no disparagement to serve Christ; he is a king, and it is no dishonour to be employed in a king's service. Some are apt to reproach the saints for their piety; but they serve the Lord Christ, he who has this inscription upon his vesture, KING OF KINGS. Theodosius thought it a greater honour to be a servant of Christ than the head of an empire. *Servire est regnare.* Christ's servants are called vessels of honour; 2 Tim ii 21; and a royal nation, 1 Pet ii 9. Serving Christ ennobles us with dignity; it is a greater honour to serve Christ than to have kings serve us.

(2.) If Christ be king, it informs us, that all matters of fact must one day be brought before him. Christ has *Jus vitæ et necis,* the power of life and death in his hand. 'The Father hath committed all judgment to the Son.' John v 22. He who once hung upon the cross shall sit upon the bench of judicature; kings must come before him to be judged; they who once sat upon the throne must appear at the bar. God has committed all judgment to the Son, and Christ's is the highest court of judicature; if this king once condemns men, there is no appeal to any other court.

(3.) When we are foiled by corruption we must go to Christ, for he is king; desire him by his kingly power to subdue our corruptions, to bind these kings with chains. Psa cxlix 8. We are apt to say of our sins, 'These sons of Zeruiah will be too strong for us;' we shall never overcome this pride and infidelity; ay, but go to Christ, he is king. Though our lusts are too strong for us, they are not for Christ to conquer; for by his Spirit he can break the power of sin. When Joshua had conquered five kings, he caused his servants to set their feet on the necks of those kings; so Christ can and will set his feet on the necks of our lusts.

Use two: Is Christ King of kings? Let all these great ones take heed how they employ their power against him. He gives them their power, and if this power shall be made use of for suppressing his kingdom and ordinances, their account will be heavy. God has laid the key of government upon Christ's shoulders, Isa ix 6, and to oppose Christ in his kingly office is as if the thorns should set themselves in battle array against the fire, or a child fight with an archangel. Christ's sword on his thigh is able to avenge all his quarrels. It is not good to stir a lion: let no man provoke the Lion of the tribe of Judah, whose eyes are a lamp of fire, and 'the rocks are thrown down by him.' Nah i 6. 'He shall cut off the spirit of princes.' Psa lxxvi 12.

Use three: If Christ be a great king, submit to him. Say not, as those Jews, 'We have no king but Cæsar,' no king but our lusts. This is to choose the bramble to rule over you, and 'out of the bramble will come forth a fire.' Judg ix 15. Submit to Christ willingly. All the devils in hell submit to Christ; but it is against their will; they are his slaves, not his subjects. Submit cheerfully to Christ's person and his laws. Many would have Christ their saviour, but not their prince; such as will not have Christ to be their king to rule over them, shall never have his blood to save them. Obey all Christ's princely commands; if he commands love, humility, good works, be as the needle that points which way soever the loadstone draws.

Use four: Let those admire God's free grace who were once under the power and tyranny of Satan, and now of slaves Christ has made them to become the subjects of his kingdom. Christ did not need subjects, he has legions of angels ministering to him; but in his love he has honoured you to make you his subjects. Oh, how long was it ere Christ could prevail with you to come under his banner! How much opposition did he meet with ere you would wear this prince's colours! At last omnipotent grace overcame you. When Peter was sleeping between two soldiers, an angel came and beat off his chains, Acts xii 7; so, when thou wast sleeping in the devil's arms, Christ by his Spirit smote thy heart, and caused the chains of sin to fall off, and made thee a subject of his kingdom. Oh admire free grace! thou who art a subject of Christ, and art sure to reign with him for ever!

6. CHRIST'S HUMILIATION IN HIS INCARNATION

'Great is the mystery of godliness, God manifest in the flesh.' 1 Tim iii 16.

QXXVII: WHEREIN DID CHRIST'S HUMILIATION CONSIST?

A: In his being born, and that in a low condition, made under the law, undergoing the miseries of this life, the wrath of God, and the cursed death of the cross.

Christ's humiliation consisted in his incarnation, his taking flesh, and being born. It was real flesh that Christ took; not the image of a body (as the Manichees erroneously held), but a true body; therefore he is said to be 'made of a woman.' Gal iv 4. As bread is made of wheat, and wine is made of the grape; so Christ is made of a woman: his body was part of the flesh and substance of the virgin. This is a glorious mystery, 'God manifest in the flesh.' In the creation, man was made in God's image; in the incarnation God was made in man's image.

How came Christ to be made flesh?

It was by his Father's special designation. 'God sent forth his Son, made of a woman.' Gal iv 4. God the Father in a special manner appointed Christ to be incarnate; which shows how needful a call is to any business of weight and importance: to act without a call, is to act without a blessing. Christ would not be incarnate, and take upon him the work of a mediator till he had a call. 'God sent forth his Son, made of a woman.'

But was there no other way for the restoring of fallen man but that God should take flesh?

We must not ask a reason of God's will; it is dangerous to pry into God's ark; we are not to dispute but adore. The wise God saw it to be the best way for our redemption, that Christ should be incarnate. It was not fit for any to satisfy God's justice but man; none could do it but God; therefore, Christ being both God and man, is the fittest to undertake this work of redemption.

Why was Christ born of a woman?

(1.) That God might fulfil that promise in Gen iii 15, 'The seed of the woman shall break the serpent's head.' (2.) Christ was born of a woman, that he might roll away that reproach from the woman, which she had contracted by being seduced by the serpent. Christ, in taking his flesh from

[192]

the woman, has honoured her sex; that as, at the first, the woman had made man a sinner; so now, to make him amends, she should bring him a saviour.

Why was Christ born of a virgin?

(1.) For decency. It became not God to have any mother but a maid, and it became not a maid to have any other son but a God.

(2.) For necessity. Christ was to be a high priest, most pure and holy. Had he been born after the ordinary course of nature he had been defiled, since all that spring out of Adam's loins have a tincture of sin, but, that 'Christ's substance might remain pure and immaculate,' he was born of a virgin.

(3.) To answer the type. Melchisedec was a type of Christ, who is said to be 'without father and without mother.' Christ being born of a virgin, answered the type; he was without father and without mother; without mother as he was God, without father as he was man.

How could Christ be made of the flesh and blood of a virgin, and yet be without sin? The purest virgin is stained with original sin.

This knot the Scripture unties. 'The Holy Ghost shall come upon thee, and overshadow thee: therefore that holy thing, which shall be born of thee, shall be called the Son of God.' Luke i 35. 'The Holy Ghost shall come upon thee,' that is, the Holy Ghost did consecrate and purify that part of the virgin's flesh whereof Christ was made. As the alchymist extracts and draws away the dross from the gold, so the Holy Ghost refines and clarifies that part of the virgin's flesh, separating it from sin. Though the Virgin Mary herself had sin, yet that part of her flesh, whereof Christ was made, was without sin; otherwise it must have been an impure conception.

What is meant by the power of the Holy Ghost overshadowing the virgin?

Basil says, 'It was the Holy Ghost's blessing that flesh of the virgin whereof Christ was formed.' But there is a further mystery in it; the Holy Ghost having framed Christ in the virgin's womb, did, in a wonderful manner, unite Christ's human nature to his divine, and so of both made one person. This is a mystery, which the angels pry into with adoration.

When was Christ incarnate?

In the fulness of time. 'When the fulness of time was come, God sent forth his Son, made of a woman.' Gal iv 4. By the fulness of time we must understand, *tempus a patre præfinitum;* so Ambrose, Luther, Cornelius a Lapide – the determinate time that God had set. More particularly, this fulness of time was when all the prophecies of the coming of the Messiah were accomplished; and all legal shadows and figures, whereby he was typified, were abrogated. This may comfort us, in regard to the church of God, that though at present we do not see that peace and purity in the church which we could desire, yet in the fulness of time, when God's time is come and mercy is ripe, then shall deliverance spring up, and God will come riding upon the chariots of salvation.

Why was Jesus Christ made flesh?

(1.) The *causa prima*, and impulsive cause, was free grace. It was love in God the Father to send Christ, and love in Christ that he came to be incarnate. Love was the intrinsic motive. Christ is God-man, because he is a lover of man. Christ came out of pity and indulgence to us: *non merita nostra, sed misera nostra*. Augustine. 'Not our deserts, but our misery' made Christ take flesh. Christ's taking flesh was a plot of free grace, and a pure design of love. God himself, though Almighty, was overcome with love. Christ incarnate is nothing but love covered with flesh. As Christ's assuming our human nature was a master-piece of wisdom, so it was a monument of free grace.

(2.) Christ took our flesh upon him, that he might take our sins upon him. He was, says Luther, *maximus peccator*, the greatest sinner, having the weight of the sins of the whole world lying upon him. He took our flesh that he might take our sins, and so appease God's wrath.

(3.) Christ took our flesh that he might make the human nature appear lovely to God, and the divine nature appear lovely to man.

(i) That he might make the human nature lovely to God. Upon our fall from God, our nature became odious to him; no vermin is so odious to us as the human nature was to God. When once our virgin nature was become sinful, it was like flesh imposthumated, or running into sores, loathsome to behold. It was so odious to God that he could not endure to look upon us. Christ taking our flesh, makes this human nature appear lovely to God. As when the sun shines on the glass it casts a bright lustre, so Christ being clad with our flesh makes the human nature shine, and appear amiable in God's eyes.

(ii) As Christ being clothed with our flesh makes the human nature appear lovely to God, so he makes the divine nature appear lovely to man. The pure Godhead is terrible to behold, we could not see it and live; but Christ clothing himself with our flesh, makes the divine nature more amiable and delightful to us. We need not be afraid to look upon God through Christ's human nature. It was a custom of old among shepherds to clothe themselves with sheepskins, to be more pleasing to the sheep; so Christ clothed himself with our flesh, that the divine nature may be more pleasing to us. The human nature is a glass, through which we may see the love and wisdom and glory of God clearly represented to us. Through the lantern of Christ's humanity we may behold the light of the Deity. Christ being incarnate makes the sight of the Deity not formidable, but delightful to us.

(4.) Jesus Christ united himself to man, 'that man might be drawn nearer to God.' God before was an enemy to us by reason of sin; but Christ having taken our flesh, mediates for us, and brings us into favour with God. As when a king is angry with a subject, the king's son marries his daughter, and so mediates for the subject, and brings him into favour with the king again; so when God the Father was angry with us, Christ married himself to our nature, and now mediates for us with his Father, and brings us to be friends again, and God looks upon us with a favourable aspect. As Joab pleaded for Absalom, and brought him to King David, and David kissed him; so Jesus Christ ingratiates us into the love and favour of God. Therefore he may well be called a peacemaker, having taken our flesh upon him, and so made peace between us and his Father.

Use one: Of instruction. (1.) See here, as in a glass, the infinite love of God the Father; that when we had lost ourselves by sin, God, in the riches of his grace, sent forth his Son, made of a woman, to redeem us. And behold the infinite love of Christ, in that he was willing thus to condescend to take our flesh. Surely the angels would have disdained to have taken our flesh; it would have been a disparagement to them. What king would be willing to wear sackcloth over his cloth of gold? but Christ did not disdain to take our flesh. Oh the love of Christ! Had not Christ been made flesh, we had been made a curse; had he not been incarnate, we had been incarcerate, and had been for ever in prison. Well might an angel be the herald to proclaim this joyful news of Christ's incarnation: 'Behold, I bring you good tidings of great joy; for unto you is born this day in the city of David a Saviour, which is Christ the Lord.' The love of Christ, in being incarcerated, will the more appear if we consider,

(i) Whence Christ came. He came from heaven, and from the richest place in heaven, his Father's bosom, that hive of sweetness.

(ii) To whom Christ came. Was it to his friends? No; he came to sinful man. Man that had defaced his image, and abused his love; man who was turned rebel; yet he came to man, resolving to conquer obstinacy with kindness. If he would come to any, why not to the angels that fell? 'He took not on him the nature of angels.' Heb ii 16. The angels are of a more noble origin, more intelligent creatures, more able for service; ay, but behold the love of Christ, he came not to the fallen angels, but to mankind. Among the several wonders of the loadstone it is not the least, that it will not draw gold or pearl, but despising these, it draws the iron to it, one of the most inferior metals: thus Christ leaves angels, those noble spirits, the gold and the pearl, and comes to poor sinful man, and draws him into his embraces.

(iii) In what manner he came. He came not in the majesty of a king, attended with his life-guard, but he came poor; not like the heir of heaven, but like one of an inferior descent. The place he was born in was poor; not the royal city Jerusalem, but Bethlehem, a poor obscure place. He was born in an inn, and a manger was his cradle, the cobwebs his curtains, the beasts his companions; he descended of poor parents. One would have thought, if Christ would have come into the world, he would have made choice of some queen or personage of honour to have descended from; but he comes of mean obscure parents, for that they were poor appears by their offering. 'A pair of turtledoves,' Luke ii 24, which was the usual offering of the poor. Lev xii 8. Christ was so poor, that when he wanted money he was fain to work a miracle for it. Matt xvii 27. When he died he made no will. He came into the world poor.

(iv) Why he came. That he might take our flesh, and redeem us; that he might instate us into a kingdom. He was poor, that he might make us rich. 2 Cor viii 9. He was born of a virgin, that we might be born of God. He took our flesh, that he might give us his Spirit. He lay in the manger that we might lie in paradise. He came down from heaven, that he might bring us to heaven. And what was all this but love? If our hearts be not rocks, this love of Christ should affect us. Behold love that passeth knowledge! Eph iii 19.

(2.) See here the wonderful humility of Christ. Christ was made flesh. *O sancta humilitas, tu filium Dei descendere fecisti in uterum, Mariæ Virginis* [O holy humility, you made the Son of God descend into the womb of the Virgin Mary]. Augustine. That Christ should clothe himself with our flesh, a piece of that earth which we tread upon; oh infinite humility! Christ's taking our flesh was one of the lowest steps of his humiliation. He humbled himself more in lying in the virgin's womb than in hanging upon the cross. It was not so much for man to die, but for God to become man was the wonder of humility. 'He was made in the likeness of men.' Phil ii 7. For Christ to be made flesh was more humility than for the angels to be made worms. Christ's flesh is called a veil in Heb x 20. 'Through the veil,' that is, his flesh. Christ's wearing our flesh veiled his glory. For him to be made flesh, who was equal with God, oh what

[196]

humility! 'Who being in the form of God thought it not robbery to be equal with God.' Phil ii 6. He stood upon even ground with God, he was co-essential and con-substantial with his Father, as Augustine and Cyril, and the Council of Nice express it; yet for all that he takes flesh. He stripped himself of the robes of his glory, and covered himself with the rags of our humanity. If Solomon wondered that God should dwell in the temple which was enriched and hung with gold, how may we wonder that God should dwell in man's weak and frail nature! Nay, which is yet more humility, Christ not only took our flesh, but took it when it was at the worst, under disgrace; as if a servant should wear a nobleman's livery when he is impeached of high treason. Besides all this he took all the infirmities of our flesh. There are two sorts of infirmities; such as are sinful without pain, and such as are painful without sin. The first of these infirmities Christ did not take upon him; as sinful infirmities, to be covetous or ambitious. But he took upon him painful infirmities as (i) Hunger. He came to the fig-tree and would have eaten. Matt xxi 18, 19. (ii) Weariness, as when he sat on Jacob's well to rest him. John iv 6. (iii) Sorrow. 'My soul is exceeding sorrowful, even unto death.' Matt xxvi 38. It was a sorrow guided with reason not disturbed with passion.(iv) Fear. 'He was heard in that he feared.' Heb v 7. A further degree of Christ's humility was, that he not only was made flesh, but in the likeness of sinful flesh. 'He knew no sin, yet he was made sin.' 2 Cor v 21. He was like a sinner; he had all sin laid upon him, but no sin lived in him. 'He was numbered among transgressors.' Isa liii 12. He who was numbered among the persons of the Trinity is said 'to bear the sins of many.' Heb ix 28. Now, this was the lowest degree of Christ's humiliation; for Christ to be reputed as a sinner was the greatest pattern of humility. That Christ, who would not endure sin in the angels, should himself endure to have sin imputed to him is the most amazing humility that ever was.

From all this learn to be humble. Dost thou see Christ humbling himself, and art thou proud? It is the humble saint that is Christ's picture. Christians, be not proud of fine feathers. Hast thou an estate? Be not proud. The earth thou treadest on is richer than thou. It has mines of gold and silver in its bowels. Hast thou beauty? Be not proud. It is but air and dust mingled. Hast thou skill and parts? Be humble. Lucifer has more knowledge than thou. Hast thou grace? Be humble. Thou hast it not of thy own growth; it is borrowed. Were it not folly to be proud of a ring that is lent? 1 Cor iv 7. Thou hast more sin than grace, more spots than beauty. Oh look on Christ, this rare pattern, and be humbled! It is an unseemly sight to see God humbling himself and man exalting himself;

to see a humble Saviour and a proud sinner. God hates the very semblance of pride. He would have no honey in the sacrifice. Lev ii 11. Indeed, leaven is sour; but why no honey? Because, when honey is mingled with meal or flour, it makes the meal to rise and swell; therefore no honey. God hates the resemblance of the sin of pride; better want parts, and the comfort of the Spirit, than humility. *Si Deus superbientibus angelis non pepercit.* 'If God,' says Augustine, 'spared not the angels, when they grew proud, will he spare thee, who art but dust and rottenness?'

(3.) Behold here a sacred riddle or paradox – 'God manifest in the flesh.' That man should be made in God's image was a wonder, but that God should be made in man's image is a greater wonder. That the Ancient of Days should be born, that he who thunders in the heavens should cry in the cradle; *Qui tonitruat in cœlis, clamat in cunabulis; qui regit sidera, sugit ubera;* that he who rules the stars should suck the breast; that a virgin should conceive; that Christ should be made of a woman, and of that woman which himself made; that the branch should bear the vine; that the mother should be younger than the child she bare, and the child in the womb bigger than the mother; that the human nature should not be God, yet one with God; this was not only *mirum* but *miraculum.* Christ taking flesh is a mystery we shall never fully understand till we come to heaven, when our light shall be clear, as well as our love perfect.

(4.) From hence, 'God manifest in the flesh,' Christ born of a virgin, a thing not only strange in nature, but impossible, learn, That there are no impossibilities with God. God can bring about things which are not within the sphere of nature to produce; as that iron should swim, that the rock should gush out water, and that the fire should lick up the water in the trenches. 1 Kings xviii 38. It is natural for water to quench fire, but for fire to consume water is impossible in the course of nature; but God can bring about all this. 'There is nothing too hard for thee.' Jer xxxii 27. 'If it be marvellous in your eyes, should it be marvellous in my eyes? saith the Lord.' Zech viii 6. How should God be united to our flesh? It is impossible to us, but not with God; he can do what transcends reason, and exceeds faith. He would not be our God if he could not do more than we can think. Eph iii 20. He can reconcile contraries. How apt are we to be discouraged with seeming impossibilities! How do our hearts die within us when things go cross to sense and reason! We are apt to say as that prince in 2 Kings vii 1, 2, 'If the Lord would make windows in heaven, might this thing be!' It was a time of famine, and now that a measure of wheat, which was a good part of a bushel, should be sold for a shekel, half an ounce of silver, how can this be? So, when things are cross, or strange, God's own people are apt to question, how they should be brought about with success? Moses, who was a man of God, and one of the brightest stars that ever shone in the firmament of God's church, was apt to be discouraged with seeming impossibilities. 'And Moses said, The people among whom I am are six hundred thousand footmen; and thou hast said, I will give them flesh, that they may eat a whole month. Shall the flocks and the herds be slain for them, to suffice them? or shall all the fish of the sea be gathered together for them, to suffice them?' Num xi 21, 22. As if he had said, in plain language, he did not see how the people of Israel, being so numerous, could be fed for a month. 'And the Lord said, Is the Lord's hand waxed short?' Verse 23. That God who brought Isaac out of a dead womb, and the Messiah out of a virgin's womb, what cannot he do? Oh let us rest upon the arm of God's power, and believe in him, in the midst of seeming impossibilities! Remember, 'there are no impossibilities with God.' He can subdue a proud heart. He can raise a dying church. Christ born of a virgin! The wonder-working God that wrought this can bring to pass the greatest seeming impossibility.

Use two: Of exhortation. (1.) Seeing Christ took our flesh, and was born of a virgin, let us labour that he may be spiritually born in our hearts. What will it profit us, that Christ was born into the world, unless he be born in our hearts, that he was united to our persons? Marvel not that I say unto you, Christ must be born in your hearts. 'Till Christ be formed in you.' Gal iv 19. Now, then, try if Christ be born in your hearts.

How shall we know that?

Are there pangs before the birth? So before Christ is born in the heart, there are spiritual pangs; pangs of conscience, and deep convictions. 'They were pricked at their heart.' Acts ii 37. I grant in the new birth – *recipere magis et minus* [Some receive more, some less] – all have not the same pangs of sorrow and humiliation, yet all have pangs. If Christ be born in thy heart, thou hast been deeply afflicted for sin. Christ is never born in the heart without pangs. Many thank God they never had any trouble of spirit, they were always quiet; a sign Christ is not yet formed in them.

When Christ was born into the world, he was made flesh; so, if he be born in thy heart, he makes thy heart a heart of flesh. Ezek xxxvi 26. Is thy heart flesh? Before, it was a rocky heart, and would not yield to God, or take the impressions of the word; *durum est quod non cedit tactui* [It is hard substances that do not yield to the touch]; now it is fleshy and tender like melted wax, to take any stamp of the Spirit. It is a sign Christ is born in our hearts, when they are hearts of flesh, when they melt in tears and in love. What is it the better that Christ was made flesh, unless he has given thee a heart of flesh?

As Christ was conceived in the womb of a virgin; so, if he be born in thee, thy heart is a virgin-heart, in respect of sincerity and sanctity. Art thou purified from the love of sin? If Christ be born in thy heart, it is a *Sanctum Sanctorum*, a holy of holies. If thy heart be polluted with the predominant love of sin, never think Christ is born there, Christ will never lie any more in a stable. If he be born in thy heart, it is consecrated by the Holy Ghost.

If Christ be born in thy heart, then it is with thee as in a birth. There is life. Faith is *principum vivens*, it is the vital organ of the soul. 'The life that I live in the flesh is by the faith of the Son of God.' Gal ii 20. There is appetite. 'As new-born babes, desire the sincere milk of the word.' 1 Peter ii 2. The word is like breast-milk, pure, sweet, nourishing; and the soul in which Christ is formed desires this breast-milk. Bernard, in one of his soliloquies, comforts himself with this, that he surely had the new birth in him, because he found in his heart such strong breathings and thirstings after God. After Christ is born in the heart, there is a violent motion: there is a striving to enter in at the strait gate, and offering violence to the kingdom of heaven. Matt xi 12. By this we may know Christ is formed in us. This is the only comfort, that as Christ was born into the world, so he is born in our hearts; as he was united to our flesh, so he is united to our person.

(2.) As Christ was made in our image, let us labour to be made in his image. Christ being incarnate was made like us, let us labour to be made like him. There are five things in which we should labour to be like Christ. (i) In disposition. He was of a most sweet disposition, *deliciæ humani generis* [the delight of human kind]. Titus Vespasian. He invites sinners to come to him. He has bowels to pity us, breasts to feed us, wings to cover us. He would not break our heart but with mercy. Was Christ made in our likeness? Let us be like him in sweetness of disposition; be not of a morose spirit. It was said of Nabal, 'he is such a son of Belial, that a man cannot speak to him.' 1 Sam xxv 17. Some are so barbarous, as if they were akin to the ostrich, they are fired with rage, and breathe forth nothing but revenge, or like those two men in the gospel, 'possessed with devils, coming out of the tombs, exceeding fierce.' Matt viii 28. Let us be like Christ in mildness and sweetness. Let us pray for our enemies, and conquer them by love. David's kindness melted Saul's heart. 1 Sam xxiv 16. A frozen heart will be thawed with the fire of love.

(ii) Be like Christ in grace. He was like us in having our flesh, let us be like him in having his grace. We should labour to be like Christ, in humility. 'He humbled himself.' Phil ii 8. He left the bright robes of his glory to be clothed with the rags of our humanity: a wonder to humility! Let us be like Christ in this grace. Humility, says Bernard, is *contemptus propriæ excellentiæ*, 'a contempt of self-excellence,' a kind of a self-anni-hilation. This is the glory of a Christian. We are never so comely in God's eyes as when we are black in our own. In this let us be like Christ. True religion is to imitate Christ. And indeed, what cause have we to be humble, if we look within us, below us, above us!

If we look *intra nos*, within us, here we see our sins represented to us in the glass of conscience; lust, envy, passion. Our sins are like vermin crawling in our souls. 'How many are my iniquities?' Job xiii 23. Our sins are as the sands of the sea for number, as the rocks of the sea for weight. Augustine cries out, *Væ mihi fæcibus peccatorum polluitur templum Domini.* 'My heart, which is God's temple, is polluted with sin.'

If we look *juxta nos*, about us, there is that may humble us. We may see other Christians outshining us in gifts and graces, as the sun outshines the lesser planets. Others are laden with fruit, perhaps we have but here and there an olive-berry growing, to show that we are of the right kind. Isa xvii 6.

If we look *infra nos*, below us; there is that may humble us. We may see the mother earth, out of which we came. The earth is the most ignoble element: 'They were viler than the earth.' Job xxx 8. Thou that dost set up thy escutcheon, and blaze thy coat of arms, behold thy pedigree; thou art but *pulvis animalus*, walking ashes: and wilt thou be proud? What is Adam? The son of dust. And what is dust? The son of nothing.

If we look *supra nos*, above us; there is that may humble us. If we look up to heaven, there we may see God resisting the proud. *Superbos sequitur ultor a tergo Deus.* [God pursues the proud in vengeance.] The proud man is the mark which God shoots at, and he never misses the mark. He threw proud Lucifer out of heaven; he thrust proud Nebuchadnezzar out of his throne, and turned him to eat grass. Dan iv 25. Oh then be like Christ in humility!

(iii) Did Christ take our flesh? Was he made like to us? Let us be made like him in zeal. 'The zeal of thy house hath eaten me up.' John ii 17. He was zealous when his Father was dishonoured. In this let us be like Christ, zealous for God's truth and glory, which are the two orient pearls of the crown of heaven. Zeal is as needful for a Christian as salt for the sacrifice, or fire on the altar. Zeal without prudence is rashness; prudence without zeal is cowardliness. Without zeal, our duties are not acceptable to God. Zeal is like rosin to the bow-strings, without which the lute makes no music.

(iv) Be like Christ, in the contempt of the world. When Christ took our flesh, he came not in the pride of flesh, he did not descend immediately from kings and nobles, but was of mean parentage. Christ was not ambitious of titles or of honour. He declined worldly dignity and greatness as much as others seek it. When they would have made him a king, he refused it; he chose rather to ride upon the foal of an ass, than be drawn in a chariot; and to hang upon a wooden cross, than to wear a golden crown. He scorned the pomp and glory of the world. He waived secular affairs. 'Who made me a judge?' Luke xii 14. His work was not to arbitrate matters of law; he came not into the world to be a magistrate, but a Redeemer. He was like a star in a higher orb, he minded nothing but heaven. Was Christ made like us? Let us be made like him, in heavenliness and contempt of the world. Let us not be ambitious of the honours and preferments of the world. Let us not purchase the world with the loss of a good conscience. What wise man would damn himself to grow rich? or pull down his soul, to build up an estate? Be like Christ in a holy contempt of the world.

(v) Be like Christ in conversation. Was Christ incarnate? Was he made like us? Let us be made like him in holiness of life. No temptation could fasten upon him. 'The prince of this world cometh, and hath nothing in me.' John xiv 30. Temptation to Christ was like a spark of fire upon a marble pillar, which glides off. Christ's life, says Chrysostom, was brighter than the sunbeams. Let us be like him in this. 'Be ye holy in all manner of conversation.' 1 Pet i 15. We are not, says Augustine, to be like Christ in working miracles, but in a holy life. A Christian should be both a loadstone and a diamond; a loadstone, in drawing others to Christ; a diamond, in casting a sparkling lustre of holiness in his life. Oh let us be so just in our dealings, so true in our promises, so devout in our worship, so unblameable in our lives, that we may be the walking pictures of Christ. Thus as Christ was made in our likeness, let us labour to be made in his.

(3.) If Jesus Christ was so abased for us; took our flesh, which was a disparagement to him, mingling dust with gold; if he abased himself so for us, let us be willing to be abased for him. If the world reproach us for Christ's sake, and cast dust on our name, let us bear it with patience. The apostles departed from the council, 'rejoicing that they were counted worthy to suffer shame for Christ's name,' Acts v 41: that they were graced to be disgraced for Christ. That is a good saying of Augustine, *Quid sui detrahit famæ, addet mercedi sua;* 'they who take away from a saint's name, shall add to his reward'; and while they make his credit weigh lighter, will make his crown weigh heavier. Oh, was Christ content to be humbled and abased for us, to take our flesh, and to take it when it was in disgrace? Let us not think much to be abased for Christ. Say as David, 'If this be to be vile, I will yet be more vile.' 2 Sam vi 22. If to serve my Lord Christ, if to keep my conscience pure, if this be to be vile, I will yet be more vile.

Use three: Of comfort. Jesus Christ, having taken our flesh, has ennobled our nature, *naturam nostram nobilitavit.* Our nature is now invested with greater royalties and privileges than in time of innocence. Before, in innocence, we were made in the image of God; but now, Christ having assumed our nature, we are made one with God; our nature is ennobled above the angelic nature. Christ taking our flesh, has made us nearer to himself than the angels. The angels are his friends, believers are flesh of his flesh, his members. Eph v 30 and chap i 23. The same glory which is put upon Christ's human nature, shall be put upon believers.

7. CHRIST'S EXALTATION

'Wherefore God also hath highly exalted him, and given him a name above every name, &c.' Phil ii 9.

We have before spoken of Christ's humiliation; we shall now speak of his exaltation. Before you saw the Sun of Righteousness in the eclipse; now you shall see it coming out of the eclipse, and shining in its full glory. 'Wherefore God hath highly exalted him;' *super exaltavit,* Ambrose. 'Above all exaltation.'

Qxxviii: WHEREIN CONSISTS CHRIST'S EXALTATION?

A: In his rising from the dead, his ascending into heaven, and his sitting at the right hand of God the Father, &c.

In what sense has God exalted Christ?

Not in respect of his Godhead, for that cannot be exalted higher than it is: as in his humiliation, the Godhead was not lower; so in his exaltation, the Godhead is not higher: but Christ is exalted as Mediator, his human nature is exalted.

How many ways is Christ exalted?

Five ways. God has exalted Christ, I. *In his titles.* II. *In his office.* III. *In his ascension.* IV. *In his session at God's right-hand.* V. *In constituting him judge of the world.*

I. God has exalted Christ in his titles.

[1] He is exalted to be a Lord. Acts xix 17. 'The name of the Lord Jesus

was magnified.' He is a Lord in respect of his sovereignty; he is Lord over angels and men. 'All power is given to him.' Matt xxviii 18. Christ has three keys in his hand, the key of the grave, to open the graves of men at the resurrection; the key of heaven, to open the kingdom of heaven to whom he will; the key of hell, to lock up the damned in that fiery prison. Rev i 18.

To this Lord all knees must bow. 'That at the name of Jesus every knee should bow.' Phil ii 10. *Name* is here put for *person;* to that holy thing Jesus, to the sceptre of that divine person, every knee shall bow. *Bowing* is put for *subjection.* All must be subdued to him as sons or captives, submit to him as to the Lord or Judge. 'Kiss the Son' with a kiss of love and loyalty. Psa ii 12. We must not only cast ourselves into Christ's arms to be saved by him, but we must cast ourselves at his feet to serve him.

[2] Christ is exalted to be a prince. 'There shall stand up Michael the great prince.' Dan xii 1. Some think it was a created angel, but it was *Angelus Fœderis,* Christ the angel of the covenant. He is a great prince. 'The prince of the kings of the earth.' Rev i 5. They hold their crowns by immediate tenure from him; his throne is above the stars, he has angels and archangels for his attendants. Thus he is exalted in his titles of honour.

II. *God has exalted Christ in his office.* He has honoured him to be *Salvator mundi,* the Saviour of the world. 'Him hath God exalted with his right hand, to be a prince and a Saviour.' Acts v 31. It was a great honour to Moses to be a temporal saviour; but what is it to be the Saviour of souls? Christ is called the horn of salvation. Luke i 69. He saves from sin, Matt i 21; from wrath, 1 Thess i 10. To save is a flower belonging only to his crown. 'Neither is there salvation in any other.' Acts iv 12. What an honour is this to Christ! How did it make heaven ring with the praises of the saints! They sing hallelujahs to Christ their Saviour. 'They sung a new song, saying, Thou art worthy to take the book and open the seals; for thou wast slain, and hast redeemed us to God by thy blood.' Rev v 9.

III. *God has exalted Christ in his ascension;* for if he be ascended, then he is exalted. Augustine says, 'Some, as the Hermians, were of opinion that Christ's body ascended into the orb and circle of the sun.' But the Scripture plainly says he ascended into heaven. Luke xxiv 51 and Eph iv 10. 'Far above all heavens;' therefore above the firmament. He is ascended into the highest part of the empyrean heaven, which Paul calls the third heaven. Concerning Christ's ascension, two things may be observed:

[1] The manner of his ascension. When Christ ascended he blessed his disciples. 'He lifted up his hands, and blessed them, and while he blessed

them, he was parted from them, and carried up into heaven.' Luke xxiv 50, 51. He did not leave them houses and lands, but he left them his blessing.

He ascended as a conqueror, in a way of triumph. 'Thou hast led captivity captive,' &c. Psa lxviii 18. He triumphed over sin, hell, and death; and his triumph is a believer's triumph. He has conquered sin and hell for every believer.

[2] The fruit of Christ's ascension. His ascension to heaven causes the descension of the Holy Spirit into our hearts. 'When he ascended up on high, he gave gifts to men.' Eph iv 8. Having ascended up in the clouds, as his triumphant chariot, he gives the gift of his Spirit to us; as a king at his coronation bestows gifts liberally on his favourites.

IV. *God has exalted Christ in his session at God's right hand.* 'After the Lord had spoken to them, he was received up into heaven, and sat upon the right hand of God.' Mark xvi 19. 'He raised him from the dead, and set him at his own right hand, far above all principality and power, and every name that is named.' Eph i 20.

What is meant by Christ sitting at God's right hand?

God really has no right-hand or left; for being a Spirit, he is void of all bodily parts; but it is a metaphor taken from the manner of kings, who were wont to advance their favourites next to their own persons, and set them at their right hand. Solomon caused a seat to be set for the queen his mother, and placed her at his right hand. 1 Kings ii 19. So for Christ to sit at the right hand of God, is to be in the next place to God the Father in dignity and honour. The human nature of Christ, being personally united to the divine, is now set down on a royal throne in heaven, and adored even by angels.

By virtue of the personal union of Christ's human nature with the divine, there is a communication of all that glory from the Deity of Christ of which his human nature is capable. Not that the manhood of Christ is advanced to an equality with the Godhead, but the divine nature being joined with the human, the human nature is wonderfully glorified, though not deified. Christ as mediator is filled with all majesty and honour, beyond the comprehension of the highest order of angels. In his humiliation he descended so low, that it was not fit to go lower; and in his exaltation he ascended so high that it is not possible to go higher. In his resurrection he was exalted above the grave, in his ascension he was exalted above the airy and starry heavens, in his sitting at God's right hand he was exalted far above the highest heavens, 'Far above all heavens.' Eph iv 10.

V. *God has exalted Christ in constituting him judge of the whole world.* 'The Father hath committed all judgment to the Son.' John v 22. At the day of judgment Christ shall be exalted supereminently. 'He shall come in the glory of his Father.' Mark viii 38. He shall wear the same embroidered robes of majesty as the Father; and he shall come with all his holy angels. Matt xxv 31. He who was led to the bar with a band of soldiers, shall be attended to the bench with a guard of angels. Christ shall judge his judges, he shall judge Pilate that condemned him; kings must leave their thrones and come to his bar. And this is the highest court of judicature, from whence is no appeal.

Use one: Of information. (1.) See the different state of Christ on earth and in heaven. Oh how is the scene altered! When he was on earth, he lay in a manger; now he sits on a throne. Then he was hated and scorned of men; now he is adored by angels. Then his name was reproached; now, 'God hath given him a name above every name.' Phil ii 9. Then he came in the form of a servant, and as a servant, stood with his bason and towel, and washed his disciples' feet; John xiii 4, 5; now he is clad in his princes' robes, and the kings of the earth cast their crowns before him. On earth he was a man of sorrows; now he is anointed with the oil of gladness. On earth was his crucifixion; now his coronation. Then his Father frowned upon him in desertion; now he has set him at his right hand. Before, he seemed to have no form or beauty in him; Isa liii 2; now he is in the brightness of his Father's glory. Heb i 3. Oh what a change is here! 'Him hath God highly exalted.'

(2.) Was Christ first humbled and then exalted? Hence learn 'the way to true honour is humility.' 'He that humbleth himself shall be exalted.' Luke xiv 11. The world looks upon humility as that which will make contemptible, but it is the ready way to honour; the way to rise is to fall; the way to ascend is to descend. Humility exalts us in the esteem of men, and it exalts us to a higher throne in heaven. 'Whosoever shall humble himself as this little child, the same is the greatest in the kingdom of heaven.' Matt xviii 4. He shall have a greater degree of glory in it.

(3.) Christ first suffered, and then was exalted. See here, that sufferings must go before glory. Many desire to be glorified with Christ, but they are not content to suffer for him. 'If we suffer with him, we shall reign with him.' 2 Tim ii 12. The wicked first reign and then suffer; the godly first suffer, and then reign. There is no way to Constantinople, but through the strait; no way to heaven, but through sufferings; no way to the crown, but by the cross. Jerusalem above is a pleasant city, streets of gold, gates of pearl; but we must travel through a dirty road to it, through many reproaches and sufferings. Acts xiv 22. We must enter into glory as Christ did; who first suffered shame and death, and then was exalted to sit at God's right hand.

Use two: Of comfort. (1.) Christ, being so highly exalted, has ennobled our nature, crowned it with glory, and lifted it above angels and arch-angels. Though, as man, he was made a little lower than the angels, Heb ii 9, yet as the human nature is united to the divine, and is at God's right hand, so the human nature is above the angels. If God has so dignified our nature, what a shame is it that we should debase it! God has exalted the human nature above the angels, and the drunkard debases the human nature below the beasts.

(2.) Christ being exalted at God's right hand, the key of government is laid upon his shoulders; he governs all the affairs of the world for his own glory. Do you think that when Christ is so highly advanced, and has all power in heaven and earth in his hand, he will not take care of his elect, and turn the most astonishing providences to the good of his church? In a clock, the wheels move cross one to another, but all make the clock strike; so Christ being at his Father's right hand, will make the most cross providences tend to the salvation of his church.

(3.) Christ being at God's right hand, we may be assured he has now finished the work of man's redemption. 'This man, after he had offered one sacrifice for sins, for ever sat down on the right hand of God.' Heb x 12. If Christ had not fully expiated sin, and satisfied God's law, he had not sat down at God's right hand, but had still lain in the grave; but now he is exalted to glory; which is an evident token that he has done and suffered all that was required of him, for working out our redemption.

(4.) Though Jesus Christ is so highly exalted in glory, yet he is not forgetful of us on earth. Some, when raised to places of honour, forget their friends; as the chief butler, when restored to his place at court, forgot poor Joseph in prison; but it is not so with Christ; though exalted to such glory in heaven, he is not unmindful of his saints on earth. Our high priest has all the names and wants of his people written upon his breast-plate. Art thou tempted? Though Christ be in glory, he knows how to pity and succour thee. 'We have not an high priest that cannot be touched with the feeling of our infirmities.' Heb iv 15. Dost thou mourn for sin? Christ, though in a glorified state, hears thy sighs, and bottles thy tears.

(5.) Christ being exalted at God's right hand is for the comfort of believers, that they may one day be exalted to that place of glory where he is. Christ's exaltation is our exaltation. He has prayed for this. 'Father, I will that all those, whom thou hast given me, be with me where I am.' John xvii 24. And he is said to go before to 'prepare a place' for believers. John xiv 2. Christ is called the head, and the church is called the body. Eph i 22, 23. The head being exalted to honour, the body mystic shall be exalted too. As sure as Christ is exalted far above all heavens, so sure will he instate believers in all that glory with which his human nature is adorned. John xvii 22. As he here puts his grace upon the saints, so shortly will he put his glory upon them. This is comfort for the poorest Christian. Perhaps thou hast scarce a house to put thy head in, yet thou mayest look up to heaven, and say, There is my house, there is my country; I have already taken possession of heaven in my head, Christ; he sits there, and it will not be long before I shall sit there with him; he is upon the throne of glory, and I have his word for it, I shall sit upon the throne with him. Rev iii 21.

Use three: Of exhortation. Has God highly exalted Christ? Let us labour to exalt him. Let us exalt, (1.) His person. (2.) His truths.

(1.) Let us exalt Christ in our hearts; believe, adore and love him. We cannot lift him up higher in heaven, but we may in our hearts. Let us exalt him in our lips; let us praise him. Our bodies are the temples of the Holy Ghost, our tongues must be the organs in these temples. By praising and commending Christ, we exalt him in the esteem of others. Let us exalt him in our lives, by living holy lives: *vera religio hæc, sine macula vivere luctant* [This is true religion, when men strive to live blameless lives]. Not all the doxologies and prayers in the world so exalt Christ as a holy life. It makes Christ renowned, and lifts him up indeed, when his followers walk worthy of him.

(2.) Let us exalt Christ's truths. Bucholcerus, in his Chronology, reports of the nobles of Polonia, that whenever the gospel is read, they lay their hands upon their swords, intimating by that, they are ready to maintain the gospel with the hazard of their lives. Let us exalt Christ's truths; maintain the truths of Christ against error; maintain the doctrine of free grace against merit; the Deity of Christ against Socinianism.

Truth is the most orient pearl in Christ's crown. Let us contend for the truth, as one would for a large sum of money, that it should not be wrested out of his hand. Christ takes it to be exalting him when we exalt his truths, wherein his glory is concerned.

8. CHRIST THE REDEEMER

Qxxx: how does the spirit apply to us the redemption purchased by christ?

A: The Spirit applies to us the redemption purchased by Christ by working faith in us, and thereby uniting us to Christ in our effectual calling.

In this answer there are two things. It is implied that Christ is the glorious purchaser of our redemption, in the words, 'The redemption purchased by Christ', and it is declared that the Spirit applies to us this purchased redemption, by working in us faith, &c.

The thing implied is, that Jesus Christ is the glorious purchaser of our redemption. The doctrine of redemption by Jesus Christ is a glorious doctrine; it is the marrow and quintessence of the gospel, in which all a Christian's comfort lies. Great was the work of creation, but greater the work of redemption; it cost more to redeem us than to make us; in the one there was but the speaking of a word, in the other the shedding of blood. The creation was but the work of God's fingers. Psa viii 3. Redemption is the work of his arm. Luke i 51. 'Having obtained eternal redemption for us.' Heb ix 12. Christ's purchasing redemption for us implies that our sins mortgaged and sold us. Had there not been some kind of mortgaging there had been no need of redemption: *redimere rursus emere*. Jerome. When we were thus mortgaged, and sold by sin, Christ purchased our redemption. He had the best right to redeem us, for he is our kinsman. The Hebrew word for Redeemer, *Goel*, signifies a kinsman, one that is near in blood. In the old law the nearest kinsman was to redeem his brother's land. Ruth iv 4. Thus Christ being near akin to us, 'Flesh of our flesh,' is the fittest to redeem us.

How does Christ redeem us?

By his own precious blood. 'In whom we have redemption through his blood.' Eph i 7. Among the Romans, he was said to redeem another who laid down a price equivalent for the ransom of the prisoner. In this sense Christ is a Redeemer; he has paid a price. Never was such a price paid to ransom prisoners. 'Ye are *pretio empti*, bought with a price; and this price was his own blood.' 1 Cor vi 20. So, in the text, 'by his own blood he entered in once into the holy place, having obtained eternal redemption for us.' This blood being the blood of that person who was God as well as man is a price sufficient for the ransom of millions.

From what does Christ redeem us?

From sin. To be redeemed from Turkish slavery is a great mercy, but it is infinitely more to be redeemed from sin. There is nothing that can hurt the soul but sin; it is not affliction that hurts it, it often makes it better, as the furnace makes gold the purer; but it is sin that damnifies. Now, Christ redeems us from sin. 'Now, once in the end of the world hath he appeared to put away sin by the sacrifice of himself.' Heb ix 26.

But how are we redeemed from sin? Do we not see corruption stirring in the regenerate; much pride and unmortified passion?

Redemption is either *incohata* or *plena; i.e.* begun redemption or perfect redemption. Sin cannot stand with a perfect redemption; but here it is begun only, and sin may stand with an imperfect redemption. There may be some darkness in the air at the sun's first rising, but not when the sun is at the full meridian. While our redemption is but begun, there may be sin; but not when it is perfect in glory.

In what sense has Christ redeemed justified persons from sin?

(1.) *A reatu,* from the guilt of sin, though not the stain. Guilt is the binding a person over to punishment. Now, Christ has redeemed a justified person from the guilt of sin; he has discharged his debts. Christ says to God's justice, as Paul to Philemon, 'If he hath wronged thee anything, or owes thee ought, put that on my account.' Verse 18.

(2.) A justified person is redeemed *à dominio,* from the power and regency of sin, though not from the presence. Sin may *furere,* but not *regnare;* it may rage in a child of God, but not reign. Lust raged in David, and fear in Peter, but it did not reign; they recovered themselves by repentance. 'Sin shall not have dominion over you.' Rom vi 14. Sin lives in a child of God, but is deposed from the throne; it lives not as a king, but a captive.

(3.) A believer is redeemed *à maledictione,* from the curse due to sin. 'Christ hath redeemed us from the curse of the law, being made a curse for us.' Gal iii 13. Christ said to his Father, as Rebecca to Jacob, 'Upon me, upon me be the curse; let the blessing be upon them, but upon me be the curse.' And now, there is no condemnation to believers. Rom viii 1. An unbeliever has a double condemnation; one from the law which he has transgressed, and the other from the gospel which he has despised. But

Christ has redeemed the believer from this malediction, he has set him out of the power of hell and damnation.

To what has Christ redeemed us?

He has redeemed us to a glorious inheritance. 'To an inheritance incorruptible and undefiled, and that fadeth not away, reserved in heaven for you.' 1 Pet i 4.

(1.) *To an inheritance.* Christ has not only redeemed us out of prison, but he has redeemed us to a state of happiness, to an inheritance; heaven is not a lease which soon expires, but an inheritance; and a glorious inheritance; called an inheritance in light. Col i 12. *Lumen producit colores;* light adorns and gilds the world. What were the world without light but a prison? The heavenly inheritance is irradiated with light. Christ, as a continual sun, enlightens it with his beams. Rev xxi 23.

(2.) *To an inheritance incorruptible.* It does not moulder away or suffer dissolution. Earthly comforts are shadowed out by the tabernacle which was transient; but heaven is set out by the temple, which was fixed and permanent, built with stone, overlaid with gold. This is the glory of the celestial inheritance; it is incorruptible. Eternity is written upon the frontispiece of it.

(3.) *Undefiled.* The Greek word for undefiled alludes to a precious stone called *Amiantus,* which cannot be blemished. Such a place is heaven, undefiled, nothing can stain it; there is no sin there to eclipse its purity. For holiness and undefiledness it is compared to pure gold, and to the sapphire and emerald. Rev xxi 19. 'The sapphire hath a virtue,' says Pliny, 'to preserve chasteness, the emerald to expel poison.' These are the lively emblems of heaven, to show the sanctity of it; no fever of lust; no venom of malice; none but pure virgin spirits inhabit it.

(4.) *It fadeth not away.* The Greek word is the name of a flower, *Amarantus,* which keeps a long time fresh and green, as Clement of Alexandria writes. Such is the heavenly inheritance, it does not lose its orient colour, but keeps its freshness and greenness to eternity; the beauty of it fadeth not away. To this glorious inheritance hath Christ redeemed the saints; an inheritance which cannot be fully described or set forth by all the lights of heaven, though every star were a sun. And that which is the diamond in the ring, the glory of this inheritance, is the eternal sight and fruition of the blessed God. The sight of God will be a most alluring, heart-ravishing object; the king's presence makes the court. 'We shall see him as he is.' 1 John iii 2. It is comfortable to see God showing himself through the lattice of an ordinance, to see him in the Word and sacrament. The martyrs thought it comfortable to see him in a prison. Oh then, what will it be to see him in glory, shining ten thousand times brighter than the sun! and not only see him, but enjoy him for ever! *Præmium quod fide non attingitur*. Augustine. Faith itself is not able fully to comprehend this reward. All this blessedness has Christ purchased through the redemption of his blood.

Use one: Of instruction. (1.) See into what a wretched deplorable condition we had brought ourselves by sin; we had sinned ourselves into slavery, so that we needed Christ to purchase our redemption. *Nihil durius servitute*, says Cicero, 'Slavery is the worst condition.' Such as are now prisoners in Algiers think it so. But by sin we are in a worse slavery, slaves to Satan, a merciless tyrant, who sports in the damnation of souls. In this condition we were when Christ came to redeem us.

(2.) See in this, as in a transparent glass, the love of Christ to the elect. He came to redeem them; and died intentionally for them. Were it not great love for a king's son to pay a great sum of money to redeem a captive? But that he should be content to be a prisoner in his stead, and die for his ransom; this were matter of wonder. Jesus Christ has done all this, he has written his love in characters of blood. It had been much for Christ to speak a good word to his Father for us, but he knew that was not enough to redeem us. Though a word speaking made a world, yet it would not redeem a sinner. 'Without shedding of blood there is no remission.' Heb ix 22.

Use two: Of trial. If Christ came to purchase our redemption, then let us try whether we are the persons whom Christ has redeemed from the guilt and curse due to sin. This is a needful trial; for let me tell you, there is but a certain number whom Christ has redeemed. Oh, say sinners, Christ is a redeemer, and we shall be saved by him! Beloved, Christ came not to redeem all, for that would overthrow the decrees of God. Redemption is not as large as creation. I grant there is a sufficiency of merit in Christ's blood to save all; but there is a difference between sufficiency and efficiency. Christ's blood is a sufficient price for all, but it is effectual only to them that believe. A plaster may have a sovereign virtue in it to heal any wound, but it does not heal unless applied to the wound. And if it be so, that all have not the benefit of Christ's redemption, but some only, then it is a necessary question to ask our own souls, *Are we in the number of those that are redeemed by Christ or not?*

How shall we know that?

(1.) Such as are redeemed are reconciled to God. The enmity is taken away. Their judgments approve, their wills incline *ad bonum*. Col i 21. Are they redeemed that are unreconciled to God, who hate God and his people (as the vine and laurel have an antipathy), who do all they can to disparage holiness? Are they redeemed who are unreconciled? Christ has purchased a reprieve for these; but a sinner may have a reprieve, and yet go to hell. John v 6.

(2.) Such as are redeemed by Christ are redeemed from the world. 'Who gave himself for our sins, that he might deliver (or redeem) us from this present evil world.' Gal i 4. Such as are redeemed by Christ are risen with Christ, Col iii 1. As birds that light upon the ground to pick up a little seed, immediately fly up to heaven again; so the redeemed of the Lord use the world, and take the lawful comforts of it, but their hearts are presently off these things, and they ascend to heaven. They live here, and trade above. Such as Christ has died for are 'dead to the world;' to its honours, profits, and preferments. What shall we think of those who say they are redeemed of the Lord, and yet are lovers of the world? They are like the tribes who desired to have their portion on this side Canaan. 'Who mind earthly things.' Phil iii 19. They pull down their souls to build up an estate. They are not redeemed by Christ, who are not redeemed from the world.

Use three: Of comfort to such as are redeemed. You are happy, the lot of free grace has fallen upon you; you were once in the devil's prison, but have broken from that prison; you were once bound in the chains of sin, but God has begun to beat off your chains, and has freed you from the power of sin, and the curse due to it. What a comfort is this! Is there any consolation in Christ? It is thine. Is there any sweet fruit growing upon the promise? Thou mayest gather it. Are there any glorious privileges in the gospel? They are thy jointure, justification, adoption, coronation. Is there any glory in heaven? Thou shalt shortly drink of that river of pleasure. Hast thou any temporal comforts? These are but a pledge and earnest of more. Thy meal in the barrel is but a meal by the way, and an earnest of that angels' food which God has prepared for thee. How mayest thou be comforted in all worldly afflictions, though the fig-tree flourish not! Nay, in case of death, it has lost its sting. *Mors abiit morte Christi* [Death takes its leave, through the death of Christ]. Death shall carry thee to thy Redeemer: fear not dying since you cannot be perfectly happy but by dying.

Use four: Of exhortation. Long for the time when you shall have a full and perfect redemption in heaven, an eternal jubilee; when you shall be freed not only from the power but from the presence of sin. Here a believer is as a prisoner that has broken prison, but walks with a fetter on his leg.

When the banner of glory shall be displayed over you, you shall be as the angels of God, you shall never have a sinful thought more; no pain or grief, no aching head or unbelieving heart. You shall see Christ's face, and lie for ever in his arms; you shall be as Joseph. Gen xli 14. They brought him hastily out of the dungeon, and he shaved himself, and changed his raiment, and came in unto Pharaoh. Long for that time, when you shall put off your prison garments, and change your raiment, and put on the embroidered garment of glory. Oh long for it! Yet be content to wait for this full and glorious redemption, when you shall be more happy than you can desire, when you shall have 'that which eye hath not seen, nor ear heard, nor can it enter into man's heart to conceive.'

V. The application of redemption

1. FAITH

'The life that I now live in the flesh, I live by the faith of the Son of God.'
Gal ii 20.

The Spirit applies to us the redemption purchased by Christ, by working faith in us.

Christ is the glory, and faith in Christ the comfort, of the gospel.

What are the kinds of faith?

Fourfold: (1.) An historical or dogmatic faith, which is believing the truths revealed in the Word, because of divine authority.

(2.) There is a temporary faith, which lasts for a time, and then vanishes. 'Yet hath he no root in himself, but dureth for a while.' Matt xiii 21. A temporary faith is like Jonah's gourd, which came up in a night and withered. Chap iv 10.

(3.) A miraculous faith, which was granted to the apostles, to work miracles for the confirmation of the gospel. This Judas had; he cast out devils, yet was cast out to the devil.

(4.) A true justifying faith, which is called 'A faith of the operation of God,' and is a jewel hung only upon the elect. Col ii 12.

What is justifying faith?

I shall show, (1.) *What it is not.* It is not a bare acknowledgment that Christ is a Saviour. There must be an acknowledgment, but that is not sufficient to justify. The devils acknowledged Christ's Godhead. 'Jesus the Son of God.' Matt viii 29. There may be an assent to divine truth, and yet no work of grace on the heart. Many assent in their judgments, that sin is an evil thing, but they go on in sin, whose corruptions are stronger than their convictions; and that Christ is excellent; they cheapen the pearl, but do not buy.

(2.) *What justifying faith is.* True justifying faith consists in three things:
(i) Self-renunciation. Faith is going out of one's self, being taken off

from our own merits, and seeing we have no righteousness of our own. 'Not having mine own righteousness.' Phil iii 9. Self-righteousness is a broken reed, which the soul dares not lean on. Repentance and faith are both humbling graces; by repentance a man abhors himself; by faith he goes out of himself. As Israel in their wilderness march, behind them saw Pharaoh and his chariots pursuing, before them the Red Sea ready to devour; so the sinner behind sees God's justice pursuing him for sin, before, hell ready to devour him; and in this forlorn condition, he sees nothing in himself to help, but he must perish unless he can find help in another.

(ii) Reliance. The soul casts itself upon Jesus Christ; faith rests on Christ's person. Faith believes the promise; but that which faith rests upon in the promise is the person of Christ: therefore the spouse is said to 'lean upon her Beloved.' Cant viii 5. Faith is described to be 'believing on the name of the Son of God,' 1 John iii 23, viz., on his person. The promise is but the cabinet, Christ is the jewel in it which faith embraces; the promise is but the dish, Christ is the food in it which faith feeds on. Faith rests on Christ's person, 'as he was crucified.' It glories in the cross of Christ. Gal vi 14. To consider Christ crowned with all manner of excellencies, stirs up admiration and wonder; but Christ looked upon as bleeding and dying, is the proper object of our faith; it is called therefore 'faith in his blood.' Rom iii 25.

(iii) Appropriation, or applying Christ to ourselves. A medicine, though it be ever so sovereign, if not applied, will do no good; though the plaster be made of Christ's own blood, it will not heal, unless applied by faith; the blood of God, without faith in God, will not save. This applying of Christ is called receiving him. John i 12. The hand receiving gold, enriches; so the hand of faith, receiving Christ's golden merits with salvation, enriches us.

How is faith wrought?

By the blessed Spirit; who is called the 'Spirit of grace,' because he is the spring of all grace. Zech xii 10. Faith is the chief work which the Spirit of God works in a man's heart. In making the world God did but speak a word, but in working faith he puts forth his arm. Luke i 51. The Spirit's working faith is called, 'The exceeding greatness of God's power.' Eph i 19. What a power was put forth in raising Christ from the grave when such a tombstone lay upon him as 'the sins of all the world'! yet he was raised up by the Spirit. The same power is put forth by the Spirit of God in working faith. The Spirit irradiates the mind, and subdues the will. The will is like a garrison, which holds out against God: the

Spirit with sweet violence conquers, or rather changes it; making the sinner willing to have Christ upon any terms; to be ruled by him as well as saved by him.

Wherein lies the preciousness of faith?

(1.) In its being the chief gospel-grace, the head of the graces. As gold among the metals, so is faith among the graces. Clement of Alexandria calls the other graces the daughters of faith. In heaven, love will be the chief grace; but, while we are here, love must give place to faith. Love takes possession of glory, but faith gives a title to it. Love is the crowning grace in heaven, but faith is the conquering grace upon earth. 'This is the victory that overcometh the world, even our faith.' 1 John v 4.

(2.) In its having influence upon all the graces, and setting them to work: not a grace stirs till faith set it to work. As the clothier sets the poor to work, sets their wheel going; so faith sets hope to work. The heir must believe his title to an estate in reversion before he can hope for it; faith believes its title to glory, and then hope waits for it. If faith did not feed the lamp of hope with oil, it would soon die. Faith sets love to work. 'Faith which worketh by love.' Gal v 6. Believing the mercy and merit of Christ causes a flame of love to ascend. Faith sets patience to work. 'Be followers of them who through faith and patience inherit the promises.' Heb vi 12. Faith believes the glorious rewards given to suffering. This makes the soul patient in suffering. Thus faith is the master-wheel, it sets all the other graces running.

(3.) In its being the grace which God honours to justify and save. Thus indeed it is 'precious faith,' as the apostle calls it. 2 Pet i 1. The other graces help to sanctify, but it is faith that justifies. 'Being justified by faith.' Rom v 1. Repentance or love do not justify, but faith does.

How does faith justify?

(1.) Faith does not justify as it is a work, which would make a Christ of our faith; but faith justifies, as it lays hold of the object, viz. Christ's merits. If a man had a precious stone in a ring that could heal, we should say the ring heals; but properly it is not the ring, but the precious stone in the ring that heals. Thus faith saves and justifies, but it is not any inherent virtue in faith, but as it lays hold on Christ it justifies.

(2.) Faith does not justify as it exercises grace. It cannot be denied, that faith invigorates all the graces, puts strength and liveliness into them, but it does not justify under this notion. Faith works by love, but it does not justify as it works by love, but as it applies Christ's merits.

Why should faith save and justify more than any other grace?

(1.) Because of God's purpose. He has appointed this grace to be justifying; and he does it, because faith is a grace that takes a man off himself, and gives all the honour to Christ and free grace. 'Strong in faith, giving glory to God.' Rom iv 20. Therefore God has put this honour on faith, to make it saving and justifying. The king's stamp makes the coin pass for current; if he would put his stamp upon leather, as well as silver, it would make it current: so God having put his sanction, the stamp of his authority and institution upon faith, makes it to be justifying and saving.

(2.) Because faith makes us one with Christ. Eph iii 17. It is the espousing, incorporating grace, it gives us coalition and union with Christ's person. Other graces make us like Christ, faith makes us members of Christ.

Use one: Of exhortation. Let us above all things labour for faith. *Fides est sanctissimum humani pectoris bonum.* 'Above all, taking the shield of faith.' Eph vi 16. Faith will be of more use to us than any grace; as an eye, though dim, was of more use to an Israelite than all the other members of his body, a strong arm, or a nimble foot. It was his eye looking on the brazen serpent that cured him. It is not knowledge, though angelic, not repentance, though we could shed rivers of tears, could justify us; only faith, whereby we look on Christ. 'Without faith it is impossible to please God.' Heb xi 6. If we do not please him by believing, he will not please us in saving. Faith is the condition of the covenant of grace; without faith, without covenant; and without covenant, without hope. Eph ii 12.

Use two: Of trial. Let us try whether we have faith. There is something that looks like faith, and is not, as a Bristol-stone looks like a diamond. Some plants have the same leaf with others, but the herbalist can distinguish them by the root and taste. Some faith may look like true faith, but it may be distinguished by the fruits. Let us be serious in the trial of our faith. Much depends upon our faith; for if our faith be not good, nothing good comes from us, even our duties and graces are adulterated.

How then shall we know a true faith?

By the noble effects. (1.) Faith is a Christ-prizing grace, it puts a high valuation upon Christ. 'To you that believe he is precious.' 1 Pet ii 7. Paul best knew Christ. 'Have I not seen Jesus Christ our Lord?' 1 Cor ix 1. He saw Christ with his bodily eyes in a vision, when he was caught up into the third heaven; and with the eye of his faith in the Holy Supper; therefore he best knew Christ. And see how he styles all things in com-

parison of him. 'I count all things but dung, that I may win Christ.'
Phil iii 8. Do we set a high estimate upon Christ? Could we be willing
to part with the wedge of gold for the pearl of price? Gregory Nazianzen
blessed God he had anything to lose for Christ's sake.

(2.) Faith is a refining grace. 'Mystery of faith in a pure conscience.'
1 Tim iii 9. Faith is in the soul as fire among metals; it refines and purifies.
Morality may wash the outside, faith washes the inside. 'Having purified
their hearts by faith.' Acts xv 9. Faith makes the heart a sacristy or holy
of holies. Faith is a virgin-grace: though it does not take away the life of
sin, yet it takes away the love of sin. Examine if your hearts be an unclean
fountain, sending out the mud and dirt of pride and envy. If there be
legions of lusts in thy soul, there is no faith. Faith is a heavenly plant,
which will not grow in an impure soil.

(3.) Faith is an obediential grace. 'The obedience of faith.' Rom xvi 26.
Faith melts our will into God's. It runs at God's call. If God commands
duty (though cross to flesh and blood) faith obeys. 'By faith Abraham
obeyed.' Heb xi 8. Faith is not an idle grace; as it has an eye to see Christ,
so it has a hand to work for him. It not only believes God's promise, but
obeys his command. It is not having knowledge that will evidence you
to be believers; the devil has knowledge, but wants obedience, and that
makes him a devil. The true obedience of faith is a cheerful obedience.
God's commands do not seem grievous. Have you obedience, and obey
cheerfully? Do you look upon God's command as your burden, or
privilege; as an iron fetter about your leg, or as a gold chain about your
neck.

(4.) Faith is an assimilating grace. It changes the soul into the image of
the object; it makes it like Christ. Never did any look upon Christ with a
believing eye, but he was made like Christ. A deformed person may look
on a beautiful object, and not be made beautiful; but faith looking on
Christ transforms a man, and turns him into his similitude. Looking on a
bleeding Christ causes a soft bleeding heart; looking on a holy Christ
causes sanctity of heart; looking on a humble Christ makes the soul
humble. As the chameleon is changed into the colour of that which it
looks upon, so faith, looking on Christ, changes the Christian into the
similitude of Christ.

(5.) True faith grows. All living things grow. 'From faith to faith.'
Rom i 17.

How may we judge of the growth of faith?

Growth of faith is judged by strength. We can do that now, which we
could not do before. When one is man-grown, he can do that which he

could not do when he was a child; he can carry a heavier burden; so thou canst bear crosses with more patience.

Growth of faith is seen by doing duties in a more spiritual manner, with more fervency; we put coals to the incense, from a principle of love to God. When an apple has done growing in bigness, it grows in sweetness; so thou performest duties in love and art sweeter, and come off with a better relish.

But I fear I have no faith.

We must distinguish between weakness of faith and no faith. A weak faith is true. The bruised reed is but weak, yet it is such as Christ will not break. Though thy faith be weak, be not discouraged.

(1.) A weak faith may receive a strong Christ. A weak hand can tie the knot in marriage as well as a strong one; and a weak eye might have seen the brazen serpent. The woman in the gospel did but touch Christ's garment, and received virtue from him. It was the touch of faith.

(2.) The promise is not made to strong faith, but to true. The promise says not whosoever has a giant-faith, that can remove mountains, that can stop the mouths of lions, shall be saved; but whosoever believes, be his faith ever so small. Though Christ sometimes chides a weak faith, yet that it may not be discouraged, he makes it a promise. *Beati qui esuriunt.* Matt v 3.

(3.) A weak faith may be fruitful. Weakest things multiply most; the vine is a weak plant, but it is fruitful. Weak Christians may have strong affections. How strong is the first love, which is after the first planting of faith!

(4.) Weak faith may be growing. Seeds spring up by degrees; first the blade, then the ear, then the full corn in the ear. Therefore, be not discouraged. God who would have us receive them that are weak in faith, will not himself refuse them. Rom xiv 1. A weak believer is a member of Christ; and though Christ will cut off rotten members from his body, he will not cut off weak members.

2. EFFECTUAL CALLING

'Them he also called.' Rom viii 30.

QXXXI: WHAT IS EFFECTUAL CALLING?

A: It is a gracious work of the Spirit, whereby he causes us to embrace Christ freely, as he is offered to us in the gospel.

[220]

In this verse is the golden chain of salvation, made up of four links, of which one is vocation. 'Them he also called.' Calling is *nova creatio*, 'a new creation,' the first resurrection. There is a two-fold call: (1.) An outward call: (2.) An inward call.

(1.) An outward call, which is God's offer of grace to sinners, inviting them to come and accept of Christ and salvation. 'Many are called, but few chosen.' Matt xx 16. This call shows men what they ought to do in order to salvation, and renders them inexcusable in case of disobedience.

(2.) There is an inward call, when God with the offer of grace works grace. By this call the heart is renewed, and the will is effectually drawn to embrace Christ. The outward call brings men to a profession of Christ, the inward to a possession of Christ.

What are the means of this effectual call?

Every creature has a voice to call us. The heavens call to us to behold God's glory. Psalm xix 1. Conscience calls to us. God's judgments call us to repent. 'Hear ye the rod.' Mic vi 9. But every voice does not convert. There are two means of our effectual call:

(1.) The 'preaching of the word,' which is the sounding of God's silver trumpet in men's ears. God speaks not by an oracle, he calls by his ministers. Samuel thought it had been the voice of Eli only that called him; but it was God's voice. 1 Sam iii 6. So, perhaps, you think it is only the minister that speaks to you in the word, but it is God himself who speaks. Therefore Christ is said to speak to us from heaven. Heb xii 25. How does he speak but by his ministers? as a king speaks by his ambassadors. Know, that in every sermon preached, God calls to you; and to refuse the message we bring, is to refuse God himself.

(2.) The other means of our effectual call is the Holy Spirit. The ministry of the word is the pipe or organ; the Spirit of God blowing in it, effectually changes men's hearts. 'While Peter spake, the Holy Ghost fell on all them that heard the word of God.' Acts x 44. Ministers knock at the door of men's hearts, the Spirit comes with a key and opens the door. 'A certain woman named Lydia, whose heart the Lord opened.' Acts xvi 14.

From what does God call men?

(1.) From sin. He calls them from their ignorance and unbelief. 1 Pet i 14. By nature the understanding is enveloped with darkness. God calls men 'from darkness to light,' as if one should be called out of a dungeon to behold the light of the sun. Eph v 8.

(2.) From danger. As the angels called Lot out of Sodom, when it was ready to rain fire; so God calls his people from the fire and brimstone of hell, and from all those curses to which they were exposed.

(3.) He calls them out of the world; as Christ called Matthew from the receipt of custom. 'They are not of the world.' John xvii 16. Such as are divinely called, are not natives here, but pilgrims; they do not conform to the world, or follow its sinful fashions; they are not of the world; though they live here, yet they trade in the heavenly country. The world is a place where Satan's throne is. Rev ii 13. It is a stage on which sin every day acts its part. Now such as are called are in the world but not of it.

To what does God call men?

(1.) He calls them to holiness. 'God hath not called us to uncleanness, but unto holiness.' 1 Thess iv 7. Holiness is the livery, or silver star which the godly wear. *Knam kodsheca*, 'The people of thy holiness.' Isa lxiii 18. The called of God are anointed with the consecrating oil of the Spirit. 'Ye have an unction from the Holy One.' 1 John ii 20.

(2.) God calls them to glory, as if a man were called out of a prison to sit upon a throne. 'Who hath called you to his kingdom and glory.' 1 Thess ii 12. Whom God calls he crowns with a weight of glory. 2 Cor iv 17. The Hebrew word for glory (*Kabod*) signifies *pondus*, a weight. The weight of glory adds to the worth, the weightier gold is the more it is worth. This glory is not transient, but permanent, an eternal weight; it is better felt than expressed.

What is the cause of the effectual call?

God's electing love. 'Whom he predestinated, them he also called.' Rom viii 30. Election is the fountain-cause of our vocation. It is not because some are more worthy to partake of the heavenly calling than others, for we were 'all in our blood.' Ezek xvi 6. What worthiness is in us? What worthiness was there in Mary Magdalene, out of whom seven devils were cast? What worthiness in the Corinthians, when God began to call them by his gospel? They were fornicators, effeminate, idolaters. 'Such were some of you, but ye are washed,' &c. 1 Cor vi 11. Before effectual calling, we are not only 'without strength,' Rom v 6, but 'enemies,' Col i 21. So that the foundation of vocation is election.

What are the qualifications of this call?

(1.) It is a powerful call. *Verba Dei sunt opera* [The words of God are works]. Luther. God puts forth infinite power in calling home a sinner to himself; he not only puts forth his voice but his arm. The apostle

[222]

speaks of the exceeding greatness of his power, which he exercises towards them that believe. Eph i 19. God rides forth conquering in the chariot of his gospel; he conquers the pride of the heart, and makes the will, which stood out as a fort-royal, to yield and stoop to his grace; he makes the stony heart bleed. Oh, it is a mighty call! Why then do the Arminians seem to talk of a moral persuasion, that God in the conversion of a sinner only morally persuades and no more; sets his promises before men to allure them to good, and his threatenings to deter them from evil; and that is all he does? But surely moral persuasions alone are insufficient to the effectual call. How can the bare proposal of promises and threatenings convert a soul? This amounts not to a new creation, or that power which raised Christ from the dead. God not only persuades, but enables. Ezek xxxvi 27. If God, in conversion, should only morally persuade, that is, set good and evil before men, then he does not put forth so much power in saving men as the devil does in destroying them. Satan not only propounds tempting objects to men, but concurs with his temptations: therefore he is said to 'work in the children of disobedience.' Eph ii 2. The Greek word, to work, signifies *imperii vim*, Camerarius, the power Satan has in carrying men to sin. And shall not God's power in converting be greater than Satan's power in seducing? The effectual call is mighty and powerful. God puts forth a divine energy, nay, a kind of omnipotence; it is such a powerful call, that the will of man has no power effectually to resist.

(2.) It is a high calling. 'I press toward the mark for the prize of the high calling of God.' Phil iii 14. It is a high calling, (i) Because we are called to high exercises of religion; to be crucified to the world, to live by faith, to do angels' work, to love God, to be living organs of his praise, to hold communion with the Father and the Son. 1 John i 3.

(ii) It is a high calling, because we are called to high privileges; to justification and adoption, to be kings and priests unto God. We are called to the fellowship of angels, to be co-heirs with Christ. Heb xii 22. Rom viii 17. They who are effectually called are candidates for heaven, they are princes in all lands, though princes in disguise. Psa xlv 16.

(3.) It is an immutable call. 'The gifts and calling of God are without repentance;' Rom xi 29; that is, those gifts that flow from election (as vocation and justification) are without repentance. God repented he called Saul to be a king; but he never repents of calling a sinner to be a saint.

Use one: See the necessity of the effectual call. A man cannot go to heaven without it. First, we must be called before we are glorified. Rom viii 30.

A man uncalled can lay claim to nothing in the Bible but threatenings: a man in the state of nature is not fit for heaven, no more than a man in his filth and his rags is fit to come into a king's presence. A man in his natural state is a God-hater, and is he fit for heaven? Rom i 30. Will God lay his enemy in his bosom?

Use two: Of trial whether we are effectually called. This we may know by its antecedent and consequent.

(1.) By the antecedent. Before this effectual call, a humbling work passes upon the soul. A man is convinced of sin, he sees he is a sinner and nothing but a sinner; the fallow ground of his heart is broken up. Jer iv 3. As the husbandman breaks the clods, then casts in the seed; so God, by the convincing work of the law, breaks a sinner's heart, and makes it fit to receive the seeds of grace. Such as were never convinced are never called. 'He shall convince the world of sin.' John xvi 8. Conviction is the first step in conversion.

(2.) By the consequents, which are two. (i) He who is savingly called answers to God's call. When God called Samuel, he answered, 'Speak, Lord, thy servant heareth.' I Sam iii 10. When God calls thee to an act of religion, dost thou run at God's call? 'I was not disobedient to the heavenly vision.' Acts xxvi 19. If God calls to duties contrary to flesh and blood, we obey his voice in everything; true obedience is like the needle, which points that way which the loadstone draws. Such as are deaf to God's call show they are not called by grace. (ii) He who is effectually called stops his ears to all other calls which would call him off from God. As God has his call, so there are other contrary calls. Satan calls by a temptation, lust calls, evil company calls; but as the adder stops its ear against the voice of the charmer, so he who is effectually called stops his ear against all the charms of the flesh and the devil.

Use three: Of comfort to those who are the called of God. This call evidences election. 'Whom he predestinated, them he also called.' Rom viii 30. Election is the cause of our vocation, and vocation is the sign of our election. Election is the first link of the golden chain of salvation, vocation is the second. He who has the second link of the chain is sure of the first. As by the stream we are led to the fountain, so by vocation we ascend to election. Calling is an earnest and pledge of glory. 'God hath chosen you to salvation, through sanctification.' 2 Thess ii 13. We may read God's predestinating love in the work of grace in our heart.

Use four: Let such as are called be thankful to God for that unspeakable blessing. Be thankful to all the persons in the Trinity, to the Father's mercy, to the Son's merit, to the Spirit's efficacy. To make you thankful, consider, when you had offended God, he called you; when God needed you not, but had millions of glorified saints and angels to praise him, he called you. Consider what you were before God called you. You were in your sins. When God called Paul, he found him persecuting; when he called Matthew, he found him at the receipt of custom; when he called Zacchaeus, he found him using extortion. When God calls a man by his grace, he finds him seeking after his lusts; as when Saul was called to the kingdom, he was seeking the asses. That God should call thee when thou wast in the hot pursuit of sin, admire his love, exalt his praise. Again, that God should call you, and pass by others, what mercy is this! 'Even so, Father, for so it seemed good in thy sight.' Matt xi 26. That God should pass by wise and noble persons, of sweeter disposition, acuter parts, guilty of less vice, and that the lot of free grace should fall upon you – oh astonishing love of God! It was a great favour to Samuel that God called to him, and revealed his mind to him, and passed by Eli, though a priest and a judge in Israel; 1 Sam iii 6; so, that God should call to thee, a flagitious sinner, and pass by others of higher birth and better morals, calls aloud for praise. As God so governs the clouds, that he makes them rain upon one place, and not upon another; so at a sermon the Lord opens the heart of one, and another is no more affected with it than a deaf man with the sound of music. Here is the banner of free grace displayed, and here should the trophies of praise be erected. Elijah and Elisha were walking together; on a sudden there came a chariot of fire, and carried Elijah up to heaven, but left Elisha behind; so, when two are walking together, husband and wife, father and child, that God should call one by his grace, but leave the other, carry up one in a triumphant chariot to heaven, but let the other perish eternally – oh infinite rich grace! How should they that are called be affected with God's discriminating love! How should the vessels of mercy run over with thankfulness! How should they stand upon Mount Gerizim, blessing and praising God! Oh begin the work of heaven here! Such as are patterns of mercy should be trumpeters of praise. Thus Paul being called of God, and seeing what a debtor he was to free grace, breaks forth into admiration and gratitude. 1 Tim i 12.

Use five: To the called. Walk worthy of your high calling. 'I beseech you, that ye walk worthy of the vocation wherewith ye are called;' Eph iv 1; in two things.

(1.) Walk compassionately. Pity such as are yet uncalled. Hast thou a child that God has not yet called, a wife, a servant? Weep over their dying souls; they are in their blood, 'under the power of Satan.' Oh pity them! Let their sins more trouble you than your own sufferings. If you pity an ox or ass going astray, will you not pity a soul going astray? Show your piety by your pity.

(2.) Walk holily. Yours is a holy calling. 2 Tim i 9. You are called to be saints, Rom i 7. Show your vocation by a Bible conversation. Shall not flowers smell sweeter than weeds? Shall not they who are ennobled with grace have more fragrance in their lives than sinners? 'As he who hath called you is holy, so be ye holy in all manner of conversation.' 1 Pet i 15. Oh dishonour not your high calling by any sordid carriage! When Antigonus was going to defile himself with women, one told him, 'he was a king's son.' Oh remember your dignity; 'called of God!' of the blood-royal of heaven. Do nothing unworthy of your honourable calling. Scipio refused the embraces of an harlot, because he was general of an army. Abhor all motions to sin, because of your high calling. It is not fit for those who are the called of God, to do as others; though others of the Jews did drink wine, it was not fit for the Nazarite, because he had a vow of separation upon him, and had promised abstinence. Though Pagans and nominal Christians take liberty to sin, yet it is not fit for those who are called out of the world, and have the mark of election upon them, to do so. Ye are consecrated persons, your bodies are the temples of the Holy Ghost, and your bodies must be a sacristy, or holy of holies.

3. JUSTIFICATION

'Being justified freely by his grace.' Rom iii 24.

Qxxxiii: WHAT IS JUSTIFICATION?

A: It is an act of God's free grace, whereby he pardons all our sins, and accepts us as righteous in his sight, only for the righteousness of Christ, imputed to us, and received by faith alone.

Justification is the very hinge and pillar of Christianity. An error about justification is dangerous, like a defect in a foundation. Justification by Christ is a spring of the water of life. To have the poison of corrupt doctrine cast into this spring is damnable. It was a saying of Luther, 'that after his death the doctrine of justification would be corrupted.' In these latter times, the Arminians and Socinians have cast a dead fly into this box of precious ointment.

I shall endeavour to follow the star of Scripture to light me through this mysterious point.

I *What is meant by justification?*

It is *verbum forense*, a word borrowed from law-courts, wherein a person arraigned is pronounced righteous, and is openly absolved. God, in justifying a person, pronounces him to be righteous, and looks upon him as if he had not sinned.

What is the source of justification?

The *causa*, the inward impellant motive or ground of justification, is the free grace of God: 'being justified freely by his grace.' Ambrose expounds this, as 'not of the grace wrought within us, but the free grace of God.' The first wheel that sets all the rest running is the love and favour of God; as a king freely pardons a delinquent. Justification is a mercy spun out of the bowels of free grace. God does not justify us because we are worthy, but by justifying us makes us worthy.

What is the ground, or that by which a sinner is justified?

The ground of our justification is Christ's satisfaction made to his Father. If it be asked, how can it stand with God's justice and holiness to pronounce us innocent when we are guilty? the answer is, that Christ having made satisfaction for our fault, God may, in equity and justice, pronounce us righteous. It is a just thing for a creditor to discharge a debtor of the debt, when a satisfaction is made by the surety.

But how was Christ's satisfaction meritorious, and so sufficient to justify?

In respect of the divine nature. As he was man he suffered, as God he satisfied. By Christ's death and merits, God's justice is more abundantly satisfied than if we had suffered the pains of hell for ever.

Wherein lies the method of our justification?

In the imputation of Christ's righteousness to us. 'This is the name whereby he shall be called,' *Jehovah Tzidkennu*, 'THE LORD OUR RIGHTEOUSNESS.' Jer xxiii 6. 'He is made to us righteousness.' 1 Cor i 30. This righteousness of Christ, which justifies us, is a better righteousness than the angels'; for theirs is the righteousness of creatures, this of God.

What is the means or instrument of our justification?

Faith. 'Being justified by faith.' Rom v 1. The dignity is not in faith as a grace, but relatively, as it lays hold on Christ's merits.

What is the efficient cause of our justification?

The whole Trinity. All the persons in the blessed Trinity have a hand in the justification of a sinner: *opera Trinitatis ad extra sunt indivisa.* God the Father is said to justify. 'It is God that justifieth.' Rom viii 33. God the Son is said to justify. 'By him all that believe are justified.' Acts xiii 39. God the Holy Ghost is said to justify. 'But ye are justified by the Spirit of our God.' 1 Cor vi 11. God the Father justifies, as he pronounces us righteous; God the Son justifies, as he imputes his righteousness to us; and God the Holy Ghost justifies, as he clears up our justification, and seals us up to the day of redemption.

What is the end of our justification?

The end is, (1.) That God may inherit praise. 'To the praise of the glory of his grace.' Eph i 6. Hereby God raises the everlasting trophies of his own honour. How will the justified sinner proclaim the love of God, and make heaven ring with his praises!

(2.) That the justified person may inherit glory. 'Whom he justified, them he also glorified.' Rom viii 30. God in justifying, not only absolves a soul from guilt, but advances him to dignity: as Joseph was not only loosed from prison, but made lord of the kingdom. Justification is crowned with glorification.

Are we justified from eternity?

No: for, (1.) By nature we are under a sentence of condemnation. John iii 18. We could never have been condemned, if we were justified from eternity.

(2.) The Scripture confines justification to those who believe and repent. 'Repent, that your sins may be blotted out.' Acts iii 19. Therefore their sins were uncancelled, and their persons unjustified, till they did repent. Though God does not justify us for our repentance, yet not without it. The Antinomians erroneously hold, that we are justified from eternity. This doctrine is a key which opens the door to all licentiousness; for what sins do they care not to commit, so long as they hold they are *ab æterno* justified whether they repent or not?

II. Before I come to the uses, *I shall lay down four maxims or positions about justification.*

[1] That justification confers a real benefit upon the person justified. The acquitting and discharging of the debtor, by virtue of the satisfaction made by the surety, is a real benefit to the debtor. A robe of righteousness, and a crown of righteousness, are real benefits.

[2] All believers are alike justified: *justificatio non recipit magis et minus.* [Justification does not apply to some more than to others.] Though

there are degrees in grace, yet not in justification; one is not justified more than another; the weakest believer is as perfectly justified as the strongest; Mary Magdalene is as much justified as the Virgin Mary. This may be a cordial to a weak believer. Though thou hast but a drachm of faith, thou art as truly justified as he who is of the highest stature in Christ.

[3] Whomsoever God justifies, he sanctifies. 'But ye are sanctified, but ye are justified.' 1 Cor vi 11. The Papists calumniate Protestants; they report them to hold that men continuing in sin are justified; whereas all our Protestant writers affirm, that righteousness imputed, for justification, and righteousness inherent, for sanctification, must be inseparably united. Holiness indeed is not the cause of our justification, but it is the attendant; as the heat in the sun is not the cause of its light, but it is the attendant. It is absurd to imagine that God should justify a people, and they should still go on in sin. If God should justify a people and not sanctify them, he would justify a people whom he could not glorify. A holy God cannot lay a sinner in his bosom. The metal is first refined, before the king's stamp is put upon it; so the soul is first refined with holiness, before God puts the royal stamp of justification upon it.

[4] Justification is *inamissibilis;* it is a fixed permanent thing, it can never be lost. The Arminians hold an apostasy from justification; to-day justified, tomorrow unjustified; to-day a Peter, to-morrow a Judas; to-day a member of Christ, to-morrow a limb of Satan. This is a most uncomfortable doctrine. Justified persons may fall from degrees of grace, they may leave their first love, they may lose God's favour for a time, but not lose their justification. If they are justified they are elected; and they can no more fall from their justification than from their election. If they are justified they have union with Christ; and can a member of Christ be broken off? If one justified person may fall away from Christ, all may; and so Christ would be a head without a body.

Use one: See from hence, that there is nothing within us that could justify, but something without us; not any righteousness inherent, but imputed. We may as well look for a star in the earth as for justification in our own righteousness. The Papists say we are justified by works; but the apostle confutes it, for he says, 'not of works, lest any man should boast.' Eph ii 9. The Papists say, 'the works done by an unregenerate man indeed cannot justify him, but works done by a regenerate man may justify.' This is most false, as may be proved both by example and reason.

(1.) By example. Abraham was a regenerate man; but Abraham was not justified by works, but by faith. Abraham 'believed God, and it was counted to him for righteousness.' Rom iv 3. (2.) By reason. How can those works justify us which defile us? 'Our righteousnesses are as filthy rags.' Isa lxiv 6. *Bona opera non præcedunt justificationem, sed sequuntur justificatum:* good works are not an usher to go before justification, but a handmaid to follow it.

But does not the apostle James say that Abraham was justified by works?

The answer is easy. Works declare us to be righteous before men, but they do not make us righteous before God. Works are evidences of our justification, not causes. The only name graven upon the golden plate of Christ our High Priest must be, THE LORD OUR RIGHTEOUSNESS.

Use two: Of exhortation. (1.) Adore the infinite wisdom and goodness of God that found out a way to justify us by 'rich grace and precious blood.' We were all involved in guilt; none of us could plead *not guilty;* and being guilty, we lay under a sentence of death. Now that the judge himself should find out a way to justify us, and the creditor himself contrive a way to have the debt paid, and not distress the debtor, should fill us with wonder and love. The angels admire the mystery of free grace in this new way of justifying and saving lost man, 1 Pet i 12, and should not we, who are nearly concerned in it, and on whom the benefit is devolved, cry out with the apostle, 'O the depth of the riches both of the wisdom and knowledge of God!' &c.

(2.) Labour for this high privilege of justification. There is balm in Gilead; Christ has laid down his blood as the price of our justification; and he offers himself and all his merits to us, to justify; he invites us to come to him; he has promised to give his Spirit, to enable us to do what is required. Why then, sinners, will ye not look after this great privilege of justification? Why starve in the midst of plenty? Why perish when there is a remedy to save you? Would not he be thought to be distracted, who having a pardon offered him, only upon the acknowledgment of his fault, and promising amendment, should bid the prince keep his pardon to himself; for his part, he was in love with his chains and fetters, and would die? Thou who neglectest justification offered thee freely by Christ in the gospel art this infatuated person. Is the love of Christ to be slighted? Is thy soul, is heaven worth nothing? Oh then look after justification through Christ's blood!

Consider (i) The necessity of being justified. If we are not justified, we cannot be glorified. 'Whom he justified, them he also glorified.' Rom viii 30. He who is outlawed, and all his goods confiscated, must be brought into favour with his prince before he can be restored to his former rights and liberties; so, we must have our sins forgiven, and be brought into God's favour by justification, before we can be restored to the liberty of the sons of God, and have a right to that happiness we forfeited in Adam.

(ii) The utility and benefit. By justification we enjoy peace in our conscience; a richer jewel than any prince wears in his crown. 'Being justified by faith, we have peace with God.' Rom v 1. Peace can sweeten all our afflictions, it turns our water into wine. How happy is a justified person who has the power of God to guard him, and the peace of God to comfort him! Peace flowing from justification is an antidote against the fear of death and hell. 'It is God that justifieth, who is he that condemneth?' Rom viii 33, 34. Therefore labour for this justification by Christ. This privilege is obtained by believing in Christ. 'By him all that believe are justified.' Acts xiii 39. 'Whom God hath set forth to be a propitiation through faith in his blood.' Rom iii 25. Faith unites us to Christ; and having union with his person we partake of his merits, and the glorious salvation which comes by him.

Use three: Comfort to the justified. (1.) It is comfort in case of failings. Alas! how defective are the godly! they come short in every duty; but though believers should be humbled under their defects, they should not despond. They are not to be justified by their duties or graces, but by the righteousness of Christ. Their duties are mixed with sin, but that righteousness which justifies them is a perfect righteousness.

(2.) Comfort in case of hard censures. The world censures the people of God as proud and hypocritical, and the troublers of Israel; but though men censure and condemn the godly, yet God has justified them, and as he has now justified them, so at the day of judgment he will openly justify them, and pronounce them righteous before men and angels. God is so just and holy a judge, that having once justified his people he will never condemn them. Pilate justified Christ, saying, 'I find no fault in him;' yet after this he condemned him; but God having publicly justified his saints, he will never condemn them; for 'whom he justified, them he also glorified.'

4. ADOPTION

'As many as received him to them gave he power to become the sons of God, even to them that believe on his name.' John i 12.

Having spoken of the great points of faith and justification, we come next to adoption.

The qualification of the persons is, 'As many as received him.' Receiving is put for believing, as is clear by the last words, 'to them that believe in his name.' The specification of the privilege is, 'to them gave he power to become the sons of God.' The Greek word for power, *exousia*, signifies dignity and prerogative: he dignified them to become the sons of God.

Our sonship differs from Christ's. He was the Son of God by eternal generation, a son before time; but our sonship is, (1.) By creation. 'We are his offspring.' Acts xvii 28. This is no privilege; for men may have God for their Father by creation, and yet have the devil for their father. (2.) Our sonship is by adoption. 'He gave them power to become the sons of God.'

Adoption is twofold. *External and federal:* as those who live in a visible church, and make a profession of God, are sons. 'The children of the kingdom shall be cast out.' Matt viii 12. *Real and gracious:* as they are sons who are God's favourites, and are heirs of glory. Before I proceed to the questions, I shall lay down three positions.

I. *Adoption takes in all nations.* A first adoption was confined to the people of the Jews, who alone were grafted into the true olive, and were dignified with glorious privileges. 'Who are Israelites, to whom pertaineth the adoption and the glory.' Rom ix 4. But now, in the time of the gospel, the charter is enlarged, and the believing Gentiles are within the line of communication, and have a right to the privileges of adoption as well as the Jews. 'In every nation he that feareth God and worketh righteousness is accepted with him.' Acts x 35.

II. *Adoption takes in both sexes, females as well as males.* 'I will be a father unto you, and ye shall be my sons and daughters.' 2 Cor vi 18. I have read, that in some countries, females are excluded from the supreme dignity, as by the Salique law in France, no woman can inherit a crown; but of spiritual privileges, females are as capable as males. Every gracious soul (of whatever sex) lays claim to adoption, and has an interest in God as a father. 'Ye shall be my sons and daughters, saith the Lord Almighty.'

III. *Adoption is an act of pure grace.* 'Having predestinated us to the adoption of children, according to the good pleasure of his will.' Eph i 5. Adoption is a mercy spun out of the bowels of free grace. All by nature are strangers, therefore have no right to sonship. God is pleased to adopt one, and not another; to make one a vessel of glory, another a vessel of wrath. The adopted heir may cry out, 'Lord, how is it, that thou wilt show thyself to me, and not unto the world?'

What is this filiation or adoption?

It is taking a stranger into the relation of a son and heir; as Moses was the adopted son of King Pharaoh's daughter, Exod ii 10, and Esther was the adopted child of her cousin Mordecai. Esth ii 7. Thus God adopts us into the family of heaven, and God in adopting us does two things:

(1.) He ennobles us with his name. He who is adopted bears the name of him who adopts him. 'I will write on him the name of my God.' Rev iii 12.

(2.) God consecrates us with his Spirit. Whom he adopts, he anoints; whom he makes sons, he makes saints. When a man adopts another for his son and heir, he may put his name upon him, but he cannot put his disposition into him; if he be of a morose rugged nature, he cannot alter it; but whom God adopts he sanctifies; he not only gives a new name but a new nature. 2 Pet i 4. He turns the wolf into a lamb; he makes the heart humble and gracious; he works such a change as if another soul dwelt in the same body.

From what state does God take us when he adopts us?

From a state of sin and misery. Pharaoh's daughter took Moses out of the ark of bulrushes in the water, and adopted him for her son. God did not take us out of the water, but out of our blood, and adopted us. Ezek xvi 6. He adopted us from slavery: it is a mercy to redeem a slave, but it is more to adopt him.

To what does God adopt us?

(1.) He adopts us to a state of excellence. It were much for God to take a clod of dust, and make it a star; it is more for him to take a piece of clay and sin, and adopt it for his heir.

(2.) God adopts us to a state of liberty. Adoption is a state of freedom; a slave being adopted is made a free man. 'Thou art no more a servant but a son.' Gal iv 7. *How is an adopted son free?* Not to do what he lists; but he is free from the dominion of sin, the tyranny of Satan, and the curse of the law. He is free in the manner of worship. He has God's free Spirit, which makes him free and cheerful in the service of God; he is 'joyful in the house of prayer.' Isa lvi 7.

(3.) God adopts us to a state of dignity. He makes us heirs of promise, he installs us into honour. 'Since thou wast precious in my sight, thou hast been honourable.' Isa xliii 4. The adopted are God's treasure; Exod xix 5; his jewels; Mal iii 17; his first-born; Heb xii 23. They have angels for their life-guards. Heb i 14. They are of the blood royal of heaven. 1 John iii 9. The Scripture has set forth their spiritual heraldry; they have their escutcheon or coat-armour; sometimes the lion for courage; Prov xxviii 1; sometimes the dove for meekness; Cant ii 14; sometimes the eagle for flight; Isa xl 31. Thus you see their coat of arms displayed.

(4.) What is honour without inheritance? God adopts all his sons to an inheritance. 'It is your father's good pleasure to give you the kingdom.' Luke xii 32. It is no disparagement to be the sons of God. To reproach the saints, is as if Shimei had reproached David when he was going to be made king. Adoption ends in coronation. The kingdom God gives his adopted sons and heirs excels all earthly monarchies.

(i) In riches. 'The gates are of pearl, and the streets of pure gold, as it were transparent glass.' Rev xxi 21.

(ii) In tranquillity. It is peaceable, and the white lily of peace is the best flower in a prince's crown. *Pax una triumphis innumeris melior* [One peace is better than innumerable triumphs]. No divisions at home, or invasions abroad; no more the noise of the drum or cannon; but the voice of harpers harping is the hieroglyphic of peace. Rev xiv 2.

(iii) In stability. Other kingdoms are corruptible; though they have heads of gold they have feet of clay; but the kingdom into which the saints are adopted runs parallel with eternity; it is a kingdom that cannot be shaken. Heb xii 28. The heirs of heaven reign for ever and ever. Rev xxii 5.

What is the organic or instrumental cause of adoption?

Faith interests us in the privilege of adoption. 'Ye are all the children of God by faith in Christ Jesus.' Gal iii 26. Before faith is wrought, we are spiritually illegitimate, we have no relation to God as a father. An unbeliever may call God judge, but not father. Faith is the affiliating grace; it confers upon us the title of sonship, and gives us right to inherit.

Why is faith the instrument of adoption more than any other grace?

Faith is a quickening grace, the vital artery of the soul. 'The just shall live by faith.' Hab ii 4. Life makes us capable of adoption, dead children are never adopted. It makes us Christ's brethren, and so God comes to be our Father.

Use one: (1.) See the amazing love of God, in making us his sons. Plato gave God thanks that he had made him a man, and not only a man but a philosopher; but it is infinitely more, that he should invest us with the prerogative of sons. It is love in God to feed us, but more to adopt us. 'Behold, what manner of love the Father hath bestowed upon us, that we should be called the sons of God!' 1 John iii 1. It is an *ecce admirantis*, a behold of wonder.

The wonder of God's love in adopting us will appear the more if we consider these six things:

(i) That God should adopt us when he had a Son of his own. Men adopt because they want children, and desire to have some to bear their name; but that God should adopt us when he had a Son of his own, the Lord Jesus, is a wonder of love. Christ is called 'God's dear Son.' Col i 13. A Son more worthy than the angels. 'Being made so much better than the angels.' Heb i 4. Now, since God had a Son of his own, and such a Son, how wonderful God's love in adopting us! We needed a Father, but he did not need sons.

(ii) Consider what we were before God adopted us. We were very deformed; and a man will scarce adopt him for his heir that is crooked and ill-favoured, but rather him that has some beauty. Mordecai adopted Esther, because she was fair. When we were in our blood God adopted us. 'When I saw thee polluted in thy blood, it was the time of love.' Ezek xvi 6, 8. God did not adopt us when we were bespangled with the jewels of holiness, and had the angels' glory upon us; but when we were black as Ethiopians, diseased as lepers, was the time of his love.

(iii) That God should be at so great expense in adopting us. When men adopt, they have only some deed sealed, and the thing is effected; but when God adopts, it puts him to a far greater expense; it sets his wisdom to work to find out a way to adopt us. It was no easy thing to make heirs of wrath, heirs of the promise. When God had found out a way to adopt, it was no easy way. Our adoption was purchased at a dear rate; for when God was about to make us sons and heirs, he could not seal the deed but by the blood of his own Son. Here is the wonder of God's love in adopting us, that he should be at all this expense to accomplish it.

(iv) That God should adopt his enemies. If a man adopts another for his heir, he will not adopt his mortal enemy; but that God should adopt us, when we were not only strangers, but enemies, is the wonder of his love. For God to have pardoned his enemies had been much; but to adopt them for his heirs, sets the angels in heaven wondering.

(v) That God should take great numbers out of the devil's family, and adopt them into the family of heaven. Christ is said to bring many sons to glory. Heb ii 10. Men adopt usually but one heir, but God is resolved to increase his family, he brings many sons to glory. God's adopting millions is the wonder of love. Had but one been adopted, all of us might have despaired; but he brings many sons to glory, which opens a door of hope to us.

(vi) That God should confer so great honour upon us, in adopting us. David thought it no small honour that he should be a king's son-in-law. 1 Sam xviii 18. But what honour to be the sons of the high God! The more honour God has put upon us in adopting us, the more he has magnified his love towards us. What honour that God has made us so near in alliance to him, sons of God the Father, members of God the Son, temples of God the Holy Ghost! that he has made us as the angels, Matt xxii 30; nay, in some sense, superior to the angels! All this proclaims the wonder of God's love in adopting us.

(2.) See the sad condition of such as live and die in unbelief. They are not the sons of God. 'To as many as received him, he gave power to become the sons of God, even to them that believe on his name.' No faith, no sonship. Unbelievers have no sign of sonship, they know not God. All God's children know their Father, but the wicked do not know him. 'They proceed from evil to evil, and know not me, saith the Lord.' Jer ix 3. Unbelievers are 'dead in trespasses.' Eph ii 1. God has no dead children; and not being children, they have no right to inherit.

Use two: Try whether you are adopted. All the world is divided into two ranks, the sons of God, and the heirs of hell. 'To them he gave power to become the sons of God.' John i 12. Let us put ourselves on a trial. It is no sign we are adopted sons, because we are sons of godly parents. The Jews boasted that they were of Abraham's seed, and thought they must needs be good, because they came of such a holy line. But adoption does not come by blood. Many godly parents have wicked sons; Abraham had an Ishmael; Isaac an Esau. The corn that is sown pure brings forth grain with a husk; so from him who is holy the child springs that is unholy. So that, as Jerome says, *non nascimur filii* [We are not born sons]; we are not God's sons as we are born of godly parents, but by adoption and grace. Well, then, let us try if we are the adopted sons and daughters of God.

The first sign of adoption is obedience. A son obeys his father. 'I set before the sons of the house of the Rechabites pots full of wine, and cups, and said unto them, Drink ye wine. But they said, We will drink no wine: for Jonadab the son of Rechab our father commanded us, saying, Ye shall drink no wine.' Jer xxxv 5. So, when God says drink not in sin's enchanted cup, an adopted child says, my heavenly Father has commanded me, and I dare not drink. A gracious soul not only believes God's promise, but obeys his command. True child-like obedience must be regular, which implies five things:

(1.) It must be done by a right rule. Obedience must have the word for its rule. *Lydius lapis* [This is the touchstone]. 'To the law and to the testimony.' Isa viii 20. If our obedience be not according to the word, it is offering up strange fire; it is will worship; and God will say, Who hath required this at your hand? The apostle condemns worshipping of angels, which had a show of humility. Col ii 18. The Jews might say that they were loath to be so bold as to go to God in their own persons; they would be more humble, and prostrate themselves before the angels, desiring them to be their mediators to God. Here was a show of humility in their angel worship; but it was abominable, because they had no word of God to warrant it; it was not obedience, but idolatry. Child-like obedience is that which is consonant to our Father's revealed will.

(2.) It must be done from a right principle, from the noble principle of faith. 'The obedience of faith.' Rom xvi 26. *Quicquid decorum est ex fide proficiscitur* [All acceptable works proceed from faith]. Augustine. A crab-tree may bear fruit fair to the eye, but it is sour because it does not come from a good root. A moral person may give God outward obedience, which to the eyes of others may seem glorious; but his obedience is sour, because it comes not from the sweet and pleasant root of faith. A child of God gives him the obedience of faith, and that meliorates and sweetens his services, and makes them come off with a better relish. 'By faith Abel offered a better sacrifice than Cain.' Heb xi 4.

(3.) It must be done to a right end. *Finis specificat actionem* [The end determines the value of the deed]; the end of obedience is glorifying God. That which has spoiled many glorious services, is, that the end has been wrong. 'When thou doest thine alms, do not sound a trumpet, as the hypocrites do, that they may have glory of men.' Matt vi 2. Good works should shine, but not blaze. 'If I give my body to be burnt, and have not charity, it profits me nothing.' 1 Cor xiii 3. The same I must say of a sincere aim; if I obey never so much, and have not a sincere aim, it profits me nothing. True obedience looks at God in all things. 'That Christ may be magnified.' Phil i 20. Though a child of God shoots short, yet he takes a right aim.

(4.) True child-like obedience must be uniform. A child of God makes conscience of one command as well as another. *Quicquid propter Deum fit æqualiter fit* [All things done for God are done with equal zeal]. All God's commands have the same stamp of divine authority upon them; and if I obey one precept because my heavenly Father commands me, by the same rule I must obey all. As the blood runs through all the veins of the body, and the sun in the firmament runs through all the signs of the zodiac; so true child-like obedience runs through the first and second table. 'When I have respect unto all thy commandments.' Psalm cxix 6. To obey God in some things of religion and not in others, shows an unsound heart; like Esau, who obeyed his father in bringing him venison, but not in a greater matter, as the choice of his wife. Child-like obedience moves towards every command of God, as the needle points that way which the load-stone draws. If God call to duties which are cross to flesh and blood, if we are children, we shall still obey our Father.

But who can obey God in all things?

Though an adopted heir of heaven cannot obey every precept per-fectly, yet he does evangelically. He approves of every command. 'I consent to the law, that it is good.' Rom vii 16. He delights in every command. 'O how love I thy law!' Psalm cxix 97. His desire is to obey every command. 'O that my ways were directed to keep thy statutes!' Psalm cxix 5. Wherein he comes short, he looks up to Christ's blood to supply his defects. This is evangelical obedience; which, though it be not to satisfaction, it is to acceptance.

(5.) True childlike obedience is constant. 'Blessed is he that doeth righteousness at all times.' Psalm cvi 3. Child-like obedience is not like a high colour in a fit, which is soon over; but like a right sanguine com-plexion, which abides; and like the fire on the altar, which was kept always burning. Lev vi 13.

The second sign of adoption is to love to be in our Father's presence. The child who loves his father is never so well as when he is near him. Are we children? We love the presence of God in his ordinances. In prayer we speak to God, in the preaching of his word he speaks to us; and how does every child of God delight to hear his Father's voice! 'My soul thirsteth for thee, to see thy glory so as I have seen thee in the sanc-tuary.' Psalm lxiii 1, 2. Such as disregard ordinances are not God's child-ren, because they care not to be in God's presence. 'Cain went out from the presence of the Lord.' Gen iv 16. Not that he could go out of God's sight, but the meaning is, 'Cain went out from the church and people of God, where the Lord gave visible tokens of his presence.'

The third sign of adoption is to have the guidance of God's Spirit. 'As many as are led by the Spirit of God, they are the sons of God.' Rom viii 14. It is not enough that the child have life, but it must be led every step by the nurse; so the adopted child must not only be born of God, but have the manuduction of the Spirit to lead him in a course of holiness. 'I taught Ephraim also to go, taking them by their arms.' Hos xi 3. As Israel was led by the pillar of fire, so God's children are led by the Spirit. The adopted ones need God's Spirit to lead them, since they are apt to go wrong. The fleshy part inclines to sin; the understanding and con-science are to guide the will, but the will is imperious and rebels; there-fore, God's children need the Spirit to check corruption and lead them in the right way. As wicked men are led by the evil spirit – the spirit of

Satan led Herod to incest, Ahab to murder, Judas to treason – so the good Spirit leads God's children into virtuous actions.

But enthusiasts pretend to be led by the Spirit, when it is an ignis fatuus, *a delusion.*

The Spirit's guidance is agreeable to the Word; enthusiasts leave the Word. 'Thy Word is truth.' John xvii 17. 'The Spirit guides into all truth.' John xvi 13. The Word's teaching and the Spirit's leading agree together.

The fourth sign is, that if we are adopted we have an entire love to all God's children. 'Love the brotherhood.' 1 Pet ii 17. We bear affection to God's children, though they have some infirmities. There are spots in God's children; Deut xxxii 5; but we must love the beautiful face of holiness though it has a scar in it. If we are adopted, we love the good we see in God's children: we admire their graces, we pass by their imprudencies. If we cannot love them because they have some failings, how do we think God can love us? Can we plead exemption? By these signs we know our adoption.

Use three: Rejoice in the benefits of adoption.

What are the benefits which accrue to God's children?

(1.) They have great privileges. King's children have great privileges and freedoms. They do not pay custom. Matt xvii 25. God's children are privileged persons, they are privileged from the hurt of everything. 'Nothing shall by any means hurt you.' Luke x 19. Hit you it may, but not hurt you. 'There shall no evil befall thee.' Psa xci 10. God says not, No affliction shall befall his children, but, No evil; the hurt and poison of it is taken away. Affliction to a wicked man has evil in it, it makes him worse; it makes him curse and blaspheme. 'Men were scorched with great heat, and blasphemed the name of God.' Rev xvi 9. But no evil befalls a child of God; he is bettered by affliction. Heb xii 10. The furnace makes gold purer. Again, no evil befalls the adopted, because no condemnation. 'It is God that justifieth; who is he that condemneth?' Rom viii 33. What a blessed privilege is this, to be freed from the sting of affliction, and the curse of the law! to be in such a condition that nothing can hurt us! When the dragon has poisoned the water, the unicorn with his horn extracts and draws out the poison; so Jesus Christ has drawn out the poison of every affliction, that it cannot injure the saints.

(2.) The second benefit, if we are adopted, is that we have an interest in all the promises. The promises are children's bread. 'Believers are heirs of the promises.' Heb vi 17. The promises are sure. God's truth, which is the brightest pearl in his crown, is pawned in a promise. The promises are suitable, like a medical garden, in which there is no disease but there is some herb to cure it. In the dark night of desertion God has promised to be a sun; in temptation, to tread down Satan. Rom xvi 20. Does sin prevail? He has promised to take away its kingly power. Rom vi 14. Oh the heavenly comforts which are distilled from the promises! But who has a right to these? Believers only are heirs of the promise. There is not a promise in the Bible but a believer may say, This is mine.

Use four: Extol and magnify God's mercy, who has adopted you into his family; who, of slaves, has made you sons; of heirs of hell, heirs of the promise. Adoption is a free gift. He gave them power, or dignity, to become the sons of God. As a thread of silver runs through a whole piece of work, so free grace runs through the whole privilege of adoption. Adoption is a greater mercy than Adam had in paradise; he was a son by creation, but here is a further sonship by adoption. To make us thankful, consider, in civil adoption there is some worth and excellence in the person to be adopted; but there was no worth in us, neither beauty, nor parentage, nor virtue; nothing in us to move God to bestow the prerogative of sonship upon us. We have enough in us to move God to correct us, but nothing to move him to adopt us, therefore exalt free grace; begin the work of angels here; bless him with your praises who has blessed you in making you his sons and daughters.

5. SANCTIFICATION

'*For this is the will of God, even your sanctification.*' 1 Thess iv 3.

The word sanctification signifies to consecrate and set apart to a holy use: thus they are sanctified persons who are separated from the world, and set apart for God's service. Sanctification has a privative and a positive part.

I. *A privative part, which lies in the purging out of sin.* Sin is compared to leaven, which sours; and to leprosy, which defiles. Sanctification purges out 'the old leaven.' 1 Cor v 7. Though it takes not away the life, yet it takes away the love of sin.

II. *A positive part, which is the spiritual refining of the soul;* which in Scripture is called a 'renewing of our mind,' Rom xii 2, and a 'partaking of the divine nature.' 2 Pet i 4. The priests in the law were not only washed in the great laver, but adorned with glorious apparel. Exod xxviii 2; so sanctification not only washes from sin, but adorns with purity.

What is sanctification?

It is a principle of grace savingly wrought, whereby the heart becomes holy, and is made after God's own heart. A sanctified person bears not only God's name, but his image. In opening the nature of sanctification, I shall lay down these seven positions:—

(1.) Sanctification is a supernatural thing; it is divinely infused. We are naturally polluted, and to cleanse, God takes to be his prerogative. 'I am the Lord which sanctify you.' Lev xxi 8. Weeds grow of themselves. Flowers are planted. Sanctification is a flower of the Spirit's planting, therefore it is called, 'The sanctification of the Spirit.' 1 Pet i 2.

(2.) Sanctification is an intrinsic thing; it lies chiefly in the heart. It is called 'the adorning the hidden man of the heart.' 1 Pet iii 4. The dew wets the leaf, the sap is hid in the root; so the religion of some consists only in externals, but sanctification is deeply rooted in the soul. 'In the hidden part thou shalt make me to know wisdom.' Psalm li 6.

(3.) Sanctification is an extensive thing: it spreads into the whole man. 'The God of peace sanctify you wholly.' 1 Thess v 23. As original corruption has depraved all the faculties – 'the whole head is sick, the whole heart faint,' no part sound, as if the whole mass of blood were corrupted – so sanctification goes over the whole soul. After the fall, there was ignorance in the mind; but in sanctification, we are 'light in the Lord.' Eph v 8. After the fall, the will was depraved; there was not only impotence to good, but obstinacy. In sanctification, there is a blessed pliableness in the will; it symbolizes and comports with the will of God. After the fall, the affections were misplaced on wrong objects; in sanctification, they are turned into a sweet order and harmony, the grief placed on sin, the love on God, the joy on heaven. Thus sanctification spreads itself as far as original corruption; it goes over the whole soul: 'the God of peace sanctify you wholly.' He is not a sanctified person who is good only in some part, but who is all over sanctified; therefore, in Scripture, grace is called a 'new man,' not a new eye or a new tongue, but a 'new man.' Col iii 10. A good Christian, though he be sanctified but in part, yet in every part.

(4.) Sanctification is an intense and ardent thing. *Qualitates sunt in subjecto intensive* [Its properties burn within the believer]. 'Fervent in spirit.' Rom xii 11. Sanctification is not a dead form, but it is inflamed into zeal.

We call water hot, when it is so in the third or fourth degree; so he is holy whose religion is heated to some degree, and his heart boils over in love to God.

(5.) Sanctification is a beautiful thing. It makes God and angels fall in love with us. 'The beauties of holiness.' Psa cx 3. As the sun is to the world, so is sanctification to the soul, beautifying and bespangling it in God's eyes. That which makes God glorious must needs make us so. Holiness is the most sparkling jewel in the Godhead. 'Glorious in holiness.' Exod xv 11. Sanctification is the first fruit of the Spirit; it is heaven begun in the soul. Sanctification and glory differ only in degree: sanctification is glory in the seed, and glory is sanctification in the flower. Holiness is the quintessence of happiness.

(6.) Sanctification is an abiding thing. 'His seed remaineth in him.' 1 John iii 9. He who is truly sanctified, cannot fall from that state. Indeed, seeming holiness may be lost, colours may wash off, sanctification may suffer an eclipse. 'Thou hast left thy first love.' Rev ii 4. True sanctification is a blossom of eternity. 'The anointing which ye have received abideth in you.' 1 John ii 27. He who is truly sanctified can no more fall away than the angels which are fixed in their heavenly orbs.

(7.) Sanctification is a progressive thing. It is growing; it is compared to seed which grows: first the blade springs up, then the ear, then the ripe corn in the ear; such as are already sanctified may be more sanctified. 2 Cor vii 1. Justification does not admit of degrees; a believer cannot be more elected or justified than he is, but he may be more sanctified than he is. Sanctification is still increasing, like the morning sun, which grows brighter to the full meridian. Knowledge is said to increase, and faith to increase. Col i 10; 2 Cor x 15. A Christian is continually adding a cubit to his spiritual stature. It is not with us as it was with Christ, who received the Spirit without measure; for Christ could not be more holy than he was. We have the Spirit only in measure, and may be still augmenting our grace; as Apelles, when he had drawn a picture, would be still mending it with his pencil. The image of God is drawn but imperfectly in us, therefore we must be still mending it, and drawing it in more lively colours. Sanctification is progressive; if it does not grow, it is because it does not live. Thus you see the nature of sanctification.

What are the counterfeits of sanctification?

There are things which look like sanctification, but are not.

(1.) The first counterfeit of sanctification is moral virtue. To be just, to be temperate, to be of a fair deportment, not to have one's escutcheon blotted with ignominious scandal is good, but not enough: it is not sanctification. A field-flower differs from a garden-flower. Heathens have attained to morality; as Cato, Socrates, and Aristides. Civility is but nature refined; there is nothing of Christ there, and the heart may be foul and impure. Under these fair leaves of civility the worm of unbelief may be hid. A moral person has a secret antipathy against grace: he hates vice, and he hates grace as much as vice. The snake has a fine colour, but a sting. A person adorned and cultivated with moral virtue, has a secret spleen against sanctity. The Stoics who were the chief of the moralized heathens, were the bitterest enemies Paul had. Acts xvii 18.

(2.) The second counterfeit of sanctification is superstitious devotion. This abounds in Popery; adorations, images, altars, vestments, and holy water, which I look upon as a religious frenzy, and is far from sanctification. It does not put any intrinsic goodness into a man, it does not make a man better. If the legal purifications and washings, which were of God's own appointing, did not make those who used them more holy; and the priests, who wore holy garments, and had holy oil poured on them, were not more holy without the anointing of the Spirit; then surely those superstitious innovations in religion, which God never appointed, cannot contribute any holiness to men. A superstitious holiness costs no great labour; there is nothing of the heart in it. If to tell over a few beads, or bow to an image, or sprinkle themselves with holy water were sanctification, and all that is required of them that should be saved, then hell would be empty, none would come there.

(3.) The third counterfeit of sanctification is hypocrisy; when men make a pretence of that holiness which they have not. As a comet may shine like a star, a lustre may shine from their profession that dazzles the eyes of the beholders. 'Having a form of godliness, but denying the power.' 2 Tim iii 5. These are lamps without oil; whited sepulchres, like the Egyptian temples, which had fair outsides, but within spiders and apes. The apostle speaks of true holiness. Eph iv 24, implying that there is holiness which is spurious and feigned. 'Thou hast a name to live, but art dead;' Rev iii 1; like pictures and statues which are destitute of a vital principle. 'Clouds without water.' Jude 12. They pretend to be full of the Spirit, but are empty clouds. This show of sanctification is a self-delusion. He who takes copper instead of gold, wrongs himself; the most counterfeit saint deceives others while he lives, but deceives himself when he dies. To pretend to holiness when there is none is a vain thing. What were the foolish virgins better for their blazing lamps, when they wanted oil? What is the lamp of profession without the oil of saving grace? What comfort will a show of holiness yield at last? Will painted gold enrich? painted wine refresh him that is thirsty? or painted holiness be a cordial at the hour of death? A pretence of sanctification is not to be rested in. Many ships, that have had the name of the Hope, the Safeguard, the Triumph, have been cast away upon rocks; so, many who have had the name of saints, have been cast into hell.

(4.) The fourth counterfeit of sanctification is restraining grace, when men forbear vice, though they do not hate it. This may be the sinner's motto, 'Fain I would, but I dare not.' The dog has a mind to the bone, but is afraid of the cudgel; so men have a mind to lust, but conscience stands as the angel, with a flaming sword, and affrights: they have a mind to revenge, but the fear of hell is a curb-bit to check them. There is no change of heart; sin is curbed, but not cured. A lion may be in chains, but is a lion still.

(5.) The fifth counterfeit of sanctification is common grace, which is a slight, transient work of the Spirit, but does not amount to conversion. There is some light in the judgment, but it is not humbling; some checks in the conscience, but they are not awakening. This looks like sanctification, but is not. Men have convictions wrought in them, but they break loose from them again, like the deer, which, being shot, shakes out the arrow. After conviction, men go into the house of mirth, take the harp to drive away the spirit of sadness, and so all dies and comes to nothing.

Wherein appears the necessity of sanctification?

In six things: (1.) God has called us to it. 'Who hath called us to glory and virtue; 2 Pet i 3; to virtue, as well as glory. 'God hath not called us to uncleanness, but unto holiness.' 1 Thess iv 7. We have no call to sin, we may have a temptation, but no call; no call to be proud, or unclean; but we have a call to be holy.

(2.) Without sanctification there is no evidencing our justification. Justification and sanctification go together. 'But ye are sanctified, but ye are justified.' 1 Cor vi 11. 'Pardoning iniquity,' Mic vii 18; there is justification. 'He will subdue our iniquities,' v 19; there is sanctification. 'Out of Christ's side came blood and water,' John xix 34; blood for justification; water for sanctification. Such as have not the water out of Christ's side to cleanse them, shall never have the blood out of his side to save them.

(3.) Without sanctification we have no title to the new covenant. The covenant of grace is our charter for heaven. The tenure of the covenant is, That God will be our God. But who are interested in the covenant, and may plead the benefit of it? Sanctified persons only. 'A new heart will I give you, and I will put my Spirit within you, and I will be your God.'

Ezek xxxvi 26. If a man makes a will, none but such persons as are named in the will can lay claim to the will; so God makes a will and testament, but it is restrained and limited to such as are sanctified; and it is high presumption for any one else to lay claim to the will.

(4.) There is no going to heaven without sanctification. 'Without holiness no man shall see the Lord.' Heb xii 14. God is a holy God, and he will suffer no unholy creature to come near him. A king will not suffer a man with plague-sores to approach into his presence. Heaven is not like Noah's ark, where the clean beasts and the unclean entered. No unclean beasts come into the heavenly ark; for though God suffer the wicked to live awhile on the earth, he will never suffer heaven to be pestered with such vermin. Are they fit to see God who wallow in wickedness? Will God ever lay such vipers in his bosom? 'Without holiness no man shall see the Lord.' It must be a clear eye that sees a bright object: only a holy heart can see God in his glory. Sinners may see God as an enemy, but not as a friend; may have an affrighting vision of him, but not a beatific vision; they may see the flaming sword, but not the mercy-seat. Oh then, what need is there of sanctification!

(5.) Without sanctification all our holy things are defiled. 'Unto them that are defiled is nothing pure.' Tit i 15. Under the law, if a man who was unclean by a dead body carried a piece of holy flesh in his skirt, the holy flesh would not cleanse him, but it would be polluted by him. Hag ii 12, 13. This is an emblem of a sinner's polluting his holy offering. A foul stomach turns the best food into ill humours; so an unsanctified heart pollutes prayers, alms, sacraments. This evinces the necessity of sanctification. Sanctification makes our holy things accepted. A holy heart is the altar which sanctifies the offering; if not to satisfaction, to acceptation.

(6.) Without sanctification we can show no sign of our election. 2 Thess ii 13. Election is the cause of our salvation, sanctification is our evidence. Sanctification is the ear-mark of Christ's elect sheep.

What are the signs of sanctification?

First, such as are sanctified can remember a time when they were unsanctified. Tit iii 3. We were in our blood, and then God washed us with water, and anointed us with oil. Ezek xvi 9. Those trees of righteousness that blossom and bear almonds, can remember when they were like Aaron's dry rod, not one blossom of holiness growing. A sanctified soul can remember when it was estranged from God through ignorance and vanity, and when free grace planted this flower of holiness in it.

A second sign of sanctification is the indwelling of the Spirit. 'The Holy Ghost which dwelleth in us.' 2 Tim i 14. As the unclean spirit dwells in the wicked and carries them to pride, lust, revenge – the devil enters into these swine, Acts v 3 – so the Spirit of God dwells in the elect, as their guide and comforter. The Spirit possesses the saints. God's Spirit sanctifies the fancy, causing it to mint holy thoughts; and sanctifies the will by putting a new bias upon it, whereby it is inclined to good. He who is sanctified has the influence of the Spirit, though not the essence.

A third sign of sanctification is an antipathy against sin. Psa cxix 104. A hypocrite may leave sin, yet love it; as a serpent casts its coat, but keeps its sting; but a sanctified person can say he not only leaves sin, but loathes it. As there are antipathies in nature between the vine and laurel, so in a sanctified soul there is a holy antipathy against sin; and antipathies can never be reconciled. Because a man has an antipathy against sin, he cannot but oppose it, and seek the destruction of it.

A fourth sign of sanctification is the spiritual performance of duties, with the heart, and from a principle of love. The sanctified soul prays out of a love to prayer, and 'calls the Sabbath a delight.' Isa lviii 13. A man may have gifts to admiration; he may speak as an angel dropped out of heaven, yet he may be carnal in spiritual things; his services may not come from a renewed principle, nor be carried upon the wings of delight in duty. A sanctified soul worships God in the Spirit. 1 Pet ii 5. God judges not of our duties by their length, but by the love from which they spring.

A fifth sign is a well-ordered life. 'Be ye holy in all manner of conversation.' 1 Pet i 15. Where the heart is sanctified the life will be so too. The temple had gold without as well as within. As in a piece of coin there is not only the king's image within the ring, but his superscription without; so where there is sanctification, there is not only God's image in the heart, but a superscription of holiness written in the life. Some say they have good hearts, but their lives are vicious. 'There is a generation that are pure in their own eyes, and yet is not washed from their filthiness.' Prov xxx 12. If the water be foul in the bucket, it cannot be clean in the well. 'The king's daughter is all glorious within.' Psa xlv 13. There is holiness of heart. 'Her clothing is of wrought gold.' There is holiness of life. Grace is most beautiful when its light so shines that others may see it; this adorns religion, and makes proselytes to the faith.

A sixth sign is steadfast resolution. He is resolved never to part with his holiness. Let others reproach it, he loves it the more. Let water be sprinkled on the fire, it burns the more. He says, as David, when Michal reproached him for dancing before the ark, 'If this be to be vile, I will yet be more vile.' 2 Sam vi 22. Let others persecute him for his holiness, he says as Paul, 'None of these things move me.' Acts xx 24. He prefers sanctity before safety, and had rather keep his conscience pure than his skin whole. He says as Job, 'My integrity I will hold fast, and not let it go,' xxvii 6. He will rather part with his life than his conscience.

Use one: The main thing a Christian should look after is sanctification. This is the *unum necessarium*, 'the one thing needful.' Sanctification is our purest complexion, it makes us as the heaven, bespangled with stars; it is our nobility, by it we are born of God, and partake of the divine nature; it is our riches, therefore compared to rows of jewels, and chains of gold. Cant i 10. It is our best certificate for heaven. What evidence have we else to show? Have we knowledge? So has the devil. Do we profess religion? Satan often appears in Samuel's mantle, and transforms himself into an angel of light. But our certificate for heaven is sanctification. Sanctification is the firstfruits of the Spirit; the only coin that will pass current in the other world. Sanctification is the evidence of God's love. We cannot know God's love by giving us health, riches, success; but by drawing his image of sanctification on us by the pencil of the Holy Ghost it is known.

Oh the misery of such as are destitute of a principle of sanctification! They are spiritually dead. Eph ii 1. Though they breathe, yet they do not live. The greatest part of the world remains unsanctified. 'The world lies in wickedness.' 1 John v 19. That is, the major par' of the world. Many call themselves Christians, but blot out the word saints. You may as well call him a man who wants reason, as him a Christian who wants grace. Nay, which is worse, some are buoyed up to such a height of wickedness, that they hate and deride sanctification. They hate it. It is bad to want it, it is worse to hate it. They embrace the form of religion, but hate the power. The vulture hates sweet smells, so do they the perfumes of holiness. They say in derision, These are your holy ones! To deride sanctification argues a high degree of atheism, and is a black brand of reprobation. Scoffing Ishmael was cast out of Abraham's family, Gen xxi 9; and such as scoff at holiness shall be cast out of heaven.

Use two: Above all things pursue after sanctification. Seek grace more than gold. 'Keep her, for she is thy life.' Prov iv 13.

What are the chief inducements to sanctification?

(1.) It is the will of God that we should be holy, as saith the text, 'This is the will of God, your sanctification.' As God's word must be the rule, so his will, the reason of our actions. This is the will of God, our sanctification. Perhaps it is not the will of God we should be rich, but it is his will that we should be holy. God's will is our warrant.

(2.) Jesus Christ has died for our sanctification. Christ shed his blood to wash off our impurity. The cross was both an altar and a laver. 'Who gave himself for us to redeem us from all iniquity.' Tit ii 14. If we could be saved without holiness, Christ needed not have died. Christ died, not only to save us from wrath, but from sin.

(3.) Sanctification makes us resemble God. It was Adam's sin that he aspired to be like God in omniscience, but we must endeavour to be like him in sanctity. It is a clear glass in which we can see a face; it is a holy heart in which something of God can be seen. Nothing of God can be seen in an unsanctified man, but you may see Satan's picture in him. Envy is the devil's eye, hypocrisy his cloven foot; but nothing of God's image can be seen in him.

(4.) Sanctification is that which God bears a great love to. Not any outward ornaments, high blood, or worldly grandeur, draws God's love, but a heart embellished with holiness does. Christ never admired anything but the beauty of holiness: he slighted the glorious buildings of the temple, but admired the woman's faith, and said, 'O woman, great is thy faith.' *Amor fundatur similitudine.* As a king delights to see his image upon a piece of coin, so where God sees his likeness he gives his love. The Lord has two heavens to dwell in, and the holy heart is one of them.

(5.) Sanctification is the only thing that makes us differ from the wicked. God's people have his seal upon them. 'The foundation of God standeth sure, having this seal, The Lord knoweth them that are his. And, Let every one that nameth the name of Christ depart from iniquity.' 2 Tim ii 19. The godly are sealed with a double seal, a seal of election, 'The Lord knoweth who are his,' and a seal of sanctification, 'Let every one that nameth the name of Christ depart from iniquity.' This is the name by which God's people are known, 'The people of thy holiness.' Isa lxiii 18. As chastity distinguishes a virtuous woman from a harlot, so sanctification distinguishes God's people from others. 'Ye have received an unction from the Holy One.' 1 John ii 20.

(6.) It is as great a shame to have the name of a Christian, yet want sanctity, as to have the name of a steward and want fidelity; or the name of a virgin, and want chastity. It exposes religion to reproach, to be baptized into the name of Christ while unholy, and to have eyes full of tears on a sabbath, and on a week-day eyes full of adultery: 2 Pet ii 14; to be so devout at the Lord's table, as if men were stepping into heaven, and so profane the week after, as if they came out of hell; to have the name of Christians while unholy is a scandal to religion, and makes the ways of God evil spoken of.

(7.) Sanctification fits for heaven: 'Who hath called us to glory and virtue.' 2 Pet i 3. Glory is the throne, and sanctification is the step by which we ascend to it. As you first cleanse the vessel, and then pour in

[248]

the wine; so God first cleanses us by sanctification, and then pours in the wine of glory. Solomon was first anointed with oil, and then was a king. 1 Kings i 39. First God anoints us with the holy oil of his Spirit, and then sets the crown of happiness upon our head. Pureness of heart and seeing God are linked together. Matt v 8.

How may sanctification be attained?

(1.) Be conversant in the word of God. 'Sanctify them through thy truth.' John xvii 17. The word is both a glass to show us the spots of our soul, and a laver to wash them away. The word has a transforming virtue in it; it irradiates the mind, and consecrates the heart.

(2.) Get faith in Christ's blood. 'Having purified their hearts by faith.' Acts xv 9. She in the gospel who touched the hem of Christ's garment was healed. A touch of faith purifies. Nothing can have a greater force upon the heart, to sanctify it, than faith. If I believe Christ and his merits are mine, how can I sin against him? Justifying faith does that in a spiritual sense which miraculous faith does, it removes mountains, the mountains of pride, lust, envy. Faith and the love of sin are inconsistent.

(3.) Breathe after the Spirit. It is called 'the sanctification of the Spirit.' 2 Thess ii 13. The Spirit sanctifies the heart, as lightning purifies the air, and as fire refines metals. *Omne agens generat sibi simile.* [The Spirit at work generates its own likeness everywhere.] The Spirit stamps the impression of its own sanctity upon the heart, as the seal prints its likeness upon the wax. The Spirit of God in a man perfumes him with holiness, and makes his heart a map of heaven.

(4.) Associate with sanctified persons. They may, by their counsel, prayers, and holy example, be a means to make you holy. As the communion of saints is in our creed, so it should be in our company. 'He that walketh with the wise shall be wise.' Prov xiii 20. Association begets assimilation.

(5.) Pray for sanctification. Job propounds a question. 'Who can bring a clean thing out of an unclean?' Job xiv 4. God can do it. Out of an unholy heart he can produce grace. Oh! make David's prayer your own, 'Create in me a clean heart, O God.' Psa li 10. Lay thy heart before the Lord, and say, Lord, my unsanctified heart pollutes all it touches. I am not fit to live with such a heart, for I cannot honour thee; nor die with such a heart, for I cannot see thee. Oh create in me a new heart! Lord, consecrate my heart, and make it thy temple, and thy praises shall be sung there for ever.

Use three: Has God brought a clean thing out of an unclean? has he sanctified you? Wear this jewel of sanctification with thankfulness. 'Giving thanks to the Father, who hath made us meet for the inheritance,'

&c. Col i 12. Christian, thou couldst defile thyself, but not sanctify thyself; but God has done it, he has not only chained up sin, but changed thy nature, and made thee as a king's daughter, all glorious within. He has put upon thee the breastplate of holiness, which, though it may be shot at, can never be shot through. Are there any here that are sanctified? God has done more for you than millions, who may be illumined, but are not sanctified. He has done more for you than if he had made you the sons of princes, and caused you to ride upon the high places of the earth. Are you sanctified? Heaven is begun in you; for happiness is nothing but the quintessence of holiness. Oh, how thankful should you be to God! Do as that blind man in the gospel did after he had received his sight, who 'followed Christ, glorifying God.' Luke xviii 43. Make heaven ring with God's praises.

6. ASSURANCE

Qxxxvi: WHAT ARE THE BENEFITS WHICH FLOW FROM SANCTIFICATION?

A: Assurance of God's love, peace of conscience, joy in the Holy Ghost, increase of grace, and perseverance therein to the end.

The first benefit flowing from sanctification is assurance of God's love. 'Give diligence to make your calling and election sure.' 2 Pet i 10. Sanctification is the seed, assurance is the flower which grows out of it: assurance is a consequent of sanctification. The saints of old had it. 'We know that we know him.' 1 John ii 3. 'I know whom I have believed.' 2 Tim i 12. Here was *sensus fidei*, 'the reflex act of faith': and 'Christ hath loved me.' Gal ii 20. Here is faith flourishing into assurance. Æcolampadius, when sick, pointed to his heart, saying, *Hic sat lucis*, Here I have light enough, meaning comfort and assurance.

Have all sanctified persons assurance?

They have a right to it, and I incline to believe that all have it in some degree before their last expiring; though their comfort may be so feeble, and their vital spirits so weak, that they cannot express what they feel. But I dare not positively affirm that all have assurance in the first moment of their sanctification. A letter may be written, when it is not sealed; so grace may be written in the heart, and the Spirit may not set the seal of assurance to it. God is a free agent, and may give or suspend assurance *pro licito*, as he pleases. Where there is the sanctifying work of the Spirit, he may withhold the sealing work, partly to keep the soul humble; partly to punish our careless walking – as when we neglect our spiritual watch, grow remiss in duty, and walk under a cloud, we quench the graces of the Spirit, and God withholds the comforts; and partly to put a difference between earth and heaven. This I the rather speak to bear up the hearts of God's people, who are dejected because they have no assurance. You may have the water of the Spirit poured on you in sanctification, though not the oil of gladness in assurance. There may be faith of adherence, and not of evidence; there may be life in the root, when there is no fruit in the branches to be seen; so faith in the heart, when no fruit of assurance.

What is assurance?

It is not any vocal or audible voice, or brought to us by the help of an angel or revelation. Assurance consists of a practical syllogism, in which the word of God makes the major, conscience the minor, and the Spirit of God, the conclusion. The Word says, 'He that fears and loves God is loved of God;' there is the major proposition; then conscience makes the minor, 'But I fear and love God;' then the Spirit makes the conclusion, 'Therefore thou art loved of God;' and this is what the apostle calls 'The witnessing of the Spirit with our spirits, that we are his children.' Rom viii 16.

Has a sanctified soul such an assurance as excludes all doubting?

He has that which bears up his heart from sinking, he has such an earnest of the Spirit, that he would not part with it for the richest prize; but his assurance, though infallible, is not perfect. There will be sometimes a trepidation, but he is safe amidst fears and doubts; as a ship lies safe at anchor, though shaken by the wind. If a Christian had no doubts there would be no unbelief in him; had he no doubts there would be no difference between grace militant and grace triumphant. Had not David sometimes his ebbings as well as flowings? Like the mariner, who sometimes cries out, *stellam video*, 'I see a star,' and then cries the star is out of sight. Sometimes we hear David say, 'Thy lovingkindness is before mine eyes.' Psa xxvi 3. At another time he is at a loss: 'Lord, where are thy former lovingkindnesses?' Psa lxxxix 49. There may fall out an eclipse in a Christian's assurance, to put him upon longing after heaven, where there shall not be the least doubting; where the banner of God's love shall be always displayed upon the soul; where the light of God's face shall be without clouds, and have no sun-setting; and where the saints shall have an uninterrupted assurance, and be ever with the Lord.

What are the differences between true assurance and presumption?

(1.) They differ in the method or manner of working. Divine assurance flows from humiliation for sin; I speak not of the measure of humiliation, but the truth. There are in Palermo reeds growing, in which there is a sugared juice; a soul humbled for sin is the bruised reed, in which grows this sweet assurance. God's Spirit is a spirit of bondage before it is a spirit of adoption; but presumption arises without any humbling word of the Spirit. 'How camest thou by the venison so soon?' The plough goes before the seed be sown; the heart must be ploughed up by humiliation and repentance, before God sows the seed of assurance.

(2.) He who has a real assurance will take heed of that which will weaken and darken his assurance; he is fearful of the forbidden fruit; he knows, though he cannot sin away his soul, yet he may sin away his assurance; but he who has the *ignis fatuus* of presumption does not fear defiling his garments, he is bold in sin. 'Wilt thou not cry unto me, My Father? Behold, thou hast done evil things as thou couldest.' Jer iii 4, 5. Balaam said, 'My God,' yet was a sorcerer. It is a sign he has no money about him, who fears not to travel all hours in the night. It is a sign he has not the jewel of assurance, who fears not the works of darkness.

(3.) True assurance is built upon a Scripture basis. The word says, 'The effect of righteousness shall be quietness and assurance for ever.' Isa xxxii 17. A Christian's assurance is built upon this Scripture. God has sown the seed of righteousness in his soul, and this seed has brought forth the harvest of assurance; but presumption is a spurious thing; it has not Scripture to show for its warrant; it is like a will without seal and witnesses, which is null and void in law. Presumption wants both the witness of the word, and the seal of the Spirit.

(4.) Assurance flowing from sanctification always keeps the heart in a lowly posture. Lord, says the soul, what am I, that, passing by so many, the golden beams of thy love should shine upon me? Paul had assurance. Is he proud of this jewel? No. 'To me who am less than the least of all saints.' Eph iii 8. The more love a Christian receives from God, the more he sees himself a debtor to free grace, and the sense of his debt keeps his heart humble; but presumption is bred of pride. He who presumes disdains; he thinks himself better than others. 'God, I thank thee that I am not as other men are . . . or even as this publican.' Luke xviii 11. Feathers fly up, but gold descends; so the heart of him who has this golden assurance descends in humility.

What may excite us to look after assurance?

To consider how sweet it is, and the noble and excellent effects it produces.

(1.) How sweet it is. This is the manna in the golden pot; the white stone, the wine of paradise which cheers the heart. How comfortable is God's smile! The sun is more refreshing when it shines out than when it is hid in a cloud; it is a prelibation and a foretaste of glory, it puts a man in heaven before his time. None can know how delicious and ravishing it is, but such as have felt it; as none can know how sweet honey is, but they who have tasted it.

(2.) The noble and excellent effects it produces.

(i) Assurance will make us love God, and praise him. Love is the soul of religion, the fat of the sacrifice; and who can love God as he who has assurance? The sun reflecting its beams on a burning-glass makes the glass burn that which is near it; so assurance (which is the reflection of God's love upon the soul) makes it burn in love to God. Paul was assured of Christ's love to him – 'Who hath loved me:' and how was his heart fired with love! He valued and admired nothing but Christ. Phil iii 8. As Christ was fastened to the cross, so he was fastened to Paul's heart. Praise is the quit-rent we pay to the crown of heaven. Who but he who has assurance of his justification can bless God, and give him the glory of what he has done for him? Can a man in a swoon or apoplexy praise God that he is alive? Can a Christian, staggering with fears about his spiritual condition, praise God that he is elected and justified? No! 'The living, the living, he shall praise thee.' Isa xxxviii 19. Such as are enlivened with assurance are the fittest persons to sound forth God's praise.

(ii) Assurance will drop sweetness into all our creature enjoyments; it will be as sugar to wine, an earnest of more; it will give a blessing with the venison. Guilt embitters our comforts; it is like drinking out of a wormwood cup; but assurance sweetens all health. The assurances of God's love are sweet riches, and with the assurance of a kingdom are delectable. A dinner of green herbs, with the assurance of God's love, is princely fare.

(iii) Assurance will make us active and lively in God's service; it will excite prayer, and quicken obedience. As diligence begets assurance, so assurance begets diligence. Assurance will not (as the Papists say) breed self-security in the soul, but industry. Doubting discourages us in God's service, but the assurance of his favour breeds joy. 'The joy of the Lord is our strength.' Neh viii 10. Assurance makes us mount up to heaven, as eagles, in holy duties; it is like the Spirit in Ezekiel's wheels, that moved them, and lifted them up. Faith will make us walk, but assurance will make us run: we shall never think we can do enough for God. Assurance will be as wings to the bird, as weights to the clock, to set all the wheels of obedience running.

[253]

(iv) Assurance will be a golden shield to beat back temptation, and will triumph over it. There are two sorts of temptations that Satan uses. (1.) He tempts to draw us to sin; but being assured of our justification will make this temptation vanish. What, Satan! shall I sin against him who has loved me, and washed me in his blood? Shall I return to folly after God has spoken peace? Shall I weaken my assurance, wound my conscience, grieve my Comforter? Avaunt, Satan! Tempt no more. (2.) Satan would make us question our interest in God, by telling us we are hypocrites, and God does not love us. Now there is no such shield against this temptation as assurance. What, Satan! have I a real work of grace in my heart, and the seal of the Spirit to witness it, and dost thou tell me God does not love me? Now I know thou art an impostor, who goest about to disprove what I sensibly feel. If faith resists the devil, assurance will put him to flight.

(v) Assurance will make us contented though we have but little in the world. He who has enough is content. He who has sunlight is content, though he is without torchlight. A man that has assurance has enough: *in uno salvatore omnes florent gemmæ ad salutem.* He has the riches of Christ's merit, a pledge of his love, an earnest of his glory; he is filled with the fulness of God; here is enough, and having enough he is content. 'The Lord is the portion of my inheritance . . . the lines are fallen to me in pleasant places, and I have a goodly heritage.' Psa xvi 5, 6. Assurance will rock the heart quiet. The reason of discontent is either because men have no interest in God, or do not know their interest. Paul says, 'I know whom I have believed.' 2 Tim i 12. There was the assurance of his interest. And, 'As sorrowful, yet alway rejoicing,' &c., 2 Cor vi 10. There was his contentment. Get but assurance, and you will be out of the weekly bill of murmurers; you will be discontented no more. Nothing can come amiss to him that has assurance. God is his. Has he lost a friend? – His Father lives. Has he lost his only child? – God has given him his only Son. Has he scarcity of bread? – God has given him the finest of the wheat, the bread of life. Are his comforts gone? – He has the Comforter. Does he meet with storms on the sea? – He knows where to put in for harbour; God is his portion, and heaven is his haven. This assurance gives sweet contentment in every condition.

(vi) Assurance will bear up the heart in sufferings, it will make a Christian endure troubles with patience and cheerfulness. With patience, I say. 'Ye have need of patience.' Heb x 36. There are some meats which are hard of digestion, and only a good stomach will concoct them; so affliction is a meat hard of digestion, but patience, like a good stomach, will be able to digest it; and whence comes patience but from assurance?

'Tribulation worketh patience, because the love of God is shed abroad in our hearts' with cheerfulness. Rom v 3, 5. Assurance is like the mariner's lantern on the deck, which gives light in a dark night. Assurance gives the light of comfort in affliction. Ye 'took joyfully the spoiling of your goods, knowing in yourselves,' &c., there was assurance. Heb x 34. He that has assurance, can rejoice in tribulation; he can gather grapes of thorns, and honey out of the lion's carcase. Latimer said, 'When I sit alone, and can have a settled assurance of the state of my soul, and know that God is mine, I can laugh at all troubles, and nothing can daunt me.'

(vii) Assurance will pacify a troubled conscience. He who has a disturbed vexatious conscience, carries a hell about him, *Eheu quis intus scorpia!* but assurance cures the agony, and allays the fury of conscience. Conscience, which before was turned into a serpent, is now like a bee that has honey in its mouth, it speaks peace; *tranquillus Deus, tranquillat omnia.* Tertullia. When God is pacified towards us, then conscience is pacified. If the heavens are quiet, and there are no winds stirring, the sea is quiet and calm; so if there be no anger in God's heart, if the tempest of his wrath does not blow, conscience is quiet and serene.

(viii) Assurance will strengthen us against the fears of death. Such as want it, cannot die with comfort; they are *in æquilibrio*, they hang in a doubtful suspense as to what shall become of them after death; but he who has assurance, has a happy and joyful passage out of the world; he knows he is passed from death to life; he is carried full sail to heaven! Though he cannot resist death, he overcomes it.

What shall they do who have not assurance?

(1.) Let such labour to find grace. When the sun denies light to the earth, it may give forth its influence; so when God denies the light of his countenance, he may give the influence of his grace.

How shall we know we have a real work of grace, and have a right to assurance?

If we can resolve two queries: (i) Have we high appreciations of Jesus Christ? 'To you that believe he is precious.' 1 Pet ii 7. Christ is all made up of beauties and delights; our praises fall short of his worth, and is like spreading canvas upon a cloth of gold. How precious is his blood and incense! The one pacifies our conscience, the other perfumes our prayers. Can we say we have endearing thoughts of Christ? Do we esteem him our pearl of price, our bright morning-star? Do we count all our earthly enjoyments but as dung in comparison of Christ? Phil iii 8. Do we prefer the worst things of Christ, before the best things of the world; the reproaches of Christ before the world's embraces? Heb xi 26. (ii) Have we the indwelling of the Spirit? 'The Holy Ghost which dwelleth in us.' 2 Tim i 14.

How may we know that we have the indwelling presence of the Spirit?

Not by having sometimes good motions stirred up in us by the Spirit; for he may work in us but not dwell; but by the sanctifying power of the Spirit in our heart the Spirit infuses, *divinam indolem*, a divine nature; it stamps its own impress and effigy on the soul, making the complexion of it holy. The Spirit ennobles and raises the heart above the world. When Nebuchadnezzar had his understanding given him, he grazed no longer among the beasts, but returned to his throne, and minded the affairs of his kingdom; so when the Spirit of God dwells in a man, it carries his heart above the visible orbs; it makes him, *superna anhelare* [pant after heavenly things], thirst after Christ and glory. If we can find this, then we have grace, and so have a right to assurance.

(2.) If you want assurance, wait for it. If the figures are graven on the dial, it is but waiting a while, and the sun shines; so when grace is engraven in the heart, it is but waiting a while, and we shall have the sunshine of assurance. 'He that believes makes not haste.' Isa xxviii 16. He will stay God's leisure. Say not, God has forsaken you, he will never lift up the light of his countenance; but rather say, as the church, 'I will wait upon the Lord, that hideth his face from the house of Jacob,' Isa viii 17. (i) Has God waited for your conversion and will you not wait for his consolation? How long did he come wooing you by his Spirit? He waited till his head was filled with dew; he cried, 'Wilt thou not be made clean? When shall it once be?' Jer xiii 27. O Christian, did God wait for thy love, and canst thou not wait for his? (ii) Assurance is so sweet and precious, that it is worth waiting for; the price of it is above rubies, it cannot be valued with the gold of Ophir. Assurance of God's love is a pledge of election, it is the angels' banquet: what other joy have they? As Micah said, 'What have I more?' Judg xviii 24; so, when God assures the soul of his eternal purposes of love, what has he more to give? Whom God kisses he crowns. Assurance is the firstfruits of paradise. One smile of God's face, one glance of his eye, one crumb of the hidden manna is so sweet and delicious, that it deserves our waiting. (iii) God has given a promise that we should not wait in vain. 'They shall not be ashamed that wait for me.' Isa xlix 23. Perhaps God reserves this cordial of assurance for a fainting time; he keeps sometimes his best wine till last. Assurance shall be reserved as an ingredient to sweeten the bitter cup of death.

How may deserted souls be comforted who are cast down for want of assurance?

(1.) Want of assurance shall not hinder the success of the saint's prayers.

Sin lived in puts a bar to our prayer; but want of assurance does not hinder prayer; we may go to God still in an humble, fiducial manner. A Christian perhaps may think, because he does not see God's smiling face, God will not hear him. This is a mistake. 'I said in my haste, I am cut off from before thine eyes: nevertheless thou heardest the voice of my supplications.' Psa xxxi 22. If we pour out sighs to heaven, God will hear every groan; and though he does not show us his face, he will lend us his ear.

(2.) Faith may be strongest when assurance is weakest. The woman of Canaan had no assurance, but a glorious faith.' 'O woman, great is thy faith.' Matt xv 28. Rachel was more fair, but Leah was more fruitful. Assurance is more fair and lovely to look upon, but a fruitful faith God sees to be better for us. 'Blessed are they that have not seen, and yet have believed.' John xx 29.

(3.) When God is out of sight, he is not out of covenant. 'My covenant shall stand fast.' Psa lxxxix 28. Though a wife does not see her husband's face for many years, yet the marriage-relation holds, and he will come again to her after a long voyage. God may be gone from the soul in desertion, but the covenant stands fast. 'The covenant of my peace shall not be removed.' Isa liv 10. *But this promise was made to the Jews, and does not belong to us!* Yes it does, for says ver 17, 'This is the heritage of the servants of the Lord.' This is true of all the servants of God, those who are now living, as well as those who lived in the time of the Jews.

What shall we do to get assurance?

(1.) Keep a pure conscience. Let no guilt lie upon the conscience un-repented of. God seals no pardon before repentance. He will not pour the wine of assurance into a foul vessel. 'Let us draw near in full assurance of faith, having our hearts sprinkled from an evil conscience!' Heb x 22. Guilt clips the wings of comfort. He who is conscious to himself of secret sins, cannot draw near to God in full assurance; he cannot call God father, but judge. Keep conscience as clear as your eye, that no dust of sin can fall into it.

(2.) If you would have assurance, be much in the exercise of grace. 'Exercise thyself unto godliness.' 1 Tim iv 7. Men grow rich by trading; so by trading in grace we grow rich in assurance. 'Make your election sure.' How? 'Add to your faith virtue, and to virtue knowledge.' 2 Pet i 5. Keep grace upon the wing; it is lively faith that flourishes into assurance. No man will set up a great sail in a small boat, but in a large vessel; so God sets up the sail of assurance in a heart enlarged with grace.

(3.) If you would have assurance, cherish the Holy Spirit of God. When David would have assurance, he prayed, 'Take not away thy Spirit from me.' Psa li 11. He knew that it was the Spirit only that could make him hear the voice of joy. The Spirit is the Comforter, that seals up assurance. 2 Cor i 22. Therefore make much of the Spirit, do not grieve it. As Noah opened the ark to receive the dove, so should we open our hearts to receive the Spirit, which is the blessed dove that brings an olive branch of assurance in its mouth.

(4.) Let us lie at the pool of the ordinances, and frequent the word and sacrament. 'He brought me to the banqueting-house, and his banner over me was love.' Cant ii 4. The blessed ordinances are the banqueting-house, where God displays the banner of assurance. The sacrament is a sealing ordinance. Christ made himself known to his disciples in the breaking of bread; so, in the holy supper, in the breaking of bread God makes himself known to us, to be our God and portion.

How should they conduct themselves who have assurance?

(1.) If you have assurance of your justification, do not abuse it. It is abusing assurance when we grow more remiss in duty; as the musician, having money thrown him, leaves off playing. By remissness, or intermitting the exercises of religion, we grieve the Spirit, and that is the way to have an embargo laid upon our spiritual comforts. We abuse assurance when we grow presumptuous and less fearful of sin. What! because a father gives his son an assurance of his love, and tells him he will entail his land upon him, shall the son be wanton and dissolute? This were the way to lose his father's affection, and make him cut off the entail. It was an aggravation of Solomon's sin that his heart was turned away from the Lord, after he had appeared to him twice. 1 Kings xi 9. It is bad to sin when one wants assurance, but it is worse to sin when one has it. Has the Lord sealed his love with a kiss? Has he left a pledge of heaven in your hand, and do you thus requite the Lord? Will you sin with manna in your mouth? Does God give you the sweet clusters of assurance to feed on, and will you return him wild grapes? It much pleases Satan, either to see us want assurance, or abuse it. We abuse assurance when the pulse of our souls beats faster in sin, and slower in duty.

(2.) If you have assurance, admire his stupendous mercy. You deserved that God should give you gall and vinegar to drink, and has he made the honeycomb of his love to drop upon you? Oh, fall down and adore his goodness! Say, Lord, how is it that thou shouldst manifest thyself to me, and not to other believers! for many whom thou lovest as the apple of thine eye thou holdest in suspense, and givest them no assurance of thy love; though thou hast given them the new name, yet not the white stone; though they have the seed of grace, yet not the oil of gladness; though they have the Holy Ghost, the Sanctifier, yet not the Holy Ghost, the Comforter. Lord, whence is it that thou shouldst manifest thyself to me, and make thy golden beams of assurance to shine upon my soul? Oh, adore God on this account! such will be the work of heaven.

(3.) Let your hearts be endeared in love to God. If God gives his people correction, they must love him: much more when he gives them assurance. 'O love the Lord, all ye his saints.' Ps xxxi 23. Has God brought you to the borders of Canaan, given you a bunch of grapes, crowned you with lovingkindness, confirmed your pardon under the broad seal of heaven? How can you be frozen at such a fire? How can you be turned into seraphims burning in divine love! Say as Augustine, *animam meam in odio haberem*, I would hate my own soul, if I did not find it loving God. Give God the cream and quintessence of your love, and show your love by being willing to lose all for his sake.

(4.) If you have assurance, improve it for God's glory. (i) By encouraging such as are yet unconverted. Tell them how sweet this hidden manna is; tell them what a good master you serve; what gales you have had; tell them God has carried you to the hill of myrrh, to the mountains of spices; he has given you not only a prospect of heaven, but an earnest. Oh, persuade sinners, by all the love and mercy of God, that they would enrol their names in his family, and cast themselves upon him for salvation. Tell them God has met with you and unlocked the secrets of free grace, and assured you of a land flowing with those infinite delights which eye has not seen. Thus, by telling others what God has done for your soul, you may make them in love with the ways of God, and cause them to turn proselytes to religion. (ii) Improve assurance, by comforting such as want it. Be as the good Samaritan to pour wine and oil into their wounds. You who have assurance, are arrived as it were at the haven, you are sure of your happiness; but do you not see others who are struggling with the waves of temptation and desertion, and are ready to sink? Oh, now sympathize with them, and do what you can to comfort them while they are in this deep ocean. 'Whether we be comforted is it, for your consolation.' 2 Cor i 6. The comfortable experience of one Christian being communicated to another much revives and bears up his fainting heart. 'Our comfort,' says the apostle, 'is for your consolation.' (iii) Improve assurance, by walking more heavenly. You should scorn the things below; you who have an earnest of heaven, should not be too earnest for the earth. You have angels' food; and it becomes not you, with the serpent, to lick the dust. The wicked are all for corn, wine and oil; but you have that which is better. God has lifted up the light of his countenance; and will you hanker after the world, when you have been feeding upon the grapes and pomegranates of the holy land? Do you now lust after the garlics and onions of Egypt? When you are clothed with the sun, will you set the moon and the stars above you? Oh let them scramble for the world, who have nothing else but husks to feed on. Have you assurance of heaven, and is not that enough? Will not a kingdom satisfy you? Such as are high in assurance, should live above the world. (iv) Improve assurance by a cheerful walking. It is for condemned persons to go hanging down their heads. But hast thou thy absolution? Does thy God smile on thee? Cheer up. 'Why art thou, being the king's son, lean?' 2 Sam xiii 4. Art thou the king's son? Has God assured thee of thy adoption, and art thou sad? Assurance should be an antidote against all trouble. What though the world hate thee? Thou art assured that thou art one of God's favourites. What though there is but little oil in the cruse, and thou art low in the world? Thou art high in assurance. Oh, then rejoice! How musical is the bird! How does it chirp and sing, though it knows not where to pick up the next crumb! and shall they be sad and discontented who have God's bond to assure them of their daily bread, and his love to assure them of heaven? Certainly those who have assurance, cannot but be of a sanguine complexion.

(5.) If you have an assurance of salvation, let it make you long after a glorified state. He who has an earnest in his hand, desires the whole sum to be paid. The soul that has tasted how sweet the Lord is, should long for a fuller enjoyment of him in heaven. Has Christ put the ring of assurance on thy hand, and so espoused thee to himself? how shouldst thou long for the marriage-supper of the Lamb! Rev xix 9. O Christian, think with thyself, if a glimpse of heaven, a smile of God's face be so sweet, what will it be, to be ever sunning thyself in the light of God's countenance! Certainly, you who have an assurance of your title to heaven, cannot but desire possession. Be content to live, but willing to die.

(6.) If you have assurance, be careful you do not lose it. Keep it, for it is your life, your *benc esse*, the comfort of your life. Keep assurance. 1st. By prayer. 'O continue thy lovingkindness.' Psa xxxvi 10. Lord, continue assurance; do not take away this privy seal from me. 2ndly. Keep assurance by humility. Pride estranges God from the soul. When you are nigh in assurance, be low in humility. Paul had assurance, and he baptized himself with the name, 'Chief of sinners.' 1 Tim i 15. The jewel of assurance is best kept in the cabinet of an humble heart.

7. PEACE

Grace unto you and peace be multiplied. 1 Pet i 2.

Having spoken of the first fruit of sanctification, assurance, I proceed to the second, viz., Peace, 'Peace be multiplied.'

What are the several species or kinds of Peace?

Peace, in Scripture, is compared to a river which parts itself into two silver streams. Isa lxvi 12.

I. *There is an external peace*, and that is, (1.) Œconomical, or peace in a family. (2.) Political, or peace in the state. Peace is the nurse of plenty. 'He maketh peace in thy borders, and filleth thee with the finest of the wheat.' Psa cxlvii 14. How pleasant it is when the waters of blood begin to assuage, and we can see the windows of our ark open, and the dove returning with an olive branch of peace! (3.) Ecclesiastical, or peace in the church. As unity in Trinity is the greatest mystery in heaven, unity in verity is the greatest mercy on earth. Peace ecclesiastical stands in opposition to schism and persecution.

II. *A spiritual peace*, which is twofold; peace above us, or peace with God; and peace within us, or peace with conscience, which is superlative: other peace may be lasting, but this is everlasting.

Whence comes this Peace?

It has the whole Trinity for its author. God the Father is 'the God of peace.' 1 Thess v 23. God the Son is the 'Prince of peace.' Isa ix 6. Peace is said to be the 'fruit of the Spirit.' Gal v 22.

(1.) God the Father is the God of peace. As he is the God of order, so he is the God of peace. 1 Cor xiv 33, and Phil iv 9. This was the form of the priest's blessing upon the people. 'The Lord give thee peace.' Numb vi 26.

(2.) God the Son is the purchaser of peace. He made peace by his blood. 'Having made peace by the blood of his cross.' Col i 20. The atonement Aaron made for the people, when he entered into the holy of holies, with blood, was a type of Christ our high priest, who by his sacrifice pacified his angry Father, and made atonement for us. Christ purchased our peace upon hard terms; for his soul was in an agony, while he was travailing to bring forth peace to the world.

(3.) Peace is a fruit of the Spirit. He seals up peace to the conscience. The Spirit clears up the work of grace in the heart, from whence arises peace. There was a well of water near Hagar, but she did not see it, therefore she wept. A Christian has grace, but does not see it, therefore he weeps. Now the Spirit discovers this well of water, it enables conscience to witness to a man that has the real work of grace, and so peace flows into the soul. Thus you see whence this peace comes – the Father decrees it, the Son purchases it, the Holy Ghost applies it.

Whether such as are destitute of grace may have peace?

No! Peace flows from sanctification, but they being unregenerate, have nothing to do with peace. 'There is no peace, saith my God to the wicked.' Isa lvii 21. They may have a truce, but no peace. God may forbear the wicked a while, and stop the roaring of his cannon; but though there be a truce, yet there is no peace. The wicked may have something which looks like peace, but it is not. They may be fearless and stupid; but there is a great difference between a stupified conscience, and a pacified conscience. 'When a strong man armed keepeth his palace, his goods are in peace.' Luke xi 21. This is the devil's peace; he rocks men in the cradle of security; he cries, Peace, peace, when men are on the precipice of hell. The seeming peace a sinner has, is not from the knowledge of his happiness, but the ignorance of his danger.

What are the signs of a false peace?

(1.) A false peace has much confidence in it, but this confidence is conceit. The sinner does not doubt of God's mercy; and from this presumptuous confidence arises some kind of quiet in the mind. The same word in the Hebrew, *cassal*, signifies both confidence and folly. Indeed a sinner's confidence is folly. How confident were the foolish virgins!

(2.) False peace separates those things which God has joined together. God joins holiness and peace, but he who has a false peace, separates the two. He lays claim to peace, but banishes holiness. 'I shall have peace, though I walk in 'the imagination of mine heart, to add drunkenness to thirst.' Deut xxix 19. The wicked are loose and vain, and yet thank God that they have peace, what a delusion! You may as well suck health out of poison, as peace out of sin.

(3.) False peace is not willing to be tried. It is a sign they are bad wares which will not endure the light; a sign a man has stolen goods, when he will not have his house searched. A false peace cannot endure to be tried by the word. The word speaks of a humbling and refining work upon the soul before peace; but false peace cannot endure to hear of this. The least trouble will shake this peace; it will end in despair. In a false peace, conscience is asleep; but when this lion of conscience shall be awakened at death, it will roar upon a man; he will be a terror to himself, and be ready to lay violent hands upon himself.

How shall we know that ours is a true peace?

(1.) True peace flows from union with Christ. *Communio fundatur in unione.* The graft or scion must first be innoculated into the tree before it can receive sap or nourishment from it; so we must first be ingrafted into Christ, before we can receive peace from him. Have we faith? By holiness we are made like Christ; by believing we are made one with Christ, and being in Christ we have peace. John xvi 33.

(2.) True peace flows from subjection to Christ. Where Christ gives peace, there he sets up his government in the heart. 'Of his government and peace there shall be no end.' Isa ix 7. Christ is called 'a priest upon his throne.' Zech vi 13. Christ as a priest makes peace; but he will be a priest upon his throne – he brings the heart in subjection to him. If Christ be our peace, he is our prince. Isa ix 6. Whenever Christ pacifies the conscience, he subdues the lust.

(3.) True peace is after trouble. First, God lets loose a spirit of bondage, he convinces and humbles the soul; then he speaks peace. Many say they have peace, but is this peace before a storm, or after it? True peace is after trouble. First there was the earthquake, and then the fire, and then the still small voice. 1 Kings xix 12. Thou who never hadst any legal bruisings, mayest suspect thy peace. God pours the golden oil of peace into broken hearts.

Have all sanctified persons this peace?

They have a title to it; they have the ground of it; grace is the seed of peace, and it will in time turn to peace; as the blossoms of a tree to fruit, milk to cream. They have a promise of it. 'The Lord will bless his people with peace.' Psalm xxix 11. They may have peace with God, though not peace in their own conscience; they have the initials and beginnings of peace. There is a secret peace which the heart has in serving God; such meltings and enlargements in duty as revive the soul, and bear it up from sinking.

But why have not all believers the full enjoyment and possession of peace? Why is not this flower of peace fully ripe and blown?

Some of the godly may not have so full a degree of peace. (1.) Through the fury of temptation, though the devil cannot destroy us, he will disturb us. He disputes against our adoption; he would make us question the work of grace in our hearts, and so disturb the waters of our peace. He is like a subtle cheater, who, if he cannot make a man's title to his land void, yet will put him to many troublesome suits in law. If Satan cannot make us ungodly, he will make us unquiet. Violent winds make the sea rough and stormy; so the winds of temptation blowing, disturb peace of spirit, and put the soul into a commotion.

(2.) The godly may not enjoy peace, through mistake and misapprehension about sin. They find so much corruption, that they think sure, if there were grace, there would not be such strong working of corruption; whereas this should be so far from discouraging Christians, and hindering their peace, that it is an argument for them. Let me ask, Whence is it that you feel sin? No man can feel sin, but by grace. A wicked man is insensible. Lay a hundredweight upon a dead man, he does not complain; but being sensible of corruption, argues a gracious principle. Rom vii 21. Again, Whence is it that there is a combat with sin, but from the life of grace? Gal v 17. Dead things cannot combat. Whence is it that the saints weep for sin? What are these tears but seeds of faith? The not understanding of this hinders a Christian's peace.

(3.) The godly may not enjoy peace, through remissness in duty: they may leave their first love. When Christians abate their fervency, God abates their peace. If you slacken the strings of a viol, the music is spoiled; so, if Christians slack in duty, they spoil the sweet music of peace in their souls. As the fire decays, the cold increases; so, as fervency in duty abates, our peace cools.

Use one: Labour for this blessed peace – peace with God and conscience. Peace with neighbour-nations is sweet. *Pax una triumphis innumeris melior* [One peace is better than innumerable triumphs]. The Hebrew word *shalom*, peace, comprehends all blessings; it is the glory of a kingdom. A prince's crown is more beautiful, when it is hung with the white lily of peace, than when it is set with the red roses of a bloody war. Oh, then, how sweet is peace of conscience! It is a bulwark against the enemy. Phil iv 7. It shall keep you as in a garrison; you may throw down the gauntlet, and bid defiance to enemies. It is the golden pot and the manna. It is the first fruits of paradise. It is still music, for want of which a Christian is in continual fear, and does not take comfort in ordinances. Hannah went up to the feast at Jerusalem, but she wept and did not eat. 1 Sam i 7; so, a poor dejected soul goes to an ordinance, but does not eat of the feast; he weeps and does not eat. He cannot take comfort in worldly blessings, health, estate, relations; he wants that inward peace, which should be a sauce to sweeten his comforts. Oh, therefore, labour for this blessed peace. Consider its noble and excellent effects. (1.) It gives boldness at the throne of grace. Guilt of conscience clips the wings of prayer, it makes the face blush, and the heart faint; but when a Christian has some lively apprehensions of God's love, and the Spirit whispers peace, he goes to God with boldness, as a child to his father. 'Unto thee, O Lord, do I lift up my soul.' Psa xxv 1. Time was when David's soul was bowed down. 'I am bowed down greatly.' Psa xxxviii 6. Now the case is altered, he will lift up his soul to God in a way of triumph. Whence was this? God has spoken peace to his soul. 'Thy lovingkindness is before mine eyes.' Psa xxvi 3. (2.) This divine peace fires the heart with love to Christ. Peace is the result of pardon. He who has a pardon sealed, cannot choose but love his prince. How endeared is Christ to the soul! Now Christ is precious indeed. 'Oh,' says the soul, 'how sweet is this rose of Sharon! Has Christ waded through a sea of blood and wrath, to purchase my peace? Has he not only made peace, but spoken peace to me? How should my heart ascend in a fiery chariot of love! How willing should I be to do and suffer for Christ!' (3.) This peace quiets the heart in trouble. 'This man shall be the peace, when the Assyrian shall come into our land, and when he shall tread in our palaces.' Mic v 5. The enemy may invade our palaces, but not our peace: this man Christ shall be the peace. When the head aches, the heart may be well; and when worldly troubles assault a Christian, his mind may be in peace and quiet. 'I will lay me down in peace, and sleep.' Psa iv 8. It was a sad time with David, he was fleeing for his life from Absalom; it was no small affliction to think that his own son should seek to take away his father's life and crown. David wept and covered his head. 2 Sam xv 30. Yet at this time he says, 'I will lay me down in peace, and sleep.' He had trouble from his son, but peace from his conscience. David could sleep upon the soft pillow of a good conscience. This is a peace worth getting.

What shall we do to attain this blessed peace?

(1.) Let us ask it of God. He is the God of peace; he beats back the roaring lion; he stills the raging of conscience: if we could call all the angels out of heaven, they could not speak peace without God. The stars cannot make day without the sun; none can make day in a dark deserted soul, but the Sun of Righteousness. As the wilderness cannot water itself, but remains dry and parched till the clouds drop their moisture, so our hearts cannot have peace till he infuse it, and drop it upon us by his Spirit. Therefore pray, 'Lord, thou who art the God of peace, create peace; thou who art the Prince of peace, command it. Give me that peace which may sweeten trouble, yea, even the bitter cup of death.'

(2.) If you would have peace, make war with sin. Sin is the Achan that troubles us, the Trojan horse. 'When Joram saw Jehu, he said, Is it peace,

Jehu? And he answered, What peace, so long as the whoredoms of thy mother Jezebel and her witchcrafts are so many?' 2 Kings ix 22. What peace, so long as sin remains unmortified? If you would have peace with God, break the league with sin; give battle to sin, for it is a most just war. God has proclaimed it: nay, he has promised us victory. 'Sin shall not have dominion.' Rom vi 14. No way to peace, but by maintaining a war with sin. *Pax nostra bellum contra dæmonem* [Our peace is a war against the Devil]. Tertullian. When Samson had slain the lion, there came honey out of the lion; so by slaying sin, we get the honey of peace.

(3.) Go to Christ's blood for peace. Some go to fetch their peace from their own righteousness, not Christ's: they go for peace to their holy life, not Christ's death. If conscience be troubled, they strive to quiet it with their duties. This is not the right way to peace. Duties must not be neglected, nor yet idolized. Look to the blood of sprinkling. Heb xii 24. That blood of Christ which pacified God, must pacify conscience. Christ's blood being sucked in by faith, gives peace. 'Being justified by faith, we have peace with God.' Rom v 1. No balm to cure a wounded conscience, but the blood of Christ.

(4.) Walk closely with God. Peace flows from purity. 'As many as walk according to this rule, peace be on them.' Gal vi 16. In the text, grace and peace are put together; grace is the root, and peace is the flower. As balm-water drops in distillation, so divine peace comes out of a gracious heart. Walk very holily. God's Spirit is a refiner before a comforter.

Use two: You who have this peace, peace above, peace within, labour to keep it: it is a precious jewel, do not lose it. It is sad to have the league of national peace broken, but it is worse to have the peace of conscience broken. Oh, preserve this peace! First, take heed of relapses. Has God spoken peace? Do not turn again to folly. Psa lxxxv 8. Besides ingratitude, there is folly in relapses. It was long ere God was reconciled and the breach made up, and will you again eclipse and forfeit your peace? Has God healed the wound of conscience, and will you tear it open again? Will you break another vein? Will you cut a new artery? This is returning indeed to folly. What madness is it to meddle again with that sin, which will breed the worm of conscience! Secondly, make up your spiritual accounts daily; see how matters stand between God and your souls. 'I commune with my own heart.' Psa lxxvii 6. Often reckonings keep God and conscience friends. Do with your hearts as you do with your watches, wind them up every morning by prayer, and at night examine whether your hearts have gone true all that day, whether the wheels of your affections have moved swiftly towards heaven. Oh, call yourselves often to account! Keep your reckonings even, for that is the way to keep your peace.

8. JOY

'The fruit of the Spirit is joy.' Gal v 22.

The third fruit of justification, adoption, and sanctification, is joy in the Holy Ghost. Joy is setting the soul upon the top of a pinnacle – it is the cream of the sincere milk of the word. Spiritual joy is a sweet and delightful passion, arising from the apprehension and feeling of some good, whereby the soul is supported under present troubles, and fenced against future fear.

I. *It is a delightful passion.* It is contrary to sorrow, which is a perturbation of mind, whereby the heart is perplexed and cast down. Joy is a sweet and pleasant affection which eases the mind, exhilarates and comforts the spirits.

II. *It arises from the feeling of some good.* Joy is not a fancy, or conceit; but is rational, and arises from the feeling of some good, as the sense of God's love and favour. Joy is so real a thing that it makes a sudden change in a person; and turns mourning into melody. As in the spring-time, when the sun comes to our horizon, it makes a sudden alteration in the face of the universe: the birds sing, the flowers appear, the fig-tree puts forth her green figs; every thing seems to rejoice and put off its mourning, as being revived with the sweet influence of the sun; so when the Sun of Righteousness arises on the soul, it makes a sudden alteration, and the soul is infinitely rejoiced with the golden beams of God's love.

III. *By it the soul is supported under present troubles.* Joy stupifies and swallows up troubles; it carries the heart above them, as the oil swims above the water.

IV. *The heart is fenced against future fear.* Joy is both a cordial and an antidote: it is a cordial which gives present relief to the spirits when they are sad; and an antidote, which fences off the fear of approaching danger. 'I will fear no evil, for thou art with me; thy rod and thy staff they comfort me.' Psa xxiii 4.

How is this joy wrought?

(1.) It arises partly from the promise. As the bee lies at the breast of the flower, and sucks out its sweetness, so faith lies at the breast of a promise, and sucks out the quintessence of joy. 'Thy comforts delight my soul;' that is, the comforts which distil from the promises. Psa xciv 19.

(2.) The Spirit of God who is called the 'Comforter,' John xiv 26, sometimes drops this golden oil of joy into the soul; the Spirit whispers to a believer the remission of his sin, and sheds God's love abroad in the heart, whence flows infinite joy and delight. Rom v 5.

What are the Seasons in which God usually gives his people divine joys?

There are five Seasons. (1.) Sometimes at the blessed Supper. The soul comes weeping after Christ in the Sacrament, and God sends it away weeping for joy. The Jews had a custom at their feasts of pouring ointment on their guests and kissing them; in the Eucharist, God often pours the oil of gladness on the saints, and kisses them with the kisses of his lips. There are two grand ends of the Sacrament, the strengthening of faith, and the flourishing of joy. Here, in this ordinance, God displays the banner of his love; here believers taste not only sacramental bread, but hidden manna. Not that God always meets the soul with joy. He may give increase of grace, when not increase of joy; but oftentimes he pours in the oil of gladness, and gives the soul a privy seal of his love; as Christ made himself known in the breaking of bread.

(2.) Before God calls his people to suffering. 'Be of good cheer, Paul.' Acts xxiii 11. When God was about to give Paul a cup of blood to drink, he spiced it with joy. 'As the sufferings of Christ abound in us, so our consolation also aboundeth.' 2 Cor i 5. This made the martyrs' flames beds of roses. When Stephen was being stoned he saw heaven open, and the Sun of Righteousness shone upon his face. God candies our wormwood with sugar.

(3.) After sore conflicts with Satan. He is the red dragon who troubles the waters; he puts the soul into frights, makes it believe that it has no grace, and that God does not love it. Though he cannot blot out a Christian's evidence, yet he may cast such a mist before his eyes, that he cannot read it. When the soul has been bruised with temptations, God will comfort the bruised reed by giving joy, *ad corroborandum titulum*, to confirm a Christian's title to heaven. After Satan's fiery darts comes the white stone. No better balm to heal a tempted soul than the oil of gladness! After Christ was tempted, an angel came to comfort him.

(4.) After desertion. Desertion is a poisoned arrow which shoots to the heart. Job vi 4. God is called a fire and a light: the deserted soul feels the fire, but does not see the light; it cries out, as Asaph, 'Is his mercy clean gone?' Psa lxxvii 8. When the soul is in this case, and ready to faint away in despair, God shines upon it, and gives it some apprehension of his favour, and turns the shadow of death into the light of the morning. God keeps his cordials for a time of fainting. Joy after desertion is like a resurrection from the dead.

(5.) At the hour of death. Of those even who have had no joy in their lifetime. God puts this sugar in the bottom of the cup, to make their death sweet. At the last hour, when all other comforts are gone, God sends the Comforter; and when their appetite to meat fails, he feeds them with hidden manna. As the wicked before they die, have some apprehensions of hell and wrath in their conscience, so the godly have some foretastes of God's everlasting favour, though sometimes their diseases may be such, and their animal spirits so oppressed, that they cannot express what they feel. Jacob laid himself to sleep on a stone and saw a vision of a ladder, and the angels ascending and descending upon it; so, when saints lay themselves down to sleep the sleep of death, they have often a vision: they see the light of God's face, and have the evidences of his love sealed up to them for ever.

What are the differences between worldly joys and spiritual?

The gleanings of the one are better than the vintage of the other.

(1.) Spiritual joys help to make us better, worldly joys often make us worse. 'I spake unto thee in thy prosperity, but thou saidst, I will not hear.' Jer xxii 21. Pride and luxury are the two worms that are bred of worldly pleasures. 'Wine takes away the heart;' it is *fomentum libidinis*, Augustine, 'the inflamer of lust.' Hos iv 11. As Satan entered in the sop, so often in the cup; but spiritual joy makes one better; it is like cordial water, which, as physicians say, not only cheers the heart, but purges out the noxious humours; so divine joy is cordial water, which not only comforts but cleanses; it makes a Christian more holy; it causes an antipathy against sin; it infuses strength to do and suffer. 'The joy of the Lord is your strength.' Neh viii 10. As some colours not only delight the eye, but strengthen the sight; so the joys of God not only refresh the soul, but strengthen it.

(2.) Spiritual joys are inward, they are heart joys. 'Your heart shall rejoice.' John xvi 22. Seneca says true joy *latet in profundo*, it is hidden within, worldly joy is *in superficie*, it lies on the outside, like the dew that wets the leaf. We read of those who 'rejoice in appearance,' in the Greek, in the face. 2 Cor v 12. It goes no farther than the face, it is not within; 'in laughter the heart is sad.' Like a house which has a gilded frontispiece, but all the rooms within are hung in mourning. But spiritual joy lies most within. 'Your heart shall rejoice.' Divine joy is like a spring of water which runs underground! Others can see the sufferings of a

Christian, but they see not his joy. 'A stranger intermeddleth not with his joy.' Prov xiv 10. His joy is hidden manna, hid from the eye of the world; he has still music which others hear not; the marrow lies within, the best joy is within the heart.

(3.) Spiritual joys are sweeter than others, they are better than wine. Cant i 2. They are a Christian's festival; they are the golden pot and the manna; they are so sweet, that they make everything else sweet: sweeten health and estate, as sweet water poured on flowers makes them more fragrant and aromatic. Divine joys are so delicious and ravishing, that they put our mouth out of taste for earthly delights; as he who has been drinking cordials tastes little sweetness in water. Paul had so tasted these divine joys, that his mouth was out of taste for worldly things; the world was crucified to him, it was like a dead thing, he could find no sweetness in it. Gal vi 14.

(4.) Spiritual joys are more pure, they are not tempered with any bitter ingredients. A sinner's joy is mixed with dregs, it is imbittered with fear and guilt: the wolf feeds in the breasts of his joy; he drinks wormwood wine; but spiritual joy is not muddled with guilt, but like a crystal stream, runs pure; it is all spirits and quintessence; it is joy and nothing but joy; it is a rose without prickles; it is honey without wax.

(5.) They are satisfying joys: 'Ask, that your joy may be full.' John xvi 24. Worldly joys can no more fill the heart than a drop can fill a cistern; they may please the palate or fancy, as Plato calls them pictures of joy, but cannot satisfy the soul. 'The eye is not satisfied with seeing, nor the ear with hearing;' Eccl i 8; but the joys of God satisfy. 'Thy comforts delight my soul.' Psa xciv 19. There is as much difference between spiritual joys and earthly, as between a banquet that is eaten and one that is painted on the wall.

(6.) They are stronger joys than worldly. 'Strong consolation.' Heb vi 18. They are strong indeed that can bear up a Christian's heart in trials and afflictions. 'Having received the word in much affliction, with joy.' 1 Thess i 6. These are roses that grow in winter, these joys can sweeten the waters of Marah; he that hath these can gather grapes of thorns, and fetch honey out of the carcase of a lion. 'As sorrowing, yet always rejoicing.' 2 Cor vi 10. At the end of the rod a Christian tastes honey.

(7.) They are unwearied joys. Other joys, when in excess, often cause loathing, we are apt to surfeit on them; too much honey nauseates; one may be tired with pleasure as well as labour. Xerxes offered a reward to him that could find out a new pleasure; but the joys of God, though they satisfy, yet they never surfeit. A drop of joy is sweet, but the more of this wine the better. Such as drink of the joys of heaven are never cloyed; the satiety is without loathing, because they still desire the joy wherewith they are satiated.

(8.) They are abiding joys. Worldly joys are soon gone. Such as crown themselves with rosebuds, and bathe in the perfumed waters of pleasure, may have joys which seem to be sweet but they are swift: they are like meteors, which give a bright and sudden flash, and then disappear. The joys which believers have are abiding; they are a blossom of eternity, a pledge and earnest of those rivers of pleasure which run at God's right hand for evermore.

Why is this joy to be laboured for?

(1.) Because it is self-existent, it can subsist in the absence of all other carnal joy. This joy depends not upon outward things. As the philosophers said, when the musicians came to them, 'Philosophers can be merry without music;' so he that has this joy can be cheerful in the deficiency of carnal joys; he can rejoice in God, in sure hope of glory, 'although the fig-tree shall not blossom.' Hab iii 17. Spiritual joy can go without silver crutches to support it. Spiritual joy is higher built than upon creatures, for it is built on the love of God, on the promises, and on the blood of Christ.

(2.) Because spiritual joy carries the soul through duty cheerfully; the Sabbath becomes a delight, and religion is a recreation. Fear and sorrow hinder us in the discharge of duty; but a Christian serves God with activity, when he serves him with joy. The oil of joy makes the wheels of obedience move faster. How fervently did they pray, whom God made joyful in the house of prayer! Isa lvi 7.

(3.) It is called the kingdom of God in Rom xiv 17, because it is a taste of that which the saints have in the kingdom of God. What is the heaven of the angels, but the smiles of God's face, the sensible perception and feeling of those joys which are infinitely ravishing and full of glory! To encourage and quicken us in seeking after them, consider, that Christ died to purchase this joy for his saints. He was a man of sorrows, that we might be full of joy; he prayed that the saints might have this divine joy. 'And now I come to thee, that they may have my joy fulfilled in themselves.' John xvii 13. This prayer he now prays in heaven; he knows we never love him so much as when we feel his love; which may encourage us to seek after this joy. We pray for that which Christ himself is praying for, when we pray that his joy may be fulfilled in us.

What shall we do to obtain this spiritual joy?

Walk consistently and spiritually. God gives joy after long and close walking with him. (1.) Observe your hours. Set time every day apart for God. (2.) Mourn for sin. Mourning is the seed, as Basil says, out of which the flower of spiritual joy grows. 'I will restore comforts to his mourners.' Isa lvii 18. (3.) Keep the book of conscience fair written. Do not by presumptuous sins blur your evidences. A good conscience is the ark in which God puts the hidden manna. (4.) Be often upon your knees, pray with life and fervency. The same Spirit that fills the heart with sighs fills it with joys. The same Spirit that indites the prayer, seals it. When Hannah had prayed, her countenance was no more sad. 1 Sam i 18. Praying Christians have much intercourse with God; and none are so like to have the secrets of his love imparted, as those who hold correspondence with him. By close walking with God we get bunches of grapes by the way, which are an earnest of future happiness.

How shall we comfort those that want joy?

Such as walk in close communion with God have more than others.

(1.) Initial joy, joy *in semine*, in the seed. 'Light (a metaphor for joy) is sown for the righteous.' Psa xcvii 11. Grace in the heart is a seed of joy. Though a Christian wants the sun, he has a day-star in his heart.

(2.) A believer has real, though not royal comforts; he has, as Aquinas says, *gaudium in Deo*, though not *à Deo;* joy in God, though not from God. Joy in God is the delight and complacency the soul takes in God. 'My soul shall be glad in the Lord.' Psa civ 34. He that is truly gracious, is so far joyful as to take comfort in God: though he cannot say, God rejoices in him, he can say, he rejoices in God.

(3.) He has supporting, though not transporting comforts. He has as much as keeps him from sinking. 'Thou strengthenedst me with strength in my soul.' Psa cxxxviii 3. If a Christian has not God's arm to embrace him, yet he has it to uphold him. Thus a Christian who walks with God, has something that bears up his heart from sinking; and it is but waiting awhile, and he is sure of those joys which are unspeakable and full of glory.

Use one: Then see that religion is no melancholy thing; it brings joy; the fruit of the Spirit is joy. *Mutatur non tollitur* [It varies, but it is not destroyed]. A poor Christian that feeds on bread and water, may have purer joy than the greatest monarch; though he fares hard, he feeds high; he has a table spread from heaven; angels' food, hidden manna; he has sometimes sweet raptures of joy, that cause jubilation of spirit; he has that which is better felt than can be expressed. 2 Cor xii 4.

Use two: If God gives his people such joy in this life, oh! then, what glorious joy will he give them in heaven! 'Enter thou into the joy of thy

Lord.' Matt xxv 21. Here joy begins to enter into us, there we shall enter into joy. God keeps his best wine till last. Heliogabalus bathed himself in sweet perfumed waters. What joy when the soul shall for ever bathe itself in the pure and pleasant fountain of God's love! What joy to see the orient brightness of Christ's face, and have the kisses of those lips which drop sweet-smelling myrrh! *Lætabitur sponsa in amplexibus Domini* [The Bride will rejoice in the embrace of her Lord]. Augustine. Oh! if a cluster of grapes here be so sweet, what will the full vintage be! How may this set us all longing for that place where sorrow cannot live, and where joy cannot die!

9. GROWTH IN GRACE

'But grow in grace.' 2 Pet iii 18.

True grace is progressive, of a spreading and growing nature. It is with grace as with light; first, there is the *crepusculum*, or daybreak; then it shines brighter to the full meridian. A good Christian is like the crocodile. *Quamdiu vivet crescit;* he has never done growing. The saints are not only compared to stars for their light, but to trees for their growth. Isa lxi 3, and Hos xiv 5. A good Christian is not like Hezekiah's sun that went backwards, nor Joshua's sun that stood still, but is always advancing in holiness, and increasing with the increase of God. 1 Cor iii 6.

In how many ways may a Christian be said to grow in grace?

(1.) He grows *vigore*, in the exercise of grace. His lamp is burning and shining: therefore we read of a lively hope. 1 Pet i 3. Here is the activity of grace. The church prays for the blowing of the Spirit, that her spices might flow forth. Cant iv 16.

(2.) A Christian grows *gradu*, in the degree of grace. He goes from strength to strength, from one degree of grace to another. Psa lxxxiv 7. A saint goes from faith to faith. Rom i 17. His love abounds more and more. Phil i 9.

What is the right manner of a Christian's growth?

(1.) It is to grow less in one's own eyes. 'I am a worm, and no man.' Psa xxii 6. The sight of corruption and ignorance makes a Christian grow into a dislike of himself; he vanishes in his own eyes. Job abhorred himself in the dust. Ch xlii 6. It is good to grow out of conceit with one's self.

(2.) The right manner of growth is to grow proportionately, to grow in one grace as well as another. 2 Pet i 5. To grow in knowledge, but not meekness, brotherly love, or good works, is not the right growth. A thing may swell and not grow; a man may be swelled with knowledge, yet may have no spiritual growth. The right manner of growth is uniform, growing in one grace as well as another. As the beauty of the body consists in a symmetry of parts, in which not only the head grows, but the arms and breast; so spiritual growth is most beautiful, when there is symmetry and proportion, and every grace thrives.

(3.) The right manner of growth is, when a Christian has grace suitable to his several employments and occasions; when corruptions are strong, and he has grace able to give check to them; burdens are heavy, and he has patience able to bear them; temptations fierce, and he has faith able to resist them. Then grace grows in the right manner.

Whence is it that true grace cannot but grow?

(1.) It is proper for grace to grow; it is *semen manens* [an enduring seed], the seed of God. 1 John iii 9. It is the nature of seed to grow: grace does not lie in the heart, as a stone in the earth, but as seed in the earth, which will spring up, first the blade, then the ear, and then the full corn in the ear.

(2.) Grace cannot but grow, from its sweetness and excellence. He that has grace is never weary of it, but would have more. The delight he has in it causes thirst. Grace is the image of God, and a Christian thinks he can never be enough like God. Grace instils peace; a Christian, therefore, strives to grow in grace that he may grow in peace.

(3.) Grace cannot but grow, from a believer's ingrafting into Christ. He who is a scion, ingrafted into this noble, generous stock, cannot but grow. Christ is so full of sap, and vivifying influence, that he makes all who are grafted into him, grow fruitful. 'From me is thy fruit found.' Hos xiv 8.

What motives or incentives are there to make us grow in grace?

(1.) Growth is the end of the ordinances. Why does a man lay out cost on ground, manure and water it, but that it may grow? The sincere milk of the word is given, that we may grow thereby. 1 Pet ii 2. The table of the Lord is on purpose for our spiritual nourishment and increase of grace.

(2.) The growth of grace is the best evidence of the truth of it. Things that have no life will not grow: a picture will not grow, a stake in the hedge will not grow; but a plant that has a vegetative life grows. The growing of grace shows it to be alive in the soul.

(3.) Growth in grace is the beauty of a Christian. The more a child grows, the more it comes to its favour and complexion, and looks more ruddy; so, the more a Christian grows in grace, the more he comes to his spiritual complexion, and looks fairer. Abraham's faith was beautiful when in its infancy, but at last it grew so vigorous and eminent, that God himself was in love with it, and crowned Abraham with this honour, to be the 'father of the faithful.'

(4.) The more we grow in grace, the more glory we bring to God. God's glory is more worth than the salvation of all men's souls. This should be our design, to raise the trophies of God's glory; and how can we do it more, than by growing in grace? 'Hereby is my Father glorified, if ye bring forth much fruit.' John xv 8. Though the least drachm of grace will bring salvation to us, yet it will not bring so much glory to God. 'Filled with the fruits of righteousness, which are to the praise of his glory.' Phil i 11. It commends the skill of the husbandman when his plants grow and thrive; it is a praise and honour to God when we thrive in grace.

(5.) The more we grow in grace, the more will God love us. Is it not that which we pray for? The more growth, the more God will love us. The husbandman loves his thriving plants; the thriving Christian is God's *Hephzibah,* or chief delight. Christ loves to see the vine flourishing, and the pomegranates budding. Cant vi 11. He accepts the truth of grace, but commends the growth of grace. 'I have not found so great faith, no, not in Israel.' Matt viii 10. Would you be as the beloved disciple that lay in Christ's bosom? Would you have much love from Christ? Labour for much growth, let faith flourish with good works, and love increase into zeal.

(6.) We need to grow in grace. There is still something lacking in our faith. 1 Thess iii 10. Grace is but in its infancy and minority, and we must still be adding a cubit to our spiritual stature. The apostles said, 'Lord, increase our faith.' Luke xvii 5. Grace is but weak. 'I am this day weak, though anointed king.' 2 Sam iii 39. So, though we are anointed with grace, yet we are but weak, and had need arrive at further degrees of sanctity.

(7.) The growth of grace will hinder the growth of corruption. The more health grows, the more the distempers of the body abate; so in spirituals, the more humility grows, the more the swelling of pride is assuaged, the more purity of heart grows, the more the fire of lust is abated. The growth of flowers in the garden does not hinder the growing of weeds, but the growing of the flower of grace hinders the sprouting of corruption. As some plants have an antipathy, and will not thrive if they grow near together, as the vine and the bay tree, so, where grace grows, sin will not thrive so fast.

(8.) We cannot grow too much in grace; there is no *nimium*, no excess

[275]

there. The body may grow too great, as in the dropsy; but faith cannot grow too great. 'Your faith groweth exceedingly.' 2 Thess i 3. Here was exceeding, yet not excess. As a man cannot have too much health, so not too much grace. Grace is the beauty of holiness. Ps cx 3. We cannot have too much spiritual beauty; it will be the only trouble at death, that we have grown no more in grace.

(9.) Such as do not grow in grace, decay in grace. *Non progredi in via est regredi* [Not to go forward in the Christian life is to turn back]. Bernard. There is no standing in religion, either we go forward or backward. If faith does not grow, unbelief will; if heavenly-mindedness does not grow, covetousness will. A man that does not increase his stock, diminishes it: so if you do not improve your stock of grace, your stock will decay. The angels on Jacob's ladder were either ascending or descending: if you do not ascend in religion, you descend.

(10.) The more we grow in grace, the more we shall flourish in glory. Though every vessel of glory shall be full, yet some vessels hold more than others. He whose pound gained ten, was made ruler over ten cities. Luke xix 17. Such as do not grow much, though they lose not their glory, they lessen it. If any shall follow the Lamb in whiter and larger robes of glory than others, they shall be such as have shone most in grace here.

Use: Lament the want of growth. Religion in many is grown into a form and profession only: this is to grow in leaves, not in fruit. Many Christians are like a body in an atrophy, which does not thrive. They are not nourished by the sermons they hear. Like the angels who assumed bodies, they ate, but did not grow. It is to be suspected where there is no growth, there wants a vital principle. Some instead of growing better, grow worse; they grow more earthly, more profane. 2 Tim iii 13. Evil men *proficient in pejus*, shall wax worse and worse. Many grow hell-ward – they grow past shame. Zeph iii 5. They are like some watered stuffs, which grow more rotten.

How shall we know whether we grow in grace?

For deciding this question, I shall show
I. *The signs of our not growing;* II. *of our growing.*

I. *The signs of our not growing in grace, but rather falling into a spiritual consumption.*

[1] When we have lost our spiritual appetite. A consumptive person has not that stomach to his meat as formerly. Perhaps, Christian, thou canst remember the time when thou didst hunger and thirst after righteousness, thou didst come to the ordinances with such a stomach as to a feast; but now

it is otherwise, Christ is not so prized, nor his ordinances so loved. This is a sad presage that grace is on the declining hand; and thou art in a deep consumption. It was a sign that David was near his grave when they covered him with clothes, and he got no heat, 1 Kings i 1; so, when a person is covered with the warm clothes of ordinances, and yet has no heat of affection to spiritual things, it is a sign that he is declining in grace.

[2] When we grow more worldly. Perhaps we once mounted into higher orbs, we set our hearts on things above, and spake the language of Canaan; but now our minds are taken off from heaven, we dig our comfort out of the lower mines, and with Satan compass the earth. This is a sign we are going down the hill apace, and our grace is in a consumption. It is observable when nature decays, and people are near dying, they grow more stooping; and truly, when men's hearts grow more stooping to the earth, and they can hardly lift up themselves to a heavenly thought, if grace be not dead, yet it is ready to die. Rev iii 2.

[3] When we are less troubled about sin. Time was when the least sin grieved us, as the least hair makes the eye weep; but now we can digest sin without remorse. Time was when we were troubled if we neglected closet prayer; now we can omit family-prayer. Time was when vain thoughts troubled us; now we are not troubled for loose practices. Here is a sad declension in religion; and truly grace is so far from growing that we can hardly perceive its pulse to beat.

II. *The signs of our growing in grace.*

[1] The first sign of our growing, is, when we have got beyond our former measures of grace. It is a sign a child thrives when he has outgrown his clothes. That knowledge which would serve us before will not serve us now; we have a deeper insight into religion, our light is clearer, our spark of love is increased into a flame; there is a sign of growth. That competency of grace we once had is too scanty for us now; we have outgrown ourselves.

[2] When we are more firmly rooted in religion. 'Rooted in him, and established:' the spreading of the root shows the growth of the tree. Col ii 7. When we are so strongly fastened on Christ, that we cannot be blown down with the breath of heretics, it is a blessed sign of growth. Athanasius was called *Adamas ecclesiæ* [the Adamant of the Church], an adamant that could not be removed from the love of the truth.

[3] When we have a more spiritual frame of heart. (1.) When we are more spiritual in our principles; when we oppose sin out of love to God,

and because it strikes at his holiness. (2.) When we are more spiritual in our affections. We grieve for the first rising of corruption, for the bubbling up of vain thoughts, and for the spring that runs underground. We mourn not only for the penalty of sin, but for its pollution. It is not a coal only that burns, but blacks. (3.) When we are spiritual in the performance of duty. We are more serious, reverent, fervent; we have more life in prayer, we put fire to the sacrifice. 'Fervent in spirit.' Rom xii 11. We serve God with more love, which ripens and mellows our duty, and makes it come off with a better relish.

[4] When grace gets ground by opposition. The fire, by an antiperistasis, burns hottest in the coldest season. Peter's courage increased by the opposition of the high priest and the rulers. Acts iv 8, 11. The martyr's zeal was increased by persecution. Here was grace of the first magnitude.

What shall we do to grow in grace?

(1.) Take heed of that which will hinder growth, as the love of any sin. The body may as well thrive in a fever, as grace can where any sin is cherished.

(2.) Use all means for growth in grace. 1st. 'Exercise yourselves unto godliness.' 1 Tim iv 7. The body grows stronger by exercise. Trading of money makes men grow rich; so the more we trade our faith in the promises, the richer in faith we grow. 2ndly. If you would be growing Christians, be humble Christians. It is observed in some countries, as in France, the best and largest grapes, which make wine, grow on the lower sort of vines; so the humble saints grow most in grace. 'God giveth grace to the humble.' 1 Pet v 5. 3rdly. Pray to God for spiritual growth. Some pray that they may grow in gifts. It is better to grow in grace than gifts. Gifts are for ornament, grace is for nourishment. Gifts edify others; grace saves ourselves. Some pray that they may grow rich; but a fruitful heart is better than a full purse. Pray that God would make you grow in grace, though it be by affliction. Heb xii 10. The vine grows by pruning. God's pruning-knife is to make us grow more in grace.

How may we comfort such as complain they do not grow in grace?

They make mistake; for they may grow, when they think they do not, 'There is that maketh himself poor, yet hath great riches.' Prov xiii 7. The sight Christians have of their defects in grace, and their thirst after greater measures of grace, make them think they do not grow when they do. He who covets a great estate, because he has not so much as he desires, thinks himself to be poor. Indeed Christians should seek after the grace they want, but they must not therefore overlook the grace they have. Let

Christians be thankful for the least growth. If you do not grow so much in assurance, bless God if you grow in sincerity; if you do not grow so much in knowledge, bless God if you grow in humility. If a tree grows in the root, it is a true growth; so if you grow in the root-grace of humility, it is as needful for you as any other growth.

10. PERSEVERANCE

'*Who are kept by the power of God through faith unto salvation.*' 1 Pet i 5.

The fifth and last fruit of sanctification, is perseverance in grace. The heavenly inheritance is kept for the saints, and they are kept to the inheritance. 1 Pet i 4. The apostle asserts a saint's stability and permanence in grace. The saint's perseverance is much opposed by Papists and Arminians; but it is not the less true because it is opposed. A Christian's main comfort depends upon this doctrine of perseverance. Take this away, and you prejudice religion, and cut the sinews of all cheerful endeavours. Before I come to the full handling and discussing of this great point, let me first clear the sense of it.

I. *When I say, Believers persevere:*

[1] I grant, that such as are so only in profession, may fall away. 'Demas hath forsaken me.' 2 Tim iv 10. Blazing comets soon evaporate. A building on sand will fall. Matt vii 26. Seeming grace may be lost. No wonder to see a bough fall from a tree that is only tied on. Hypocrites are only tied on Christ by an external profession, they are not ingrafted. Who ever thought artificial motions would hold long? The hypocrite's motion is only artificial, not vital. All blossoms do not ripen into fruit.

[2] I grant that if believers were left to stand on their own legs, they might fall finally. Some of the angels, who were stars full of light and glory, actually lost their grace; and if those pure angels fell from grace, much more would the godly, who have so much sin to betray them, if they were not upheld by a superior power.

[3] I grant that, although true believers do not fall away actually, and lose all their grace, yet their grace may fail in degree, and they may make a great breach upon their sanctification. Grace may be *moritura, non mortua;* dying, but not dead. 'Strengthen the things which are ready to die.' Rev iii 2. Grace may be like fire in the embers; though not quenched, yet the flame is gone out. This decay of grace I shall show in two particulars.

(1.) The lively actings of grace may be suspended. 'Thou hast left thy first love.' Rev ii 4. Grace may be like a sleepy habit; the godly may act faintly in religion, the pulse of their affections may beat low. The wise virgins slumbered. Matt xxv 5. The exercise of grace may be hindered; as when the course of water is stopped. (2.) Instead of grace working in the godly, corruption may work; instead of patience, murmuring; instead of heavenliness, earthliness. How did pride put forth itself in the disciples, when they strove who should be the greatest! How did lust put forth itself in David! Thus lively and vigorous may corruption be in the regenerate; they may fall into enormous sins. But though all this be granted, yet they do not, *penitus exeidere*, fall away finally from grace. David did not quite lose his grace: for then, why did he pray, 'Take not away thy holy spirit from me'? He had not quite lost the Spirit. As Eutychus, when he fell from a window (Acts xx) and all thought he was dead – 'No, saith Paul, there is life in him;' so David fell foully, but there was the life of grace in him. Though the saints may come to that pass that they have but little faith, yet not to have no faith. Though their grace may be drawn low, yet it is not drawn dry; though grace may be abated, it is not abolished; though the wise virgins slumbered, yet their lamps were not quite gone out. Grace, when at the lowest, shall revive and flourish; as when Samson had lost his strength, his hair grew again, and his strength was renewed. Having thus explained the proposition, I come now to amplify this great doctrine of the saint's perseverance.

II. *By what means do Christians come to persevere?*

[1] By the help of ordinances, as of prayer, the word, and the sacraments. Christians do not arrive at perseverance when they sit still and do nothing. It is not with us as with passengers in a ship, who are carried to the end of their voyage while they sit still in the ship; or, as it is with noblemen, who have their rents brought in without their toil or labour; but we arrive at salvation in the use of means; as a man comes to the end of a race by running, to a victory by fighting. 'Watch and pray.' Matt xxvi 41. As Paul said, 'Except ye abide in the ship, ye cannot be saved.' Acts xxvii 31. Believers shall come to shore at last, arrive at heaven; but 'except they abide in the ship,' viz., in the use of ordinances, 'they cannot be saved.' The ordinances cherish grace; as they beget grace, so they are the breast-milk by which it is nourished and preserved to eternity.

[2] *Auxilio Spiritus,* by the sacred influence and concurrence of the Spirit. The Spirit of God is continually at work in the heart of a believer, to carry on grace to perfection. It drops in fresh oil, to keep the lamp of grace

burning. The Spirit excites, strengthens, increases grace, and makes a Christian go from one step of faith to another, till he comes to the end of his faith, which is salvation. 1 Pet i 9. It is a fine expression of the apostle, 'The Holy Ghost which dwelleth in us.' 2 Tim i 14. He who dwells in a house, keeps the house in repair; so the Spirit dwelling in a believer, keeps grace in repair. Grace is compared to a river of the water of life. John vii 38. This river can never be dried up, because God's Spirit is the spring that continually feeds it.

[3] Grace is carried on to perfection by Christ's daily intercession. As the Spirit is at work in the heart, so is Christ at work in heaven. Christ is ever praying that the saint's grace may hold out. *Conserva illos;* ' "Father, keep those whom thou hast given me:" keep them as the stars in their orbs: keep them as jewels, that they may not be lost. "Father keep them." ' John xvii 11. That prayer which Christ made for Peter, was the copy of the prayer he now makes for believers. 'I have prayed for thee, that thy faith fail not,' that it be not totally eclipsed. Luke xxii 32. How can the children of such prayers perish?

III. *Arguments to prove the saint's perseverance.*

[1] *A veritate Dei*, 'from the truth of God.' God has both asserted it, and promised it. (1.) God has asserted it. 'His seed remaineth in him.' 1 John iii 9. 'The anointing ye have received of him abideth in you.' 1 John ii 27. (2.) As God has asserted it, so he has promised it. The truth of God, the most orient pearl of his crown, is laid as a pawn in the promise. 'I will give unto them eternal life, and they shall never perish.' John x 28. 'I will make an everlasting covenant with them, that I will not turn away from them to do them good, but I will put my fear in their hearts, that they shall not depart from me.' Jer xxxii 40. God will so love his people, that he will not forsake them; and they shall so fear him, that they shall not forsake him. If a believer should not persevere, God would break his promise. 'I will betroth thee unto me for ever, in righteousness and loving-kindness.' Hos ii 19. God does not marry his people unto himself, and then divorce them; he hates putting away. Mal 2 16. God's love ties the marriage-knot so fast, that neither death nor hell can break it asunder.

[2] The second argument is, *a potentia Dei*, 'from the power of God.' The text says, we 'are kept by the power of God unto salvation.' Each Person in the Trinity has a hand in making a believer persevere. God the Father establishes. 2 Cor i 21. God the Son confirms, 1 Cor i 8. God the Holy Ghost seals. Eph i 13. So that it is the power of God that keeps us. We are not kept by our own power. The Pelagians held that man by his own

power might overcome temptation and persevere. Augustine confutes them. 'Man,' says he, 'prays unto God for perseverance, which would be absurd, if he had power of himself to persevere.' 'And,' says Augustine, 'if all the power be inherent in a man's self, then why should not one persevere as well as another? Why not Judas as well as Peter?' So that it is not by any other than the power of God that we are kept. The Lord preserved Israel from perishing in the wilderness, till he brought them to Canaan; and the same care will he take, if not in a miraculous manner, yet in a spiritual invisible manner, in preserving his people in a state of grace, till he bring them to the celestial Canaan. As the heathens feigned of Atlas, that he bears up the heavens from falling: the power of God is that Atlas which bears up the saints from falling. It is disputed, whether grace of itself may not perish, as Adam's; yet sure I am, grace kept by the power of God cannot perish.

[3] The third argument is taken, *ab electione*, 'from God's electing love.' Such as God has from all eternity elected to glory, cannot fall away finally; but every true believer is elected to glory, therefore he cannot fall away. What can frustrate election, or make God's decree void? This argument stands like Mount Sion, which cannot be moved; insomuch that some of the Papists hold, that those who have absolute election cannot fall away. 'The foundation of God standeth sure, having this seal, the Lord knoweth them that are his.' 2 Tim ii 19. The foundation of God is nothing else but God's decree in election; and this stands sure; God will not alter it, and others cannot.

[4] The fourth argument is taken, *ab unione cum Christo*, 'from believers' union with Christ.' They are knit to Christ as the members to the head, by the nerves and ligaments of faith, so that they cannot be broken off. Eph v 23. What was once said of Christ's natural body is true of his mystical. 'A bone of it shall not be broken.' As it is not possible to sever the leaven and the dough when they are once mingled and kneaded together, so it is impossible for Christ and believers, when once united, ever to be separated. Christ and his members make one body. Now, is it possible that any part of Christ should perish? How can Christ lose any member of his mystic body, and be perfect? In short, *si unus excidat, quare non et alter?* If one believer may be broken off from Christ, then, by the same rule, why not another. Why not all? And so Christ would be a head without a body.

[5] The fifth argument is taken, *ab emptione*, 'from the nature of a purchase.' A man will not lay down his money for a purchase which may be lost, and the fee-simple alienated. Christ died that he might purchase us as

a people to himself for ever. 'Having obtained eternal redemption for us.' Heb ix 12. Would Christ, think ye, have shed his blood that we might believe in him for a while, and then fall away? Do we think Christ will lose his purchase?

[6] The sixth argument is, *a victoria supra mundum*, 'from a believer's victory over the world.' The argument stands thus: He who overcomes the world perseveres in grace; but a believer overcomes the world; therefore a believer perseveres in grace. 'This is the victory that over-cometh the world, even our faith.' 1 John v 4. A man may lose a single battle in the field, yet win the victory at last. A child of God may be foiled in a single battle against temptation, as Peter was, but he is vic-torious at last. Now, if a saint be crowned victor, if the world be con-quered by him, he must needs persevere.

IV. *I come next to answer some objections of the Arminians.*

[1] The first objection of Arminians is, *If a believer shall persevere in grace, to what purpose are admonitions in Scripture, such as 'Let him take heed lest he fall;' 1 Cor x 12; and, 'Let us fear, lest any of you seem to come short.' Heb iv 1? Such admonitions seem to be superfluous, if a saint shall certainly persevere.*

These admonitions are necessary to caution believers against careless-ness; they are as goads and spurs to quicken them to greater diligence in working out their salvation. They do not imply the saints can fall away, but are preservatives to keep them from falling away. Christ told some of his disciples they should abide in him, yet he exhorts them to abide in him. John xv 4. His exhorting them was not in the least to question their abiding in him, but to awaken their diligence, and make them pray the harder, that they might abide in him.

[2] The second objection is, *It is impossible for those who were once en-lightened, and have tasted of the heavenly gift, and were made partakers of the Holy Ghost, and have felt the powers of the world to come, if they shall fall away, to renew them again to repentance.* Heb vi 4.

This place of Scripture has no force in it, for the apostle here speaks of hypocrites; he shows how far they may go, and yet fall away. (1.) *They who were once enlightened.* Men may have great illuminations, yet fall away. Was not Judas enlightened? (2.) *They have been made partakers of the Holy Ghost;* the common gifts of the Spirit, not the special grace. (3.) *They have tasted the good word of God.* Tasting here is opposed to eating: the hypocrite may have a kind of taste of the sweetness of religion, but his taste does not nourish. There is a great deal of difference between one that takes a gargle and a cordial: the gargle only washes his mouth – he tastes it, and puts it out again; but a cordial is drunk down, which nourishes and cherishes the spirits. The hypocrite, who has only some smack or taste of religion, as one tastes a gargle, may fall away. (4.) *And have felt the powers of the world to come;* that is, they may have such apprehensions of the glory of heaven as to be affected with it, and seem to have some joy in the thoughts of it, yet fall away; as in the parable of the stony ground. Matt xiii 20. All this is spoken of the hypocrite; but it does not therefore prove that the true believer, who is effectually wrought upon, can fall away. Though comets fall, it does not follow that true stars fall. That this Scripture speaks not of sound believers, is clear from ver 9: 'But we are persuaded better things of you, and things that accompany salvation.'

Use one: For instruction. (1.) See the excellence of grace. It perseveres. Other things are but for a season; health and riches are sweet, but they are but for a season; but grace is the blossom of eternity. The seed of God remains. 1 John iii 9. Grace may suffer an eclipse, not a dissolution. It is called substance, for its solidity, Prov viii 21; and durable riches, for its permanence. Prov viii 18. It lasts as long as the soul, as heaven lasts. Grace is not like a lease which soon expires, but it runs parallel with eternity.

(2.) See here that which may excite in the saints everlasting love and gratitude to God. What can make us love God more than the fixedness of his love to us? He is not only the author of grace, but finisher; his love is perpetual and carried on to our salvation. 'My sheep hear my voice, and I know them, and they follow me: and I give unto them eternal life.' John x 27, 28. *My sheep*, there is election; *hear my voice*, there is vocation; *and I know them*, there is justification; *and they follow me*, there is sanctification; *and I give unto them eternal life*, there is glorification. How may this make us love God, and set up the monuments and trophies of his praise! How much have we done to cause God to withdraw his Spirit, and suffer us to fall finally! yet that he should keep us, let his name be blessed, and his memorial eternalized, who keepeth the feet of his saints. 1 Sam ii 9.

(3.) See whence it is that saints persevere in holiness. It is to be ascribed solely to the power of God; we are kept by his power, kept as in a garrison. It is a wonder that any Christian perseveres, if you consider: (i) *Corruption within*. The tares are mingled with the wheat; there is more sin than grace, yet grace be habitually predominant. Grace is like a spark in the sea, a wonder that it is not quenched. It is a wonder that sin does not destroy grace; that it does not do, as sometimes the nurse to the infant, overlay it, and so this infant of grace be smothered and die. (ii) *Temptations without.* Satan envies us happiness, and he raises his militia, and stirs up persecution. He shoots his fiery darts of temptations, which are called darts for their swiftness, fiery for their terribleness. We are every day beset with devils. As it was a wonder that Daniel was kept alive in the midst of the roaring lions, so there are many roaring devils about us, and yet we are not torn in pieces. Now, whence is it that we stand against these powerful temptations? We are kept by the power of God. (iii) *The world's golden snares, riches and pleasure.* 'How hardly shall they that have riches enter into the kingdom of God?' Luke xviii 24. How many have been cast away upon these golden sands, as Demas! 2 Tim iv 10. What a wonder any soul perseveres in religion, that the earth does not choke the fire of all good affections? Whence is this, but from the power of God? We are kept by his power.

Use two: For consolation. This doctrine of perseverance is as a bezoar stone; it is a sovereign cordial to keep up the spirits of the godly from fainting. (1.) There is nothing that more troubles a child of God than that he fears he shall never hold out. 'These weak legs of mine,' he says, will never carry me to heaven.' But perseverance is an inseparable fruit of sanctification. *Once in Christ, for ever in Christ.* A believer may fall from some degrees of grace, but not from the state of grace. An Israelite could never wholly sell or alienate his inheritance. Lev xxv 23. So our heavenly inheritance cannot be wholly alienated from us. How despairing is the Arminian doctrine of falling from grace! To-day a saint, to-morrow a reprobate; to-day a Peter, to-morrow a Judas. This must needs cut the sinews of a Christian's endeavour, and be like boring a hole in a vessel: to make all the wine of his joy run out. Were the Arminian doctrine true, how could the apostle say, the seed of God remains in him, and the anointing of God abides? 1 John iii 9; 1 John ii 27. What comfort were it to have one's name written in the book of life, if it might be blotted out again? But be assured, for your comfort, grace, if true, though never so weak, shall persevere. Though a Christian has but little grace to trade with, yet he need not fear breaking, because God not only gives him a stock of grace, but will keep his stock for him. *Gratia concutitur, non excutitur.* Augustine. 'Grace may be shaken with fears and doubts, but it cannot be plucked up by the roots.' Fear not falling away. If anything should hinder the saints' perseverance, it must be either sin or temptation: but neither of these can. (i) Not the sin of believers. That which humbles them shall not damn them; but their sins humble them.

They gather grapes off thorns; from the thorn of sin they gather the grape of humility. (ii) Not temptation. The devil lays the train of his temptation to blow up the fort of a saint's grace; but he cannot do it. Temptation is a medicine for security; the more Satan tempts, the more the saints pray. When Paul had the messenger of Satan to buffet him, he said, 'For this I besought the Lord thrice, that it might depart from me.' 2 Cor xii 8. Thus nothing can break off a believer from Christ, or hinder his perseverance. Let this wine be given to such as are of a heavy heart. (2.) This perseverance is comfort. (i) In the loss of worldly comforts. When our goods may be taken away, our grace cannot. 'Mary hath chosen the better part, which cannot be taken from her.' Luke x 42. (ii) In the hour of death. When all things fail, friends take their farewell of us, yet still grace remains. Death may separate all things else from us but grace. A Christian may say on his death-bed, as Olevianus, 'Sight is gone, speech and hearing are departing, but the lovingkindness of God will never depart.'

Use three: For exhortation. *What motives and incentives are there to make Christians persevere?*

(1.) It is the crown and glory of a Christian to persevere. *In Christianis non initia sed fines laudantur* [It is not the beginning of the Christian life that gets glory but the end of it]. 'The hoary head is a crown of glory, if found in the way of righteousness.' Prov xvi 31. When grey hairs shine with golden virtues, it is a crown of glory. The church of Thyatira was best at last. 'I know thy patience and thy works, and the last to be more than the first.' Rev ii 19. The excellence of a building is not in having the first stone laid, but when it is finished: the glory and excellence of a Christian is when he has finished the work of faith.

(2.) You are within a few days' march of heaven. Salvation is near to you. 'Now is our salvation nearer than when we believed.' Rom xiii 11. Christians, it is but a while and you will have done weeping and praying, and be triumphing; you shall put off your mourning, and put on white robes; you shall put off your armour, and put on a victorious crown. You who have made a good progress in religion, you are almost ready to commence and take your degree of glory; now is your salvation nearer than when you began to believe. When a man is almost at the end of a race, will he tire, or faint away? O labour to persevere, your salvation is now nearer; you have but a little way to go, and you will set your foot in heaven! Though the way be up-hill and full of thorns, yet you have gone the greatest part of your way, and shortly shall rest from your labours.

(3.) How sad is it not to persevere in holiness! You expose yourself to the reproaches of men, and the rebukes of God. First, to the reproaches of men. They will deride both you and your profession. 'This man began to build, and was not able to finish.' Luke xiv 30. Such is he who begins in religion, and does not persevere: he is the *ludibrium* and derision of all. Secondly, to the rebukes of God. God is most severe against such as fall off, because they bring an evil report upon religion. Apostasy breeds a bitter worm in the conscience; (what a worm did Spira feel!); and it brings swift damnation; it is a drawing back to perdition. Heb x 39. God will make his sword drunk with the blood of apostates.

(4.) The promises of mercy are annexed only to perseverance. 'He that overcometh shall be clothed in white raiment; and I will not blot out his name out of the book of life.' Rev iii 5. *Non pugnanti sed vincenti dabitur corona.* Augustine. The promise is not to him that fights, but that overcomes. 'Ye are they which have continued with me, and I appoint unto you a kingdom.' Luke xxii 28, 29. The promise of a kingdom, says Chrysostom, is not made to them that heard Christ or followed him, but that continued with him. Perseverance carries away the garland; no man has the crown set upon his head, but he who holds out to the end of the race. O therefore, be persuaded by all this to persevere. God makes no account of such as do not persevere. Who esteems corn that sheds before harvest, or fruit that falls from the tree before it be ripe?

What expedients or means may be used for a Christian's perseverance?

(1.) Take heed of those things which will make you desist and fall away. 1st. Take heed of presumption. Do not presume upon your own strength; exercise a holy fear and jealousy over your own hearts. 'Be not high-minded, but fear.' Rom xi 20. 'Let him that thinketh he standeth take heed lest he fall.' 1 Cor x 12. It was Peter's sin that he leaned more upon his grace than upon Christ, and then he fell. A Christian has cause to fear lest the lust and deceit of his heart betray him. Take heed of presuming. Fear begets prayer, prayer begets strength, and strength begets steadfastness. 2ndly. Take heed of hypocrisy. Judas was first a sly hypocrite, and then a traitor. 'Their heart was not right with God, neither were they steadfast in his covenant.' Psa lxxviii 37. If there be any venom or malignity in the blood, it will break forth into a plague-sore. The venom of hypocrisy is in danger of breaking out into the plague-sore of scandal. 3rdly. Beware of a vile heart of unbelief. 'Take heed lest there be in any of you an evil heart of unbelief, in departing from the living God.' Heb iii 12. Whence is apostasy but from incredulity? Men do not believe the truth, and therefore they fall from the truth. Unbelieving and unstable go together. 'They believed not in God.' 'They turned back.' Psa lxxviii 22, 41.

(2.) If you would be pillars in the temple of God, and persevere in sanctity;

(i) Look that you enter into religion upon a right ground; be well grounded in the distinct knowledge of God. You must know the love of the Father, the merit of the Son, and the efficacy of the Holy Ghost. Such as know not God aright will by degrees fall off. The Samaritans sided with the Jews when they were in favour, but disclaimed all kindred with them when Antiochus persecuted the Jews. No wonder they were no more fixed in religion, if you consider what Christ says of them: 'Ye worship ye know not what.' John iv 22. They were ignorant of the true God. Let your knowledge of God be clear, and serve him purely out of choice, and then you will persevere. 'I have chosen the way of truth. . . I have stuck unto thy testimonies.' Psa cxix 30, 31.

(ii) Get a real work of grace in your heart. 'It is a good thing that the heart be established with grace.' Heb xiii 9. Nothing will hold out but grace; it is only this anointing abides; paint will fall off. Get a heart-changing work. 'But ye are washed, but ye are sanctified.' 1 Cor vi 11. Be not content with baptism of water, without baptism of the Spirit. The reason men persevere not in religion, is for want of a vital principle; a branch must needs wither that has no root to grow upon.

(iii) If you would persevere, be very sincere. Perseverance grows only upon the root of sincerity. 'Let integrity and uprightness preserve me.' Psa xxv 21. The breastplate of sincerity can never be shot through. How many storms was Job in! The devil set against him; his wife tempted him to curse God; his friends accused him of being a hypocrite: here was enough, one would think, to have made him desist from religion; but for all this, he perseveres. What preserved him? It was his sincerity. 'My righteousness I hold fast, and will not let it go; my heart shall not reproach me so long as I live.' Job xxvii 6.

(iv) If you would persevere, be humble. Chrysostom calls humility the mother of all the graces. God lets a poor, humble Christian stand, when others of higher parts, and who have higher thoughts of themselves, fall off by apostasy. They are most likely to persevere, to whom God gives most grace. 'But he gives grace to the humble.' 1 Pet v 5. They are most likely to persevere, who have God dwelling in them. 'But God dwells in the humble soul.' Isa lvii 15. *Non requiescet Spiritus Sanctus nisi super humilem* [The Holy Spirit will only come to rest over a humble soul]. Bernard. The lower the tree roots in the earth, the firmer it is; so the more the soul is rooted in humility, the more established it is, and is in less danger of falling away.

(v) Would you persevere? Cherish the grace of faith. Faith is able *stabilere animum* [to support the spirit]. 'By faith ye stand.' 2 Cor i 24. Faith knits us to Christ, as the members are knit to the head by nerves and sinews. Faith fills us with love to God. 'It works by love.' Gal v 6. He who loves God will rather die than desert him; as the soldier who loves his general will die in his service. Faith gives us a prospect of heaven; it shows us an invisible glory; and he who has Christ in his heart, and a crown in his eye, will not faint away. O cherish faith! Keep your faith, and your faith will keep you. While the pilot keeps his ship, his ship keeps him.

(vi) Would we persevere? Let us seek God's power to help us. We are kept by the power of God. The child is safest when it is held in the nurse's arms; so are we, when we are held in the arms of free grace. It is not our holding God, but his holding us, that preserves us. When a boat is tied to a rock, it is secure; so, when we are fast tied to the Rock of Ages, we are impregnable. O engage God's power to help you to persevere. We engage his power by prayer. Let us pray to him to keep us. 'Hold up my goings in thy path, that my footsteps slip not.' Psa xvii 5. It was a good prayer of Beza, *Domine quod cepisti perfici, ne in portu naufragium accidat:* 'Lord, perfect what thou hast begun in me, that I may not suffer shipwreck when I am almost at the haven.'

(vii) If you would persevere, set before your eyes the noble examples of those who have persevered in religion: *Quot martyres, quot fideles in cælis, jam triumphant!* [How many martyrs, how many faithful souls are even now rejoicing in Heaven!]. What a glorious army of saints and martyrs have gone before us! How constant to the death was Paul! Acts xxi 13. How persevering in the faith were Ignatius, Polycarp, and Athanasius! They were stars in their orbs, pillars in the temple of God. Let us look on their zeal and courage, and be animated. 'Seeing we are compassed about with so great a cloud of witnesses, let us run with patience the race that is set before us.' Heb xii 1. The crown is set at the end of the race; and if we win the race, we shall wear the crown.

VI. Death and the last day

1. THE DEATH OF THE RIGHTEOUS

'For to me to live is Christ, and to die is gain.' Phil i 21.

Paul was a great admirer of Christ. He desired to know nothing but Christ, and him crucified. 1 Cor ii 2. No medicine like the blood of Christ; and in the text, 'For to me to live is Christ, and to die is gain.'

I. *For to me to live is Christ.* We must understand Paul of a spiritual life. *For to me to live is Christ, i.e.*, Christ is my life; so Gregory of Nyssa; or thus, my life is made up of Christ. As a wicked man's life is made up of sin, so Paul's life was made up of Christ: he was full of Christ. That I may give you the sense of the text more fully, take it in these three particulars:—

[1] *For to me to live is Christ, i.e.*, Christ is the principle of my life. I fetch my spiritual life from Christ, as the branch fetches its sap from the root. 'Christ liveth in me.' Gal ii 20. Jesus Christ is a head of influence; he sends forth life and spirits into me, to quicken me to every holy action. Thus, *for to me to live is Christ:* Christ is the principle of my life; from his fulness I live, as the vine branch lives from the root.

[2] *For to me to live is Christ, i.e.*, Christ is the end of my life; I live not to myself but to Christ. So Grotius and Casaubon, *Christo servio,* 'For me to live is Christ;' all my living is to do service to Christ. 'Whether we live, we live unto the Lord.' Rom xiv 8. When we lay out ourselves wholly for Christ: as the factor trades for the merchant, so we trade for Christ's interest: we propagate his gospel; the design of our life is to exalt Christ, and make the crown upon his head flourish. It may then be said, *for to us to live is Christ;* our whole life is a living to Christ.

[3] *For to me to live is Christ, i.e.*, Christ is the joy of my life. 'God my exceeding joy,' or the cream of my joy. Psa xliii 4. A Christian rejoices in Christ's righteousness. He can rejoice in Christ when worldly joys are gone. When the tulip in a garden withers, a man rejoices in his jewels;

when relations die, a saint can rejoice in Christ, the pearl of price. In this sense, *For to me to live is Christ;* he is the joy of my life; if Christ were gone, my life would be a death to me.

It should exhort us all to labour to say as the apostle, *For to me to live is Christ:* Christ is the principle of my life, the end of my life, the joy of my life. If we can say, *For to me to live is Christ,* we may comfortably conclude, that to die shall be gain.

II. *And to die is gain.* To a believer death is great gain. A saint can tell what his losses for Christ are here, but he cannot tell how great his gains are at death. 'To me to die is gain.' Death to a believer is *crepusculum gloriae*, the daybreak of eternal brightness. To show fully what a believer's gains are at death were a task too great for an angel; all hyperboles fall short of it; the reward of glory exceeds our very faith. Let me give you some dark views and imperfect lineaments only of that infinite glory the saints shall gain at the hour of death. 'To me to die is gain.'

[1] Believers at death shall gain a writ of ease from all sins and troubles; they shall be in a state of impeccability: sin expires with their life. I think sometimes what a happy state that will be, never to have another sinful thought, and to have a *quietus* from all troubles. Here David cried out, 'My life is spent with griefs, and my years with sighing.' Psa xxxi 10. *Quid est diu vivere, nisi diu torqueri* [Long life is merely long torment]. Augustine. Life begins with a cry, and ends with a groan; but at death all troubles die.

[2] Believers at death shall gain the glorious sight of God. They shall see him; (1.) Intellectually with the eyes of their mind, which divines call the beatific vision. If there were not such an intellectual sight of God, how do the spirits of just men, made perfect, see him?

(2.) They shall behold the glorified body of Jesus Christ; and if it be pleasant to behold the sun, how blessed a sight will it be to see Christ, the Sun of Righteousness, clothed with our human nature, shining in glory above the angels! Through Christ's flesh, as through a transparent glass, some bright rays and beams of the Godhead shall display themselves to glorified eyes. The sight of God through Christ will be very delightful; for the terror of God's essence will be taken away; his majesty will be mixed with beauty, and sweetened with clemency. It will be infinitely delightful to the saints to see the amiable aspects and smiles of God's face.

[3] The saints at death shall not only have a sight of God, but shall enjoy his love. There shall be no more a vail on God's face, nor shall his smiles be chequered with frowns, but his love shall discover itself in all its orient

beauty and fragrant sweetness. Here the saints pray for his love, and they have a few drops; but there they shall have as much as their vessels can receive. To know the love that passeth knowledge will cause a jubilation of spirit, and create such holy raptures of joy in the saints, as are superlative, and would soon overwhelm them, if God did not make them able to bear it.

[4] Believers at death shall gain a celestial palace, a house not made with hands. 2 Cor v 1. Here the saints are straitened for room; they have but mean cottages to live in; but they shall have a royal palace to live in hereafter. Here is their sojourning house, there in heaven is their mansion-house, a house built high above all the visible orbs, bespangled with light, and enriched with pearls and precious stones. Col i 12, and Rev xxi 19. It is not their landlord's house, but their Father's house, and stands upon consecrated ground. John xiv 2. It is represented by transparent glass, to show its holiness. Rev xxi 21.

[5] Believers at death shall gain the sweet society of glorified saints and angels; which will add to the felicity of heaven, as every star adds some lustre to the firmament. (1.) The society of the glorified saints. We shall see them in their souls, as well as in their bodies. Their bodies will be so clear and bright, that we shall see their souls shining through them, as wine through the glass. Believers at death will have close converse with glorified saints. How delightful will it be, to be freed from all the sinful corruptions, pride, envy, passion and censoriousness, which as scars disfigured them here! In heaven there will be perfect love among the saints; as the olive and myrtle, they will sweetly embrace each other. If in the transfiguration Peter knew Moses and Elias, whom he never saw before, Matt xvii 3, much more, in the glorified state, will saints perfectly know one another, though they never saw each other before. (2.) The saints at death will behold the angels with the glorified eye of their understandings. The wings of the cherubims (representing the angels) were made of fine gold, to denote both their sanctity and splendour. Angels are compared to lightning, Matt xxviii 3, because of those sparkling beams of majesty, which as lightning shoot from them. When saints and angels meet and sing together in concert in the heavenly choir, what divine harmony, what joyful triumphs will there be!

[6] Believers at death shall gain perfection of holiness. Here grace is but *in cunabulis*, 'in its cradle,' very imperfect; so that we cannot write a copy of holiness without blotting: here believers receive but *primitias Spiritus*, 'the first fruits of the Spirit.' Rom viii 23. At death the saints will arrive at perfection; their knowledge will be clear; their sanctity perfect; their

sun will be in its full meridian splendour. They need not then pray for increase of grace; for they shall love God as much as they would love him, and as much as he desires to have them love him. They shall be in respect of holiness as the angels of God.

[7] At death, the saints will gain a royal magnificent feast. I told you before what a glorious palace they shall have; but a man may starve in a house, if there be no cheer. The royal banquet which saints have at death is sha-dowed out in Scripture by a marriage-supper. Rev xix 9. Bullinger and Gregory the Great understand by the marriage-supper of the Lamb, the stately, magnificent festival the saints will have in heaven, when they shall feed on the tree of life. Rev xxii 2. They shall have the heavenly nectar and ambrosia, 'the spiced wine, and the juice of the pomegranate.' Cant viii 2. This royal supper of the Lamb will not only satisfy hunger, but prevent it. 'They shall hunger no more.' Rev vii 16. Nor can there be any surfeit at this feast, because a fresh course will be continually served. New and fresh delights will spring from God; therefore the tree of life in paradise is said to bear twelve sorts of fruit. Rev xxii 2.

[8] Believers at death shall gain honour and dignity; they shall reign as kings. We read therefore of the ensigns of their royalty, their white robes and crowns celestial. Rev iv 4. We read that the doors of the holy of holies were made of palm-trees and open flowers, covered with gold. 1 Kings vi 35. An emblem this of the victory and triumph, and the golden garland of honour wherewith God invests the saints glorified. When all worldly honour shall lie in the dust, the mace, the star, the robe of ermine, the imperial diadem, then shall the saints' honour remain; not one jewel shall be plucked out of their crown. At death they shall gain a blessed eternity. If the saints could have the least suspicion or fear of losing their glory, it would much cool and imbitter their joy; but their crown fadeth not away. 1 Pet v 4. As the wicked have a worm that never dies, so the elect have a crown that never fades. Ever, is a short word, but it has no end. *In fine erit gaudium sine fine* [At the last our joy shall be never-ending]. Bernard. 'The things which are not seen are eternal.' 2 Cor iv 18. 'At thy right hand are pleasures for evermore.' Psa xvi 11. Who can span eter-nity? Millions of ages stand but for ciphers in eternity. Ever in Christ's bosom is the *elah*, or highest strain of the saint's glory.

How come the saints to have all this gain?

They have a right to all this gain at death upon several accounts, as by virtue of the Father's donation, the Son's purchase, the Holy Ghost's earnest, and faith's acceptance. Therefore the state of future glory is called the saint's proper inheritance. Col i 12. They are heirs of God and have a right to inherit.

Use one: See the great difference between the death of the godly and the wicked. The godly are great gainers, but the wicked are great losers at death. They lose four things:—

(1.) They lose the world; and that is a great loss to the wicked. They laid up their treasure upon earth, and to be turned out of it all at once is a great loss.

(2.) They lose their souls. Matt xvi 26, 27. The soul was at first a noble piece of coin, upon which God stamped his own image. This celestial spark is more precious than the whole globe of the world; but the sinner's soul is lost: not that the souls of the wicked are annihilated at death, but tormented.

(3.) They lose heaven. Heaven is *sedes beatorum*, the royal seat of the blessed; it is the region of happiness, the map of perfection. There is the manna which is angels' food; there is the garden of spices, the bed of perfumes, the river of pleasure. Sinners at death, lose all these.

(4.) They lose all hope. Though they lived wickedly, they hoped God would be merciful, and they hoped they should go to heaven. Their hope was not an anchor, but a spider's web. At death they lose their hopes, and see they did but flatter themselves into hell. 'Whose hope shall be cut off.' Job viii 14. It is sad to have life and hope cut off together.

Use two: If saints gain such glorious things at death, well may they desire it. Does not every one desire preferment? *Nemo ante funera felix* [No-one is content before his death]. Faith gives a title to heaven: death gives the possession. Though we should be desirous of doing service here, yet we should be ambitious of being with Christ. Phil i 23. We should be content to live, but willing to die. Is it not a blessed thing to be freed from sin, and to lie for ever in the bosom of divine love? Is it not a blessed thing to meet our godly relations in heaven, and to be singing divine anthems of praise among the angels? Does not the bride desire the marriage day, especially if she has the prospect of a crown? What is the place we now live in, but a place of banishment from God? We are in a wilderness, while angels live at court. Here we are combating with Satan, and should we not desire to be out of the bloody field, where the bullets of temptation fly fast, and receive a victorious crown? Think what it will be to have always a smiling look from Christ's face! to be brought into the banqueting-house, and have the banner of his love displayed over us! O ye saints, desire death; it is your ascension-day to heaven. *Egredere, anima, egredere!* said Hilarion on his death-bed, 'Go forth, my soul, Go

forth!' Another holy man said, 'Lord, lead me to that glory which I have
seen as through a glass; haste, Lord, and do not tarry.' Some plants thrive
best when they are transplanted; so believers, when transplanted by death,
cannot but thrive, because they have Christ's sunbeams shining upon
them. What though the passage through the valley of the shadow of
death be troublesome! who would not be willing to pass a tempestuous
sea, if he were sure to be crowned so soon as he came to shore?

Use three: We may here find comfort in the loss of dear and pious relations. They are not only taken away from the evil to come, but are
great gainers by death. They leave a wilderness, and go to a paradise;
they change their complaints into thanksgivings; they leave their sorrows
behind, and enter into the joy of their Lord. Why should we weep for
their preferment? Believers have not their portion paid till the day of their
death. God's promise is his bond to make over heaven in reversion to
them; but though they have his bond, they do not receive their portion
till the day of death. Oh! rejoice to think of their happiness who die in
the Lord: to them 'to die is gain.' They are as rich as heaven can make
them.

2. A BELIEVER'S PRIVILEGE AT DEATH

'For to me to live is Christ, and to die is gain.' Phil i 21.

Hope is a Christian's anchor, which he casts within the veil. 'Rejoicing
in hope.' Rom xii 12. A Christian's hope is not in this life, but he 'hath
hope in his death.' Prov xiv 32. The best of a saint's comfort begins when
his life ends; but the wicked have all their heaven here. 'Woe unto you
that are rich! for ye have received your consolation.' Luke vi 24. You may
make your acquittance, and write 'Received in full payment.' 'Son,
remember that thou in thy lifetime receivedst thy good things.' Luke xvi
25. But a saint's happiness is in reversion. 'The righteous hath hope in his
death.' God keeps the best wine till last. If Cato, the heathen, said, 'To
me to die is gain:' he saw mortality to be a mercy: what, then, may a
believer say! 'The day of death is better than the day of one's birth.'
Eccl vii 1. A queen of this land said she preferred her coffin before her
cradle.

What benefits do believers receive at death?

I. *The saints, at death, have great immunities and freedoms.* An apprentice,
when out of his time, is made free: so, when the saints are out of their
time of living, they are made free! they are not made free till death. [1] At

death they are freed from a body of sin. There are in the best *reliquiæ peccati* [the remnants of sin], some remainders and relics of corruption. 'O wretched man that I am! who shall deliver me from this body of death?' Rom vii 24. By the body of death is meant the *congeries*, the mass and lump of sin. It may well be called a body for its weightiness, and a body of death for its noisomeness. (1.) It weighs us down. Sin hinders us from doing good. A Christian – like a bird that would be flying up, but has a string tied to its legs to hinder it – would be flying up to heaven with the wings of desire, but sin hinders him. 'The good that I would, I do not.' Rom vii 19. He is like a ship under sail, and at anchor! grace would sail forward, but sin is the anchor that holds it back. (2.) Sin is more active in its sphere than grace. How stirring was lust in David, when his grace lay dormant! (3). Sin sometimes gets the mastery, and leads a saint captive. 'The evil that I would not, that I do.' Rom vii 19. Paul was like a man carried down the stream, and could not bear up against it. How often is a child of God overpowered with pride and passion! Therefore Paul calls sin a law in his members. Rom vii 23. It binds as a law; it has a kind of jurisdiction over the soul, as Caesar had over the senate. (4.) Sin defiles the soul; like a stain to beauty, it turns the soul's azure brightness into sable. (5.) Sin debilitates us, disarms us of our strength. 'I am this day weak, though anointed king.' 2 Sam iii 39. Though a saint be crowned with grace, and anointed a spiritual king, he is weak. (6.) Sin is ever restless. 'The flesh lusts against the spirit.' Gal v 17. It is an inmate that is always quarrelling; like Marcellus, that Roman captain, of whom Hannibal said, whether he beat or was beaten, he would never be quiet. (7.) Sin adheres to us, we cannot get rid of it. It may be compared to a wild fig-tree growing on a wall, the roots of which are pulled up, but some fibres of it are left in the joints of the stone-work, which cannot be got out. (8.) Sin mingles with our duties and graces. It makes a child of God weary of his life, and makes him water his couch with his tears, to think that sin is so strong a party, and he often offends the God he loves. This made Paul cry out, *Miser ego homo!* 'O wretched man that I am!' He did not cry out for his affliction, or his prison-chain, but for the body of sin. Now a believer at death is freed from sin; he is not taken away in, but from his sins; he shall never have a vain, proud thought more; he shall never grieve the Spirit of God any more. Sin brought death into the world, and death shall carry sin out of the world. The Persians had a certain day in the year in which they killed all serpents and venomous creatures; such a day will the day of death be to a believer; it will destroy all his sins, which, like so many serpents, have stung him. Death smites a believer as the angel did Peter, and made his chains fall off. Acts xii 7.

Believers at death are made perfect in holiness. 'The spirits of just men made perfect.' Heb xii 23. At death the souls of believers recover their virgin purity. Oh! what a blessed privilege is this, to be *sine macula et ruga*, without spot or wrinkle; to be purer than the sunbeams; to be as free from sin as the angels! Eph v 27. This makes a believer desirous to have his passport and to be gone; he would fain live in that pure air where no black vapours of sin arise.

[2] At death the saints shall be freed from all the troubles and incumbrances to which this life is subject. 'Sin is the seed sown, and trouble is the harvest reaped.' Euripides. Life and trouble are married together. There is more in life to wean us than to tempt us. Parents divide a portion of sorrow to their children, and yet leave enough for themselves. 'Man is born to trouble;' he is heir to it, it is his birth-right; you may as well separate weight from lead, as trouble from the life of man. Job v 7. King Henry's emblem was a crown hung in a bush of thorns. There is a far greater proportion of bitterness than pleasure in this life. 'I have perfumed my bed with myrrh, aloes, and cinnamon.' Prov vii 17. For one sweet ingredient there were two bitter; for the cinnamon, there were myrrh and aloes. A man's grace will not exempt him from troubles. 'Few and evil have the days of the years of my life been.' Gen xlvii 9. Thus said a godly patriarch, though he had met with God. He named 'the name of the place Peniel; for I have seen God face to face:' Gen xxxii 30; and yet he had his troubles. There are many things to imbitter life and cause trouble, but death frees us from all. (1.) Care. The mind is full of perplexed thoughts, how to bring about such a design; how to prevent such an evil. The Greek word for care comes from a primitive in the Greek, that signifies, *To cut the heart in pieces.* Care excruciates the mind; wastes the spirits. No such bitter bread as the bread of carefulness. Ezek xii 19. Care is a spiritual canker, which eats out the comfort of life: death is its only cure. (2.) Fear. Fear is the ague of the soul, which sets it shaking. 'There is torment in fear.' 1 John iv 18. Fear is like Prometheus's vulture gnawing the heart. There is a mistrustful fear, a fear of want; and a distracting fear, a fear of danger; and a discouraging fear, a fear God does not love us. These fears leave sad impressions upon the mind. At death a believer is freed from these torturing fears; he is as far from fear as the damned are from hope. The grave buries a Christian's fear. (3.) Labour. 'All things are full of labour.' Eccl i 8. Some labour in the mine, others among the Muses. God has made a law, 'In the sweat of thy face thou shalt eat bread;' but death gives a believer a *quietus;* it takes him off from his day-labour. 'Blessed are the dead that die in the Lord: they rest

from their labours.' Rev xiv 13. What needs working, when they have their reward? What needs fighting, when the crown is set on their head? 'They rest from their labours.' (4.) Suffering. Believers are as a lily among thorns; as the dove among birds of prey. The wicked have an antipathy against them; and secret hatred will break forth into open violence. 'He that was born after the flesh, persecuted him that was born after the Spirit.' Gal iv 29. The dragon is described with seven heads and ten horns. Rev xii 3. He plotteth with the one, and pusheth with the other. But at death the godly shall be freed from the molestations of the wicked; they shall never more be pestered with these vermin. 'There (viz., in the grave) the wicked cease from troubling.' Job iii 17. Death does to a believer, as Joseph of Arimathaea did to Christ, it takes him down from the cross, and gives him a writ of ease. The eagle that flies high, cannot be stung with the serpent. Death gives the soul the wings of an eagle, to fly above all the venomous serpents here below. (5.) Temptation. Though Satan be a conquered enemy, yet he is a restless enemy. 1 Pet v 8. He walketh about; he is always going about his diocese; he has his snares and his darts; one he tempts with riches, another with beauty. It is no small trouble to be continually followed with temptations; it is as bad as for a virgin to have her chastity daily assaulted; but death will free a child of God from temptation, so that he shall never be vexed more with the old serpent. After death has shot its dart, the devil will have done shooting his. Grace puts a believer out of the devil's possession, but death only frees him from the devil's temptation. (6.) Sorrow. A cloud of sorrow often gathers in the heart, and drops into tears. 'My life is spent with grief, and my years with sighing.' Psa xxxi 10. It was part of the curse, 'In sorrow thou shalt bring forth.' Gen iii 16. Many things occasion sorrow: sickness, law-suits, treachery of friends, disappointment of hopes, and loss of estate. 'Call me not Naomi, call me Mara: I went out full, and the Lord hath brought me home again empty.' Ruth i 20, 21. Sorrow is the evil spirit that haunts us. The world is a *Bochim*. Judges ii 4. Rachel wept for her children: some grieve that they have no children, and others grieve that their children are undutiful. Thus we spend our years with sighing: it is a valley of tears; but death is the funeral of all our sorrows. 'And God shall wipe away all tears.' Rev vii 17. Then Christ's spouse puts off her mourning; for how can the children of the bride-chamber mourn, when the bridegroom is with them? Matt ix 15. Thus death gives a believer his *quietus;* it frees him from sin and trouble. Though the apostle calls death the last enemy, 1 Cor xv 26, yet it is the best friend. 'To me to die is gain.'

See here that which may make a true saint willing to die. Death will set him out of gunshot, and free him from sin and trouble. There is no cause for weeping to leave a valley of tears – a stage on which sin and misery are acted. Believers are here in a strange country, why then should they not be willing to go out of it? Death beats off their fetters of sin, and sets them free. Who goes weeping from a gaol? Besides our own sins, there are the sins of others. The world is a place where Satan's seat is; a place where we see God daily dishonoured. Lot, who was a bright star in a dark night, felt his righteous soul vexed with the unclean conversation of the wicked. 2 Pet ii 7. To see God's Sabbaths broken, his truths adulterated, his glory eclipsed, wounds a godly heart. It made David cry out, 'Woe is me, that I sojourn in Mesech, that I dwell in the tents of Kedar.' Psa cxx 5. Kedar was Arabia, where were Ishmael's posterity. It was a cut to David's heart to dwell there. O then be willing to depart out of the tents of Kedar.

II. *The bodies of believers are united to Christ in the grave, and shall rest there till the resurrection.* They are said to sleep in Jesus. 1 Thess iv 14. The dust of believers is part of Christ's mystic body. The grave is a dormitory or place of rest to the saints, where their bodies quietly sleep in Christ, till they are awakened out of their sleep by the trumpet of the archangel.

How shall we know that at death we shall be freed from sin and trouble, and have our bodies united to Christ in the grave?

'To me,' says Paul, 'to die is gain;' to me, *quatenus* a believer [insofar as I am a believer]. Are we such? Have we this blessed faith? Faith, wherever it is, is operative. Lapidaries say there is no precious stone but has *virtutem insitam*, some hidden virtue in it: so I may say of faith, it has some secret virtue in it; it anchors the soul on Christ; it has both a justifying and sanctifying virtue; it fetches blood out of Christ's side to pardon, and water out of his side to purge; it works by love; it constrains to duty; it makes the head study for Christ, the tongue confess him, and the hands work for him. I have read of a father who had three sons, and left in his will all his estate to that son who could find his ring with the jewel which had a healing virtue. The case was brought before the judges; the two elder sons counterfeited a ring, but the younger son brought the true ring, which was proved by the virtue of it, whereupon his father's estate went to him. To this ring I may compare faith. There is a counterfeit faith in the world: but if we can find this ring of faith which has the healing virtue in it to purify the heart, it is the true faith which gives us an interest in Christ, and entitles us to all these privileges at death, to be freed from sin and sorrow, and to have our bodies united to Christ, while they are in the grave.

[299]

III. *At death the souls of believers pass into glory.* Death brings *malorum omnium ademptionem; omnium adeptionem* [Death brings the removal of all evils, and the attainment of all things]; it is the daybreak of eternal brightness. Here I shall lead you to the top of Mount Pisgah and give you a glimpse of the Holy Land.

What is comprehended in glory?

Glory is *status omnium bonorum aggregatione perfectus* [a state made perfect by the gathering together of everything good]. Boethius. It is a perfect state of bliss, which consists in the accumulation and heaping together all the good things of which immortal souls are capable. And truly here I am at a loss; for all I can say falls short of the celestial glory. Appelles' pencil cannot delineate it; angels' tongues cannot express it. We shall never understand glory fully till we are in heaven. Let me give you some dark views only, and some imperfect lineaments of that state of glory at which saints shall arrive after death.

[1] The first and most sublime part of the glory of heaven is the full and sweet fruition of God. *Ipse Deus sufficit ad præmium.* Augustine. We are apt to think the happiness of heaven is in being free from pain and misery; but the very essence of happiness is the enjoyment and fruition of God. God is an infinite inexhaustible fountain of joy; and to have him, is to have all. The enjoyment of God implies three things.

The enjoyment of God implies our seeing him. 'We shall see him as he is.' 1 John iii 2. Here we see him as he is not; mutable, mortal: there as he is.

How shall we see God?

(1.) We shall see him intellectually, with the eyes of the mind. This divines call the beatific vision. We shall have a full knowledge of God, though not know him fully. If there were not such an intellectual sight of God, how could the spirits of just men made perfect see God? This sight of God will be very glorious; as when a king, on his coronation-day, shows himself in all his royalty and magnificence.

(2.) We shall corporally behold the glorified body of Jesus Christ. And if it be a pleasant thing to behold the sun, how blessed a sight will it be to behold the Sun of Righteousness! to see Christ clothed in our human nature, sitting in glory above the angels! Solomon says, 'The eye is not satisfied with seeing.' Eccl i 8. But surely the eyes of saints will be satisfied with seeing that orient brightness which shall shine from the beautiful body of Christ! It must needs be satisfying, because through Christ's flesh some rays and beams of the Godhead will gloriously display themselves. God's excellent majesty would overwhelm us; but through the vail of Christ's flesh we shall behold the divine glory.

(3.) Our seeing God will be transforming. We shall so see him, as to be in some measure assimilated and changed into his image. 'We shall be like him.' 1 John iii 2. If, when Moses was with God on the Mount, and had but some imperfect sight of his glory, 'Moses' face shined', Exod xxxiv 35, how shall the saints glorified shine, being always in God's presence, and having some beams of his glory put upon them! 'We shall be like him.' One that is deformed may look on beauty, and not be made beautiful; but the saints shall so see God, as that sight shall transform them into his likeness. 'When I awake, I shall be satisfied with thy likeness.' Psa xvii 15. Not that the saints shall partake of God's essence; for as the iron in the fire is made fiery, yet remains iron still, so the saints, by beholding God's majesty, shall be made glorious creatures, but are creatures still.

(4.) Our seeing God in heaven will be without weariness. Let a man see the rarest sight that is, he will soon be cloyed; as when he comes into a garden, and sees delicious walks, fair arbours, pleasant flowers, within a little while he grows weary; but it is not so in heaven; there is no surfeit there; *ibi nec fames nec fastidium.* Bernard. The saints will never be weary of seeing God; for, God being infinite, there shall be every moment new and fresh delight springing from him into their souls.

The second thing implied in enjoying God, is loving him. It is a saint's grief that his heart is like the frozen ocean, and he can melt no more in love to God; but in heaven he shall be like the seraphims, burning with divine love. Love is a pleasant affection; 'fear hath torment.' 1 John iv 18. Love has joy in it. To love beauty is delightful. God's amazing beauty will attract the saints' love, and it will be their heaven to love him.

The third thing implied in enjoying God is God's loving us. Were there glory in God, yet, if there were not love, it would much eclipse the joys of heaven; but 'God is love.' 1 John iv 16. The saints glorified cannot love so much as they are loved. What is their love to God's? What is their star to this Sun? God loves his people on earth, when they are black as well as comely. If now they have their imperfections, oh, how entirely will he love them when they are 'without spot or wrinkle'! Eph v 27.

This is the felicity of heaven, to be in the sweet embraces of God's love; to be the *Hephzibah*, the delight of the King of Glory; to be sunning ourselves in the light of God's countenance. Then the saints shall know that love of Christ which passeth knowledge. Eph iii 19. From this glorious manifestation of God's love will flow infinite joy into the souls of the blessed; therefore heaven is called 'entering into the joy of our Lord,'

Matt xxv 21. The seeing God, loving God, and being beloved of God will cause a jubilation of spirit, and create such holy raptures of joy in the saints, that are unspeakable and full of glory. 1 Pet i 8. *In Deo quodam dulcidene delectatur anima, imo rapitur* [There is a certain sweetness about God's person which delights, nay, rather, ravishes the soul]. Augustine. Now the saints spend their years with sighing; they weep over their sins and afflictions: then their water shall be turned into wine – the vessels of mercy shall be filled and run over with joy; they shall have their palm-branches and harps in their hand, in token of their triumphs and rejoicing. Rev xiv 2.

[2] The second thing comprehended in glory is the good society there. There are the angels. Every star adds to the light. Those blessed cherubims will welcome us to paradise. If the angels rejoiced at the conversion of the elect, how will they rejoice at their coronation! There is the company of the saints. 'The spirits of just men made perfect.' Heb xii 23.

Will the saints in glory know each other?

Certainly they shall; for our knowledge in heaven shall not be diminished, but increased. We shall not only know our friends and godly relations, but those glorified saints whom we never saw before. It must be so; for society without acquaintance is not comfortable. Of this opinion were Augustine, Anselm, and Luther. Indeed, the Scripture seems to hint as much to us; for, if Peter in the transfiguration knew Moses and Elias, whom he never saw before, Matt xvii 3, then surely in heaven the saints shall know one another, and be infinitely delighted in each other's company.

[3] The third thing comprehended in glory is perfection in holiness. Holiness is the beauty of God and angels; it makes heaven. What is happiness but the essence of holiness? Here a Christian's grace is imperfect. At death believers shall arrive at perfection of grace. Then this sun shall be in its meridian splendour; then shall they not need to pray for increase of grace, for they shall be as the angels; their light shall be clear, and their joy shall be full.

[4] The fourth thing in glory is dignity and honour. They shall reign as kings. Therefore glorified saints are said to have their *insignia regalia*, their ensigns of royalty, their white robes and their crown. Rev vii 9. Cæsar, after his victories, in token of honour, had a chair of ivory set for him in the senate, and a throne in the theatre; so the saints, having obtained their victories over sin and Satan, will be enthroned with Christ

in the empyrean heaven. To sit with Christ denotes safety; to sit on the throne; dignity. 'This honour have all the saints.' Psa cxlix 9.

[5] The fifth thing in glory is the harmony and union among the heavenly inhabitants. The devil cannot get his cloven foot into heaven; he cannot conjure up any storms of contention there. There shall be perfect union; there Calvin and Luther are agreed; there is no jarring string in the heavenly music; there is nothing to make any difference – no pride or envy there. Though one star may differ from another, one may have a greater degree of glory, yet every vessel shall be full. There shall the saints and angels sit as olive-plants round about their Father's table in love and unity. Then shall they join together in concert, then shall the loud anthems of praise be sung in the heavenly choir.

[6] The sixth thing in glory is a blessed rest. 'There remains a rest.' Heb iv 9. *Felix transitus a labore ad requiem* [A happy transition from toil to rest]. Here we can have no rest, tossed and turned as a ball on racket. 'We are troubled on every side.' 2 Cor iv 8. How can a ship rest in a storm? But after death the saints get into their haven. Everything is quiet in the centre. God is *centrum quietativum animæ*, as the schoolmen say, 'the centre where the soul doth sweetly acquiesce.' A Christian, after his weary marches and battles, shall put off his bloody armour, and rest himself upon the bosom of Jesus, that bed of perfume. When death has given the saints the wings of a dove, then they shall fly away to paradise and be at rest.

[7] The seventh thing in glory is eternity. 'An eternal weight of glory.' 2 Cor iv 17. Glory is a weight. The Hebrew word for glory is a weight. God must make us able to bear it. An eternal weight. Glory is such a manna as does not breed worms. If the saints' glory in heaven were but for a time, and they were in fear of losing it, it would eclipse and imbitter the joys of heaven; but eternity is written upon their joys. The garland made of flowers of paradise fades not. 1 Pet v 4. I have read of a river called the Day-river, at which time it runs with a full torrent, but at night is dried up. Such are all earthly comforts; they run with a full stream all the daytime of life, but at the night of death they are dried up. The glorified saints shall drink of the rivers of pleasure for evermore. Psa xvi 11. Eternity is the heaven of heavens; *in fine gaudium erit sine fine* [At the last our joy shall be never-ending]. Bernard. The joys of heaven are overflowing and everlasting.

When do believers enter upon possession of glory?
They pass immediately after death into glory. Some hold, with the

Platonists and Lucianists, that the soul dies; but many of the sober heathens believed the soul's immortality. The Romans, when their great men died, caused an eagle to be let loose, and fly about in the air, signifying hereby that the soul was immortal, and did not die with the body. Christ tells us the soul is not capable of being killed, therefore not of dying. Matt x 28. And as the soul does not die, so neither does it sleep in the body for a time. If the soul at death be absent from the body, it cannot sleep in the body. 2 Cor v 8. There is an immediate passage from death to glory; it is but the twinkling of an eye, and we shall see God. 'This day shalt thou be with me in paradise.' Luke xxiii 43. By paradise is meant heaven: the third heaven, into which Paul was taken. 2 Cor xii 4. Christ said to the thief on the cross, 'This day shalt thou be with me in paradise.' His body could not be there, for it was laid in the grave; but it was spoken of his soul, that it should be, immediately after death, in heaven. Let none be so vain as to talk of purgatory: a soul purged by Christ's blood needs no fire of purgatory, but goes immediately from a deathbed into a glorified state.

Use one: See what little cause believers have to fear death, when it brings such glorious benefits. Why should the saints fear their preferment? Is it not a blessed thing to see God, to love God, and to lie for ever in the bosom of divine love? Is it not a blessed thing to meet our godly relations in heaven? Why should the saints be afraid of their blessings? Is a virgin afraid to be matched unto the crown? Now is but the contract: at death is the marriage-supper of the Lamb. Rev xix 9. What hurt does death, but take us from among fiery serpents, and place us among angels? What hurt does it do, but to clothe us with a robe of immortality? Has he any wrong done him that has his sackcloth pulled off, and has cloth of gold put upon him? Fear not dying, ye who cannot live but by dying.

Use two: You who are real saints, whose hearts are purified by faith, spend much time in musing upon those glorious benefits which you shall have by Christ at death. Thus might you, by a contemplative life, begin the life of angels here, and be in heaven before your time. Eudoxius was so affected with the glory of the sun, that he thought he was born only to behold it. What should we contemplate but celestial glory, when we shall see God face to face! David was got above the ordinary sort of men; he was in the altitudes when he said, 'I am ever with thee.' Psalm cxxxix 18. A true saint every day takes a turn in heaven; his thoughts and desires are, like cherubims, flying up to paradise. Can men of the world delight in looking upon their bags of gold, and fields of corn, and shall not the heirs of heaven take more delight in contemplating their glory in reversion? Could we send forth faith as a spy, and every day view the glory of the

Jerusalem above, how would it rejoice us, as it does the heir to think of the inheritance which is to come into his hand shortly?

Use three: This may comfort the saints in two cases.

(1.) Under their wants. They abound only in wants: the meal is almost spent in the barrel; but be patient till death, and you shall have a supply of all your wants; you shall have a kingdom, and be as rich as heaven can make you. He who has the promise of an estate, after a few years have expired, though at present he has nothing to help himself, comforts himself with this, that shortly he shall have an estate come into his hand. 'It doth not yet appear what we shall be;' but we shall be enamelled with glory, and be as rich as the angels. 1 John iii 2.

(2.) A true saint is, as Luther says, *Hæres crucis* [an heir of the Cross]. It may make us go cheerfully through our sufferings, that there are great things laid up in store; there is glory coming, which eye hath not seen; we shall drink of the fruit of the vine in the kingdom of heaven. Though now we drink in a wormwood cup, yet there is sugar to sweeten it. We shall taste of those joys of paradise, which exceed our faith, and may be better felt than they can be expressed.

3. THE RESURRECTION

'*Marvel not at this: for the hour is coming, in the which all that are in the graves shall hear his voice, and shall come forth; they that have done good, unto the resurrection of life; and they that have done evil, unto the resurrection of damnation.*' John v 28, 29.

Qxxxviii: WHAT BENEFITS DO BELIEVERS RECEIVE FROM CHRIST AT THE RESURRECTION?

A: At the resurrection, believers being raised up in glory, shall be openly acknowledged and acquitted in the day of judgment, and made perfectly blessed in the full enjoyment of God to all eternity.

I. *The bodies of believers shall be raised up to glory.* The doctrine of the resurrection is a fundamental article of our faith. The apostle puts it among the first principles of the doctrine of Christ. Heb vi 2. The body shall rise again; we are not so sure to rise out of our beds as we are to rise out of our graves. The saved body shall rise again. Some hold that the soul shall be clothed with a new body; but then it were improper to call it a resurrection, it would be rather a creation. 'Though worms destroy this body, yet in my flesh shall I see God.' Job xix 26. Not in another

flesh, but my flesh. 'This corruptible must put on incorruption.' 1 Cor xv
53.

By what arguments may the resurrection be proved?

(1.) By Scripture. 'I will raise him up at the last day.' John vi 44. 'He
will swallow up death in victory.' Isa xxv 8. That is, by delivering our
bodies from the captivity of the grave, wherein death for a time had
power over them. 'Them which sleep in Jesus, will God bring with him.'
1 Thess iv 14.

(2.) Christ is risen; therefore the bodies of the saints must rise. Christ
did not rise from the dead as a private person, but as the public head of the
church; and the head being raised, the rest of the body shall not always lie
in the grave. Christ's rising is a pledge of our resurrection. 'Knowing that he
which raised up the Lord Jesus, shall raise up us also by Jesus.' 2 Cor iv 14.
Christ is called the first-fruits of them that sleep. 1 Cor xv 20. As the
first-fruits is a sure evidence that the harvest is coming, so the resurrection
of Christ is a sure evidence of the rising of our bodies from the grave.
Christ cannot be perfect as he is Christ mystical, unless his members be
raised with him.

(3.) In respect of God's justice. If God be a just God, he will reward the
bodies of the saints as well as their souls. It cannot be imagined that the
souls of believers should be glorified, and not their bodies. They have
served God with their bodies; their bodies have been members of holiness;
their eyes have dropped tears for sin; their hands have relieved the poor;
their tongues have set forth God's praise; therefore justice and equity
require that their bodies should be crowned as well as their souls: and
how can that be unless they are raised from the dead?

(4.) If the body did not rise again, a believer would not be completely
happy; for, though the soul can subsist without the body, yet it has
appetitus unionis; 'a desire of reunion' with the body; and it is not fully
happy till it be clothed with the body. Therefore, undoubtedly, the body
shall rise again. If the soul should go to heaven, and not the body, then a
believer would be only half saved.

*But some say, as the Virgin Mary to the angel, 'How can this be?' How can it
be, that the body, which is consumed to ashes, should rise again?*

It does not oppose reason, but transcends it. There are some resem-
blances of the resurrection in nature. The corn, which is sown in the
ground, dies before it springs up. 'That which thou sowest is not quickened, except it die.' 1 Cor xv 36. In winter the fruits of the earth die:
in spring there is a resurrection of them. Noah's olive-tree springing after
the flood, was a lively emblem of the resurrection. After the passion of

our Lord, many of the saints which slept in the grave arose. Matt xxvii 52. God can more easily raise the body out of the grave, than we can wake a man out of sleep.

But when the dust of many are mingled together; how is it possible that a separation should be made and the same numerical body arise?

If we believe God can create, why not distinguish the dust of one body from another? Do we not see that the chemist, out of several metals mingled together, as gold, silver, alchymy, can extract one from the other, the silver from the gold, the alchymy from silver, and can reduce every metal to its own kind? And shall we not much more believe, that when our bodies are mingled and confounded with other substances, the wise God is able to reinvest every soul with its own body?

Shall none but the bodies of the righteous be raised?

All that are in the grave shall hear Christ's voice, and shall come forth. 'There shall be a resurrection of the dead, both of the just and unjust.' Acts xxiv 15. 'I saw the dead, small and great, stand before God.' Rev xx 12. But though all shall be raised out of their graves, yet all shall not be raised alike.

(1.) The bodies of the wicked shall be raised with ignominy. Those bodies which on the earth tempted and allured others with their beauty, shall at the resurrection be loathsome to behold; they shall be ghastly spectacles. 'They shall be an abhorring unto all flesh.' Isa lxvi 24. But the bodies of the saints shall be raised with honour. 'It is sown in dishonour, it is raised in glory.' 1 Cor xv 43. The saints' bodies then shall shine as sparkling diamonds. Then shall the righteous shine forth as the sun.' Matt xiii 43.

(2.) The bodies of the saints shall rise out of their graves with triumph; but the bodies of the wicked with trembling. The one, as about to receive their fatal doom; the other, awake from the dust too, shall sing for joy. 'Awake and sing, ye that dwell in the dust.' Isa xxvi 19. When the archangel's trumpet sounds, the bodies of believers shall come out of the grave to be made happy, as the chief butler came out of the prison, and was restored to all his dignity at the court; but the bodies of the wicked shall come out of the grave, as the chief baker out of prison, to be executed. Gen xl 21, 22.

Use one: Believe this doctrine of the resurrection; that the same body that dies shall rise again, and with the soul be crowned. Without the belief of this, *tota corruit religio,* 'all religion falls to the ground.' If the dead rise not, then Christ is not risen, and then our faith is vain. 1 Cor xv 14.

[307]

Use two: The body shall rise again. This was Job's comfort. 'Though worms destroy this body, yet in my flesh shall I see God.' Job xix 26. The body is sensible of joy, as well as the soul; and indeed, we shall not be in all our glory, till our bodies are reunited to our souls. Oh consider what joy there will be at the reuniting of the body and the soul at the resurrection! Look what sweet embraces of joy were between old Jacob and Joseph, when they first saw one another; such, and infinitely more, will there be when the body and soul of a saint shall meet together at the resurrection. Gen xlvi 29. How will the body and soul greet one another! What a welcome will the soul give to the body! Oh, blessed body! When I prayed, thou didst attend my prayers with hands lifted up, and knees bowed down; thou wert willing to suffer with me, and now thou shalt reign with me; thou wert sown in dishonour, but now art raised in glory. Oh, my dear body! I will enter into thee again, and be eternally married to thee.

Use three: The resurrection of the body is a cordial when a Christian is dying. Thy body, though it drop into the sepulchre, shall revive and flourish as a herb in the resurrection. The grave is a bed of dust, where the bodies of saints sleep; but they shall be awakened by the trump of the archangel. The grave is your long home, but not your last home. Though death strips you of your beauty, at the resurrection you shall have it restored again. As when David found Saul asleep, he took away his spear and cruse of water, but when Saul awoke he restored them again, 1 Sam xxvi 22; so, though at death all our strength and beauty be taken away, at the resurrection God will restore all again in a more glorious manner.

But how shall we know that our bodies will be raised to a glorious resurrection?

If we have a part in the first resurrection. 'Blessed is he that hath a part in the first resurrection. Rev xx 6. *What is meant by this?* It is rising by repentance out of the grave of sin. He who lies buried in sin, can have little hope of a joyful resurrection; his body shall be raised, but not in glory. O then, ask conscience, have you a part in the first resurrection? Has the Spirit entered into you, and lifted you up? Has he raised you out of your unbelief? Has he raised your hearts above the earth? This is the first resurrection; and if your souls are thus spiritually raised, your bodies shall be gloriously raised; and shall shine as stars in the kingdom of heaven. Regeneration makes way for a glorious resurrection.

Use four: Seeing you expect your bodies shall rise to glory, keep them unspotted from sin. Shall a drunken body rise to glory? Shall an unclean

[308]

body rise to glory? Shall a thievish body steal into heaven? O keep your bodies pure! Keep your eyes from unchaste glances, your hands from bribes, your tongues from slander. Defile not your bodies, which you hope shall rise one day to glory. Your bodies are the members of Christ. Hear what the apostle says: 'Shall I take the members of Christ, and make them the members of an harlot? God forbid.' 1 Cor vi 15. O keep your bodies unspotted; let them be instruments of righteousness. 'Glorify God in your body.' 1 Cor vi 20. If your bodies glorify God, God will glorify your bodies.

But seeing our bodies must be laid in the grave, and may lie many years rotting there before the resurrection, what support and comfort have we in this case?

(1.) That God will not leave his people in the grave. Our friends bring us to the grave and leave us there, but God will not. He will go to the grave with us, and watch over our dead bodies, and take care of our ashes. Rizpah watched over the dead bodies of the sons of Saul, and guarded them against the ravenous fowls of the air. 2 Sam xxi 10. Thus the Lord watches over the dead bodies of the saints, and looks to it that none of their dust be missing. Christian, thou hast a God to watch over thy body when thou art dead.

(2.) The bodies of the saints in the grave, though separated from their souls, are united to Christ. The dust of a believer is part of Christ's mystic body.

(3.) When the bodies of the saints are in the sepulchre, their souls are in paradise; the soul does not sleep in the body, 'but returns to God who gave it.' Eccl xii 7. The soul immediately partakes of those joys the blessed angels do. When the body returns to dust, the soul returns to rest; when the body is sleeping, the soul is triumphing; when the body is buried, the soul is crowned. As the spies were sent before to taste of the fruits of the land, so at death the soul is sent before into heaven, to taste of the fruit of the holy land. Numb xiii 20.

(4.) When God's time is come, the 'graves shall deliver up their dead.' Rev xx 13. When the judge sends, the jailor must deliver up his prisoners. As God said to Jacob, 'I will go down with thee into Egypt, and I will surely bring thee up again;' Gen xlvi 4, so the Lord will go down with us into the grave, and will surely bring us out again.

(5.) Though the bodies of the saints shall rot and be loathsome in the grave, yet afterwards they shall be made illustrious and glorious. The bodies of the saints, when they arise, shall be comely and beautiful. The body of a saint in this life may be deformed; those even whose minds are adorned with virtue, may have misshapen bodies – as the finest cloth may have the coarsest list; but those deformed bodies shall be amiable and beautiful. This beauty consists in two things, (i) Perfection of parts. There shall be a full proportion of all the members. In this life there is often a defect of members: the eye is lost, the arm is cut off; but in the resurrection all parts of the body will be restored again; therefore the resurrection is called the time of restoring all things. Acts iii 21. Malchus' ear cut, *restituit* [He restored]. (ii) Splendour. The bodies of the saints shall have a graceful majesty in them; they shall be like Stephen, whose face shone as if it had been the face of an angel. Acts vi 15. Nay, they will be made like Christ's glorious body. Phil iii 21.

The bodies of the saints, when they arise, shall be free from the necessities of nature, as hunger and thirst. 'They shall hunger no more.' Rev vii 16. Moses on the mount was so filled with the glory of God, that he needed not the recruits of nature. Much more in heaven shall the bodies of the saints be so filled with God's glory, as to be upheld without food.

The bodies of the saints, when they arise, shall be swift and nimble. Our bodies on earth are dull and heavy in their motion; then they shall be swift, and made fit to ascend, as the body of Elias, in the air. Now the body is a clog: in heaven it shall be a wing. We shall be as the angels. Matt xxii 30. And how nimble are they? The angel Gabriel in a short time came from heaven to the earth. Dan ix 21. As the helm turns the ship instantly whither the steersman wills, so the body in an instant will move which way the soul wills.

The bodies of the saints, at the resurrection, shall be firm and strong. 'It is raised in power.' 1 Cor xv 43. Through frequent labour and sickness, the strongest body begins to languish: but at the resurrection we shall be of a strong constitution; there will be no weariness in the body, nor faintness in the spirits. This may comfort you who now conflict with many bodily weaknesses. This weak body shall be raised in power; the body, which is now a weak reed, shall be like a rock.

The bodies of the saints, at the resurrection, will be immortal. 'This mortal shall put on immortality.' 1 Cor xv 53. Our bodies shall run parallel with eternity. 'Neither can they die any more.' Luke xx 36. Heaven is a healthful climate, there is no bill of mortality there. If a physician could give you a recipe to keep you from dying, what sums of money would you give! At the resurrection Christ shall give the saints such a recipe. 'There shall be no more death.' Rev xxi 4.

II. *They shall be openly acquitted at the day of judgment.*

[1] This is to be laid down for a proposition, that there shall be a day of judgment. 'For we must all appear before the judgment-seat of Christ.'

2 Cor v 10. This is the grand assize; the greatest appearance that ever was. Adam shall then see all his posterity at once. We must all appear; the greatness of men's persons does not exempt them from Christ's tribunal; kings and captains are brought in trembling before the Lamb's throne. Rev vi 15. We must all appear, and appear in our own persons; not by proxy.

How does it appear that there shall be a day of judgment?

Two ways. (1.) By the testimony of Scripture. 'For God shall bring every work into judgment, with every secret thing.' Eccl xii 14. 'For he cometh, for he cometh to judge the earth.' Psa xcvi 13. The reduplication denotes the certainty. 'I beheld till the thrones were cast down, and the Ancient of days did sit, whose garment was white as snow. . . . The judgment was set, and the books were opened.' Dan vii 9, 10.

(2.) It appears from the petty sessions kept in a man's own conscience. When a man does virtuously, conscience excuses him; when evil, conscience arraigns and condemns him. Now, what is this private session kept in the court of conscience, but a certain forerunner of that general day of judgment, when all the world shall be summoned to God's tribunal?

Why must there be a day of judgment?

That there may be a day of retribution, in which God may render to every one according to his work. Things seem to be carried very unequally in the world: the wicked to prosper, as if they were rewarded for doing evil; and the godly to suffer, as if they were punished for being good. Therefore, for vindicating the justice of God, there must be a day wherein there shall be a righteous distribution of punishments and rewards to men, according to their actions.

Who shall be judge?·

The Lord Jesus Christ. 'The Father hath committed all judgment to the Son.' John v 22. It is an article of our creed, that 'Christ shall come to judge the quick and the dead.' It is a great honour put upon Christ; he who was himself judged, shall be judge: he who once hung upon the cross, shall sit upon the throne of judgment. He is fit to be judge, as he partakes of both the manhood and Godhead.

(1.) Of the manhood. Being clothed with the human nature, he may be visibly seen of all. It is requisite the judge should be seen. 'Behold, he cometh with clouds, and every eye shall see him.' Rev i 7.

(2.) As he partakes of the Godhead. He is of infinite knowledge to understand all causes brought before him; and of infinite power to execute offenders. He is described with seven eyes. Zech iii 9, to denote his wisdom; and a rod of iron, Psa ii 9, to denote his power. He is so wise that he cannot be deluded, and so strong that he cannot be resisted.

When will the time of judgment be?

The *quando*, or time of the general judgment, is a secret kept from the angels. 'Of that day and hour knoweth no man, no, not the angels of heaven.' Matt xxiv 36. But it cannot be far off. One great sign of the approach of the day of judgment, is, 'That iniquity shall abound,' Matt xxiv 12. Sure then that day is near at hand, for iniquity never more abounded than in this age, in which lust grows hot, and love grows cold. When the elect are all converted, then Christ will come to judgment. As he that rows a ferry-boat, stays till all the passengers are taken in, and then rows away, so Christ stays till all the elect are gathered in, and then he will hasten away to judgment.

What shall be the modus, or manner of trial?

(1.) The citing of men to the court. The dead are cited as well as the living. Men, when they die, avoid the censure of our law-courts; but at the last day, they are cited to God's tribunal. 'I saw the dead, small and great, stand before God.' Rev xx 12. This citing of men will be by the sound of a trumpet. 1 Thess iv 16. This trumpet will sound so loud, that it will raise men from their graves. Matt xxiv 31. Such as will not hear the trumpet of the gospel sound 'repent, and believe,' shall hear the trumpet of the archangel sounding, 'arise, and be judged.'

(2.) The approach of the judge to the tribunal.

(i) This will be terrible to the wicked. How can a guilty prisoner endure the sight of the judge? If Felix trembled when Paul preached of judgment, Acts xxiv 25, how will sinners tremble when they shall see Christ come to judgment! Christ is described, sitting in judgment, with a fiery stream issuing from him. Dan vii 10. The Lamb of God will then be turned into a lion, the sight of whom will strike terror into sinners. When Joseph said to his brethren, 'I am Joseph, your brother, whom ye sold into Egypt,' 'they were troubled at his presence.' Gen xlv 4. How did their hearts smite them for their sin! So, when Christ shall come to judgment, and say, 'I am Jesus, whom ye sinned against; I am Jesus, whose laws ye have broken, whose blood ye despised. I am now come to judge you.' Oh, what horror and amazement will take hold of sinners! How they will be troubled at the presence of their judge!

(ii) The approach of Christ to the bench of judicature will be comfortable to the righteous. Christ will come in splendour and great glory. His first coming in the flesh was obscure. Isa liii 2. He was like a prince in disguise; but his second coming will be illustrious – he shall come in the glory of his Father, with the holy angels. Mark viii 38. Oh, what a bright day will that be, when a vast number of angels, those morning stars, shall appear in the air, and Christ the Sun of Righteousness shall shine in splendour above the brightest cherub! He will come as a friend. Indeed, if the saints' judge were their enemy, they might fear to be condemned; but he who loves them, and prayed for them, is their judge; he who is their husband is their judge, therefore they need not fear but all things shall go well on their side.

(3.) The trial itself, which has a dark and a light side. A dark side. It will fall heavy on the wicked, when the judge being set, the books shall be opened, the book of conscience, and the book of God's remembrance. Rev xx 12. The sinners' charge being read, all their sins laid open, their murder, drunkenness, and uncleanness, Christ will say, 'What can you plead for yourselves, that the sentence of death should not pass?' Then, being convicted, they will be speechless. Then follows the dismal sentence: *Ite maledicti*, 'depart from me, ye cursed, into everlasting fire, prepared for the devil and his angels.' Matt xxv 41. He that said to God, 'Depart from me', Job xxi 14, and to religion, '*Depart from me,*' must now hear that word pronounced from his judge, '*Depart from me*' – a dreadful, but a righteous sentence. Psa li 4. The sinner himself shall cry: 'Guilty!' Though he has a sea of wrath, he has not one drop of injustice. When once the sentence is passed, it is irreversible; there is no appealing to a higher court. The trial has also a light side. It will increase the joy and happiness of the righteous. The day of judgment will be a day of jubilee to them.

[2] At that day Christ their judge will own them by name. Those whom the world scorned, and looked upon as madmen and fools, Christ will take by the hand, and openly acknowledge to be his favourites. What is his 'confessing of men,' but his openly acknowledging them to be precious in his eyes? Luke xii 8.

Christ as judge will plead for them. It is not usual to be both judge and advocate, to sit on the bench and plead; but it shall be so at the day of judgment.

(1.) Christ will plead his own blood for the saints. 'These persons I have purchased; they are the travail of my soul; they have sinned, but my soul was made an offering for their sin.'

(2.) Christ will vindicate them from all unjust censures. They were strangely misrepresented in the world, as proud, hypocritical, factious; as Paul was called a seditious man, the head of a faction. Acts xxiv 5. But at the day of judgment Christ will clear their innocence; he will 'bring forth their righteousness as the light.' Ps xxxvii 6. He will wipe off tears from their eyes, and dust from their names. When Moses was charged with taking too much upon him, he comforted himself with this, 'To-morrow will the Lord show who are his.' Numb xvi 5. So the saints, when reproached, may comfort themselves with the day of judgment, in which Christ will say who are his, and they shall come forth as the wings of a dove covered with silver.

(3.) Christ as judge will absolve his people before men and angels. As Pilate said of Christ, 'I find no fault in this man', John xviii 38; so will Christ say of the elect, 'I find no fault in them, I pronounce them righteous.' Then follows, 'Come, ye blessed of my Father, inherit the kingdom.' Matt xxv 34. As if Christ should say, 'O ye happy ones, the delight of my soul, the fruit of my sufferings, stand no longer at the bar. Ye are heirs apparent to the crown of heaven, enter and take possession.' At the hearing of this sentence, with what ravishing joy will the saints be filled! This word, 'Come, ye blessed,' will be music to their ear, and a cordial to their heart.

(4.) Christ will mention before men and angels all the good deeds the saints have done. 'I was an hungred, and ye gave me meat; I was thirsty, and ye gave me drink.' Matt xxv 35. You that have wept in secret for sin, that have shown any love for Christ's name, that have been rich in good works, Christ will take notice of it at the last day, and say, 'Well done, good and faithful servant.' He himself will be the herald to proclaim your praises; thus it shall be done to the man whom Christ delights to honour.

(5.) Christ will call his saints from the bar, to sit upon the bench with him to judge the world. 'Behold, the Lord cometh with ten thousands of his saints, to execute judgment upon all.' Jude 14. 'Know ye not that the saints shall judge the world?' 1 Cor vi 2. The saints shall sit with Christ in judgment as justices of peace with the judge; they shall applaud Christ's righteous sentence on the wicked, and, as it were, vote with Christ. As it is a great honour to the saints, so it must needs add to the sorrows of the wicked, to see those whom they once hated and derided, sit as judges upon them.

(6.) The saints shall be fully crowned with the enjoyment of God for ever. They shall be in his sweet presence, 'in whose presence is fulness of joy', Psa xvi 11, and this shall be for ever. The banner of God's love shall be eternally displayed. The joys of heaven shall be without intermission and expiration, 'and so shall we ever be with the Lord.' 1 Thess iv 17.

Use one: It is sad news to the wicked, that they shall 'not stand in judgment', Psa i 5; that they shall come to judgment, but shall not stand in judgment; they shall not stand acquitted, they shall not stand with boldness, but sneak and hang down their heads, and not be able to look their judge in the face; but it is great consolation to the godly. When the apostle had said, 'The Lord shall descend from heaven with a shout, with the voice of the archangel, and the trump of God,' he presently adds, 'Wherefore comfort one another with these words.' 1 Thess iv 16, 18.

(1.) The day of judgment is comfort in respect of weakness of grace. A Christian is ready to be troubled to see his grace so minute and imperfect; but, at the last day, if Christ find but a drachm of true grace, it shall be accepted. If thine be true gold, though it be many grains too light, Christ will put his merits into the scales, and make it pass current.

(2.) What a comfort is it to such of the saints who have met with unrighteous judgment in the world, who have been wronged of their estates in lawsuits, or had their lives taken away by an unrighteous sentence: Christ will judge things over again, and will give a righteous sentence. If your estates have been taken away wrongfully, you shall be restored a thousandfold at the day of judgment. If you have lost your lives for Christ, you shall not lose your crown; you shall wear a garland made of the flowers of paradise, which fade not away.

Use two: Meditate much upon the day of judgment. Feathers swim upon the water, but gold sinks into it; so, light, feathery Christians float in vanity; they mind not the day of judgment; but serious spirits sink deep into the thoughts of it.

(1.) The meditation of this last day should make us very sincere. We should labour to approve our hearts to God, the great judge and umpire of the world. It is easy to carry it fair before men, but there is no dissembling or prevaricating with God. He sees what the heart is, and will accordingly pass his verdict.

(2.) The meditation of Christ's coming to judge us, should keep us from judging our brethren. We are apt to judge the final state of others; which is for men to step into Christ's place, and take his work out of his hand. 'Who art thou that judgest another?' James iv 12. Thou that passest a rash sentence upon another, thou must come thyself shortly to be judged, and then, perhaps, he may be acquitted, and thou condemned.

Use three: So demean and carry yourselves that, at the last day of judgment, you may be sure to be acquitted, and have the glorious privileges with which the saints shall be crowned.

How is that?

(1.) If you would stand acquitted at the day of judgment, then (i) Labour to get into Christ. 'That I may be found in him.' Phil iii 9. Faith implants us into Christ, it engarrisons us in him, and then 'there is no condemnation.' Rom viii 1. There is no standing before Christ, but by being in Christ. (ii) Labour for humility, which is a kind of self-annihilation. 'Though I be nothing.' 2 Cor xii 11. Christian, hast thou parts and abilities, and dost thou cover them with the veil of humility, as Moses, when his face shone, put a veil over it? If thou art humble, thou shalt be acquitted at the day of judgment. 'He shall save the humble person.' Job xxii 29. An humble man judgeth himself for his sins, and Christ will acquit those who judge themselves.

(2.) If you would stand acquitted at the last day, keep a clear conscience. Do not load yourself with guilt, and furnish your judge with matter against you. 'The Lord,' says Paul, 'hath appointed a day in which he will judge the world.' Acts xvii 31. How would Paul fit himself for that day? 'Herein do I exercise myself, to have always a conscience void of offence toward God and toward men.' Acts xxiv 16. Be careful of the first and second table; be holy and just. Have hearts without false aims, and hands without false weights. Keep conscience as clear as your eye, that no dust of sin fall into it. They that sin against conscience, will be shy of their judge; as such as take in prohibited goods cannot endure to see the searchers that are appointed to open their packs. Christian, thy pack will be opened at the last day, I mean, thy conscience (and Christ is the searcher), to see what sins, what prohibited goods thou hast taken in; and then he proceeds to judgment. Oh! be sure to keep a good conscience; which is the best way to stand with boldness at the day of judgment. The voice of conscience is the voice of God. If conscience, upon just grounds, acquits us, God will acquit us. 'If our heart condemn us not, then have we confidence toward God.' 1 John iii 21.

(3.) If you would stand acquitted at the last day, trade with your talents for God's glory; lay out yourselves for him; honour him with your substance; relieve Christ's members, that you may be acquitted. He that had five talents traded with them, and made them five talents more; 'His lord said unto him, Well done, good and faithful servant.' Matt xxv 21.

(4.) If you would stand acquitted at the day of judgment, get a sincere love to the saints. Love is the truest touchstone of sincerity. To love grace for grace, shows the spirit of God to be in a man. Does conscience witness for you? Are you perfumed with this sweet spice of love? Do you delight most in those in whom the image of God shines? Do you reverence their graces? Do you bear with their infirmities? A blessed evidence that you shall be acquitted in the day of judgment. 'We know that we have passed from death to life, because we love the brethren.' 1 John iii 14.